PLANET TACO

OXFORD
UNIVERSITY PRESS

A GLOBAL HISTORY OF MEXICAN FOOD

Jeffrey M. Pilcher

Planet Taco

OXFORD
UNIVERSITY PRESS

Oxford University Press is a department of the University of Oxford. It furthers the University's
objective of excellence in research, scholarship, and education by publishing worldwide.

Oxford   New York
Auckland   Cape Town   Dar es Salaam   Hong Kong   Karachi
Kuala Lumpur   Madrid   Melbourne   Mexico City   Nairobi
New Delhi   Shanghai   Taipei   Toronto

With offices in
Argentina   Austria   Brazil   Chile   Czech   Republic France   Greece
Guatemala   Hungary   Italy   Japan   Poland   Portugal   Singapore
South Korea   Switzerland   Thailand   Turkey   Ukraine   Vietnam

Oxford is a registered trade mark of Oxford University Press in the UK and certain other countries.

Published in the United States of America by
Oxford University Press
198 Madison Avenue, New York, NY 10016

Pilcher, Jeffrey M., 1965–
    Planet taco: a global history of Mexican food / Jeffrey M. Pilcher.
    p. cm.
Includes bibliographical references and index.
    ISBN 978-0-19-974006-2 (hardcover : alk. paper)   1. Cooking, Mexican—History.
2. Cooking, Mexican—Social aspects—History.   3. Food habits—Mexico—History.
4. Ethnicity—Mexico.   5. Tacos—History.   6. Mexican Americans—Food—History.
7. Sovereignty—Social aspects—Mexico—History.   8. Globalization—Social aspects—History.
I. Title.
    TX716.M4P543 2012
    641.5972—dc23

1 3 5 7 9 8 6 4 2

Printed in the United States of America
on acid-free paper

To Donna

CONTENTS

ACKNOWLEDGMENTS

During a decade of traveling the world eating tacos, I met countless home cooks, professional chefs, restaurant owners, waitstaff, and fellow diners. Their stories have animated this book, and I am sorry there are not enough pages to include all of them here or even to acknowledge the storytellers by name. To everyone who has shared their tales and tacos, I offer a heartfelt thank you.

In addition to oral histories and ethnography, this book is based on research in libraries and archives. I appreciate the helpful assistance I received at the institutions listed in the bibliography, as well as a few that do not appear there: the Immigration History Research Center; the Lilly Library at Indiana University; the New York Public Library; the Schlesinger Library at Harvard University; and the Special Collections and Chicano Studies Library at UCLA. As always, I am grateful to interlibrary loan librarians everywhere. For permission to reproduce illustrations, I thank El Museo de América, Madrid; Elsevier; the Fototeca of the Instituto Nacional de Antropología e Historia; the Library of Congress; the Los Angeles Public Library; the New York Public Library; the Palace of the Governors Photo Archives; the New Mexico History Museum, Santa Fe; the United States Patent and Trademark Office; the University of Santa Clara; and the University of Texas at San Antonio Institute of Texas Cultures. Daniel Arreola, a pioneer in the study of Mexican food, was particularly generous in sharing and discussing materials from his border postcard collection. Thanks also to Dan Strehl, another early scholar of Mexican food, formerly of the Los Angeles Public Library, for allowing me access to important materials.

It may sound a bit questionable using as evidence newspaper stories to which I have contributed as a source. Nevertheless, I have always learned as much in my conversations with journalists as they have from me, and I have done my best to keep the sources of information distinct. I would particularly like to thank Dave Roos, who asked me a telling question at an early stage in this project. I am also grateful to Eric Asimov, Glenn Collins, Øyvend Holen, Matthew Huisman, David McLemore, Davia Nelson, David Olson, Patricia Sharpe, Nikki Silva, Jennifer Steinhauer, and Robb Walsh.

Those who oppose support for research in the humanities and social sciences, considering it a frivolous waste of taxpayer dollars, will be relieved to learn that I used no federal funds in order to buy tacos in exotic places. I did receive assistance from the Citadel Development Foundation and from the University of Minnesota, for which I am deeply grateful.

In writing this book, I have found that public lectures and undergraduate classrooms are ideal places to practice the art of combining critical history with good storytelling. For their help in working through these stories and for suggesting many new ones, I thank the students of History 3417 and 3418 as well as the people who attended talks at Adelaide University; Allegheny College; Arizona State University; Bowling Green State University; the British Museum; the College of William and Mary; Columbia University; the Culinary Institute of America (Greystone and San Antonio campuses); DePauw University; Gettysburg College; the Haffenreffer Museum at Brown University; the Hagley Museum and Library; the IACP conferences at Williams College and the University of the Pacific; Indiana University; Lehigh University; Ohio Wesleyan University; Oregon State University; the University of Arizona; the University of California at Irvine; the University of Iowa; the University of Minnesota Bell Museum, IHRC, and LACIS; the University of Nevada at Reno; the University of Puget Sound; the University of Texas at Austin Institute of Latin American Studies; the University of Toronto Monck Center; the University of Warwick; the Walters Art Museum, and Yale University. I am particularly grateful to the colleagues and friends who made those events possible.

Parts of this book have appeared previously and I appreciate the permission to reprint material from the following works: "'Chili Queens' and Checkered Tablecloths: Public Dining Cultures of Italians in New York City and Mexicans in San Antonio, Texas, 1870s–1940s," Donna R. Gabaccia, co-author, *Radical*

History Review 110 (Spring 2011): 109–26; "Eating Mexican in a Global Age: The Politics and Production of Ethnic Food," in *Food Chains: From Farmyard to Shopping Cart*, ed. Warren Belasco and Roger Horowitz (Philadelphia: University of Pennsylvania Press, 2009), 158–76; "From 'Montezuma's Revenge' to 'Mexican Truffles': Culinary Tourism across the Rio Grande," in *Culinary Tourism*, ed. Lucy M. Long (Lexington: The University Press of Kentucky, 2004), 76–96; "The Globalization of Mexican Cuisine," *History Compass* 6, no. 2 (March 2008): 529–51 (available online at: http://www.blackwell-synergy. com/doi/abs/10.1111/j.1478–0542.2007.00509.x?journalCode=hico); "Taco Bell, Maseca, and Slow Food: A Postmodern Apocalypse for Mexico's Peasant Cuisine?" in *Fast Food/Slow Food: The Cultural Economy of the Global Food System*, ed. Richard Wilk (Walnut Creek, Calif.: Altamira Press, 2006), 69–81; "'¡Tacos, joven!' Cosmopolitismo proletario y la cocina nacional mexicana," *Dimensión Antropológica* 13, no. 37 (mayo-agosto 2006): 87–125; "Los tacos que envuel-ven al mundo: Aproximaciones a una historia global de la cocina mexicana," in *Tendencias del consumo en Mesoamérica*, ed. Juan José Marín Hernández and Patricia Vega Jiménez (San José: Editorial Universidad de Costa Rica, 2008), 67–86; "Tex-Mex, Cal-Mex, New Mex, or Whose Mex? Notes on the Historical Geography of Southwestern Cuisine," *Journal of the Southwest* 43, no. 4 (Winter 2001): 659–79; "Was the Taco Invented in Southern California?" *Gastronomica: The Journal of Food and Culture* 8, no. 1 (Winter 2008): 26–38; "Who Chased Out the 'Chili Queens'? Gender, Race, and Urban Reform in San Antonio, Texas, 1880–1943," *Food and Foodways* 16, no. 3 (July 2008): 173–200.

Clearly, I have been flogging this project for too long! But as a result I have benefited from working with some exceptional editors. I thank Warren Belasco, Carole Counihan, Darra Goldstein, Roger Horowitz, Lucy Long, Vincent Peloso, Phil Scranton, Patricia Vega Jiménez, Mark Wasserman, Richard Wilk, and Andrew Wood. Susan Ferber, my editor at Oxford, held me up to very exacting standards, and this is a better book as a result.

I also received excellent suggestions from the following diligent readers: Susan Deeds, Víctor Macías-González, M. J. Maynes, Enrique Ochoa, Carla Philips, Wim Philips, the University of Minnesota Agri-Food Reading Group, and the anonymous referees for Oxford University Press. Neil Foley, James Garza, Martín González de la Vara, Cynthia Radding, Vicki Ruiz, and Fritz Schwaller provided introductions and assistance at critical moments.

I have been blessed with wonderful colleagues at both The Citadel and at the University of Minnesota. Special thanks to David Van Riper of the Minnesota

Population Center for his help mapping tacos and to IPUMS ambassador Bob McCaa for his far-flung taco reports. Another benefit of moving to Minnesota has been working with some truly outstanding research assistants: Fernando Calderón, Melanie Huska, Jodi Larson, Erika Martínez, and Marianne Samoya.

Donna Gabaccia has been an enthusiastic supporter, trenchant critic, and treasured companion on my taco world tour. I dedicate this book to her.

What is authentic Mexican food? Surveys show that Mexican is one of the top three ethnic foods in the United States, along with Chinese and Italian. But just as chop suey and pepperoni pizza are not typical of the foods of China and Italy, few people in Mexico actually eat the burritos (made with wheat flour tortillas) and taco shells (prefried corn tortillas) that often pass for Mexican cooking in the United States. Although there are growing numbers of cookbooks and websites, celebrity chefs and migrant restaurants all claiming to offer "authentic" Mexican, as opposed to Americanized food, when traveling across the country—or around the world—burritos and taco shells still predominate.

The global presence of Americanized tacos has provoked outrage from many Mexicans, who take patriotic pride in their national cuisine. But beyond a common distaste for "gloopy" North American versions, there is surprisingly little consensus about what is properly Mexican, even in Mexico. Every region and virtually every town has its own distinct specialties, which are regarded with deep affection by residents. Indeed, the first attempt to write a national history of Mexican food, Salvador Novo's *Cocina mexicana, o historia gastronomica de la Ciudad de México* (*Mexican Cuisine, or Gastronomic History of the City of Mexico*, 1967), asserted boldly that the foods of the capital constituted the national cuisine.[1] Mexican diets vary widely by ethnic group and social class as well as by region, and more critical histories, including one of my own, have shown how the national cuisine has been used for ideological purposes. Nineteenth-century cookbooks sought to establish cultural boundaries of citizenship by excluding dishes that were not considered respectable, particularly indigenous foods made of maize.[2] In the twentieth century, the national cuisine has been politicized through inclusion as well as exclusion. The Yucatán, for example, has been a culturally distinctive region since the days of rival Maya and Aztec empires. Its foods were virtually invisible in nineteenth-century Mexican cookbooks, but they have recently been subsumed within the national cuisine, despite the resistance of Yucatecans who reject the label "Mexican."[3]

Contemporary national boundaries do not provide any better guide to authenticity than do lines of region, ethnicity, or class. Cuisines grow organically from the local climate and soil and from global movements of trade and migration. By contrast, national borders are fixed artificially at a particular place and time, often through war and diplomacy. When the United States invaded Mexico in 1846 and imposed the Treaty of Guadalupe Hidalgo, it annexed South Texas without regard for its Mexican population and history. Although the Lower Rio Grande is at the center of a common agricultural region and local cuisine, it divides two nations. A dish served on the south bank of the river is the national cuisine; on the north bank, it is ethnic food. For families on both sides, it is simply home cooking.

The search for authentic Mexican food—or rather, the struggle to define what that means—has been going on for two hundred years, and some of the most important sites of contention have been outside of Mexico. Notions of authenticity have been contested through interactions between insiders and outsiders, they have changed over time, and they have contributed to broader power relations. The very idea of Mexico was first conceived by Creoles, people of European descent who were born in the Americas and who imagined a shared past with Aztec monarchs in order to claim political autonomy within the Spanish empire. Nevertheless, the Creoles scorned native foods made of corn, as well as the lower-class people who ate them. When independence came in the nineteenth century, attempts to forge a national cuisine were split between nostalgia for Creole traditions and the allure of European fashions. Foods considered to be Indian were largely ignored, along with yet another variant of Mexican cooking that emerged in the northern territories conquered by Yankee invaders. With the U.S. rise to global power in the twentieth century, this Tex-Mex cooking was industrialized and carried around the world. Mexican elites, confronted with the potential loss of their culinary identity to this powerful neighbor, then sought to ground their national cuisine in the pre-Hispanic past. This book tells the story of how a particular idea of authentic Mexican food was invented in the global marketplace by promoters of culinary tourism in order to compete against industrial foods from the United States.

The struggle between industrialized Tex-Mex foods and Mexican peasant cuisines is one front in the much larger battle between globalization and national sovereignty. It is all the more bitter because Mexico's national rival, the United States, embodies the forces of globalization. But an exclusive focus on this national rivalry ignores important chapters in the history of Mexican food, notably the food-processing corporations of Mexico and the home cooking of Mexican Americans. Moreover, an interpretation equating nations with foods, particularly the foods of marginalized groups—the United States and Mexican Americans on the one hand, Mexico and peasants on the other—obscures social inequality and racial discrimination in both countries. *Planet Taco* offers instead a global history that reveals these power relations and recognizes not a single "authentic" cuisine but rather multiple variations of Mexican food.

PLANET TACO

A TALE OF TWO TACOS

INTRODUCTION

As a historian of Mexican food, I have eaten my fair share of tacos. In Mexico City, I am always on the lookout for *tacos al pastor*, slices of pork from a vertical rotisserie served on small corn tortillas with bits of pineapple and *guajillo* chile salsa. Sitting on the beaches of Cancún, I have tasted sublime fish tacos with succulent white flesh, delicately fried batter, and a splash of lime and *pico de gallo*. At home in Minneapolis, while shopping at the Mercado Central on Lake Street, I often grab some *tacos de barbacoa*, shreds of tender meat enlivened by a fresh tomatillo salsa. But feeling that I had not truly experienced *carne asada*, the grilled beef that is the centerpiece of *norteño* (northern) cuisine, I recently traveled to Hermosillo, 250 miles south of Tucson, Arizona, in the heart of Sonora's cattle country. Getting there was no easy task, for although it is a state capital, it is poorly served even by Mexican airlines. Once I arrived, however, I had no trouble enlisting a local guide for the city's fine dining.

Miguel Angel Rascón is a librarian at the Colegio de Sonora, Hermosillo's elite postgraduate institution, but his real love is teaching cooking classes to neighborhood children, including his young son, Miguelito. When he offered to take me to the best tacos in town, he started at a Chinese restaurant. That may sound strange, but chop suey has been a local favorite since the late nineteenth century, when it was brought by Asian migrants, who were headed for the

United States but took a detour through northwestern Mexico to evade customs officials enforcing the Chinese Exclusion Act of 1882. We also stopped for coffee—drive-through Starbucks was all the rage in Hermosillo—but still no tacos. Finally, we headed down the main tourist boulevard and approached an outdoor restaurant crowded with fashionable young people. Having eaten there the night before, I felt smugly satisfied about my instinct for Mexican food, that is, until Miguel downshifted and turned the corner. He drove for another five minutes, through a maze of dark side streets, before stopping in front of a taco cart, operated by a young couple and illuminated by a street lamp. After introducing me to the chef and his wife, Miguel ordered tacos of carne asada for both of us.

There are two theories on carne asada: the thick and the thin. Some cooks use large slabs of meat, perhaps chuck roast, called *diezmillo* in Spanish, while others prefer the thinnest of butterflied steaks, known as *sábana*, literally, sheets. Neither are fancy cuts, the kind reserved for restaurants and the export market, but they are always fresh and flavorful. Regardless of size, the meat is grilled over a very hot fire until beads of juice appear on the surface. It is then salted, turned once, and when the drops begin to form again, it is finished. Our host came from the thin school. As he placed the marinated strips of beef down to sizzle on the hot grill, I glanced at my watch. It was 9:45, still quite early for a Mexican supper. Scarcely a minute later, the tell-tale sweat began to appear, and he turned the meat, revealing a nicely browned surface. At this point, he placed some flour tortillas to warm on the other side of the grill. He chopped the meat directly on the metal surface, and assembled the tacos on Styrofoam plates. With a sprinkling of diced onion and cilantro, he handed them over. I checked my watch again. Elapsed time: about two minutes. That was fast food.

Our chef did not drive a fancy taco truck, like the polished chrome models that frequent street corners and work sites in the United States, but he had transformed his simple cart into a comfortable restaurant with a circle of lawn chairs. His wife handed us each a beer from the ice chest located on one side of the cart, and we proceeded to the well-equipped salsa bar on the other side. I opted for a smooth avocado sauce, not the rustic guacamole made in a mortar, with bits of tomato, onion, and chile, but the taco-shop version, creamy and pale green. Miguel liked to mix his own salsa, adding pico de gallo and a bit of guajillo to the guacamole and topping it off with a garnish of radish and pickled chiles—a baroque feast of tacos. We spent nearly as much time saucing the tacos as it took to make them, but we ate them very quickly. I cannot say if it was the best carne asada in Hermosillo, but it was definitely worth the trip.

Back in the United States, I decided to continue my comparative taco experiment with a visit to Taco Bell. I headed for not just any neighborhood franchise, but East Los Angeles. That might sound a little perverse. Cruising down Whittier Boulevard, under the landmark steel arch, I had my choice of places serving *birria* (braised goat) from Guadalajara, Ensenada fish tacos, Salvadoran *pupusas*, and a dozen other regional specialties. My friend María Muñoz insisted that I was wasting my time. There was no Taco Bell in her hometown, the Chicana capital of East L.A. It must have been across the border, in Boyle Heights. But I found it, several blocks from the city center, on a corner facing a beauty salon, a travel agency, and a strip mall. The restaurant shared a menu with Pizza Hut Express—both are subsidiaries of the Yum! Corporation—and pizza seemed to be the favorite of the predominantly middle-aged women on lunch break.

A Mexican American teenager greeted me at the counter. Behind her, the Taco Bell side of the menu listed several options: hard tacos, soft tacos, even the double decker, a hard taco wrapped in a soft taco. I wondered briefly what Miguel would make of that. Then, in the interests of scientific comparison, I ordered two soft, grilled steak tacos. The cashier touched the screen of her computer, and the order flashed up on a monitor above the stainless steel production line. As another young woman in latex gloves started to work on my tacos, I recalled a description of the chain's kitchen routine given to a journalist from *The New Yorker* by an anonymous employee: "My job is I, like, basically make the tacos! The meat comes in boxes that have bags inside, and those bags you boil to heat up the meat. That's how you make tacos."[1]

I missed that step, watching from across the counter, because the meat was already waiting in a steam tray, far from any grill. I did see the young woman place the flour tortillas in a small overhead oven, about the size of a microwave. A short time later, she pulled them out and positioned them on sheets of paper laid out on the grooved work surface designed to support either hard tacos upright or soft tacos laid flat. She arranged the meat on top and slid the tacos down the line to the next station, which was equipped with various trays of prepared condiments. Presumably, the kitchen was designed for maximum efficiency through a division of labor, but they seemed to be understaffed, and the poor woman was moving back and forth along the line. She added lettuce, tomato, and cheese. Then for a final flourish, she pulled out a caulking gun and squirted "creamy lime sauce" on my tacos. Meanwhile, the cashier had offered me little foil-wrapped packets of hot sauce. Instead of Mexican salsas like pico de gallo, guajillo, or guacamole, the "flavors" were mild, hot, and fire. When the harried employee set the tray with two paper-wrapped tacos on the counter and called my number, I checked my watch. Elapsed time: a little less than two minutes.

So which was the fast food, the carne asada from Hermosillo or the grilled steak from Taco Bell? Both delivered a quick meal for about the same price. Yet the labor that produced them—not to mention the experience of dining— could hardly have been more different. The industrial taco, mass-produced in a central commissary and served under a fiberglass mission bell, seemed worlds away from the taco grilled to order and eaten under the open skies of Mexico.

It is the ersatz version that has shaped the global image of Mexican cuisine. The sociologist George Ritzer has attributed this outcome to the technological rationalization of kitchen labor, a corporate logic of standardization and efficiency that he dubbed "McDonaldization."[2] Or in the words of Taco Bell's founder, Glen Bell, a former hot-dog vendor who had first sampled tacos in Mexican-owned restaurants in California: "If you wanted a dozen . . . you were in for a wait. They stuffed them first, quickly fried them and stuck them together with a toothpick. I thought they were delicious, but something had to be done about the method of preparation."[3] That something was the creation of the "taco shell," a prefried tortilla that could be stored indefinitely in plastic wrap and filled on demand for waiting customers.

Yet there are problems with this interpretation of Yankee ingenuity transforming a Mexican peasant tradition. As connoisseurs of global street cuisine can attest—and as my experiment readily confirmed—fast food in the United States is not particularly fast. Street vendors can prepare elaborate dumplings, noodles, sandwiches, and, of course, tacos as quickly as any chain restaurant can serve a nondescript hamburger, never mind the time spent waiting in line at the drive-through window. Moreover, this contrast between North American modernity and non-Western tradition assumes an authentic taco that has existed unchanged from time immemorial, a dubious historical claim. Once I began researching, I found to my surprise that the taco was as much a modern phenomenon in Mexico as it was in the United States.

The unexpected novelty of the taco raises larger questions about the nature of globalization. The growth of global interconnection is often described as a contemporary trend, historically unprecedented, and brought about by the latest technologies of communication and transportation. The nation appears, by contrast, as a historic entity whose boundaries and traditional cultures may be threatened by new forms of global exchange. The competition between these two versions of tacos provides a textbook example of this recent conflict between globalization and the nation. As late as the 1960s, tacos were virtually unknown outside of Mexico and its former territories in the Southwest. Fifty years later, U.S. corporations had shipped taco shells everywhere from Alaska to Australia and from Morocco to Mongolia. NASA had even blasted soft tacos into orbit to feed astronauts on the International Space Station. But if the taco shop is new to Mexico as well, then the sharp distinction between authentic national cuisines and modern globalized food begins to break down.

In fact, Mexican food has been globalized from the very beginning. As historians have pointed out, there have been earlier eras of global interconnection, beginning in 1492 with Columbus and the rise of oceanic navigation, then again in the nineteenth century with steamships and telegraphs. One such episode of globalization, the Spanish conquest of the Aztec Empire, initiated dramatic culinary changes through the introduction of Mediterranean crops and livestock to the Americas. Globalization continued to exert a powerful influence on Mexicans seeking to forge a national cuisine after independence in 1821, although the international food of the nineteenth century was French haute cuisine rather than North American fast food. The present-day battle over the meaning of authentic Mexican food has high economic stakes because taco-shell stereotypes confound efforts by Mexican tourism and agriculture to gain international distinction and raise the value of their exports. Yet, as a French historian has observed, a national cuisine is "a mirror question, a question of how [a people] and others see themselves and their cuisine."[4] For Mexicans, the fast-food taco must seem like a funhouse mirror, distorting their cuisine beyond all recognition. *Planet Taco* examines this conflict between globalization and the nation as a battle of images between how foreigners think about Mexican food and how Mexicans understand their own national cuisine. In particular, it seeks to show how Mexicans imagined a version of pre-Hispanic authenticity in order to heighten the contrast with globalized industrial dishes from the United States.

The importance of a global perspective becomes apparent when tracing the history of the taco. People have been eating corn tortillas with bits of meat or beans rolled up inside for more than a millennium, but the taco achieved national hegemony only in the twentieth century. Traditionally, every region in Mexico had its own distinctive snack foods, collectively known as *antojitos* (little whimsies), made of corn dough, formed in countless ingenious shapes, and given a wide variety of local names. The now ubiquitous "taco" label is a modern usage, probably deriving from a Spanish root, in contrast to such dishes as tamales and pozole that have a clear lineage to indigenous languages.[5] European meats, including beef, pork, and chicken, are the most common taco fillings, which would seem to make the taco part of Mexico's mestizo or mixed Spanish-Indian heritage, a central tenet of modern nationalist ideology. Indeed, Salvador Novo's national history of Mexican food imagined that this process of culinary mixing began with the first taco, a combination of Spanish pork and Indian corn—"*carnitas* in taco, with hot tortillas"—served to the conquistador Cortés.[6] Novo could only imagine this scene because documentary references to edible tacos are nonexistent for the three centuries of colonial rule. To understand the historical emergence of the taco, it is necessary to step outside the Mexican nation and consider evidence from Europe.

The Spanish word "taco," like the English "tack," is common to most Romantic and Germanic languages. The first known reference, from 1607, appeared in French and signified a cloth plug used to hold in place the ball of an *arquebus*, an early firearm.[7] Eighteenth-century Spanish dictionaries also defined "taco" as a ramrod, a billiard cue, a carpenter's hammer, and a gulp of wine—a combination recalling the English colloquialism, a "shot" of liquor. Only in the mid-nineteenth century did the Spanish Royal Academy expand the meaning to encompass a small bite of food. The specific Mexican version was not acknowledged until well into the twentieth century.[8] Nor did tacos appear in early Mexican dictionaries, most notably Melchor Ocampo's vernacular work of 1844, wryly entitled "Idiotismos Hispano-Mexicanos" (Hispano-Mexican idiocies).[9]

National histories offer little insight on the taco until the late nineteenth century. Cookbooks reflected the elite preference for Spanish and French cuisine over indigenous dishes, although *El cocinero mexicano* (*The Mexican chef*, 1831) provided a long list of street foods, including quesadillas and *chalupas* (canoes), enchiladas and their rustic kin *chilaquiles*, and *envueltos*. The envuelto (Spanish for "wrap") comes closest to what would now be called a taco, but it is crossed with an enchilada, with chile sauce poured over the fried tortilla. Most extravagant were the *envueltos de Nana Rosa* (Granny Rosa's wraps), stuffed with *picadillo* (chopped meat) and garnished profusely.[10] Mexico's *costumbrista* literature of social manners provides additional information about nineteenth-century street foods. The first national novel, José Joaquín Fernández de Lizardi's *El periquillo sarniento* (*The mangy parrot*, 1816), likewise made no mention of tacos but did describe a lunch cooked by Nana Rosa "consisting of envueltos, chicken stew, *adobo* [marinated meat], and *pulque* [a native wine made of fermented maguey] flavored with prickly pears and pineapple."[11] Tacos gained widespread attention only in 1891, with the publication of Manuel Payno's masterpiece, *Los bandidos de Río Frío* (*The bandits of Cold River*). In an early scene in the novel, set during the festival of the Virgin of Guadalupe, a group of Indians danced in honor of the national saint, while feasting on "*chito* [fried goat] with tortillas, drunken salsa, and very good pulque...and the children skipping, with tacos of tortillas and avocado in their hand."[12] Although this culinary meaning of taco had certainly been in popular use for some time, with Payno's benediction, it quickly received official recognition in Feliz Ramos I. Duarte's 1895 *Diccionario de mejicanismos*, which attributed the geographical origin of the term to Mexico City.[13]

To understand how a Spanish word, newly used for a generic snack, became associated with a particular form of rolled tortilla requires a shift to the silver mines that connected colonial Mexico with the global economy. Mexican and Peruvian silver formed the lifeblood not just for the Spanish empire but for world trade in the early modern era. Endless chests of treasure passed successively from the Spanish crown to German and Genoese bankers, Dutch and Portuguese merchants, and finally Indian and Chinese workshops. The fabled Manila galleon also shipped Mexican silver pesos directly across the Pacific from Acapulco. Although the early boomtowns of Zacatecas and Potosí had gone bust by the mid-seventeenth century, the newly installed Bourbon dynasty mobilized technicians and workers from Europe and the Americas to revive the industry in the late eighteenth century. Real del Monte, the greatest of these new mines, was discovered near the town of Pachuca, sixty miles north of Mexico City. By linguistic chance, mine workers called their explosive charges of gunpowder wrapped in paper "tacos," a reference that derived both from the specific usage of a powder charge for a firearm and from the more general meaning of plug, because they prepared the blast by carving a hole in the rock before inserting the explosive taco.[14] In retrospect, it is easy to see the similarity between a chicken taquito with hot sauce and a stick of dynamite.

The national struggle for independence of the 1810s and subsequent civil wars and economic unrest struck the silver districts particularly hard, forcing many to migrate in search of work. Unemployed miners brought their tacos with them to Mexico City, where urban workers found them a portable and convenient lunch, just as the miners did. One of the first visual records of the taco, a photo from the early 1920s, shows a woman selling *tacos sudados* ("sweaty tacos") to a group of paperboys. These foods were made by frying tortillas briefly, stuffing them with a simple mixture, often just potatoes and salsa, and keeping them warm in their own steam in a basket, thus, *tacos de canasta* ("tacos from a basket"). The chronicler Jesús Flores y Escalante confirmed the mining connection by pointing out that tacos sudados originally carried the sobriquet *tacos de minero*. The latter was a common phrase among the taco stands that first proliferated on Mexico City street corners at the beginning of the twentieth century. Once it was established among the working classes of the capital, the taco spread across the country and up the social ladder. The taco thus emerged as a new and modern variety of antojito, with a distinctive culture of its own, embodied in the taquería and associated with Mexico City. Its twentieth-century spread around the country, at times displacing regional antojitos, exemplified the emerging cultural dominance of the capital over the national life.[15]

Long before the taco became a street-corner icon, Mexican food had its origins in the mestizo blending of Native American and Spanish foods, but this colonial encounter has been hopelessly romanticized by modern nationalist ideology. The fairy tale of *mole de guajolote*, for example, celebrates the invention of a turkey and chile sauce dish in the colonial convents of Puebla as a mixture of Old World spices with New World chiles and chocolate. The history of colonial *mestizaje*, however, was not a romantic marriage but rather a racial hierarchy that separated urban Spaniards who ate wheat bread from rural Indians subsisting on corn tortillas. The mestizo castes themselves, including people of mixed race, African slaves, and some Asian migrants as well, inhabited a social limbo of urban slums and sweatshops. Creoles derived status from their European heritage and acknowledged neither the authenticity of indigenous culture nor the social blending of mestizaje.

Meanwhile, a parallel history of early globalization, the travels of maize and other indigenous crops around the world, further muddled the image of Mexican food. Although prolific and versatile, maize has significant nutritional defects, particularly the lack of niacin, a B vitamin essential for human health. Native cooks learned to overcome this flaw through the technology of *nixtamal*, a method of alkaline processing that magnified the plant's nutritional value while also yielding dough for tortillas and tamales. Because the seeds traveled

Figure I.1. An early image of Mexico City paperboys eating tacos for brunch, c. 1920. Col. SINAFO-INAH. Inventory number 155025. Courtesy of the Instituto Nacional de Antropología e Historia, Mexico.

globally without the local knowledge of vitamin fortification, epidemics of pellagra followed the spread of maize in the centuries after 1492. Mexican food came to be seen in Europe not only as plebeian but also as a potential menace to human health.

Regional differentiation has been yet another historical source of confusion about the nature of Mexican food. Mexicans generally trace their national history to the Indian societies of Mesoamerica, a broad cultural region stretching from present-day central Mexico through the Yucatán to the highlands of Central America, and in particular to Tenochtitlán, the island capital of the Aztec Empire. Nevertheless, the Mexica, who founded the Aztec Empire, were themselves migrants, "barbarians" who settled in the Valley of Anáhuac just a few centuries before Cortés. There was an ongoing exchange of goods and people between the self-styled "civilized" people of Mesoamerica and their northern rivals, the "Chichimecas." This term, meaning "children of dogs," was applied to diverse nomadic and semisedentary peoples as well as to agrarian societies in what is now the U.S. Southwest. The Ancestral Pueblos, for example, borrowed the Mesoamerican technology of nixtamal, but local cooks improvised their own recipes, preparing it as piki bread instead of tortillas. With the coming of the Spaniards, this northern frontier retained its culinary distinctiveness through the invention of the wheat flour tortilla, blending Spanish and Indian cultures in new ways. Although the Southwest was only briefly part of the Mexican nation, from independence in 1821 until it was annexed by the United States in 1848, its local cuisines eventually became the model for a globalized version of Mexican food.

In the nineteenth century, Mexicans tried to make sense of their conflicted national cuisine in opposition to the global culinary hegemony of France. This struggle ran from the "Pastry War" of 1838, a gunboat action to collect debts, to the French invasion of 1862–67 and the Imperial court of Maximilian and Carlota, and culminated in the fin de siècle dictatorship of Porfirio Díaz, who feasted on French food and champagne. This period was also when tacos first appeared as a subversive symbol of a popular national cuisine. Francophile Porfirians have been denounced for their unpatriotic tastes, but diplomats and bankers used knowledge of continental cuisine to claim a seat at the banquet table of "civilized nations," even while privately longing for street foods that were unfashionable at home.

The nostalgia of exile also shaped reactions to the regional Mexican cuisine prepared in the United States after the Treaty of Guadalupe Hidalgo.

Wealthy Mexican visitors to San Antonio, Texas, expressed a sharp aversion to the local favorite, chili con carne, which they wrongly associated with the Americanization of their compatriots. Condescension toward the working classes also surely influenced the elite Mexicans' image of street foods. Anglo tourists and settlers created their own, equally negative stereotypes of Mexican vendors. Dubbed the "Chili Queens of San Antonio," these vendors were depicted as sirens of the Old Southwest, seducing unwary visitors with hot tamales and rapacious sexuality, thereby spreading "Montezuma's Revenge" and racial contamination. Such ambivalent images, dangerous and alluring, spurred the industrialization of Mexican food by non-Mexican businessmen, who made fortunes selling chili powder, canned chili, and other purportedly hygienic knockoffs as novelties for a mass market. By the 1920s, parallel commercial networks crossed the continent to supply two distinct markets: canned chili and tamales for mainstream housewives eager for something new, and dried chiles and chocolate for migrant workers hungry for a taste of home.

The quest for authentic food acquired new meaning in the mid-twentieth century as industrial foods began replacing home-cooked meals. Packaged foods were originally developed in part to supply migrant workers, who had the cash to purchase goods unavailable to peasants back home. Mexico's rural, subsistence society was drawn into commercial networks by the Green Revolution of industrial agriculture and by the invention of tortilla factories and dehydrated tortilla flour. The commodification of maize caused an upheaval in gendered labor, because women did the hard work of making tortillas, while also encouraging the gentrification of peasant foods among a self-styled revolutionary, mestizo middle class. As workers shifted to mass-produced industrial tortillas, artisanal versions patted out by hand acquired new cachet in Mexico City restaurants. Middle-class Mexican American restaurateurs and cookbook authors meanwhile codified particular versions of Tex-Mex and Cal-Mex regional cuisines around midcentury. Glen Bell actually borrowed technologies from Mexican entrepreneurs and made his fortune catering to Anglos who were curious about Mexican food but may not have wanted to enter Mexican neighborhoods.

The contemporary globalization of Mexican food began during the Cold War, when people familiar with Tex-Mex and Cal-Mex food began to travel the world, taking their taco shells and burritos with them. Two groups in particular had the knowledge and opportunity to initiate this global migration: U.S. military personnel who had been stationed in the Southwest, and surfers

Figure I.2. Artisanal crafts create social distinctions in a nascent age of industrial tortillas. Women making tortillas in a restaurant, c. 1957. Col. SINAFO-INAH. Inventory number 170840. Courtesy of the Instituto Nacional de Antropología e Historia, Mexico.

who ate tacos and drank Corona longnecks on Baja beaches. Taco Bell, Old El Paso, and other corporate brands followed a trail that these two groups blazed, and profited from stereotypes that they established. Moreover, the Mexican companies most successful in global marketing have been those that adopted an Americanized image, most notably Corona beer and Cuervo tequila, which advertised Mexico as a Spring Break destination. The increasing sophistication of Mexican tourism markets provoked a backlash, beginning in the 1980s with the rise of the "nueva cocina mexicana," a contemporary gourmet movement that sought to reimagine the authenticity of Aztec and Maya cuisines using the professional techniques of continental chefs. Yet even this self-consciously nationalist project was part of a larger transnational phenomenon. Tourists were an initial market, as the Mexican middle classes had been forced to tighten their belts during a painful economic crisis in the 1980s. Meanwhile, chefs in the United States were creating their own version of upscale Mexican dishes as "New Southwestern," ironically appropriating foods they had once disdained as part of a broader search for authentic "American regional cuisines."

These trends would seem to herald a dim future for Mexican cuisine on a global stage: gentrified peasant cooking for a sophisticated, international elite; factory-made tortillas or Taco Bell for the masses, both in Mexico and abroad. Yet there remains a basic problem with the theory of McDonaldization, its ahistorical focus on "the highest stage of fast food," to quote one acute observer.[16] By ignoring the industry's uncertain early history, and by discounting the revolutionary potential of future technological change and global migration, fast-food corporations appear as invincible titans, gobbling up world markets and Americanizing everything in their path. Nevertheless, globalization is not only a top-down phenomenon, imposed from above by political and corporate bosses. Globalization can also transform societies from the bottom up, by way of human migration and social movements. One consequence of the great proletarian migration from Latin America, beginning with the regional crisis of the 1980s and seemingly ending with the financial crash of 2008, was a renaissance for family restaurants serving Mexican regional cooking throughout the United States. Moreover, peasant farmers have begun to mobilize and challenge corporate control over agriculture and to demand democratic governance and food sovereignty. It is hard to predict the outcome of these movements at a time of virulent anti-immigrant politics and widespread food shortages. But at least the era of the taco shell may be waning. Although this invention was essential for creating international markets for Mexican food, it is increasingly being replaced by soft corn tortillas, even if made with dehydrated tortilla flour.[17]

Understanding Mexican food requires not only global and local perspectives but also ethnic and business histories. The postwar association of Mexican food with the taco shell was determined as much by material considerations as by ethnic stereotypes. Making tortillas by hand involves skilled labor, even with the assistance of mechanical nixtamal mills and folding presses. Moreover, tortillas, like donuts, are best eaten fresh, preferably within a few hours off the griddle. In Mexico, tortilla factories have been largely a cottage industry, conveniently located on any street corner, and operating sporadically throughout the day for customers who line up before breakfast, lunch, and dinner. This just-in-time business model, however, fit poorly in the postwar "Fordist" era of giant factories pursuing economies of scale. Mass production was needed to achieve profits on low-value commodities, and there are few consumer goods cheaper than a corn tortilla. Commercial supplies of fresh tortillas were simply uneconomical in markets without regular demand from knowledgeable consumers, which basically meant everywhere except Mexico, Central America, and a few cities in the United States. By contrast, taco shells could be produced in bulk, wrapped in plastic, stored in warehouses, and shipped around the world, albeit with some breakage. They were also easier to eat than fresh corn tortillas, at least for consumers unpracticed in the deft art of rolling their own tacos.

These considerations of technological efficiency and gendered labor suggest the usefulness of approaching Mexican food from a commodity-chain analysis, with its comprehensive perspective on production, distribution, and consumption.[18] Of course, Mexican food requires many ingredients with different material properties and cultural associations. Maize, the economic foundation for ancient Mesoamerican societies, had spread from its site of domestication in southwestern Mexico across the tropics of South America and the temperate woodlands of North America before Columbus arrived. After 1492, its high productivity and pioneering ability to grow on rugged slopes made it a valuable crop for marginal farmers everywhere from southern Europe to the foothills of the Himalayas. Other ingredients in the Mexican kitchen grow only in limited climates, and elaborate commodity chains were needed to convey them to market. Chocolate was so valuable that the Aztec Empire conquered the distant province of Soconusco to ensure reliable supplies. Spanish conquistadors, who navigated the Pacific Ocean to satisfy their taste for Asian spices, carried chocolate with them to Manila. In the history of globalization, the difference between products like maize that travel as cultivars and trade goods such as spices and chocolate turns out to be highly significant.

Commodity chains have become still more lengthy and contentious today. The North American Free Trade Agreement (NAFTA), implemented in 1994, allowed the free entry of subsidized maize from the Midwestern United States, undermining family farms in Mexico and forcing many to migrate north in search of work. Then, in 2007, a rush to convert corn into biofuel caused sudden inflation in the cost of tortillas for the poorest Mexican consumers.[19] In a tragic irony of global capitalism, the loss of food security in Mexico coincided with the increasing presence of fresh corn tortillas in markets around the world.

Changing fashions for Mexican food within the international food service industry—for example, corn tortillas in place of taco shells—reflect shifting notions of Mexican ethnicity. Anthropologists now conceptualize group identities, whether ethnic, racial, national, or otherwise, as a process that is constantly evolving, and foods provide tangible collective representations of these affiliations. Cuisines can serve to police group boundaries either through the rules created by insiders such as Jewish dietary laws or through stereotypes ascribed by outsiders, for example, "frogs," "krauts," and "beaners." Nevertheless, foods can also offer enticing bridges between societies, encouraging outsiders to sample an unfamiliar culture in a relatively risk-free situation. Culinary tourism, the intentional exploration of the foods of another group, has become a rapidly growing industry. The ideal of authenticity, of getting food prepared the way it is supposed to be, is central to the experience.[20]

The differences between "inside" and "outside" meanings invariably reflect unequal relations of power.[21] Corporate advertisements often sell ethnic food to mainstream consumers by using exotic and demeaning images such as the Frito Bandito and the Taco Bell dog, conveying images of Mexicans as outlaws or animals. Even when popular culture representations are more respectful, well-financed corporate chains may crowd out ethnic entrepreneurs to the edges of the market.[22] National cuisines, which are also imagined through a process of culinary tourism, likewise manipulate the foods of regional and ethnic minorities for ideological and commercial purposes. In the nineteenth century, Indian foods were largely excluded from notions of proper Mexican cuisine. Today, ancient Aztec and Maya images provide authenticity for the national cuisine, although the foods of living Indians are often kept at a distance. Ethnic distinctions also intersect with notions of class and gender, compounding inequalities. Anglos equated the chili queens' food with deviant sexuality; elite Mexicans' views of Indian food are colored by pervasive rural poverty. Nevertheless, minorities often resist efforts to appropriate and denigrate their cooking. As early as the 1930s, for example, New Mexico matrons Cleofas Jaramillo and Fabiola Cabeza de Vaca wrote cookbooks to refute distorted images of their foods that were appearing in recipes of North American mass-market women's magazines.[23] The belief that people have the right to determine their own identities and manners of expressing themselves is basic to the ideal of cultural citizenship.[24]

But is authenticity obligatory? Are ethnic entrepreneurs "selling out" if they change a recipe to market food to a wider audience? And can ethnicity be acquired secondhand? After all, the postwar travels of Mexican food around the world offer a classic immigrant story. The cooks just happened not to be, for the most part, Mexican. To answer these questions, one must first remember that iconic recipes exist only on the pages of cookbooks; in practice, they are adapted constantly to suit available ingredients. What cultural groups share is a general idea of the appropriate flavors, proportions, and combinations that belong in any particular dish, say, the traditional spices in a *recado negro* (Yucatecan spice mixture), or the proper balance of meat to tortilla for tacos al pastor, or the right variety of cheese for marketplace enchiladas.[25] These opinions vary among regions, social classes, families, and even with the particular *sazón*, or taste, of an individual cook. One woman's secret ingredient ruins the entire dish for another. Working-class Mexican and Mexican American women are often uninterested in notions of authenticity. That concept is more useful for claiming social distinction or for marketing restaurants and cookbooks than for getting dinner on the table.[26]

The Mexican poet Octavio Paz famously declared, "the melting pot is a social idea that, when applied to culinary art, produces abominations."[27] In exalting Mexican regional cuisine as authentic and scorning Tex-Mex foods as a bastardization, he denounced the Mexican Americans who blended two cultures in their everyday lives. By contrast, the Chicana poet Gloria Anzaldúa called for an awareness of people who live between or across the borders that separate nations, races, and genders.[28] "Tex-Mex," which has been used to denote any form of inauthentic Mexican food, more properly describes a regional variant of Mexican culture from Texas, with Anglo Saxon and Central European influences, just as Veracruz is a melting pot of Afro-Mexican culture and Sonorans have a taste for Chinese.[29] Such a consciousness allows for the recognition of endless varieties of Mexican food. Norteño cooks often make soft tacos with tortillas of wheat flour instead of corn because of regional patterns of agriculture. Ground beef, iceberg lettuce, and cheddar cheese were the most readily available ingredients from the U.S. food-processing industry. Contrary to corporate myth, Mexican Americans even invented the taco shell, back when Glen Bell was still boiling weenies. Instead of the fast-food taco, it should be called the Mexican American taco, as a tribute to the creativity of hardworking ethnic cooks.

Planet Taco shows how images of authenticity have been invented to promote culinary tourism and nationalist ideology. People use food to think about others, and popular views of the taco as cheap, hot, and potentially dangerous have reinforced racist images of Mexico as a land of tequila, migrants, and tourists' diarrhea. Moreover, colonial stereotypes about Mexicans and their food, which took shape in the southwestern United States, have been transmitted around the world. But it makes no sense to exchange the Anglo mythology of chili queens and the Taco Bell dog for a Manichean nationalist ideology prescribing romanticized peasant food as an antidote to McDonaldization. Either conclusion would be far too neat. The history of tacos, like eating tacos, is a messy business.

PART I

Proto-Tacos

MAIZE AND THE MAKING OF MEXICO

CHAPTER 1

When searching for authentic Mexican food, people often look to the ancient civilizations of the Aztecs and Maya. Culinary tourists seek out native foods to experience the taste of pre-Hispanic culture as they visit the pyramids of Teotihuacán and Chichén Itzá. Chefs meanwhile turn to the Florentine Codex, an account of indigenous culture given by the children of Aztec nobles to a Spanish priest, for further links between past and present. Foods described in the sixteenth-century Codex, such as lobster in red chile sauce, tamales with greens served in crab sauce, and tortillas made with cactus fruit, have become menu items in trendy Mexico City restaurants.[1] The desire of chefs and tourists to feel connected to a "deep Mexico" is understandable in an era when industrial fast food is commonplace. A sense of authenticity, based on historic traditions of foods tied to particular locations, can be a welcome refuge from the threat of global homogenization.[2] Nevertheless, efforts to trace a genealogy for a national cuisine confront basic historical problems, starting with the fact that pre-Hispanic peoples were not "Mexican." Although nationalist ideologues have often attributed contemporary identities to primordial peoples—for example, a German folk spirit among the Saxon and Swabian tribes of classical Europe—such accounts say more about modern nationalism than about ancient societies. Idealized views of an Indian past have likewise shaped modern notions of authentic Mexican food. But as a product of the encounter between Native Americans and Spanish conquistadors, Mexican food was globalized from the very beginning.

In tracing the lineage of Mexican cuisine back to pre-Hispanic times, contemporary chefs have followed a well-established trend in Mexican historiography. Before the conquest, there was no place called Mexico. Linguistic groups such as the Nahuas, Zapotecs, and Maya, each with their own distinct lands, cultures, and histories, were given the common label of "Indians" in the colony of New Spain. When the Creole descendants of conquistadors came to perceive a separate identity from the European-born Spaniards who dominated the colony politically, they adopted an indigenous past and gave the land the indigenous name of Mexico. The historian Enrique Florescano explained that this group "attempted to create a common memory of the land it shared with other ethnic groups... [and] proposed to make the memories and historical traditions of the other ethnic groups its own." Like today's culinary nationalists, Creole patriots of the colonial era imagined themselves to be the heirs to Aztec emperors, but their attitudes toward indigenous foods were very different. Catholic missionaries had actually sought to eradicate the indigenous staple maize, with its pagan religious associations, and to propagate instead a gospel of wheat as the symbol and sustenance of Christianity. Although the campaign failed, corn tortillas were relegated to the indigenous and mestizo lower classes, while wheat bread became a status symbol for the urban, Hispanic elite. Bridging this cultural gap to create a national cuisine required a leap of historical imagination, just as "the formation of Mexican national conscience," according to Florescano, was the result "of the decision made by some segments of society to impose their own image of the past on others, of the decision of many indigenous communities to preserve their own identity, and, finally, of many things forgotten."[3]

Along with the long-standing disdain for indigenous culture, another thing that is often forgotten in Mexican nationalist ideology is the diverse parentage of the mestizo nation. The duality of the Spanish conquistador and his Indian concubine actually deviates from the original ideal of a universal "cosmic race" formulated by José Vasconcelos in the 1920s, and historians now reemphasize the global, cosmopolitan nature of New Spain's colonial society.[4] In addition to Indians and Spaniards, African slaves contributed to the multiracial mixture, particularly within coastal regions and urban areas. Immigrants also arrived

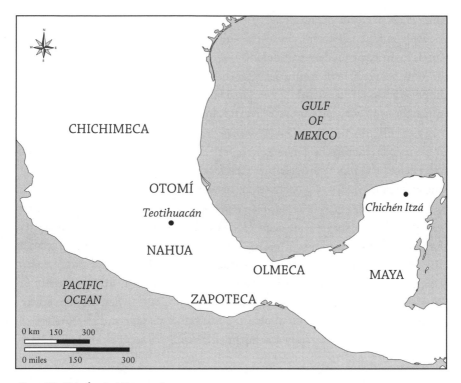

Figure 1.1. Map of ancient Mesoamerica.

from Asia by way of the Manila galleon in larger numbers than had previously been thought. The culinary influence of Africans and Asians can be difficult to document directly because of the circulation of foodstuffs before 1492; for instance, it is impossible to say with certainty whether rice arrived in New Spain from Europe, Africa, Asia, or all three. Moreover, European migrants to the colony were not all of Iberian origin. Catholic priests, in particular, were often recruited from Italy and the Habsburg territories of Central Europe. There were also profound culinary distinctions among indigenous societies, especially between the Maya of the Yucatán Peninsula and the Nahua of the central highlands. Taken together, these diverse influences produced more fluid social and political boundaries than modern nationalist ideologies often acknowledge.

Finally, although national histories have given little attention to the early modern globalization of Mesoamerican crops, this outward movement set important patterns in the global history of Mexican food. Three items in particular—corn, chiles, and chocolate—illustrate the varied reception of new foods in the early modern world. Maize, as a sturdy and productive crop, spread around the world in the centuries after contact, but because of its usefulness to impoverished farmers working marginal lands, it acquired a plebeian image. In much the same way, prolific and flavorful chile peppers attracted a wide following as a spice for the poor. Only chocolate attained elite status in Europe, and it went no farther in the early modern period, gaining little ground in Africa or Asia before the nineteenth century. The foods that spread most widely during the early modern age of globalization traveled steerage, not first class.

Whether at home or abroad, maize played a crucial role in what might be called the prehistory of Mexican food, establishing images that shaped its local and global meanings after 1821, when political independence initiated the process of inventing a Mexican national cuisine. Before that time, as this chapter shows, there was no authentic Mexican food, but rather a variety of cuisines, deeply divided by region and culture. Moreover, when Mesoamerican foods did travel, they acquired plebeian images of danger and immorality, in part because they were rarely accompanied by indigenous cooking knowledge.

Pre-Hispanic Origins

Maize held deep significance as the source of life for Native American societies, and three critical moments in the culinary history of corn coincide neatly with turning points in the archaeological record of Mesoamerica. First, around 7000 BCE, the original maize plant was "born" from a remarkable genetic mutation. This unique event probably took place along the Balsas River in what is now southwestern Mexico, and it was likely overseen by a human midwife. It began a cooperative relationship between plants and people that encouraged both biological and social expansion. Next, around 1500 BCE, the first corn and bean stew was cooked in a newly invented ceramic pot, somewhere along the Gulf Coast. Starch and legumes, when eaten together, offered a protein-rich vegetarian diet capable of supporting sedentary, agrarian societies. The Olmecs, first to devise this recipe, became the "base culture" that established patterns for the future development of Mesoamerica. Finally, in the early centuries of the Common Era, corn was first *nixtamalized*, or simmered with alkaline ash, which remedied its vitamin deficiency. This nourishing recipe yielded plump, soft kernels that could be ground on a *metate* (grinding stone) and cooked as tortillas, offering sustenance for large-scale urbanization in the first American metropolis, Teotihuacán.

According to the *Popol Vuh*, the sacred "Council Book" of the Quiché Maya of highland Guatemala, corn was present at the creation of the human race by the "Sovereign Plumed Serpent," known elsewhere as Quetzalcoatl. As dawn approached on the first day, the gods gathered at the "Split Place, Bitter Water Place," a cave in the mountains with a nearby spring, located along the modern-day border with Mexico, where a tall grass called *teosinte* grows in abundance. The maize used for creating human flesh was supplied by animals such as a fox, coyote, parrot, and crow, each a well-known thief in Maya fields. The goddess Xmucane ground the corn nine times into smooth dough and then modeled it into flesh as "human legs and arms."[5]

Recent biological research indicates that the fantastic myth of the *Popol Vuh* may well have happened, but in reverse, with humans taking an active role in the creation of maize. While most crops were domesticated through a mundane process of gradual experimentation, often on multiple occasions, the origins of maize were little short of miraculous. Botanists once thought that maize, like its cousin teosinte, was derived from a common ancestral plant, now extinct. However, recent genetic analysis has shown that it was domesticated directly from teosinte through a single, incredibly rare mutation. Computer modeling of corn's "family tree" dates this unique parent to around 9,000 years ago, while DNA comparisons with contemporary teosinte suggest the Balsas River Valley as the site of domestication. Moreover, some scholars conclude that this remarkable "Maizoid Eve" must have been discovered by humans. Unlike an ear of corn with a removable husk, teosinte seeds are encased in a thick woody sheath, which disperses for reproduction when consumed by herbivores. Left alone, the naked cobs of this first maize plant were an evolutionary dead end, destined to perish in the digestive tract of passing animals. Instead, a human gathering teosinte stalks must have observed the distinctive ears and recognized their importance, perhaps showing them off to her companions like precious jewels. That this early "botanist" was a woman seems likely given the gendered division of labor between female gatherers and male hunters, whose survival depended on a deep knowledge of the growing seasons and migratory patterns of plants and animals. Crossed back with neighboring stands of teosinte, to propagate the mutation, maize flourished under human protection, and to this day, it cannot reproduce in the wild.[6]

Maize domestication did not produce a "Neolithic revolution" immediately transforming archaic hunters and gatherers into sedentary farmers. Instead, these early foragers continued migrating for thousands of years, consuming the tiny ancestral corncobs as one component of an omnivorous diet, even while they selected larger and more productive plants in a process that would culminate with the large ears of modern maize. Many plants now associated with the Mexican kitchen such as chiles and tomatoes were originally domesticated in South America. During the ecological tumult at the end of the last ice age, when forest began displacing grass in the tropical lowlands of the Amazon and Caribbean, foragers took the first steps toward agriculture by propagating wild tubers and gourds. By 6000 BCE, early horticulturalists had begun to reclaim the tropical forest, slashing and burning the overgrowth to open land for their preferred cultigens. Even with more productive fields, humans continued to forage widely, retracing their steps to harvest plants when they had matured.[7] National and civilizational histories tend to skip quickly over these millennia between the domestication of plants and the rise of sedentary societies. Yet archaeologists have questioned progressive narratives of change and emphasized instead the stability of hunting and gathering, which yielded more varied and healthy diets than did farming, and for much less work. The real question is why humans ever abandoned a life of leisure to earn their meals by the sweat of the brow.[8]

The Mesoamerican kitchen required labor-intensive and sophisticated technology in order to maximize its nutritional yield. Although banging rocks together may not sound terribly advanced, Stone Age cooks were quite ingenious at using available resources, and they periodically redesigned their tools to create new recipes and food-processing techniques. With mortars and pestles, for example, the one-handed design and careful shaping allowed cooks to shift position and relieve muscle stress.[9] Maize needed multiple forms of food processing to achieve its nutritional potential. Grinding on a metate produced a denser, more caloric food than alternatives like popcorn. While maize and beans alone lack vital amino acids, cooking them together complements the value of their proteins as well as their tastes. The invention of ceramic vessels was therefore important to the development of the sedentary, agrarian Olmec society in the absence of protein from domesticated animals.[10] A final nutritional defect of maize is the shortage of usable niacin, a vitamin needed to prevent the disease pellagra, which is characterized by skin rash, intestinal problems, insanity, and death. Maize could not become the dietary staple for dense urban populations until cooks discovered the nixtamal process in which limestone or wood ash freed the chemically bound vitamin. However nutritionally sound, the recipe for tortillas required enormous physical labor from women. Arguably, they worked as hard grinding corn on the metate as did the men they fed who constructed the physical monuments of Teotihuacán, the pyramids of the Sun and the Moon.[11]

As Mesoamerican populations grew, they took full advantage of the material resources of the land through innovative recipes and omnivorous tastes. The Maya, for example, prepared nixtamal as porridges and tamales with various wrappings and fillings. Archaeologists debate whether the Maya patted out tortillas in pre-Hispanic times. They did not use the same earthenware *comales* (griddles) as the Nahuas but may have cooked similar thin cakes in other ways, for example, on heated stones. The Maya certainly had their own unique recipes for nixtamal, including beers that were fermented like South American *chicha*, in contrast to the agave beer called pulque favored elsewhere in Mesoamerica. The Maya also cultured a "sour dough" nixtamal with bacteria that improved its nutritional value, just as yogurt does for milk.[12] In contrast to the sedentary Maya, the Mexica were originally a tribe of nomads who invaded the central highlands from the northwest around 1250 as part of a post-classical movement known collectively as the Aztlán migrations. They went on to found the Aztec Empire and, by 1500, received tribute from throughout Mesoamerica. These luxury goods provided the basis for an elaborate court cuisine, consisting of hundreds of separate dishes prepared daily for Moctezuma and served with freshly made tortillas. The rich variety reflected not only imperial power but also the omnivorous appetites of a people without cattle, sheep, hogs, or chickens. The emperor's chile pepper stews contained deer and geese, salamanders and grasshoppers, ant eggs and lake algae, and the two indigenous domesticated animals, turkeys and small, hairless canines. In the days of the Aztecs, the Taco Bell dog would have been *in* the gorditas.[13]

Although ancient cooks were remarkably skilled in making the most of limited resources, the particular forms of gendered labor that evolved to support dense populations in the arid environment of Mesoamerica were not inevitable. The Mississippian culture independently invented hominy (nixtamal) near Cahokia about 800 CE and, with this improved nutritional base, expanded across the eastern woodlands. But they did not employ the labor-intensive grinding of tortilla dough because they simply stewed the kernels whole. In South America and the Caribbean, potatoes and cassava root were the primary staples, and the alkali treatment of corn never caught on.[14] It is also important to keep in mind the inevitable cycles of expansion and contraction within human societies. Declining population is often perceived as a sign of failure—the collapse of civilization—but such a perspective tends to privilege the elites, who do not perform the hard labor needed to support complex societies. To state the obvious, ordinary workers may prefer not to spend their leisure time building pyramids, just as women might wish to have less labor-intensive forms of food preparation. The causes of decline for the Olmecs, Teotihuacán, and classical Maya are still debated; climate change, ecological overreach, war, and revolution are all possible factors. But the resistance of subject peoples is clearly evident in the fall of the Aztec Empire, because large numbers of Indians chose to ally with the Spanish conquistadors against their former oppressors. Scholars have only begun to explore the connections between household labor and the fate of empires. Nevertheless, what is known of this history should discourage attempts to trace an inevitable and progressive path of civilization from ancient foragers to modern kitchens—without even considering the upheavals of the conquest, which toppled maize from its place of honor in Mesoamerica.

Culinary Conquistadors

Although Mexican food is often considered an iconic example of global fusion, the initial encounters between Spanish and Native American palates were marked by mutual disgust. Moctezuma's emissaries reported that European bread tasted "like dried maize stalks," while Bernal Díaz del Castillo complained of the "misery of maize cakes" that served as rations while on campaign.[15] Food even became an instrument of conquest; cattle and sheep, let loose to forage, often preceded the Spanish armies, devouring indigenous crops. The founding of wheat farms later helped to institutionalize European control over native land and labor. Animal and human incursions met with fierce resistance from Indians, who fought in court to preserve their fields for maize. By the end of the colonial era, this battle had reached a stalemate, both geographic and social, that left a strong regional imprint on the cuisines of New Spain. Native staples predominated in rural areas, especially in the south, where the indigenous population was heaviest before the conquest, while Hispanic foods gained the upper hand in urban areas and in the sparsely settled north. Despite colonial efforts to segregate Europeans and Indians in distinct societies, native women working as domestic servants and concubines were conquistadors of a sort, seducing the Spaniards with the piquant flavors of their cooking.

Taste was only one of many reasons that settlers sought to transplant the Mediterranean complex of wheat, olive oil, and wine to New Spain. Food was heavily freighted with markers of status and identity in the early modern era. Colonists feared that without access to European foods their bodies would degenerate in the climate of the Americas, eventually transforming them into Indians. Perceiving themselves as a new aristocracy, conquistadors claimed the privilege of wheat bread and Oriental spices. Missionaries were equally intent on culinary change for evangelical purposes. Wheat was the only grain that could be used for the Eucharist according to medieval Church doctrine, while wine signified the blood of Christ, and olive oil was essential to sacraments and celebrations. Unfortunately for colonists, the life cycle of European plants did not match the climate of New Spain, where the rain came in summer instead of winter, causing fungus to grow on wheat and diluting the sugar in grapes, which made for insipid wines.[16]

Eager to maintain status, Spaniards willingly purchased foods they could not grow themselves. Customs receipts from Veracruz, reported by the German naturalist Alexander von Humboldt, indicate that wine and brandy alone accounted for nearly 20 percent of colonial imports from Spain in 1802. Olives, capers, nuts, and spices were also significant expenditures. This picture of conspicuous consumption of luxury goods was confirmed by rare menus from judicial archives indicating that colonial elites spent lavish sums—and occasionally walked out on the bills—for *pucheros* (stews), salads dressed with oil and vinegar, Jerez sherry and claret wine, and, for Christmas Eve, the traditional Iberian salt cod.[17]

If Spanish colonists paid dearly for most familiar foods, meat was cheap by comparison with the homeland, at least in the early days. The catastrophic decline of Indian populations from disease and abuse allowed European livestock to take over abandoned fields. This herbivorous invasion had serious environmental consequences. For example, the Mezquital Valley, northeast of Mexico City, was overrun by sheep in the 1550s. With neither predators nor competition, they denuded the hills and encouraged erosion, rendering the land unfit for farming or herding. Eventually the soil adjusted to the new demands, supporting smaller numbers of livestock than during the boom years. Meanwhile, Native Americans overcame their initial aversion and began to raise animals and eat meat, particularly chicken, but it rarely constituted a significant part of their diet.[18]

Maize remained the foundation of indigenous livelihoods, in part because it was less expensive and more reliable than its European competitor at every step from the field to the table. Unlike the low yields of wheat, a single seed of corn produced hundreds of grains on each of several ears, all protected from disease by sturdy husks. Moreover, wheat required substantial capital investments, teams of oxen to plow the soil, mills to grind the grain into flour, and ovens to bake it into bread. By contrast, corn could be grown and cooked with only the simplest of tools: a digging stick for planting, and a metate and comal for cooking. Maize was particularly favorable on the hilly landscapes, and terraced agriculture flourished on mountainsides that farmers could never plow. Some native communities did grow wheat for sale to urban markets, just as some indigenous nobles ate bread in imitation of European rulers. Spanish priests also did their best to incorporate wheat bread into village festivals, but on a daily basis, maize was the grain of choice in rural Mexico in the sixteenth century, and it remains so in the twenty-first.

Social and culinary hierarchies were more complicated in cities because of widespread race mixture. Although the technical definition of a mestizo was the offspring of a Spaniard and an Indian, in practice, the legitimate children of wealthy parents were accepted as Spaniards, while those abandoned by their fathers often remained in their mothers' communities as de facto Indians. Over time, an urban underclass emerged comprising poor Spaniards, African slaves, unattached Indians, and assorted mestizos. To make sense of these people who did not conform to the expectations of either Spaniards or Indians, colonial officials devised an elaborate "system of castes" with bizarre, bestial categories such as *coyote* mestizo and *zambaigo* (literally "son of Sambo," the offspring of mixed Indian and African parents), in an attempt to divide and rule this variegated society.[19]

Definitions of race therefore depended as much on culture as on physical appearance, and the baker's guild of Mexico City reinforced this artificial hierarchy by producing breads appropriate for every rank and income. In the eighteenth century, the purest wheat was milled and cleaned by hand, kneaded with shortening and a little leavening, and then baked into delicate loaves called *pan frances* or *pan español* (French bread or Spanish bread). Just two master bakers had permission to make this special variety; one worked on consignment for the viceroy, the other for the archbishop. Wealthy Creoles purchased *pan floreado* (flowered bread), made of select wheat, and shaped in round or

Figure 1.2. Casta painting with tamales. "From Indian and Basina, Zambayga" ("De indio y basina, zambayga") by Miguel Cabrera. Inventory number 00010. Courtesy of El Museo de América, Madrid.

ring loaves. Large commercial bakeries used lower-quality wheat, maize, and other flours to produce coarse *pan común* and even less desirable *pambazos* and *cemitas*, thereby matching mixed-grain breads to people of mixed race, at least in theory. At the bottom of this hierarchy were Indians, who, even in Mexico

City, consumed large quantities of corn tortillas, as did many other plebeians unable to afford the cheapest bread. Of course, both racial and gastronomical castes emerged from the Spanish imagination and only approximated the complicated social realities.[20]

Foods crossed social boundaries in multiple directions in colonial New Spain. Some culinary borderlands were close to home, such as the kitchen gardens where Indian women planted aromatic European vegetables—onions, carrots, and garlic—to supplement their chiles and squash. Native cooks also learned to beat pork fat into the corn dough for tamales, giving a lighter texture to these steamed cakes. Other mixtures took place in commercial production, such as the use of European distilling technology to transform fermented pulque into a highly potent alcohol called *mezcal*. By the eighteenth century, colonial brewers had raised the ire of Spanish moralists with a wide range of beverages, Hispanic *aguardiente* (sugar cane brandy), hybrid *charagua* (pulque fermented with sugar syrup and chile colorado), and native *sangre de conejo* (literally, "rabbit blood," a bright red cocktail of pulque and prickly pear juice, named for the Nahua deity of drunkenness, 400 Rabbits).[21] Europeans also made dietary accommodations to the new environment and culture. Pork fat became a widespread substitute for expensive olive oil, and indigenous frijoles replaced chickpeas in Spanish pucheros. The native beverage chocolate quickly gained a following among Creoles, particularly women, who depended on it as a stimulant for Catholic fast days and even drank it during mass. Perhaps the most creative result of New Spain's mestizo kitchen was the perennial festival dish, mole de guajolote, a thick turkey stew blending chile peppers and chocolate with the spicy banquet foods of medieval Europe.

Despite this widespread fusion, distinctive Creole and indigenous cooking styles persisted throughout the colonial period. Fields of corn and wheat were the most obvious culinary symbols of separate Spanish and Indian societies, but domestic gardens reveal more subtle differences, for example, in the curious history of coriander, an herb called cilantro or *culantro* in Spanish. A native of the Mediterranean, it was known to the ancient Egyptians, and its aromatic seeds have been found in the tomb of Tutankhamen. The Roman cookbook of Apicius used both seeds and leaves; the former were pounded in a mortar with pepper and other spices, while the latter were cooked with leeks and mint. Coriander was also taken up in the spice trade and carried to India, where the seeds became part of the mixture known as *garam masala*. By the early modern period, changing European tastes had caused the leaves to fall out of favor,

---

Box 1.1 Recipe for Avocados in Guacamole

Peel and seed the avocados, chop with a knife of silver or wood—metal gives them a bad taste and bad color—arrange on a platter and serve with oil, vinegar, onion, oregano, and chile ancho. There are persons who mash the avocados and convert them into a paste. This platter can be eaten with all sorts of grilled meats and with stew.

Source: Vicenta Torres de Rubio, *Cocina michoacana* (Zamora: Imprenta Moderna, 1896), 18.

---

perhaps because many people considered them to have an unpleasant soapy flavor. Europeans ignored the herb until the nineteenth century, when it reappeared in Asian cookery under the exotic name of Chinese parsley. Nevertheless, coriander seeds continued to be used as a spice and indeed became a standard component in the Creole moles of New Spain. By contrast, Native Americans fit cilantro into their own culinary system in the category of *quelites*, assorted greens that were eaten wild as a snack, cooked in broth, or added to their own moles. The fragrant leaves proved to have a natural affinity for chile peppers, and today they are considered an essential ingredient in guacamole. But as late as the nineteenth century, the Creole version of guacamole—the recipe that appeared in cookbooks—was basically an avocado salad with chiles and onion, often chopped rather than mashed in a basalt mortar, and dressed with oil and vinegar.[22]

The cultural encounters of New Spain were not limited to Europeans and Native Americans; instead, this gastronomic system of castes incorporated cooks and cuisines from around the world. Tracing the origins of any given dish is difficult, not least because of the imprint left on Iberian cooking by eight centuries of Muslim rule, from 711 to 1492. Delicately perfumed Arab stews, roasts, and meatballs were taken up by European medieval courts and eventually carried to New Spain as the inspiration for mole de guajolote. Muslim traders also introduced sugar along with many Asian plants, and Indians learned to make candy with everything from sweet potato (*camote*) to coconut (*cocada*) and amaranth seeds (*alegría*). The convent kitchens of New Spain also reproduced Middle Eastern marzipan, nougat, and custard. Another Arabic cooking practice that became common was the vinegar marinade *escabeche*, used to preserve vegetables, fish, and meat. Even the Day of the Dead bread, formed in the shape of skulls, had parallels in an ancient Persian custom for celebrating the Spring Equinox.[23]

African slaves worked in the fields and kitchens of New Spain, but their influence is difficult to discern because of this complicated history of culinary blending. The most important—and for some scholars controversial—African contribution to the foods of the Americas was rice. A common rice dish, for example, was called *morisqueta*, referring to the Moors. Yet the precise origins of this rice are unclear, for although Muslims had transplanted Asian rice (*Oryza sativa*) to North Africa, indigenous African varieties (*O. glaberrima*) were also grown in the Senegambia region of West Africa, an important source for slave traders in the sixteenth century. In any event, slaves in the Caribbean quickly began to combine rice with local beans, creating the highly nutritious combination now known as *moros y cristianos*.[24] The taste for spices and greens, two other characteristics of African regional cuisines, likewise blended with local ingredients in the Americas; thus, African cooks replaced malaguetta pepper with indigenous chiles. Such Afro-Indian blends became increasingly common over time; for example, Mónica de la Cruz, a *mulata* accused of sorcery by the Inquisition in 1652, was a vendor of tamales.[25]

Asians also made subtle contributions to the globalization of culture and cuisine in New Spain. The principal source of contact was the Manila galleon, an enormous trading ship that sailed once a year to the Spanish colony of the Philippines. Its landing in Acapulco, like the arrival of the silver fleet at Veracruz, occasioned a boisterous trade fair where merchants bargained for goods from around the world. In addition to ceramics and other items, Asian slaves and servants were imported legally or smuggled into New Spain. Asian sailors and even a few Japanese samurai warriors who served as mercenary guards settled in Pacific coastal towns and married local women. These *chino* immigrants numbered between 50,000 and 100,000 over the course of the colonial era and came from a variety of Asian lands, including China, Japan, the Philippines, India, and Southeast Asia. Also known as *chinos indios*, they often worked as peddlers because they could legally cross the boundaries between Spanish and Indian communities. In 1638, the Indians of Atalcomulco expelled a chino baker who forced them to buy bread against their will. Perhaps more popular with local consumers were the alcoholic coconut spirits that Asian migrants introduced. Asian cooks may even have introduced the *comiscal*, a version of tandoor oven along the southern coast, where it is still used in present-day

Juchitán.[26] Colonial officials, on the other hand, were more eager to transplant Asian spices than people or ovens, but experiments proved disappointing. Ginger took root, but Caribbean producers dominated the market for this
commodity. Although the principal spices—clove, nutmeg, and pepper—failed
to grow, the introduction of other Asian plants, including cinnamon, coconut,
tamarind, and mango, greatly enriched the local cuisine.[27]

The globalization of food in New Spain was largely a story of conquest, but
it unfolded in a highly uneven fashion. The continued reliance on maize by the
majority of the population, including large numbers of mestizos and down-
wardly mobile Spaniards, illustrated the limits of culinary colonialism. Foods
moved across social boundaries and entered at the margins of both native
and European culinary systems. In rural areas, maize remained the foundation of everyday subsistence, while imported livestock and spices gained high
status through their consumption during religious festivals, perhaps once a
year, when a single animal might be slaughtered to feed an entire community.
Meanwhile, those on the edge of urban Hispanic society generally ate a more
indigenous diet, confirming their lower status. Even the elite, who could afford
expensive wheat bread, soon acquired a taste for native condiments such as
chiles and chocolate. Although the dual tyrannies of nature and status determined the broad outlines of food distribution, according to where crops would
grow and who could afford to purchase them, cooks nevertheless had considerable latitude in shaping the flavors of New Spain. Despite this culinary blending, one looks in vain for an authentic Mexican cuisine in the colonial era.

The Globalization of Corn, Chiles, and Chocolate

Few around the world who came to eat the foods of Mesoamerica in the early
modern era understood them to be Mexican. Maize circled the globe in the
company of strangers and inspired mystery at every turn. In his prescient global history of corn, the anthropologist Arturo Warman has shown that the
plant was everywhere an interloper, its origins unknown. Europeans called it
"Turkish wheat," while Turks dubbed it "Egyptian grain"; it spread to India as
"Mecca corn" and circled back to the Swahili Coast as "Indian sorghum." In
China, it was considered the "Western barbarian wheat," and in the Congo, the
"white man's grain." Along with confusion came low social status, as Warman
explained: "Corn carried the stigma of being alien, strange, poor. The wealthy
judged corn and declared it to be guilty. The poor, on the contrary, opened their

doors to it, embraced it, and adopted it."[28] Indeed, its prolific yields, particularly on marginal lands, made corn a precious commodity for some of the most destitute people in the world. But precisely because they "adopted it"—and cooked it using their own recipes—many eventually fell victim to the nutritional curse of pellagra. This tragedy resulted from the historical circumstances that rapidly globalized the seeds of maize but left behind the practical knowledge of Mesoamerican cooks, including the skill of making nixtamal.

The important contributions of the foods of the Americas to the cuisines of the world are well known—just try to imagine Italian cooking without tomato sauce or Indian curry before chile peppers. But it is more difficult to say how these transfers took place and why particular foods became so vital to local cuisines. The historian Alfred Crosby first tried to explain this historical moment of globalization, which he called the "Columbian exchange," in broad demographic terms. The terrible mortality caused by Old World diseases assisted the conquistadors in planting their foods in the Americas. Yet the reverse movement from New World to Old is not so clear. Crosby resorted to ecological and Malthusian determinism in concluding that American plants took root wherever they would grow and that their superior productivity spurred early modern population growth around the world.[29] Of course, ecology and demography helped shape the outcome of the Columbian exchange, but they do not fully explain local variations in culinary history. Just as Native Americans defied their colonial masters by cultivating maize, even while mixing pork fat into tamales, farmers and cooks in the Old World selected new foods that complemented existing practices. Recent research suggests that Crosby may have gotten the relationship backward; population often determined the spread of crops, rather than vice versa. In China, for example, peasants embraced productive American cultigens already in the early seventeenth century, a time of famine and social unrest at the end of the Ming Dynasty. In Mughal India, by contrast, relatively dispersed settlement and considerable available land allowed most people to ignore these novelties until pressured by British imperialists in the nineteenth century. Although a global process, the Columbian exchange was negotiated at the local level.[30]

Following the movement of three basic ingredients—corn, chiles, and chocolate—from the Mesoamerican kitchen out into the wider world can help to reveal the emergence of material and cultural patterns that later contributed to Mexican food's worldwide reputation. Already in the early modern era, these foods acquired vastly different images among elite and popular sectors. The importance of social distinctions can readily be seen in the case of yet another New World plant, the tomato. A history based exclusively on elite writings might conclude that Europeans did not eat the tomato for much of the early modern era because medical authorities warned of its resemblance to the poisonous nightshade. Only at the end of the seventeenth century did cookbook authors recommend them in Italian tomato sauce. Yet significant numbers of Spaniards who had lived in the New World acquired a taste for the plant, and archival documents from Seville's Hospital de la Sangre demonstrate the consumption of tomatoes already at the beginning of the seventeenth century: apparently they were served in salads with cucumber. Patients in charitable hospitals were invariably poor, because all but the most destitute families cared for relatives at home in early modern Europe, but clearly tomatoes were recognized as edible. By the 1650s, they had also begun to appear on elite tables in Andalucía.[31]

Maize spread through Europe primarily at the initiative of industrious peasants farming marginal lands. Like other American emigrants, the plant first made landfall in Seville and was cultivated in the royal gardens of the Alcazar, an old Moorish palace used to acclimatize New World plants to the Mediterranean. It was quickly passed along to local kitchen gardens, but it did not catch on as a field crop along the southern coast of Spain, perhaps because rice and millet were already well established as summer cereals. Instead, corn was first planted on a large scale in the remote northwestern provinces of Asturias and Galicia and in neighboring Portugal. This mountainous terrain, once used only for sheep pasture, was cleared and planted with maize on terraced fields. By the eighteenth century, the region had become densely populated farmland, and corn had become a standard summer crop throughout the Iberian Peninsula and southern France. Meanwhile, in the 1520s, corn began to revolutionize agrarian relations in the countryside around Venice, where annual spring floods had severely limited the production of winter wheat. Peasants discovered they could feed themselves and their livestock with a summer planting of corn after the floodwaters had receded, thereby breaking the stranglehold of Venetian landlords, who demanded wheat bread. By the nineteenth century, the productive crop had been planted down the flanks of the Apennine Mountains to Sicily and across the Alps into eastern France and the Austro-Hungarian Empire.[32]

The European reception of maize was shaped not only by its productivity, but also by its properties when cooked. Although highly versatile in the field, maize

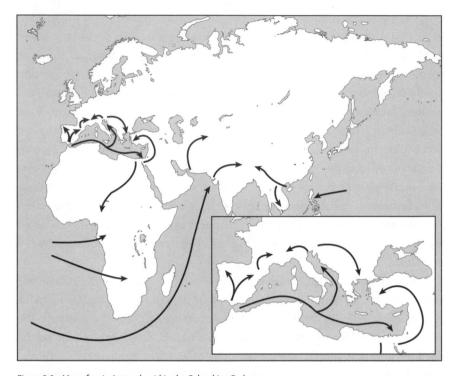

Figure 1.3. Map of maize's travels within the Columbian Exchange.

lacks gluten, the protein that allows wheat bread to rise. As a result, peasants made it into porridge, plebeians consumed it in flatbreads, and the wealthy spurned it as worthless. In rural Italy, where a thick porridge sometimes called polenta was made with everything from semolina to chickpea and chestnut flour, maize became a common ingredient for the dish. Urban bakers likewise employed a variety of different grains, and recipes from eighteenth-century Milan illustrate their experiments with the novel food as well as the tepid response of local consumers to the taste of maize. "To 48 ounces of the flour of this [Indian] corn, 2 ounces of rye corn is added as it will not adhere without it. . . . [The baker] divides it into saleable cakes of 12 ½ ounces, made round, and about an inch and a half thick in the middle." Another recipe suggested "potatoe meal improves the quality of the dough, promotes the fermentation or rising of it, and weakens or destroys the peculiar taste of the Indian corn."[33]

Enlightenment physicians soon diagnosed the nutritional limitations of maize and documented widespread health problems among populations that depended on it. In the 1750s, Dr. Gaspar Casal first linked excessive maize consumption to the *mal de la rosa*, a skin irritation resembling sunburn that had become common among the peasants of Asturias. The disease was elsewhere known as the *mal del monte*, a reference to the mountainous countryside bordering Portugal. A few decades later, Dr. Francisco Frapolli of Milan named the disease pellagra and described its progression from "repulsively disfigured" skin to "trouble in the head," followed by "colliquative diarrhoea most resistant to all remedies," and finally "a ghastly wasting [as] they approach the last extremity."[34] By the nineteenth century, reports of endemic disease constituted a veritable map of European maize consumption, snaking from the Iberian Atlantic seaboard to southern France and northern Italy, then across the Austrian Tyrol to Romania. Scattered cases of pellagra also appeared in southern Italy, the Austro-Hungarian Empire, and southwestern Russia and Poland.[35]

Chile peppers, like corn, raised suspicion among naturalists and physicians, but they nevertheless gained devoted followings across much of Europe. John Parkinson, a sixteenth-century English herbalist, described them as "so fiery hot and sharp biting in taste, that they burn and enflame the mouth and throat." José de Acosta gave a more balanced appraisal, suggesting that moderate consumption could aid digestion but warning that "much use of it in the young is prejudicial to health, especially to that of the soul, for it heightens sensuality."[36] Spanish merchants made occasional shipments of chiles from the Indies to Seville in the late sixteenth century, but commerce was sporadic, perhaps because the plants could be grown easily in kitchen gardens. The Dutch botanist Charles de L'Escluse reported finding them in two locations, Castile and Moravia, in the Czech territory neighboring Hungary, which also became an important consumer of paprika. In Italy, they gained their greatest popularity in Calabria, yet another Habsburg territory, where the heat of the chile was widely considered a homeopathic treatment against malarial fevers.[37]

Europeans generally considered chiles as a substitute for East Indian pepper that could be grown in any warm, sunny garden, but chiles' favor among the lower classes limited their appeal to elites, who had already begun to abandon the heavily spiced stews of the Middle Ages in favor of more subtle and purportedly natural dishes. Parkinson, despite his reservations, provided one of the few written recipes for chiles, dried and ground like black pepper and other spices, as opposed to the Mexican technique of grinding the pods fresh or, in the case of dried chiles, after reconstituting in water. By contrast, chiles received little attention from early modern diet guides and cookbooks, which were launching a revolution in European cooking—the first nouvelle cuisine—based on the ideal of unobtrusive flavors. Henceforth, sauces were made of the concentrated cooking juices of meat rather than bread crumbs and ground nuts, and flavored with fresh herbs instead of exotic spices. From a European perspective, mole de guajolote was already becoming an anachronism, although it was only just emerging on the other side of the Atlantic through the fusion of two older culinary traditions.[38]

Chocolate's popularity among the European aristocracy provides a curious counterpoint to the experience of corn and chiles, illustrating how a Mesoamerican food could gain status for its exoticism. The favored drink of Indian nobles, it was savored by Cortés and his band of conquistadors in the palace of Moctezuma. Merchants and priests also acquired a taste for chocolate while living in the colonies, and by the end of the sixteenth century, they had carried it home to Spain. Soon it was taken up by the court in Madrid, and from there it spread through the noble houses of Europe. As it traveled, the bitter drink of the Aztecs was transformed through the addition of sugar, spices, and other flavorings. Italians may have been the first to make chocolate ice cream, and less memorably, they experimented with grating it on polenta instead of cheese. Chocolate's exotic origins and distant sources added to the appeal for European consumers. Unlike chiles and corn, the tropical cacao tree was not easily transplanted to Europe, and it became an important article of transatlantic trade. Spaniards relied at first on supplies from Tabasco and Soconusco, at the southern tip of the old Aztec Empire, but growing demand prompted the establishment of plantations in Venezuela and Ecuador. The most valuable cacao was grown in Soconusco and Caracas, while the more abundant product of Guayaquil was considered the "chocolate of the poor."[39]

Europeans nevertheless looked with some ambivalence on the morality and healthfulness of chocolate. Both production and consumption continued to rely on pre-Hispanic technology, including heated metates, lacquered gourds (xícaras), and wooden whisks for frothing (molinillos). Its popularity as a mild stimulant increased after 1636, when a papal encyclical pronounced that it did not violate the Catholic fast. Nevertheless, moralizing sermons railed against the beverage; for example, Father Giuseppe Girolamo Semenzi warned: "Both Spain and Holland manufacture frothy ambrosias for a vain and gluttonous thirst; ... it inflames the blood parched by too much heat and too many aromas and taste turns remedy to poison."[40] Nobles certainly agreed with this sensual view. In the early eighteenth century, the Marqués de Castelvell commissioned an elaborate tile painting of bewigged nobles flirting over cups of chocolate for his palace courtyard near Barcelona. Meanwhile, Antonio Hurtado de Mendoza's racy "Couplets of Chocolate" posed the question: "What is it that embraces at the boiling point/So as to enjoy the perfect culmination?"[41]

Between Acosta's fears of chile-inflamed passions, Frapolli's diagnosis of pellagra from maize, and Hurtado's allusions to sex in a frothy cup of chocolate, Europeans perceived danger and transgression in every bite of food from the Americas. These reactions were fueled by sensationalist literature of the Indies, conquistadors' tales and moralizing sermons about pre-Hispanic cannibalism, or lurid accounts of Moctezuma drinking chocolate before visiting his concubines. Outside of Europe, these specific stereotypes had much less currency, and new plants tended to be associated with whoever happened to introduce them, whether they were long-distance traders or neighboring farmers. As a result, crops gained acceptance when they complemented but did not compete directly with existing cuisines. Chiles were perhaps the most successful of American plants within the wide tropical belt from North Africa to Southeast Asia, where nouvelle European ideas never supplanted age-old culinary traditions valuing spice. Meanwhile, corn proved to be an excellent pioneer crop, growing well in marginal lands, and as a result came to be associated with the impoverished people who inhabited these lands. By contrast, Spaniards failed to gain converts of any kind for chocolate, at least among cultures that already favored coffee or tea. Only with nineteenth-century industrialization and colonialism did cacao become a plantation crop in Africa and Southeast Asia.[42]

Chiles spread along the global networks of trade that had been developed in the early sixteenth century. Portuguese merchants took the lead in marketing the plants, calling them Pernambuco peppers after the Brazilian colony where they were first encountered after 1500. Traders had no trouble selling this novel spice in Africa, where "grains of paradise," or malagueta peppers, were already a widespread condiment. From ports along the Atlantic and the Swahili Coast, chile seeds became an item of trade throughout the continent. Likewise in India, a central hub of the spice trade, the chile was eagerly planted and named after local variants of black pepper. Unlike the latter, which predominated in the south, chiles flourished throughout the subcontinent and were eagerly taken up by gardeners. Already in the mid-sixteenth century, at least three varieties were grown and traded on the Malabar Coast. A South Asian poet declared this of chiles: "Saviour of the poor, enhancer of good food, fiery when bitten."[43] Chiles may have reached China from two directions: by overland trade from India and from Portuguese spice merchants in South China. The seeds became particularly important in the western and southern regions of Sichuan and Hunan. The plant also spread through Southeast Asia from the north through Burma and from the Portuguese fortress at Malacca. In Siam, later Thailand, chiles supplemented the black pepper and garlic that had formerly been used to flavor rice. Through a curious independent invention, Southeast Asian and Native American cooks happened on the same flavor combination of chiles and cilantro, as the two plants crossed paths during the Columbian exchange.[44]

If chiles became ubiquitous and chocolate was ignored in the tropics of Africa and Asia, then corn followed the most idiosyncratic global trajectory. After landing in Europe, the plant first reached the Ottoman Empire by sea in Egypt and later traveled overland from Venice into the Balkans. In North Africa, the grain was often made into a form of couscous, and it largely replaced less productive millet and sorghum in the Nile Valley. In the Balkans, Turkish landlords fed their Greek and Serbian tenants maize while selling wheat in markets. Eventually, this hardy crop allowed peasants to live year-round in remote mountain valleys that had formerly been useful only as summer sheep pastures, thereby escaping Ottoman authority.[45] In sub-Saharan Africa, Portuguese merchants introduced maize and cassava up and down the coasts, but linguistic evidence indicates a simultaneous overland diffusion along the trade and pilgrimage routes to Cairo. The plant spread widely as a garden vegetable in the early modern era but became a basic staple for only a few groups, such as the Asante of West Africa, who made it a symbol of the state and of military power. A novel rotation of maize, cassava, and cocoyam fit into the local ecology, allowing Asante farmers to clear new land and attract more labor, both migrants and slaves. Over time, Asante warriors expanded across a range of habitats, ranging from the coastal forest to interior savanna, all climates that readily supported maize.[46] By contrast, in Asia maize was eaten primarily by poor people living in mountainous areas. From Portuguese enclaves, the plant spread upland along an arc from the Hindu Kush through the Himalayas and into the Shan of Burma, as well as Sichuan and Yunnan in China and highland areas of Southeast Asia. Meanwhile, a distinct variety of "Persian maize" spread through the Transcaucasus region into Central Asia. Throughout Asia, maize was prominent among minority populations, who often used slash-and-burn agriculture and hand tools rather than the plows of lowland farmers. Although local cooking methods may have resembled Mesoamerican dishes, as with the tortilla-like Punjabi flatbreads called *makkai ki roti*, they were not nix-tamalized. Fortunately, pellagra did not become a widespread problem outside the Mediterranean basin because growers supplemented maize with hunting, gathering, and other crops.[47]

Some unique permutations of early modern globalization appeared in the Spanish colonies of the Pacific. New World ingredients understandably became separated from their original cultural contexts when passing through successive hands in Europe, Africa, and Asia, but Mesoamerican cuisine also underwent significant changes when carried directly to the Philippines by conquistadors from Acapulco. In 1564, a fleet under the Basque Admiral Miguel López de Legazpi y Gurruchátegui occupied Manila with little military opposition from the Filipinos, who numbered at the time only one or two million people, dispersed across thousands of islands. King Philip II originally hoped to use the colony as a staging ground for capturing the Spice Islands, but trade with China ultimately proved more lucrative. With only a few thousand Spaniards, Manila was more of a trade entrepôt than a settler colony, and European culture left relatively little imprint on the decentralized Filipino society. Moreover, the tropical climate was ill-suited to the Mediterranean staples of wheat, wine, and olives. Sacramental wine and communion wafers had to be imported from Acapulco, while Chinese bakers supplied the colony's daily bread. Mesoamerican crops fared better in the Philippines, but although the natives acquired a taste for avocados and tropical fruit, they produced maize only under compulsion for sale to Hispanic markets. Thus, both the Mesoamerican crop and the mestizos from New Spain who consumed it simultaneously achieved social mobility, becoming Spanish conquistadors in the Philippines.[48]

Skeptics may point to linguistic evidence of more thorough implantation of Hispanic and Mesoamerican foods in the Philippines. Adobo, for example, is often referred to as the Filipino national dish, and tamales have also become common in the archipelago. But these names are misleading; in Manila, adobo is not so much a marinade for meats as a chicken stew flavored with soy sauce, vinegar, and garlic. Likewise, Filipino tamales are made of rice flour and steamed in banana leaves, although the occasional use of yellow dye gives them a certain resemblance to the Mesoamerican original. The most common maize dish is porridge with coconut milk, further illustrating the subjugation of alien plants to local cooking techniques. The conquistadors may have consumed Asian foods more often than the reverse. A friar guardedly reported back to colonial authorities that, in the Chinese district of Manila, "there are also many eating-houses where the [Chinese] and the natives take their meals; and I have been told that these are frequented even by Spaniards."[49] One final mark of culinary influence can be found in "flavor principles," the basic mixtures of ingredients that immediately evoke the taste and smell of a culture. The fundamental essence of Filipino cuisine is not savory corn and fiery chiles, but, rather, in the words of one food writer, "twenty theoretical ways of making fish taste sour."[50]

A very different pattern emerged with the Spanish conquest of Guam, the largest of the Mariana Islands, 1,600 miles east of Manila. Visited briefly by the navigator Magellan in 1521, the island became a regular stopping point on the route from Acapulco to the Philippines, but Spaniards took little notice of the Polynesian natives until the Jesuits established a mission in 1668. Unlike the Filipinos, the Chamorro inhabitants of Guam fiercely resisted Spanish authority for thirty years and were annihilated in a brutal war of conquest. The few surviving Chamorros intermarried with colonists who came from Spain, Mesoamerica, and the Philippines, and a new mestizo culture soon predominated on the island. Unable to cultivate wheat in the tropical environment, the Jesuits pragmatically planted maize and encouraged the use of Mesoamerican kitchen tools, including the metate and comal. Chamorro women ground the dough standing up rather than kneeling, and they called their flatbreads *tortijas*. The introduction of nixtamal by Catholic priests in the Pacific, like the treatment of chinos in the Americas, illustrates the conflation of Native Americans and Asians within the category of "indio" by the Spanish colonial mentality. As a result, Mexican food, which was created by colonialism and globalization, finally achieved its own colonial hegemony in one of the most remote locations in the world.[51]

People have been confused about the nature of Mexican food for hundreds of years. Certainly there was no authentic Mexican food in pre-Hispanic times. Although the Creoles who first conceived of the idea of Mexico considered themselves to be the heirs of Aztec emperors, they had little desire to inherit Moctezuma's dinner. The indigenous cuisine of maize, while nutritious, diverse, and sophisticated, was more often associated with poor Indians living in the countryside than with the grandeur of pre-Hispanic civilizations. There were a few exceptions. Creoles eagerly adopted chocolate, the drink of the ancient nobility, and chiles, with their addictive spicy flavors. But ambivalence about the indigenous culinary heritage continued to frustrate efforts to define a

Figure 1.4. Native girl making tortillas in Guam. Photographic postcard from the 1920s, unknown photographer. Courtesy Daniel Arreola Collection.

Mexican national cuisine throughout the nineteenth century. Meanwhile, corn and chiles spread widely around the world, but they were often associated with poverty, illness, and immorality. Perhaps it was just as well that they were seldom considered to be Mexican.

CHAPTER 2

Although the taco first emerged in Mexico City, many other foods that are now usually considered to be Mexican had their origins in the northern borderlands. The burrito exemplifies this peculiar geography of global Mexican, eaten widely around the world, but virtually unknown in most of Mexico. Wrapped in a wheat flour tortilla, it is a distinctive product of the frontier, unlike the corn-based dishes popular in the rest of the country. The use of animal fat in making flour tortillas also sets them off from the vegetarian corn variety. While the wrapper is norteño, burrito fillings often are not; for example, the combination of beans and rice is more characteristic of the Caribbean than of northern Mexico. When deep-fried, a technique more often found in U.S. fast food than in Mexican cooking, they are called *chimichangas*, which is a nonsense word in Spanish. The "Mission burrito," a popular variety that is wrapped in aluminum foil to keep from bursting under the weight of the stuffing, derives its name from the Mission District of San Francisco rather than from Catholic evangelization on the northern frontier. A final indication of the burrito's Americanization can be found in its enormous girth; one observer declared it "possibly the single heaviest fast-food item in the world."[1]

Literally meaning the "little donkey," the burrito's origins are as obscure as those of the taco. Early Spanish dictionaries offer no culinary definitions for the word, although donkeys bearing food were a common motif in colonial popular culture. At Christmas time, in particular, burros carried loads of tropical fruit from the *tierra caliente* (coastal zones). The first known culinary reference, from Feliz Ramos's *Diccionario de mejicanismos* (1895), the volume that also introduced the taco to linguists, defined the burrito as a "rolled tortilla with meat or other thing inside, which in Yucatán is called *cosito*, and in Cuernavaca and Mexico [City], *taco*."[2] Ramos made no mention of a wheat flour tortilla, implying instead that it was made of corn, and he attributed the term not to the north but rather to Guanajuato, in central Mexico. To confuse things still further, a book of historic California cookery published in 1938 by Ana Bégué de Packman suggested that wheat and corn tortillas were interchangeable for making burritos; either could be used with a little leftover stew or some frijoles and cheese. She recalled tales of vendors in Old California selling burritos out of a basket, like the tacos de canasta of Mexico City, while singing the refrain "Los burritos para las bonitas!" (The little donkeys for the little beauties!).[3] That the once far-flung and diverse Mexican burrito became almost exclusively associated with a flour tortilla in the U.S. Southwest hints at the ways that borders and nation building can erase regional usages.

The origins of the wheat flour tortilla are likewise a mystery. Spanish historical documents provide ample information about agricultural production, which was gendered male, but they typically remain silent about the female labor of food preparation. Missionaries and settlers wrote with great pride about their success in planting wheat throughout the north, and they considered golden fields of the grain to be a sign of civilization on a savage frontier. Historians are left to infer, as did Eugenio del Hoyo, that archival references to the founding of flour mills in early seventeenth-century Nuevo León indicate that "the taste for flour tortillas [is] very old."[4] Nevertheless, wheat was a commercial crop on the northern frontier, as in Mexico City, and farmers generally sold it to towns to be baked as bread. Flour tortillas appeared at some point in the colonial period, but it is unclear whether they were an invention of Indian women forced to cook for Spanish conquistadors or whether they came from a recipe carried over by Mediterranean migrants with a long tradition of eating flatbreads such as pita. To understand the origins of the burrito, and of the distinctive version of Mexican food that Anglos first encountered in the Southwest and later carried around the world, it is necessary to examine this earlier history of cultural exchange in northern New Spain.

Even before Columbus, the arid country of the north was distinct from the heartland of Mesoamerica. Both semisedentary tribes of Chichimecas and cliff-dwelling Ancestral Pueblo farmers cultivated maize, although they prepared it quite differently from their Aztec cousins. Cultural blending was particularly complex during the colonial era because of the presence of three separate cultural groups: Chichimecas, Spaniards, and "indigenous conquistadors" from Mesoamerica. The Crown recruited warriors from Tlaxcala, Cortés's first allies, to settle in the north and "civilize" the Chichimecas. As a result, norteño cooking included a blend of Mesoamerican corn tortillas and chile pepper stews with the wheat bread and wine of Catholic missionaries. For the first two centuries of colonial occupation, a largely indigenous, subsistence society remained dominant on the frontier, and even rural Spaniards ate corn on a daily basis as tortillas or simply roasted grains known as *ezquites*. Hispanic culture came of its own during an economic boom of the Bourbon era in the late eighteenth century, the same time when silver miners were using explosive tacos at Real del Monte. On the borderlands, this cultural renaissance found expression in the emergence of distinctive regional cuisines, which would later be called Tex-Mex, New Mexican, Sonoran, and Cal-Mex. Although these cooking styles reflected cultural blends, frontier settlers generally considered themselves to be Spaniards and ignored the indigenous heritage.[5]

Maize in the *Gran Chichimeca*

Weary from hard travel and bad food on an odyssey across northern Mexico in the 1920s, José Vasconcelos exclaimed that "civilization ends where carne asada begins."[6] Four centuries earlier, Moctezuma would surely have recognized this gastronomic frontier between the chile stews of the Aztecs and the grilled meat of nomadic Chichimecas. The Florentine Codex divided these people into three categories, starting with the neighboring Otomí, who ate the same maize and chiles as the Aztecs but supposedly harvested their corn green, before it matured, and got drunk on pulque. Farther north lived the Tamime, "shooters of arrows," a seminomadic people who "made their homes in caves, in gorges; in some places they established small grass huts and small corn fields." While growing some food, they subsisted primarily by hunting game and gathering roots, mushrooms, and peyote. Finally, in the "grassy plains, the deserts, among the crags," lurked the Teochichimeca, the "extreme Chichimeca." A wandering people who knew nothing of Mesoamerican refinements, they ate whatever they found in the arid landscape: cactus paddles and fruits, yucca, maguey, and roots, wild honey and bees, too, and "all the meats—rabbit, snake, deer, wild animals."[7]

Figure 2.1. Map of Ancient Arid America and Oasis America.

Carne asada has now eclipsed mole de guajolote in the global repertoire of Mexican food, an outcome that Vasconcelos would surely have lamented. Nevertheless, while offering scornful descriptions in the Florentine Codex, the children of Aztec nobles had forgotten the Mexican's own nomadic history as well as their taste for "all the meats." The border between civilization and barbarism was fluid, and people crossed in both directions. A terrible famine in the year One Rabbit (1454) must have driven many to abandon their farms in the Valley of Anáhuac and migrate in search of food. Likewise, the neighboring Otomí could never rest easy waiting for the harvest, and they gathered maize early lest it wither on the stalk. Indeed, for thousands of years, the people of Mesoamerica maintained connections of trade and migration with the nomadic

49

and semisedentary inhabitants of "Arid America," a neutral phrase for this northern region, coined by geographers to avoid the negative cultural connotations of the name "Chichimeca."[8] These borderlands also extend to the agrarian enclaves of "Oasis America"—the Pueblos built along the Colorado River and the Rio Grande; the Hohokam societies centered on the Salt and Gila Rivers of Arizona; and the Mogollon, who reached their apogee along the Rio Casas Grandes and Rio Sonora in what is now north-central and northwestern Mexico. The diverse approaches to maize cookery across the ancient Americas confirm yet again that there never has been a singular, authentic Mexican cuisine.

Hunters and gatherers had carried maize and other tropical domesticates to Arid and Oasis America by around 2000 BCE, and they were quickly incorporated into local dietary patterns. On the Colorado Plateau, archaic peoples added maize and squash to their seasonal round of foraging, with little change to their migratory patterns.[9] Farther south, in the Sonoran desert, the grain helped to spur a dramatic social transformation by allowing people to settle year-round in fertile river valleys. By 1000 BCE, they were building irrigation canals. Scholars differ on the origins of this desert agricultural revolution: some believe that maize was carried directly from Mesoamerica by long-distance migrants with advanced farming skills. Others contend that the plant was simply passed from one group to the next and that, by the time it arrived, natives had already domesticated varieties of goosefoot, amaranth, panic grass, and Indian rice grass. Local farmers were also soon cultivating the tepary bean, a hardy legume capable of withstanding the desert environment. Recent archaeological work at Cerro Juanaqueña in northwestern Chihuahua has revealed yet another, more militarized, settlement pattern of large hilltop entrenchments overlooking floodplain maize and amaranth fields. Certainly, the move from foraging to farming took multiple paths rather than a direct march of agriculture from the south.[10]

Nixtamal is absent from the archaeological record of Oasis America in the first millennium of the Common Era, when sedentary villages began to differentiate the region from the hunter-gatherer bands of Arid America. Social complexity increased significantly among Hohokam communities around 300 CE, followed a short time later by the development of Ancestral Puebloan and Mogollon settlements. Maize was already becoming a dietary staple in all three areas, and frijoles also arrived from Mesoamerica around this time. Women adapted to the new demands of food processing by shifting to large, rectangular metates of hard volcanic rock and two-handed manos, which ground maize more efficiently than did smaller tools that had been used for mesquite and other seeds.[11] Despite the distances, these cultures maintained contact with societies farther south by way of the Chalchihuites, a militaristic people living on the frontiers of Mesoamerica. Beginning in present-day Zacatecas around the year 600, these warriors conquered an extensive empire and may have controlled the lucrative turquoise trade all the way to the Colorado Plateau. They also introduced the ceremonial Mesoamerican ballcourt to the Hohokam, even as they spread their own distinctive icon, a sacred flutist Kokopelli, throughout the region. Nevertheless, the Chalchihuites seem to have had little time for patting out tortillas, and by 850, with the waning of Teotihuacán's power, they migrated south to rule over wealthier lands in Mesoamerica. The low population density and continued importance of gathering and hunting simply made alkali treatment unnecessary in Arid and Oasis America.[12]

Even as northern societies reached a demographic peak in the eleventh and twelfth centuries, they remained far smaller than the cities of Mesoamerica. Encouraged by steady rains, the Ancestral Puebloans built dramatic cliff dwellings and ceremonial *kivas* (sweat lodges) at Chaco Canyon and Mesa Verde. Although numbering only a few hundred residents, these villages continued to trade turquoise with agrarian societies to the south. For a brief time, they even received payment in cacao, one of the most valuable commodities of Mesoamerica. At Pueblo Bonito in Chaco Canyon, chocolate was prepared in cylindrical jars like those of the Maya, who frothed the beverage by pouring it from one vessel held high above another. Fewer than two hundred such jars have been found in the entire Pueblo region, indicating the rarity of cacao at such a distance from its tropical origins. Meanwhile, the Hohokam lived in large, oval houses, made of adobe and clustered in villages of up to one or two thousand people along the Salt and Gila rivers. These skillful farmers celebrated their harvests at the mounds and plazas of Snaketown, where they roasted maize, maguey (century plants), and cholla cactus buds. Mogollon culture reached its apogee somewhat later, between 1200 and 1450, at Paquimé, along the Casas Grandes River in northwestern Chihuahua. The city housed perhaps 2,500 people in four-story apartment complexes, with numerous outlying settlements. Often considered a trade center for luxury goods from Mesoamerica, Paquimé had numerous ballcourts and plazas, with pit ovens capable of roasting large quantities of maguey hearts.[13]

But the good times did not last long. A series of social and ecological crises, beginning in the mid-twelfth century and culminating with an extreme drought in the late thirteenth century, spurred migrations throughout the Americas. People stopped building homes in Chaco Canyon by 1140, about the same time that floods devastated Hohokam irrigation systems and the temples of Snaketown were abandoned. The residents of Mesa Verde held on longer, but by 1300, the Colorado Plateau had been largely depopulated. Some rebuilt their pueblos along the Rio Grande and among the high plains and mountains at Hopi and Zuni. Other refugees descended to the Mogollon Rim and the valleys below, perhaps building the fortresslike structures at Casa Grande.[14] This was also the time of the Aztlán migrations, which launched the Mexica on their path to imperial grandeur in the Valley of Anáhuac.

Women responded to these social and environmental shocks by taking on new forms of kitchen labor. The archaeologist David Snow has proposed that nixtamal was introduced among the Pueblos after 1300 and that the heightened nutritional value of alkali-treated maize allowed them to prosper in difficult times. Evidence comes from the appearance of new kitchen technologies such as earthenware comales and the increasing prevalence of high-flour maize varieties, which made better tortillas than the previously widespread popcorns.[15] Paquimé, a northern outpost of Mesoamerican culture, apparently served as the conduit for this new technology; archaeologists have uncovered complete sets of kitchen utensils, including metates, comales, and nixtamal cooking pots, pitted inside from alkali. The tortilla recipe may also have passed to Hohokam women at Casa Grande and Los Muertos, on the Salt River near modern Tempe, where comales have also been found from the thirteenth century. Survival through these turbulent years may have depended as much on female labor, squeezing the greatest possible nutritional value from maize, as it did on male warriors guarding the parapets against invaders.[16]

It is impossible to say exactly how the Hohokam and Mogollon peoples cooked their nixtamal, because they abandoned their homes nearly a century before the Spaniards arrived in 1540. Nevertheless, ethnographic evidence from the Pueblos indicates subtle adaptations to Mesoamerican recipes. A conquistador, Francisco Vázquez de Coronado, wrote enthusiastically that at Zuni: "They eat the best tortillas I have seen anywhere." Of course, his appetite had been aroused by a long, hungry march in which at least two North Africans had died from eating poisonous plants. But he also praised the cooks' industry at the metate: "One woman from among the people of this land grinds as much as four [women] from among the Mexica."[17] Unlike the latter, who soaked the maize first and ground the resulting nixtamal into a wet dough,

Figure 2.2.   Four young Hopi women grinding grain. Edward S. Curtis Collection. Reproduction No.
LC-USZ62–94089. Courtesy of Library of Congress.

Puebloan women apparently ground it dry, in teams, using multiple metates.
Pedro de Castañeda de Nájera, another Spaniard, described "a separate room or
small secluded room where they have a large grinding bin with three stones set
in mortar, where three women go, each one to her stone. One of them breaks
the grain, the next grinds [it], and the next grinds [it] again." The resulting
corn flour may have kept better in the arid climate than in Mesoamerica,
where maize was dried on the cob for storage. Puebloan milling techniques
may have also prompted a new recipe for cooking, perhaps one that yielded
tortillas unacceptable to Nahua connoisseurs. Castañeda de Nájera continued:
"On a single occasion they grind a large quantity [of flour], because they make
all their bread, like wafers (*obleas*), from flour mixed with hot water."[18] Thus,
Puebloan women added the alkali just before cooking, producing a dry wafer.
Because this differed from the soft tortillas of Mesoamerica, the piki may have
tasted more familiar to the Spaniards, who were accustomed to communion
wafers. Unfortunately, there is no way to confirm this hypothesis because the

conquistadors did not record the reactions of their dinner companions—the Indian allies who made up the bulk of the expedition.[19]

In crossing the Mogollon Rim, the tortilla may have been transformed into that most distinctive of Puebloan festival foods—the piki bread eaten at kachina dances. This change lends further credence to the nixtamal connection proposed by Snow. Even today, masked Hopi dancers regale visitors with thin, blue corn wafers as part of a ceremony originally intended to bring rain and build solidarity. Archaeologists have traced the kachina cult to the social upheavals of the thirteenth century, when communal mechanisms for sharing food were established to help preserve the Puebloan communities.[20] Although a ceremonial food today, piki bread was likely an everyday staple of residents within fourteenth-century pueblos and was prepared on distinctive black stones. The oldest known examples, dating from around 1300, have been found at Homolovi, on the Little Colorado River, just north of the Mogollon Rim. Unlike the round comales of Mesoamerica and the Hohokam, square piki stones were greased before each use with sunflower oil or animal fat, reaching a smooth black patina over time. Cooks mixed finely ground corn meal with an ash solution to form a thin nixtamal batter, determining the correct alkali balance by the blue color. After testing the hot stone with a drop of water to see that it sizzled, they spread a thin layer of batter over the griddle using their bare hands. When the bread had set, they peeled it off the stone and stacked it to preserve moisture. Frank Hamilton Cushing, who lived among the Zuni in the 1880s, declared: "No bread is lighter or more tempting."[21]

As maize became increasingly vital for subsistence, societies acknowledged their nutritional dependence with religious rituals. Corn Maidens, a basic symbol of fertility, began appearing in Mogollon petroglyphs and pottery after 1200. Puebloans trace their lineages back to foundational moments when the gods revealed the secret of planting maize, whose different colors represented the cardinal directions orienting the cosmos. Like the peoples of post-classical Mesoamerica, Puebloans equated the growth of maize with the human life cycle. Priests sprinkled corn pollen in fertility ceremonies, and young women of childbearing age were called by the same word as the corn seeds saved for planting. The Zuni did not consider women eligible for marriage until they had developed callused hands for making piki bread. Even the mundane work of grinding corn was imbued with religious rituals, some of which may have had roots in the seventh-century arrival of the Chalchihuites and the sacred flutist,

Figure 2.3. Hopi woman making piki bread. Edward S. Curtis Collection. Reproduction No. LC-USZ62–115802. Courtesy of Library of Congress.

Kokopelli. Castañeda de Nájera observed: "Before [the women] go through the door, they remove their shoes and gather up their hair. They shake their clothes and cover their heads. While they grind, a man is seated at the door playing [music] with a flute. To the melody they draw their stones and sing in three parts."[22]

Yet not everyone persisted with the relentless labor needed to maintain a sedentary existence in the unforgiving desert. The great city of Paquimé was burned to the ground around 1450, and its inhabitants retreated to defensible hilltop trenches or perhaps sought refuge in the Sierra Tarahumara. The Hohokam also abandoned their homes as stress and malnutrition made everyday subsistence difficult, returning to a seminomadic existence of farming the floodplains during rainy seasons and gathering desert plants in dry years. The Europeans' arrival brought additional upheavals to regional subsistence patterns.[23]

Globalization and Subsistence on the Northern Frontier

In 1760, the newly anointed Bishop of Durango, Pedro Tamarón y Romeral, toured the vast diocese in order to strengthen the Catholic Church's presence on the northern frontier. In Pueblos such as Pecos, he ceremoniously confirmed the Indians while privately admonishing priests to greater efforts in their evangelical work. Tamarón's concerns were justified, for after he departed, a Pecos Indian named Agustín Guichí reenacted the Episcopal visitation in elaborate detail. Fashioning a mitre, cape, and vestment, the headman performed mock ceremonies for three days, blessed residents, and "in imitation of communion distributed pieces of wheat flour tortillas."[24] On the fourth day, he concluded the spoof and returned to his cornfield, where he was promptly mauled by a bear. Guichí reportedly survived only long enough to confess his sins to a genuine priest and receive last rites. The bishop believed this to be a divine warning to an errant flock, while modern scholars have interpreted it in the Pueblo tradition of "sacred clowns" ridiculing supernatural powers.[25] Although it is difficult to determine the motivations of Guichí—or the bear—this episode does provide one of the first documentary references to wheat flour tortillas, a norteño culinary icon that resulted from the frontier tension between globalization and subsistence.

Despite the distance from Mexico City, the northern borderlands were open to culinary globalization as diverse settlers transplanted their traditional foods. Silver mines were the most prominent connection with the wider world, and those who struck it rich imported luxury goods ranging from Asian spices to European wines. Meat was also readily available as the vast plains were converted to ranchland. Sheep grazed widely in the central highlands while cattle predominated along the coastal plains. European crops likewise fared better in the north than elsewhere in New Spain: wheat was less susceptible to fungus in the dry, irrigation-fed soils; grapes ripened in temperate valleys; and even olives grew in the Mediterranean climate of the Californias. Oxcarts and colonial roads also brought Mesoamerican foods that had not been common in pre-Hispanic times to the frontier. Franciscans provisioned their missions in New Mexico with chile peppers from central New Spain. Tlaxcalan colonists introduced pulque, candied prickly pear, and other treats. Yet even with access to commercial networks, chocolate was one of the few luxuries available for most settlers in the first two centuries of colonization. Catholic missionaries and presidio garrisons relied largely on supplies from Mexico City. Farmers sold the bulk of their wheat to itinerant merchants and then ate the more dependable maize on an everyday basis. Rural folk might share in edible by-products, such as the meat from cattle slaughtered for tallow and hides, but subsistence consumption remained an important limitation on early globalization.

The colonial frontier advanced fitfully northward, driven by the boom and bust of silver mining and by the rise and decline of Catholic missions. Prospectors discovered Zacatecas in 1547, less than a decade after the Vázquez de Coronado expedition, beginning a rush of Spaniards and Mesoamerican Indians into the once-forbidding Chichimeca territory. The province of Nueva Vizcaya expanded along the eastern foothills of the Sierra Madre Occidental with each new bonanza: Santa Bárbara (1567), Parral (1631), and Santa Eulalia (1704). Settlers built *estancias* in the surrounding valleys to supply meat and grain to the boomtowns, and even territories without silver such as Nuevo León became important for raising livestock. But the inevitable decline of mines, beginning with Zacatecas in 1620, had a ripple effect through the regional economy, causing farmers to fall back on subsistence production.[26] Meanwhile, Catholic priests also helped to push back the frontier, as Franciscans evangelized the Pueblos of New Mexico and Jesuits opened the colonies of Sonora and Baja California. Missions soon ranked among the leading agricultural producers in the region, with ready access to Indian labor. The savvy fathers marketed food to mining towns and commercial centers. Yet resident Indians, who suffered from disease, abuse, and the loss of customary practices, resisted the demands of mission life. Spanish authorities put down a series of rebellions in the late seventeenth century, but the missions never fully recovered. The colony was increasingly secular as it reached its greatest extent, in the eighteenth century, with the founding of settlements in Texas and Alta California.[27]

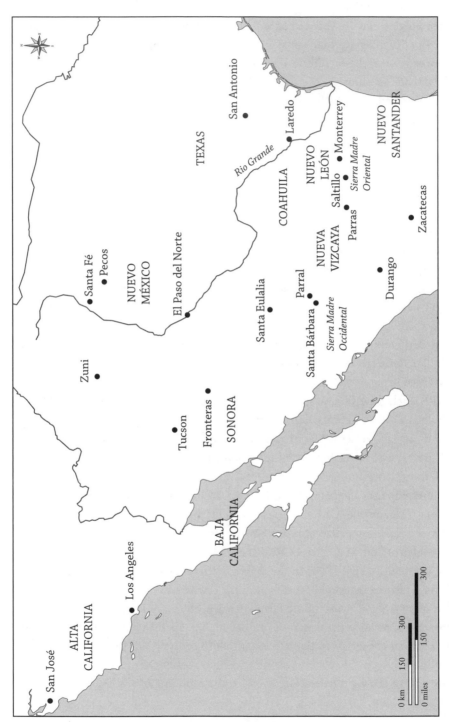

Figure 2.4. Map of Northern New Spain.

European settlers introduced many foods to the northern frontier. Livestock and wheat were the most important staples, not only providing nourishment for Spanish settlers, but also reshaping the landscape and helping to displace the indigenous population. Catastrophic overgrazing, which had already devastated the Mezquital Valley near Mexico City, was repeated around Zacatecas. The Nahuatl word *Zacatlan*, meaning "grassland," gives an idea of how these plains may have looked before the cattle herds arrived; today, the desert landscape supports little more than cacti.[28] Spaniards reserved the fertile river valleys around Durango and San Bartolomé for grain production, and even Saltillo in the northeast shipped large quantities of wheat to Zacatecas. When possible, farmers built their own water-powered mills because grain merchants paid a premium for flour.[29]

European settlers also produced specialty crops for urban markets. Peach, apple, and fig orchards flourished in the highlands of Nueva Vizcaya as did citrus, chickpeas, melons, and sugar in the coastal plains of Sonora. In the seventeenth century, missionaries succeeded in growing olives in the Mediterranean climate of Baja California, and a hundred years later, cuttings were transplanted to Alta California. Temperate northern latitudes also proved suitable for making wine from the Mission grape, known as the Mónica in Spain. The Parras Valley, a sandy oasis with a climate similar to Andalucía, became the leading wine region in New Spain. In the eighteenth century, the Marques de Aguayo owned several vineyards along with a retail shop in Mexico City. Missions and haciendas throughout the north raised grapes for local consumption. Bishop Tamarón praised the vintners of El Paso for making "fine wines [*vinos generosos*] even better than those from Parras."[30] Angélica, an aptly named California mission brandy, was described by the German naturalist Georg von Langsdorff as an "excellent wine, sweet and resembling Malaga."[31]

Lengthy commodity chains connected merchants in northern New Spain with wholesale suppliers in Mexico City and even more distant producers. As a result, even small-scale shopkeepers in seventeenth-century Parral stocked ham and pork fat from Toluca and Puebla, along with dried fish, shrimp, and oysters from the Pacific coast. Store accounts listed a range of spices, including pepper, mustard, cinnamon, saffron, and cloves, as well as chocolate, cheese, nuts, honey, vinegar, olive oil, dried figs, bananas, and tomatoes. The records that survive in colonial archives were generally drawn up for probate cases, and they provide little information about the distribution of food, much less its preparation. But judging from the quantities listed on inventories—"Item,

1 small skin containing about ½ almud [2½ liters] of olive oil... 1 ounce of very bad saffron in a little jar... 2 ounces of cinnamon"—few on the frontier could afford to reproduce the baroque stews of Mexico City. Regular demand from Catholic fast days ensured more plentiful, if not necessarily fresher, supplies of seafood: "Item, 1 *arroba* [25 pounds] of dried shrimp... about 2 or 3 *arrobas* of oysters."[32]

Provincial mining towns also had multiple *panaderías* competing to feed the Hispanic population, even if they could not quite provide the range of breads available in the viceregal capital. At the height of the silver bonanza in Zacatecas, Bishop Alonso de la Mota y Escobar noted the discerning appetites of wealthy miners and merchants. "The bread they eat is of the finest wheat, and very white and tasty," he wrote, and "the wines of Castile are esteemed more highly in this city than in any other part."[33] Eighteenth-century Chihuahua City had a large, informal bakers' guild dominated by peninsular masters, as well as many smaller shops, some owned by single women.[34] Some wealthy landowners, such as the seventeenth-century founders of the Sanchez estancia, twenty-five miles south of Santa Fe, New Mexico, constructed domed ovens called *hornos* to bake wheat bread, although they also ate corn tortillas on a regular basis.[35] Colonial documents refer to *bizcochos* eaten by travelers, mission priests, presidio garrisons, and others who did not have regular access to bakeries. Like sailors' hardtack, these biscuits were made of flour and water without shortening, kneaded extensively, and baked twice for prolonged storage.[36]

The introduction of European baking customs to the frontier may also have included wheaten flatbreads. Such breads were common throughout the Mediterranean, from the Arabic *khubz* to Italian pizza, which was originally prepared without sauce or cheese.[37] In northern Mexico, oral tradition attributes the flour tortilla to Iberian Jews, who settled on the frontier after Isabel and Ferdinand expelled non-Catholics from Spain in 1492. The conquistador of Nuevo León, Luis de Carbajal, for example, came from a Portuguese Jewish family and eventually died in an Inquisition prison. According to this interpretation, flour tortillas had provided a substitute for *matza*, the unleavened bread eaten for Passover. Yet ordinary corn tortillas would have satisfied Sephardic tradition, and Carbajal's nephew confessed under torture that he resorted to this expedient when traveling during the Holy Days.[38] Flour tortillas may also have been eaten for the seder, but they are unlikely to have originated with that purpose. Catholic priests certainly would not have introduced a crypto-Jewish food to Pecos Pueblo.

Most workers in mining towns were Indians, either drafted into service by colonial courts or lured by the offer of cash wages. Their daily meals consisted of *pozole*, a hominy stew flavored with meat and chile. Although the menu varied little, mine owners often supplied abundant rations to maintain productivity. At Santa Eulalia, the weekly allotment of meat may have been gone by Tuesday, but miners also received chocolate to help see them through to the next payday. Workers received a brief respite during religious feast days, when the mines closed and communities pooled their resources to celebrate. Town fathers sponsored not only fireworks and bullfights but also banquet tables in public plazas that served festive treats such as *buñuelos*, deep-fried pastries sprinkled with sugar and cinnamon. Annual trade fairs provided another opportunity for public dining from vendors who improvised street kitchens to feed the visiting throngs.[39]

The contrasting currents of globalization and subsistence were also present on the missionary frontier. Catholic priests recognized the importance of food to their work in a cynical statement about Indian religious beliefs quoted by the historian Vito Alessio Robles: "It's good [to have] religion and be a Christian, while there's something to eat, and bad when it's lacking."[40] The friars could not carry out their evangelical mission without first transforming nomads into cultivators, a difficult task given the scarce resources of the region. Rightly fearing that Indians would relapse into pagan ways if they left the missions to hunt and gather, priests tried to keep their charges well-fed so they would not stray. But available lands were often quite marginal for farming, even if the natives had been accustomed to the strenuous labor of peasant agriculture. Moreover, the Crown insisted that missions be self-supporting, and food produced by Indians was often sold to urban markets to pay for the priests' vestments and chocolate.

The introduction of European foods contributed relatively little to indigenous subsistence, despite the priests' belief in the superiority of Spanish agriculture. In seventeenth-century New Mexico, for example, each mission kept a herd of sheep along with smaller numbers of cattle. Pueblo Indians tended the animals, driving sheep high into the Sangre de Cristo Mountains for summer pasture. But when distributing the meat, friars doled out small portions of beef to the Indians and reserved the more valued mutton for Spanish colonists. Colonial provisions compensated for these losses at first, but the breakdown of Franciscan supply caravans to New Mexico may have contributed to the Great Rebellion of 1680, when the Pueblos united to drive out the Spaniards for a decade. The rebels showed their contempt for Spanish agriculture by uprooting the colonists' crops. Overgrazing also limited indigenous access to meat from mission herds. When the Jesuits introduced cattle to the fertile valleys of Sonora's piedmont, the herds multiplied rapidly at first but then collapsed just as suddenly when the grasses were depleted. Thereafter, the animals spent much of the year wandering among the desert scrub. Wheat harvests were likewise sold to market or used as tithe payments, leaving the indigenous staple pozole as the basic ration for mission Indians.[41]

Despite the grain's low yields, Catholic rituals required wheat, and the fathers taught natives to build ovens and bake bread for religious celebrations. Frank Cushing described this practice at Zuni in the late nineteenth century: "While the oven is heating outside, the most buxom young woman of the family...kneels down and prepares for kneading." Taking a yeast sponge prepared the night before, she added hot tallow and worked in flour, pushing through the center of the dough and pulling at the edges, alternating rhythmically. After sweeping embers out of the oven, she placed round loaves inside with a wooden peel and sealed the opening with stone and plaster. Half an hour later, the loaves were "crisp, brown, and very light, having almost doubled in size during the baking." The choice of a woman rather than the more typical European male baker hints at possible associations between rising bread and fertility, but this may also have been part of the friars' campaign to confine women to household labor as agricultural work routines grew more intense. Cushing observed that "some of the dough used for a bread-making is always reserved and made into flat cakes like [tortillas]."[42] Rather than being a shortcut for everyday bread, the Indians at Zuni connected wheat flour tortillas with Catholic celebrations, a religious significance that Guichí mocked in distributing his communion wafers.

Spanish reliance on native women for domestic service ensured that the process of culinary exchange went both ways. Although the fathers received allotments of biscuits and chocolate from church supplies, and perhaps some wheat from the congregation, maize remained the everyday staple for priests and parishioners alike. Documents contain numerous references to priests employing local women to prepare tortillas or receiving the indigenous griddlecakes as tribute.[43] The difficulty of assuring adequate rations also made it impossible for priests to hold the Indians on the missions permanently. Residents wandered off to forage, hunt feral cattle, gather cactus fruits in season, or simply to enjoy a *tesgüinado* (maize beer bash) out of sight of the clergy. On the other

Figure 2.5. Zuni woman kneading dough for wheat bread. Frank Hamilton Cushing, *Zuñi Breadstuff*, vol. 8 of *Indian Notes and Monographs* (New York: Museum of the American Indian Heye Foundation, 1920), 374.

hand, Indians who remained nomadic, such as the Cunca'ac (Seri), who lived on the coastal deserts of Sonora, often settled temporarily on missions during bad years.[44]

To encourage the process of native acculturation, the imperial government recruited Tlaxcalan warriors to populate the frontier. In 1591, the viceroy signed a generous charter establishing several settlements, including San Esteban de Nueva Tlaxcala near Saltillo. Other native peoples—the Mexica, Otomí, and Purépecha—also joined the movement to colonize Chichimeca lands, but usually as wage laborers, without the legal privileges given to Cortés's loyal allies. Indigenous settlers introduced the rich cuisines of Mesoamerica to the northern frontier, while also borrowing elements of European material culture. Tlaxcalans brought sheep, goats, and chickens along with indigenous turkeys, and they cooked tortillas on iron griddles instead of on fragile earthenware comales. Still, they planted fields in the native fashion, mixing corn, beans, squash, and chiles together with greens that many Spaniards considered to be weeds: *quelites* (lamb's quarters), *verdolagas* (purslane), and *epazote*. Individual plots were divided by rows of domesticated maguey and nopal, which also served as important foods. The maguey sap was fermented into pulque, while the sweet nectar from prickly pear was boiled down to make candies called *queso de tuna*. Tlaxcalan pioneers also grew wheat and fruit for sale to Hispanic towns, and in Santa María de las Parras, they cultivated grapes and made Spanish wine and brandy, skills learned from the Jesuits. Their irrigation works combined pre-Hispanic and European technologies. In the 1770s, Fray Juan Agustín de Morfi wrote that "their lands are perfectly cultivated" and that Spaniards in Saltillo depended on them for "vegetables, fruit, milk, etc."[45]

Interactions between local Indians and Mesoamerican settlers may have had more influence on borderland cooking than did the instruction of Spanish friars. The Rarámuri, for example, may have learned to make tortillas and tamales from Mesoamerican migrants while adapting to a new life in the Tarahumara Mountains, where they fled the advances of Spanish colonialism during the seventeenth century. In making these dishes, they added distinctive local touches, using green or pink corn, and wood ash instead of limestone for nixtamal. Like many novelties, the Rarámuri prepared tortillas only for ceremonial occasions and ate *pinole* (maize porridge) for everyday meals.[46] Meanwhile, in many New Mexican Pueblos, piki was replaced as an everyday staple not by wheat bread but rather by Mesoamerican-style tortillas. Women skilled in making tortillas had already accompanied Vázquez de Coronado's native allies in 1540, and although Tlaxcalans never became a significant presence on the upper Rio Grande, other central Mexican Indians did settle there. These newcomers also had to make adjustments to their cuisine. Archaeologists at a seventeenth-century rancho near Cochiti Pueblo have excavated a comal made of local sandstone, probably an improvisation required by the lack of appropriate clay in order to make hard-fired earthenware. The Puebloan kitchen was therefore an arena of culinary innovation in which two new recipes, maize tortillas and wheat bread, may have appeared at about the same time. Perhaps in the experimental process of learning to prepare these new foods, Puebloan women independently invented the wheat flour tortillas that Cushing praised and Bishop Tamarón denounced.[47]

By the late eighteenth century, secular Hispanic society had become dominant throughout the northern borderlands. The expulsion of the Jesuits in 1767 and the continued decline of the Franciscan order had placed many mission lands in the hands of settlers—Spaniards, mestizos, and Indians alike. Unable to rely on the Church for protection, Native Americans chose different paths, alternately fleeing to remote locations such as the Tarahumara Mountains or performing wage labor for Spanish overseers. Even those who retreated from colonial society adopted some elements of European material culture. The Rarámuri learned to herd sheep and sold grain and poultry to Spanish miners. Even the Pueblo Indians, who had destroyed all markers of Spanish colonialism in 1680, made an exception for livestock. After Spanish troops had contained the Indian rebellions of the seventeenth century, Apache and Comanche warriors continued to devastate frontier settlements until the 1780s. But once these nomadic raiders had made peace, a new era of prosperity spread across the borderlands, encouraging the consolidation of new regional cuisines.[48]

Regional Cuisines and Ethnic Identities

At least four distinctive norteño regional cuisines took shape during an economic boom of the late colonial period, and particular dishes from this era came to figure in the industrial versions of Mexican food that later circled the globe. Although not as complex as the chile and spice stews of Mesoamerica, these borderland cuisines were nevertheless more elaborate than the subsistence foods eaten during the first two centuries of frontier settlement. The chronicler of Nuevo León, Alonso de León illustrated the hunger and adversity of the early days with the tale of a Spanish official who asked a neighboring priest for something to eat, if only a plate of ezquites. The famished messenger who carried the request consumed half the ration of toasted maize, grain by grain, on the walk home, whereupon the governor ate the rest as if it were "the most delicate and suave dish of the finest *hosteria* [inn] of Italy."[49] Yet this image of frontier equality, a European dignitary and an Indian servant sharing a handful of corn kernels, was disappearing by the late eighteenth century, if it had ever really existed. The consolidation of Spanish society and the conclusion of peace treaties with nomadic Indians encouraged agricultural production and economic growth. Wheat became increasingly available not only in mining centers but also for small towns and ranchos, whose inhabitants may have lacked the means to bake bread yet nevertheless remained proud of their Hispanic lineage—whether real or imagined. Such folk could raise their social status in an everyday way by replacing corn with wheat tortillas.

These borderland regional cuisines were not the product of Americanization; they took shape in the late eighteenth century, before the arrival of merchant ships on the California coast or wagon trains from the Santa Fe Trail. Outsiders contributed relatively little to the frontier diet except for a few bottles of champagne that survived the bumpy ride from Missouri. It was the expansion of local agriculture rather than foreign novelties that transformed the region and spread prosperity. As subsistence yielded to comfort and even luxury, at least four distinct regional cuisines emerged—in the Northeast, New Mexico, Sonora, and California. These foods were still rustic but remain popular to this day. Because of the racial dynamics of this frontier society, the wheat flour tortillas that Guichí used to spoof colonial authority eventually helped to obscure the Pueblo Indians from the historical memory of the Hispanic frontier.

The northeastern provinces of New Spain, lacking in mineral wealth, depended on livestock for economic prosperity. Although *cabrito* (barbecued kid) is the favorite dish of tourist restaurants in modern Monterrey, goat was considered "*la vaca del pobre*" (the poor man's cow), and goats grazed only on land that would support nothing else. Mutton held the greatest distinction in Hispanic culture, and even cattle were preferable both for their valuable by-products and as a more efficient source of urban supply. In the mid-seventeenth century, shepherds discovered excellent winter pasture in the highlands of Nuevo León. A hundred years later, the province supported upward of a million head of sheep, a quarter of those on the vast estates of the Marques de Aguayo alone. But overgrazing took its toll, and by the nineteenth century, shepherds often had to clean the thorns off nopal cactuses with a knife to feed their flocks. Such environmental degradation may well have helped to create the rural nostalgia portrayed by twentieth-century cabrito restaurants.[50]

By contrast, longhorns dominated the coastal plains of Texas and Nuevo Santander, a province extending from Tampico north to the Nueces River.

These great herds were the feral descendants of cattle turned loose by early conquistadors. Ranching meant simply rounding up unbranded animals. San Antonio stockmen organized their first cattle drives to Saltillo in the 1770s and also smuggled cattle and horses to French Louisiana. Within a few decades, colonial commerce and Indian raids depleted the wild herds, prompting city fathers to ban the clandestine sale of livestock. The ranching economy developed more fully in the Lower Rio Grande Valley, where late colonial population growth encouraged stockmen to breed their own cattle rather than rely on round-ups. But in the late 1830s, Nuevo Santander was also devastated by the combination of Apache raids and rustlers from the newly independent Texas. With such a marginal economic basis, no great landowners comparable to Aguayo emerged along the Gulf Coast.[51]

Agriculture and commerce were even less developed than ranching, and farmers in Texas and Nuevo Santander subsisted on maize rather than risk the low yields of wheat. When a group of Canary Islanders arrived in San Antonio in 1731, colonial officials issued each family a metate to help the women accommodate the difficult labor of the frontier. Despite sporadic attempts to plant wheat, the town's residents had not bothered to construct a flour mill as late as 1778. The subsistence diet changed little in the next half century, as a military inspector, Juan Nepomuceno Almonte, noted in 1834: "The most general provisions in Texas, among the Mexicans, are corn tortillas, beef and venison, chicken, eggs, cheese and milk, and sometimes they can get bread, chocolate, coffee, and tea."[52] Moreover, these foods were often prepared and served in ceramics made by local Coahuilteca Indians, both on and off the missions. Indigenous influences also appeared in prickly pear candies, introduced by Tlaxcalan presidio troops stationed along the Rio Grande, which remained a popular festival food in nineteenth-century Laredo.[53]

The most renowned of Texas dishes, chili con carne, was surely present on the frontier. In 1842, William Bollaert wrote that a "sort of stew made of beef, chicken or any other sort of meat, with pumpkin and a large quantity of red pepper is one of their favorite dishes."[54] Although modern-day purists might turn up their noses at chicken or pumpkin in their chili, they would probably recognize the condiments available to frontier cooks—chiles intercropped with maize, *chiltepines* harvested in the wild, hardy native oregano, and perhaps a bit of cumin, a Mediterranean spice that naturalized to Texas. In contrast to the rich combinations of Mesoamerican moles, this handful of ingredients remains the distinctive taste profile of Tex-Mex cooking.

The regional cuisine of New Mexico meanwhile emerged around the head-waters of the Rio Grande with the unique flavor of distinctive local chile peppers, often called "New Mexican" or "long green." Scientists have only begun to trace the ancestry of this variety from its origins in central Mexico among chiles known variously as *guajillo*, *ancho*, and *pasilla*. Nevertheless, a pioneering study in molecular biology has recently found that a sample of land-race chiles, grown for hundreds of years in northern New Mexico and highly adapted to the local climate, exhibited little genetic diversity from one pueblo to the next. Moreover, these chiles were closely related to different varieties grown in Mexican geographical regions running from Chihuahua to Morelos and Oaxaca—a north-south "axis of chile" that likely followed seventeenth-century Franciscan supply routes. These ancestral plants presumably converged through hybridization to create the renowned New Mexico chile. More research is needed to determine the precise origins of the local *chile verde*, but this study does support the picture of a regional cuisine developing in isolation during the colonial era.[55]

Nineteenth-century travel accounts provide a glimpse of how these chiles were prepared, although the fiery heat of New Mexico cooking often left newcomers insensitive to local nuance. Passing through Santa Fe in the 1820s, a fur trapper named James O. Pattie failed to notice the social distinctions between wheat and maize when he described the grains as interchangeable: "Tortillas are a thin cake made of corn and wheat ground between two flat stones by the women."[56] Susan Magoffin, the wife of an overland merchant who arrived in the summer of 1846, first tasted *"chilly verde"* in the home of simple rancheros. This dish comprised green chiles, meat, and onion, boiled together and accompanied by blue corn tortillas. "We had neither knives, forks, or spoons, but made as good substitutes as we could by doubling a piece of *tortilla*, at every mouthful—but by the by there were few mouthfuls taken, for I could not eat a dish so strong, and unaccustomed to my palate."[57] Later that fall, as the piquant flavors grew more familiar, she sampled a more elaborate version of Hispanic provincial cooking at the feast of the patron saint San Gabriel. The meal had taken a week to prepare and ran through multiple courses, beginning with roasted mutton, perhaps flavored with red chile adobo, followed by stewed chicken with onions, and for dessert, bread pudding (*capirotada*) with half-dried grapes (*pasas*) from the recent harvest instead of the raisins more commonly available at Christmas or Lent.

Figure 2.6. Mexican mill near La Boca, Colorado, c. 1900. Rev. John Columbia Gullette. Negative number 13254. Courtesy Palace of the Governors Photo Archives, New Mexico History Museum (NMHM/DCA), Santa Fe.

Even this feast seemed rustic in comparison with the entertainments given by Santa Fe's merchant elite. At one event, Magoffin dined on oyster soup, vermicelli, multiple courses of meat, and champagne "without reserve."[58] The local gentry similarly impressed Lt. William Emory, who inspected the provincial capital in 1848 shortly after the war. "The supper was served very much after the manner of a French dinner, one dish succeeding another in endless variety. A bottle of good wine from the Paso del Norte, and a loaf of bread was placed at each plate." Alongside the abundant meat, bread, and wine, a taste for New Mexican chiles was ubiquitous in even the finest homes. Emory described local peppers as "the chef-d'oeuvre of the cuisine" and recalled that "the first mouthful brought the tears truckling down my cheeks, very much to the amusement of the spectators with their leather-lined throats."[59] Rural folk, unable to produce loaves of bread on a daily basis, associated New Mexico chiles with wheat flour tortillas in the local historical—and taste—memory. In Chimayó, the oral historian Don Usner found this connection indelibly marked in the granite of nineteenth-century gristmills used to grind both chiles and flour. "It was impossible to rid the millstones of the pungent residues of chile and the wheat flour often carried a sharp edge of chile flavor."[60]

Flour tortillas have become even more emblematic of the regional cuisine of Sonora, but they are noticeably absent from the accounts of colonial observers.

The mid-eighteenth century was a particularly difficult period, plagued by constant Apache raids and mission Indian rebellions that forced Hispanic settlers to abandon hundreds of ranches. Writing at this time, Father Ignaz Pfefferkorn observed "little difference between the food of the Indian and that of the common Spaniard in Sonora." The only meat available to residents was *tasajo* (dried beef), cut into thin strips, salted, and hung in the sun. "This is the beef which appears every noon on the table; this is the roast; of it, soup is brewed and ragout prepared." Although priests placed a high priority on wheat production, even pastries were made with maize flour. Pfefferkorn described wreath-shaped *puchas* made with sugar, cinnamon, and egg yolks "so tender that they melt in the mouth" and hard-baked *biscochuelos*, "extraordinarily good" with chocolate. The German Jesuit found corn tortillas "in the most aristocratic households"; for weddings and funerals, Spaniards "served chocolate and tortillas instead of the customary wheat bread."[61] Even humble ezquites would have been considered a feast at the presidio of Fronteras, where troops were paid so poorly that they left their guard stations to forage for roots and herbs, and the most desperate traded their horses and clothes to Indians for food.[62]

The mingling of European and Native American foods also extended to rustic *mezcal*, distilled from the wild maguey of the province. When the viceroy prohibited this alcohol in 1777, as part of the Bourbon moral reforms, local officials protested that the ban placed an unfair burden on the poor, both Indians and Spaniards alike, who could not afford imported wine and depended on the mezcal for medicinal purposes and daily sustenance. Even the military commander of the interior provinces, Brigadier Teodoro de Croix, argued on behalf of the drink, noting that it "fortifies their children from the hour of birth, serves as breakfast to conserve their health, encourages their appetites at noon, and counsels sweet and tasty dreams at night." He concluded this lyric testimonial on a practical note, explaining that the bootleggers "produce it in the most inaccessible mountains in such abundance that no penalties would suffice to extinguish it."[63] The crown relented in 1782 and legalized the agave moonshine, at least in Sonora.

When the threat of nomadic Indian raids declined, the frontier society became increasingly stratified around the turn of the nineteenth century. The loss of mission lands prompted many sedentary Indians to adopt mestizo identities, even as the introduction of new irrigation technologies encouraged the production of wheat.[64] As divisions grew between hacienda owners and peasant farmers, women cultivated the art of making ever more elaborate wheat flour tortillas in order to contribute not only to their family's subsistence but also to their Hispanic status. The results of this female labor were apparent to a cattleman who passed through Tucson, Arizona, in 1854, and sampled the "thin and well baked flour Tortilla, common to this country."[65] Eventually, wheat flour became a stereotype of the frontiersmen of the northwest in the minds of Mexicans living farther south, as the poet Ignacio Ramírez quipped:

Look at those Sonorans. They fill
Every bag with flour. It's their pinole;
Their breakfast and their dinner;
Their soft drinks, tortillas, bread, and atole.
At times they eat beef, but unaware;
They like it grilled and, at weddings, in mole.[66]

The late eighteenth-century settlement of Upper California by missionaries and presidio troops from Sonora allowed even greater reach for the culinary imagination. Under the priests' guidance, mission Indians tended livestock and cultivated abundant fields of wheat, maize, and all manner of fruits and vegetables. The neophytes also learned to make artisanal foods including European olive oil, wine, and cheese, as well as Mesoamerican tortillas and tamales. Eulalia Pérez, a former housekeeper at the San Gabriel Mission, recalled breakfasts of "*champurrado* [chocolate with maize *atole*] with sweets and bread on festive days, on other days pozole with meat."[67] The Franciscans marketed the abundant surpluses to nearby presidios and used the revenue to purchase goods from central New Spain. Georg von Langsdorff described a visit at the Mission of Santa Clara: "At dinner we were regaled with an excellent soup of pulse and vegetables, with roasted fowls, a leg of mutton, different vegetables dressed in various ways, salad, pastry, preserved fruits, and many very nice sorts of food, the produce of the dairy." To accompany the meal, they drank local wine, imported tea, and "super-excellent chocolate."[68]

Californios, as settlers were called in the towns of Los Angeles and San José, were equally generous hosts. With the assistance of Indian labor, hired away from the friars, they took over the provisioning of Spanish presidios and even began exporting grain back to the colonial heartland in 1801, although the lucrative trade ended a decade later with the wars of independence. In the 1830s, settlers inherited great herds of mission cattle and began selling hides and tallow to New England and European merchants. Midcentury visitors praised the extravagant hospitality of wealthy Californios but were less thrilled by the cooking. "It was a festive eve at the Don's," wrote the Anglo settler Walter Colton sarcastically, and "coffee and tortillas went round" instead of bread or pastry.[69] An Englishman named George Simpson added, "we saw more than once, in one and the same dish, beef, and tongue"—perhaps a reference to the *barbacoa de cabeza de vaca*, an entire cow's head, pit-roasted—along with multiple vegetables; "every mouthful was poisoned with the everlasting compound of pepper and garlick."[70] But locals viewed the rich and spicy cuisine of California as a source of deep pride. When asked about the early days of the Gold Rush, old timer José Fernández recalled that miners slept in their carts and ate on the ground, but he waxed enthusiastic about the content of their meals: "the most common foods were pork with frijoles, wheat tortillas, and boiled rice; also carne asada was obtained in abundance as well as deer, hares, and rabbits."[71]

Even as frontier communities reoriented their commercial ties toward the United States in the mid-nineteenth century, this newly formed borderland cuisine remained predominant throughout the region, albeit with local exceptions. In 1854, the landscape designer Frederick Law Olmsted noted Southern pork and cornpone in east Texas as well as German farmsteads and lager beer around New Braunfels, Texas.[72] Meanwhile, the '49ers transformed San Francisco into a cosmopolitan city of elegant French and Chinese restaurants. But outside these enclaves, newcomers tended to blend into the established Hispanic culture, at least for the first generation. Marriage alliances with wealthy local families offered an easy way to acquire land and market connections. Irish and Catholic migrants in particular, such as Bryan Callaghan, who was elected mayor of San Antonio in 1846, and the cattle barons Mifflin Kenedy and Richard King, assimilated with the local elite. Moreover, local women were often quite successful in negotiating matters of business and inheritance, not to mention food choices. The historian Jovita González observed in the 1930s: "The descendants of the Americans who married Mexican wives in the 1800s are more Mexicanized than the Mexicans."[73]

Yet the influx of trade goods from the United States gradually began to transform diets on both sides of the newly defined border. Ceramics from England and New England took the place of Hispanic majolica and indigenous earthenware in food preparation and service. Even simple manufactured goods could have a significant impact on the region, as an author, Gustave Aimard, related in an 1871 story of Hermosillo rancheros. "Father Sanchez had taken up the handmill, and was grinding the wheat, while his wife, after sifting the wheat,

Figure 2.7. Cooking tortillas at Fort Bliss, Texas. Photographic postcard from 1910, Otis A. Aultman, photographer. Courtesy Daniel Arreola Collection.

pounded it, and formed it into light cakes, called tortillas, which, after being griddled, would form the solid portion of the breakfast."[74] Although Aimard tossed off the scene as mere local color, it represented a revolutionary change in social relations. The new mechanical mill transformed the exclusively female labor of grinding grain on the metate, which was deeply symbolic of gender oppression, into a shared family task. Because flour tortillas conveyed more of the status of baking bread than of grinding corn *masa*, even men commonly prepared them when working alone on ranches and mines.[75]

North American influence spread most widely with little cans of Royal baking powder, a Fort Wayne, Indiana, brand that advertised heavily from the 1870s and became ubiquitous throughout Latin America. Even as many women appreciated the newfound ease of making flour tortillas in the early twentieth century, others were nostalgic for an earlier day. "My mother made the Sonora tortillas too—light, thin, big tortillas. Oh boy, there's nothing like it!" exclaimed Virginia Gastelum, while carefully distinguishing the family recipe from newfangled versions. "She just used lard and flour and water and a little bit of salt. No baking powder."[76]

In little more than a century, the flour tortilla had gone full circle from being a rare novelty to a regional staple and finally a lost art—at least in

---

Box 2.1 Recipe for Flour Tortillas from Sra. Dolores Espinoza de Astiazaran

Mix the flour with water and salt, until it forms a smooth dough; form balls that are not too big, and rub lard on each ball, allow it to rest for a while; then to make them extend with both hands until they are big and thin, put them on the griddle which should be very hot, and be careful to turn them without leaving them long on the fire so that they stay soft, because if left on the heat they brown and afterwards they cannot be rolled to form burritos or tacos.

Source: Josefina Velázquez de León, *Cocina de Sonora* (Mexico City: Ediciones Velázquez de León, 1958), 95–96.

---

its "traditional" form. Although earlier versions surely existed, this hybrid food became common only in the late eighteenth century, as Bourbon economic expansion made wheat available to an increasingly status-conscious rural society. As a result, women's labor in the kitchen could simultaneously affirm family connections to a particular locality and to a broader tradition of Hispanic civilization. But even as the flour tortilla was helping to forge regional ethnic identities, norteño society had already begun to fracture further with the growing presence of newcomers from the United States.

Crafting Icons on the Borderlands

Although the origins of the flour tortilla may be lost, the meanings that it had for the people of northern New Spain need not be. From a material perspective, it was a relatively easy way for rural women to prepare wheat without the time and expense of making either risen bread or corn tortillas, as the folklorist Arthur Campa has noted. "Wheat tortillas replaced the corn product in Hispanic homes in northern Mexico and most of the Southwest. It was considerably easier and faster for the housewife to prepare the biscuit-like dough and roll it out than go through the long process of making nixtamal," he explained. "With wheat tortillas she could have bread on the table in a matter of minutes."[77] Convenience was certainly important for hardworking frontier women, but such a calculation was valid only when both grains were affordable, a late colonial phenomenon at best. Symbolically, wheat and

corn held very different meanings: the former was the food of Spanish conquistadors; the latter was associated with lower-class Indians. Even today in
New Mexico, the choice of tortillas can be a political statement—many
status-conscious Hispanic women would not be caught dead making them
out of Indian corn. Moreover, these associations vary across the north; flour
tortillas may have arrived last in northeastern New Spain, the leading center
of Jewish settlement in the colonial period. Home economists found that
Mexicans in the Lower Rio Grande Valley of Texas were just making the transition from corn to flour tortillas in the 1930s.[78]

Border residents often take great pride in their Hispanic origins, but Indians
also made vital contributions to the cuisines of northern Mexico. Despite
the priests' tireless proselytism of wheat bread and wine, pioneer women of
Mesoamerican origin were just as successful in spreading corn tortillas and
chile pepper stews to the region. Spaniards were also influenced by native cooking practices, for example, during a famine of 1590 in which a Spanish official
ordered two oxen to be pit-roasted in an indigenous manner as "*barbacoa de mezcal*."[79] Nor were the native inhabitants of the frontier passive in these cultural
exchanges. They provided crucial knowledge of local foods to both Spaniards
and Mesoamerican Indians alike. While adapting new foods and practices to survive in a landscape irrevocably changed by colonialism, the Pueblos, Rarámuri,
Cunca'ac, and others succeeded in preserving their cultural integrity.

Even Spaniards lived simply on the colonial frontier, with few luxuries
beyond the inevitable cup of chocolate. Wealthy mining towns absorbed the
bulk of agricultural surpluses, and most settlers depended on maize for subsistence. Only at the end of the eighteenth century did the wheat flour tortilla emerge as a product of an artistic renaissance in the borderlands. These
cooking practices eventually coalesced into distinct regional cuisines through
a process of selective historical memory that assigned iconic foods to local
identities—dried beef as symbolic of Sonoran vaqueros, lamb adobo emblemiz-
ing New Mexican shepherds—even though colonial New Mexicans salted beef
and Sonorans also used adobo.[80] A similar process of forgetting contributed
to the creation of globalized Mexican food in the twentieth century. Although
the borderlands provided the basic menu that was later industrialized by food
processors in the United States, many local dishes dropped out, including chile
verde and carne seca. Meanwhile, through the twists of globalization, another
deeply local dish, burritos made of wheat flour tortillas, came to symbolize the
foods of all Mexicans.

PART II

National Tacos

FROM THE PASTRY WAR
TO PARISIAN MOLE

n the novel *Los bandidos de Río Frío*, Manuel Payno described three separate versions of the Mexican national cuisine—indigenous, Creole, and, paradoxically, French—although he left no doubt about his own preferences. He began by lampooning the Mexicanized examples of Parisian haute cuisine that were passed off on unsuspecting customers in fin de siècle restaurants, where the ignorance of proper French usage betrayed the inauthentic cooking. "The reader should not expect to find here ribs *a la Saint Menehould*, nor filet mignon *a la Jean Bart*, nor salmon in *sauce riche*." Although more sympathetic to the indigenous and mestizo lower classes, he depicted them as rustics dancing before the Virgin of Guadalupe and feasting on goat, *pulque*, and tacos—in one of the first literary references to a dish that would become a national standard. Payno considered the true soul of Mexican cuisine to be neither the foods of pagan peasants nor of Francophile moderns, but rather the Creole delicacies of his youth in Mexico City. As a tribute to "domestic history," he recalled such a dinner from half a century earlier, in the 1840s: "A thick bread soup, adorned with boiled egg, chickpeas, and parsley, *tornachiles* [yellow chiles, stuffed] with cheese, beef tongue with olives and capers, roast kid with lettuce salad, and to crown the work, a plate of mole de guajolote on one side and green mole on the other." The desserts that followed evoked the sweet memories of colonial convent kitchens, camote with pineapple, conserves of mamey (*ate*), and candied egg yolks (*yemitas*). Concluding the menu, he predicted that "more than one reader will lick their lips, however Parisian they may be."[1]

Despite the modest disclaimer of "domestic history," Payno offered a culinary parable for nation building in nineteenth-century Mexico. These different versions of the national cuisine represented opposing visions of Mexican society in the early republic. Divided by regionalism and ethnicity, Mexicans held little sense of common identity except perhaps for devotion to the Virgin of Guadalupe. Mexico gained its independence in 1821, and civil conflict contributed to instability for decades thereafter, reaching a low point in 1848 when the United States conquered half the national territory. Politicians tried to unite the nation around the European ideologies of conservatism and liberalism, a struggle that led to yet another foreign intervention: the 1862 alliance of Mexican conservatives with Napoleon III to place the Austrian Archduke Maximilian on the throne. Even after liberal armies defeated the invaders, French cultural influences persisted under the government of Porfirio Díaz (1876–1911), who had led a cavalry charge against Napoleon's army at the battle of Cinco de Mayo (May 5, 1862). While inviting foreign capitalists to modernize the Mexican economy, Porfirian technocrats, called *científicos* (scientific ones), adopted the latest Parisian fashions, including haute cuisine. The liberal Payno questioned their ostentatious banquets, but he was equally suspicious of the illiterate mestizo and indigenous lower classes. Mexico would achieve its destiny only under the guidance of educated elites who were respectful of the nation's cultural heritage, and Payno harkened back to the nostalgic pleasures of mole de guajolote and candied sweet potato to entice contemporaries away from their foreign infatuations.

Although Payno did not actually use the term "Creole" to describe the meal, his account fit perfectly with the historian Florescano's summary of Creole patriotism, which was held by those who "had not rejected the *puchero* of their grandparents, nor did they consider ordinary the dishes that were served in the fabulous palaces of the Aztec kings." [2] Payno thereby brought together colonial and pre-Hispanic cuisines, while carefully distinguishing them from the supposedly decadent foods of living Indians. Moreover, although these Creole images of the national cuisine were regional in nature, he knew little of such northern specialties as wheat flour tortillas.

Even the distinctions among French, Creole, and Indian cuisines were difficult to pin down in practice because they changed according to the situation and the observer. Mexicans perceived infinite variety in a dish such as mole de guajolote. Every town and village boasted a different version, and every individual cook added her unique *sazón*, or taste. By contrast, foreigners often could not distinguish between Payno's three broad categories, because indigenous festive meals and urban Creole luncheons seemingly featured the same turkey in hot sauce. Even a platter of, say, *dindonneau à la Toulousaine* (young turkey breast in brown sauce) served in a French restaurant in Mexico City might be spiced beyond all recognition, making it taste like just another mole de guajolote, at least to outsiders. The shock of chiles accounted for much of the problem, because the first bite of capsicum can paralyze the inexperienced palate, muting nuances of spice and flavor. Equally important was the social construction of taste: people acquire their eating preferences as learned or "constructed" cultural traits, of course, but also the social context of any meal, the situation in which it is served and consumed, powerfully determines the sensory experience of the food. Unfamiliar with local cultural associations, foreigners tended to collapse the national cuisine into Payno's exotic indigenous category, an unpleasant thought for Mexicans wishing to appear fashionably Parisian.

Even for Mexicans, the national cuisine was a product of the imagination, a menu of what they thought they should be eating as well as a catalog of what they actually consumed. While engaging in culinary tourism to explore the regional diversity that made up the new nation, they also projected their aspirations and fears, for example, to become sophisticated Europeans by eating fancy French cuisine or to regress to Aztec barbarism by consuming indigenous food. Although these images were founded largely on class distinctions, they were not crude materialist categories of an indigenous working class, a Creole middle class, and a Francophile aristocracy. Rather, foods were considered appropriate for particular social situations. A Porfirian *lagartijo* (dandy) might eat Creole mole for *almuerzo* (brunch) at home in the morning, French *bifstek* during the *comida* (dinner) at a restaurant in the afternoon, and indigenous tacos for *cena* (supper) while cruising the streets late at night. As this example demonstrates, the social boundaries around food consumption were artificial, fluid, and readily transgressed, whether by elites slumming among the lower classes or through the mingling of different plebeian groups.

Tacos entered the national cuisine in the late nineteenth century and were seen as a potential danger to both health and morality. Although appearing at a time of industrialization, when labor migrants filled the streets, they were perceived not as an expression of modernity but rather as part of an indigenous invasion of Mexico City. Wealthy residents did not care that most of these workers had arrived from provincial towns and considered themselves to be mestizos. They were rustic newcomers and a threat to Porfirian order and progress, right down to the foods they ate.[3] Adapting the newly developed science of nutrition, intellectuals blamed the nation's perceived backwardness on the supposed inferiority of the indigenous staple, maize. Senator Francisco Bulnes declared that "the race of wheat is the only truly progressive one" and that "maize has been the eternal pacifier of America's indigenous races and the foundation of their refusal to become civilized."[4] This "tortilla discourse" was based on spurious nutritional calculations, but at least it did not attribute the problem to racial inferiority, as was common in the North Atlantic world. Instead, the científicos assigned environmental causes to socioeconomic problems, in particular, the unequal distribution of land, which prevented rural communities from feeding themselves adequately.[5] Ultimately, the Porfirian elite took an ambivalent attitude toward the foods they considered to be indigenous, while ignoring the distinctive foods of the northern borderlands. Aspiring to become a European nation, they craved a European diet. Nevertheless, they still followed a Creole historical narrative that placed the nation's roots in native soil. Perceiving the taco to be deeply Mexican, they sought to tame it and make it their own.

The Pastry War, or Foreigners in the National Cuisine

However nationalist his taste, Manuel Payno was also a cosmopolitan, comfortable at the banquet tables of the Victorian era. Born into an aristocratic family, he held diplomatic postings on three continents, and *Los bandidos de Río Frío*, his masterpiece of local customs, was inspired by the example of Honoré de Balzac. He even published the novel while posted as a Mexican consul in Barcelona, which may help to explain his nostalgic desire for Creole foods. For Payno and his contemporaries, keeping up with the latest scientific and cultural developments was essential for securing Mexico's place among the so-called civilized nations. At the table, that meant learning French, the language of gastronomy in the Victorian world. Eager to demonstrate their savoir faire, wealthy Mexicans imported French champagne, cookbooks, and even chefs. Such skilled European migrant workers not only contributed to Mexico's stock of cultural capital, but they were also welcomed in the hopes that they would counterbalance the indigenous races and "whiten" the nation. The elite infatuation with French goods and their apparent disdain for the national heritage became the subject of popular mockery. Despite Payno's quip, the Porfirians did not unconsciously swallow an inauthentic version of another nation's cuisine; instead, they actively appropriated the global culture of the nineteenth century and made it their own.

Critics had already begun to comment unfavorably on the French food served in Mexico in the decades before the arrival of Maximilian. In 1840, Fanny Calderón de la Barca described the creations of one Parisian chef, working in an aristocratic home, as resembling mining slag. Brantz Mayer complained about the "two Frenchified meals" served daily at his hotel, La Gran Sociedad. Meanwhile, liberal journalists at *El Siglo XIX* smirked at ostentatious political banquets featuring "monstrous pastries like those of the Middle Ages, inside of which appear handsome portraits of the latest distinguished personalities."[6] Like foreign travelers and newspaper reporters, Mexican commoners were quick to mock elite pretensions. In 1838, a French fleet occupied the Port of Veracruz to collect on defaulted sovereign loans and personal damages to citizens residing in Mexico. When word spread that the claimants included the French baker Emile Lefort, whose renowned empanadas had allegedly been looted a decade earlier by revolutionaries, popular wit immortalized the episode as the "pastry war."[7]

Yet criticism did not deter the Mexican elite from their pursuit of haute cuisine, particularly when Maximilian introduced the pomp of European court life in the 1860s. Even after the emperor's death, the republican government of Benito Juárez continued to use the imperial dinnerware and tablecloths; his monogrammed "M" thus haunted Mexican state banquets for another decade. Menus from the period also testify to the prevalence of continental cuisine. On September 21, 1891, for example, 588 distinguished guests gathered at the National Theater to celebrate President Díaz's birthday. With their wives looking on from the balcony above, the delegates dined on soup *à l'espagnole*, fish *à la princesse*, truffled *vol-au-vent*, and beef *à la valencienne*.[8] The patriotic occasion merited only one course served *à la mexicaine*, although it is unclear precisely how this dish was prepared, because the language of French cuisine was still in flux during the nineteenth century. Auguste Escoffier later defined "mexicaine" in his influential guide, first published in 1903, as a dish served with grilled pimentos, mushrooms, and "very thick Tomato Fondue."[9] A garnish of pimento is a long way from mole de guajolote, but many in the nineteenth century may have preferred such a bland representation of their cuisine. European gourmets often refused to tolerate

Menu

Haut Sauterne		Clovisses
	Gombo printanière	Crème d'Oseille
Amontillado Pasado		
	Mousse de Jambon à la Venitienne	
Radis	Olives	Céléri	Amandes salées
	Filet de Bass à la Joinville	
Rauenthaler Berg, 1883	Tomates farcies aux concombres	
Moët-Chandon Imperial Brut	Paniere de Ris-de-Veau, Royale	
	Selle d'Agneau, Sauce Colbert	
Pommes Palestine		Petits pois nouveaux
	Ailes de Volaille à la Mexicaine	
	Sorbet Fantaisie	
Chambertin, 1878	Pigrannaux desossé sauté	
		Salade à la Waldorf
	Pèches glacés	Petits Fours
Old East India Madeira	Fromage	Fruits
Liqueurs	Café	

The Waldorf-Astoria   *August le 17, 1899*

CAMERON & BULKLEY, N.Y.

Figure 3.1. "Ailes de Volaille [chicken wings] à la Mexicaine" at a dinner at the Waldorf-Astoria, August 17, 1899, in honor of the South-Eastern Railroad Co. of Yucatán by Rafael Peón y Loza. Miss Frank E. Buttolph American Menu Collection, 1851–1930. New York Public Library. Stephen A. Schwarzman Building Rare Book Division. Image ID 4000006353.3. Courtesy of New York Public Library.

even the mildest of stimulants, which left Mexicans sensitive to accusations of savage cookery. Such a reputation had spread as far as Russia, where a banquet guest described a dash of cayenne pepper as the "fiery nectar of the Mexicans."[10]

Diplomatic representatives abroad took pains to downplay Mexican popular foods in order to project a more civilized image. Manuel M. de Zamacona, who served as a minister to Washington, D.C., in the late 1870s, hired the city's leading chefs to cater events at his elegant brownstone residence. The press corps dutifully reported on banquet tables loaded with baked salmon, foie gras, sandwiches, and pyramids of crystallized fruits. Zamacona assured journalists that he provided simply "a reproduction of such entertainments when given in the city of the Montezumas," although the turkey was served roasted rather than in mole. The only hint of Mexican popular culture appeared as ornaments in the shapes of eagles and serpents on the table and in murals of folkloric Indian women making tortillas and selling *refrescos* (fruit drinks) along with men selling poultry and tapping maguey plants to make pulque. The legation thus provided a glimpse of exotic Mexico without the risk of offending delicate palates.[11]

Zamacona was not exaggerating when he suggested that visitors to Mexico City could find continental cuisine in exclusive restaurants, social clubs, and private homes. Chef Gustave Montaudon's Restaurant de Paris, for example, was renowned for serving only the finest seafood, carried fresh from the coasts by express train. Meanwhile, guests at the Iturbide could rest assured that the *maître d'hôtel* Charles Récamier maintained the most exacting service in the dining room. Even provincial cities offered cosmopolitan cuisine; the Russian geographer S. K. Patkanov reported a tasteful French restaurant in Mérida, Yucatán. The Moctezuma Brewery hired Philippe Suberbie to manage the Brasserie d'Orizaba, where aficionados could sample Alsatian *choucrout* (sauerkraut) along with the house brew, Siglo XX, which became known simply as Dos Equis when the twentieth century lost its novelty. Social clubs provided another venue for elite socializing and business deals. The Casino Español, Casino Alemán, and le Cercle Français were frequented not only by Spanish, German, and French expatriates but also by prominent Mexicans. The most exclusive institution of the day was the Jockey Club, founded in 1881 and located in the House of Tiles, a magnificent edifice bordering the fashionable Alameda Park. A French chef presided over the kitchen, while General Francisco Zacarías Mena, a personal friend of don Porfirio, administered the club's vast wine cellar. Members of Díaz's inner circle, including General Bernardo Reyes, also took pride in employing French chefs. The president himself retained a German, Hermann Bellinghausen, who had formerly cooked for Kaiser Wilhelm II. Sylvain Daumont, the most renowned chef in Porfirian Mexico, arrived from Paris in 1891 to run the kitchen of Ignacio de la Torre y Mier, noted bon vivant and Díaz's son-in-law. The chef was celebrated so lavishly that he left private service within a year to open a restaurant called simply Sylvain; the house specialty was filet of venison with chestnut purée.[12]

Imported goods as well as skilled professionals were essential for recreating continental cuisine in Mexico, and Escoffier aptly described the French chefs who worked abroad as "traveling salesmen in high white toques."[13] For the monthlong centennial celebrations of September 1910, Mexican politicians and visiting dignitaries reportedly consumed hundreds of cans of French asparagus, mushrooms, truffles, and foie gras, along with more than one thousand cases of wine, including Jerez, Pouilly, Mouton Rothschild, and Martell Cognac, plus 450 more cases of champagne.[14] Wealthy Mexicans also provided regular employment for brigades of kitchen workers and waiters, who in 1893 organized a local chapter of the Société Française des Cuisiniers, Pâtissiers, et Confiseurs, a fraternal society intended to assist members and to help place new arrivals in appropriate kitchens.[15] Parisian publishing houses even dominated the production of Mexican cookbooks, ensuring that French cuisine was well represented alongside recipes for mole.[16]

Despite French cuisine's cosmopolitan image, many of Mexico's leading restaurants were run by migrants from other nations. Just as Swiss Italians founded Delmonico's of New York, Porfirian Mexico City's most storied restaurant, La Concordia, was run by the Omarinis, a family originally from the Swiss border region of northwestern Italy. One critic described the restaurant as a memorial for the fine dining of Maximilian's Empire, with "Austrian and French officers stalking down through the mirrored rooms," even though it had not actually opened until 1868, a year after the republic was restored.[17] Agostino Fulceri (Hispanicized to Fulcheri) expanded a simple Venetian coffeehouse and ice cream shop into an elegant Italian restaurant specializing in oyster soup, ravioli, and roast kid. Madrid-born Alejandro Pardo Landa parlayed his Parisian training and experience as a sous chef under Sylvain Daumont to become a noted author and cooking teacher to Mexico City high society. Those with bohemian tastes could visit boisterous German beer gardens, pseudo-Chinese chop suey joints, and Middle Eastern restaurants. For a more sedate crowd, several Mexico City hotels offered American-style dining, although *Campbell's Guide* warned that "with few exceptions, the restaurant advertised as English or American is to be avoided."[18]

This cosmopolitanism was not entirely welcome to elites who feared that the wrong sorts of immigrants would undermine their efforts to improve both the national cuisine and the Mexican race. The Chinese, in particular, with their rice-based diet, inspired fears of degeneration. As the second-largest foreign colony in Porfirian Mexico, prominent as retailers and restaurateurs in Mexico City and the North, the Chinese were villainized by nativists. One such author,

La noche de bodas.....

y cinco años después

Figure 3.2. "The wedding night and five years later." Anti-Chinese propaganda by José Angel Espinoza, *El ejémplo de Sonora* (Mexico City: N.p., 1932), 36.

José Angel Espinoza, graphically depicted the fate of Mexican women ensnared by Chinese men. The first scene illustrated the wedding night of a voluptuous young Mexican bride with flowing skirts and bobbed hair, as she is ogled from behind a screen by a demonic Chinese husband. In the second scene, five years later, the woman looks gaunt and haggard with three malnourished children. The husband, having failed to provide for them, appears in the background wearing stylish clothes, presumably in pursuit of other vulnerable Mexican women. Anti-Chinese xenophobia also found expression in popular culture through tales of rat eating and other disgusting foods.[19]

Foreigners not only ran many restaurants and groceries, but they also contributed significantly to modernizing the local food industry. The foremost name in prepared Mexican food, Clément Jacques, came to Mexico in 1880 with an ambitious scheme for manufacturing cork from the oak forests of Campeche to supply the international bottling industry. Although Mexican trees could not match the quality of true Mediterranean cork, Jacques developed a successful business importing European wine, oil, and foods for the local elite. Meanwhile, Central European immigrants provided the expertise for an emerging Porfirian beer industry. Because each large city supported an independent brewery, diverse European traditions of ale and lager were overlaid on Mexican culinary regionalism, according to the origins of the brew master. The Yucatecan León was modeled on a Munich dark beer, Dos Equis was styled after a Viennese lager, and Monterrey's Cuauhtemoc Brewery crafted a pilsner in its Bohemia brand. But not all new imported food-processing technologies took root; the Mexican taste for freshly slaughtered meat helped to undermine efforts by Chicago investors to construct refrigerated packinghouses. Moreover, many migrants contributed to the Mexican food industry without introducing new technology. For example, Basques controlled the bread supply of Porfirian Mexico City by using traditional baking methods, although they did employ modern milling techniques. Even more old-fashioned were the Mennonites, Dutch reform Protestants who arrived in the 1920s by way of Canada. They founded a remote colony in Chihuahua but eventually gained fame throughout the republic for their soft, white cheese, which became known as *queso chihuahua.*[20]

The development of local food industries, together with the growth of importers, brought European foods within the reach of Mexico's growing middle classes. Cookbooks proliferated during the Porfirian era, revealing the secrets of French cuisine to housewives and their servants. Even those who lacked the skills or equipment at home had access to professional caterers, charcuterie, and bakeries. El Globo, founded in 1884 by Monsieur and Madame Emile Hommel, continues to sell flaky croissant and rich brioche to this day. Imported delicacies were also available for middle-class consumers in the provinces. In April 1883, the Guaymas merchant Franz Seldner received a shipment from Hamburg containing 120 kilograms of sausage, 80 of perfume, and a small quantity of chocolate truffles (*pastel trufado*). The shipment was recorded in state judicial archives when customs officials impounded the goods and charged him with smuggling, although Seldner eventually took delivery, assuring that the women of Sonora had access to imported luxuries.[21]

Much of the criticism for Porfirian Francophilia in the works of Payno and other authors betrayed an aristocratic scorn for the arriviste middle classes, who sought to rise above their station by acquiring foreign tastes. The dangers of social climbing were clearly portrayed in José Tomás de Cuéllar's satiric novella, *Baile y cochino* (Having a ball, 1889). When a colonel from the provinces threw a party to introduce his daughter into Mexico City society, a well-connected friend, Don Saldaña, generously offered to arrange the invitations and catering: Westphalia hams, oyster vol-au-vent, aspic, champagne, liquors, silverware, and tablecloths—all for a hefty kickback. But the elegant Creole ladies at the dance turned out to be mestizo strumpets in pancake makeup. Saldaña was exposed as a pretender when a guest revealed that "for lunch he buys mole de guajolote and spends a few reales on pulque."[22] The next morning, the colonel surveyed the damage to his house caused by drunken party crashers and swore off his social aspirations. Similar views of the nouveaux riches were common in elite circles of New York City, London, and Paris, as well as in Mexico City.

The Porfirian elite has also been lampooned for mimicking French haute cuisine, but table manners were simply part of the protocol of diplomacy and business in the globalized age of the Victorians. Although many resented Gallic supremacy at the table, in London and New York as well as in Mexico City, rejecting it on patriotic grounds would have been unthinkable for cosmopolitans. More important, from the perspective of culinary history, is the creativity that Mexicans brought to this global cuisine. Although derided by many at the time, the addition of chile peppers and the use of local produce and cooking techniques—in short, the Mexicanization of European cuisine— constituted a form of culinary innovation. Nor were such changes limited to Mexican apprentices taking liberties with the artistry of French masters; even some immigrant chefs experimented with local flavors and became aficionados of chiles. Alejandro Pardo followed his celebrated guide to European cuisine with a volume on Mexican cookery, including an early recipe for tacos. Italians such as Agostino Fulceri likewise were naturalized in their new home, and not just by changing the spelling of their names. A writer for the *Mexican Herald* observed that Italian restaurants also "are becoming, in a way, Mexican, in their desire to obtain Mexican patronage."[23] After all, French chefs constructed *la grande cuisine* by borrowing from various countries and transformed their dishes, including ones designated *à la mexicaine*; Mexicans were simply returning the favor. Gourmets today celebrate such culinary blending as avant-garde, and at least some modernists recognized this at the time. The poet and gourmet José Juan Tablada, for one, had a ready answer to critics of Porfirian cosmopolitanism: "Our imitation of the French was therefore not ridiculous and grotesque, but rather by its exaggeration, the French models adopted, *but adapted*, have been and will be fecund in our soil."[24] While the middle classes experimented with French versions of the national cuisine, foods that were seen as indigenous proved more controversial but ultimately triumphed among the masses.

The Insurgent Taco, or Indigenous Images of Mexico

Although Manuel Payno introduced the taco to many readers in the 1890s, there was at least one prior literary reference to the snack, which likewise revealed ambiguities and social divisions within the national cuisine. This earlier mention, by another liberal author, Guillermo Prieto, came at a critical moment in Mexican history—the Cinco de Mayo victory at the Battle of Puebla by largely indigenous troops over the French invaders. But rather than exalting a national dish, Prieto used the taco to spoof the Europeans and bring them down to the level of Indians. Throughout the nineteenth century, elites perceived indigenous food as a shameful category within the national cuisine; such food was undoubtedly Mexican but associated with Aztec barbarism and backwardness. It was not a treasure to celebrate but rather a condition to overcome on the path to modernity. Nevertheless, an alternate current within Porfirian thought, running alongside the faith in imported progress, believed it was possible to redeem the indigenous culture and create a mestizo nation. This *indigenista* attitude, which achieved dominance with the Revolution of 1910 against the regime of Díaz, sought to appropriate the taco and cleanse it of its plebeian associations. Thus, the taco inspired a struggle between elites and masses over how to define the national cuisine.

Even before Mexico achieved independence, Enlightenment thinkers maintained two rival images of Native Americans: the noble savage and the barbarous cannibal. The former view predominated in Father Francesco Saviero Clavigero's *History of Mexico* (1780–81), written from exile in Italy following the Jesuit expulsion. He described the corn tortilla as "extremely wholesome and substantial, and when fresh made of a good taste, [although it] becomes rather disagreeable when stale." Yet he also recounted in detail the indigenous taste for "*Axolotl* [salamander], *Atetepiz* [insect egg], *Atopinan* [marsh grasshopper], and other such little animals [*animalitos*], inhabitants of the water; but even ants, marsh-flies, and the very eggs of the same flies." Clavigero explained the difficult circumstances of the Aztec capital's founding on a rocky lake outcropping and noted that "historians who have tasted this food, pronounce it not disagreeable." Nevertheless, he considered it "wonderful that the Mexicans, and especially the poor among them, were not subject to numberless diseases, considering the quality of their food."[25]

Anglo-Saxon writers, lacking Clavigero's local knowledge and affection, employed food to convey various negative images of Mexican society. In his *History of America* (1777), William Robertson portrayed Native Americans as a stunted race and dismissed even the Aztec warriors as "feeble" on account of "their scanty diet, on poor fare, sufficient to preserve life, but not to give

Figure 3.3. "Mexican method of making bread." Francesco Saverio Clavigero, *The History of Mexico*, trans. Charles Cullen, 2 vols. (London: J. Johnson, 1807), 1:432.

firmness to their constitution."[26] By contrast, William Prescott's popular *History of the Conquest of Mexico* (1843) followed the Spaniards' descriptions of a magnificent empire of great pyramids and haute cuisine. "Aztec *artistes*," he observed, "had penetrated deep into the mysteries of culinary science." But admiring accounts of Moctezuma's banquets, consisting of hundreds of finely seasoned dishes, delicate tortillas, and frothy chocolate, served only to highlight the barbarism of human sacrifice and ceremonial cannibalism. Prescott concluded indignantly: "Cannibalism in the guise of an Epicurean science, becomes even the more revolting."[27] In an essay entitled "Montezuma's Dinner" (1876), the ethnologist Lewis H. Morgan chided Prescott for a romantic and uncritical reading of the conquistadors. He insisted mistakenly that the Aztec Empire was the social equivalent of an Iroquois village and that Moctezuma's banquets were little more than a pot of hominy.[28] Descriptions of ancient foods therefore allowed writers to project contemporary Mexico into the pre-Hispanic past.

Travel writers meanwhile imagined themselves living in the days of Moctezuma. The French naturalist Lucien Biart, author of a popular history of the ancient Aztecs, also wrote about his adventures in Mexico, including the hardships of dining in the countryside: "Don Bernardo invited me to dinner, when I partook of two or three dishes, the composition of which I dared not inquire into. In one of them there was certainly turpentine and onions, unfortunately there was not enough onion, and the turpentine had been too freely used. At dessert, I was obliged to crunch some ant's eggs, a sweetmeat I do not recommend to any one."[29] The German traveler Carl Sartorius described Mexico City's plebeian tenement houses, "ground-floor smoky places, where queer cookery is going on. As the street-doors stand wide open, earthen vessels are observed on huge fires, in which bubble red broth and black beans." Exploring further, he discovered kitchens "in which rows of brown women, the upper part of the body quite naked, or but indifferently covered, kneel on the floor, and crush maize on flat stones, whilst others prepare the mass with their hands for tortillas, and bake them in flat earthen pans."[30] Pulque also featured prominently in the accounts of foreign visitors, particularly in the letters of Fanny Calderón de la Barca, who was disgusted at first by the "rancid odour" but later became a connoisseur of the native beverage, visiting the finest maguey haciendas to sample varieties. One of her tasting notes read "sweet taste and a creamy froth."[31]

Mexican elites displayed a similar blend of fascination and abhorrence at the foods of the popular classes. Liberal intellectuals and gourmets such as Manuel Payno, Guillermo Prieto, and Antonio García Cubas were regular visitors in the *pulquerías* of the early republic, and in their memoirs and fiction, they ranked the finest street food vendors and tavern enchilada makers. But despite their praise for a few cooks, they looked with dismay on the diet of the lower classes.[32] A satiric poem by Prieto, written around 1862 as propaganda during the war against France, illustrates this haughty attitude. Mexican troops had repulsed Napoleon's first invasion in May at the Battle of Puebla, but reinforcements arrived in September under the command of Élie Forey. While awaiting the coronation of Maximilian, the general appointed a regency council including Juan Nepomuceno Almonte, who had led the diplomatic mission to Napoleon and unilaterally declared himself ruler of Mexico—from behind French lines. In a parody entitled "Glorias de Juan Pamuceno," Prieto described the traitorous Almonte serving indigenous food and drink to the French general:

Good Forey!
You drank wine of the maguey
until you lost your head:
ate pipián and *tamalli*,
tlemolito with *xumiles*,
and tired yourself of *mextlapiles*
in your tacos of *tlaxcalli*.[33]

In these brief verses, Prieto first spoofed the Frenchman for going native, getting drunk on pulque while eating tamales, pumpkin seed sauce (pipián), and, most degrading of all, stinkbugs (xumiles) in chile broth (tlemolito). Unspoken in the text, but obvious to contemporaries, was an equally cruel jibe at Almonte, the illegitimate son of a Native American woman, Brígida Almonte, and the priest and independence war hero Father José María Morelos. Although the conservative diplomat moved comfortably in European royal courts, speaking fluent English and French, Prieto dismissed him with racist stereotypes of the ancient Aztecs. As a final insult, the taco served to emasculate General Forey. The mextlapil on which he tired himself was a stone rolling pin, used to grind corn by hand for making tortillas (tlaxcalli), the most stereotypically feminine task in Mexican society and one that no self-respecting man would ever be seen undertaking. What may be the first recorded taco thus served as propaganda in the campaign to expel French invaders and restore the Mexican Republic. Yet Prieto was not celebrating the indigenous troops who had helped to defeat the French. Like Payno, he lumped Indians and French together in opposition to Creole liberals, who were portrayed as the true defenders of the nation.

Despite the scorn of liberal intellectuals, tacos soon spread from plebeian obscurity to become an omnipresent food in Mexico City. By the early 1900s, municipal authorities had taken notice of this fad, and their efforts to license and inspect the growing number of taquerías provide some of the first archival records of the taco. Unfortunately, while officials dutifully noted taxes paid and fines imposed, they rarely bothered to describe the kinds of tacos on offer in these informal neighborhood restaurants. Among specific references, tacos de barbacoa appeared most commonly, while documents also mentioned tacos de minero, generic meat tacos, enchiladas, and *gordas* (fat, stuffed tortillas). A number of vendors provided their customers with refrescos (soft drinks), because alcohol was forbidden, and Natalia López even sold ice cream with her tacos. There are hints of regional specialties among the taquerías, perhaps

Figure 3.4. People eating tacos during the fiesta of the Virgin of Guadalupe, c. 1952. Nacho López. Col. SINAFO-INAH. Inventory number 374177. Courtesy of the Instituto Nacional de Antropología e Historia, Mexico.

catering to recent migrants homesick for childhood favorites. At least two shops specialized in pozole, the hominy stew typical of Guadalajara, Jalisco. Railroad transportation also made seafood available to the working classes, and diners could choose between oyster shops, fried fish stands, and a restaurant called Pesca de Alvarado after the port town in Veracruz renowned for its fresh fish and sharp-talking women. Other culinary delights might have been recorded had the municipal government employed restaurant critics instead of tax collectors.[34]

While the presence of unattached male workers created a demand for vendors, Mexico City's cosmopolitan street foods depended on the labor of female migrants. Esther Torres, a native of Guanajuato who arrived in the city in 1910, recalled that it was widely known that women could find work in the capital.[35] Although most preferred the higher wages available in textile factories and other light industries, vending provided a fallback for those of modest circumstances. For example, documents in the Historical Archive of Mexico City record the sojourn of Jovita Ruiz, who sold tacos in a doorway behind the National Palace around 1920 to support her children while petitioning for the pension of her husband, a revolutionary veteran who had died in battle.[36]

Ruiz may have returned home when her case was decided, but other migrants settled in the city. Beatriz Muciño Reyes came to the capital from San Mateo Tazcaliatac and likewise set up shop in the doorway of an office building. After several moves, in 1907 she rented a small storefront on Uruguay Street, where she remained for another four decades before passing the business to a cousin. Tacos Beatriz is remarkable for its longevity as it is still in operation today, but its modest origins are common in the social history of the taco.[37]

Mexico City taquerías allowed for an inexpensive form of culinary tourism, an opportunity for ordinary people to explore exotic delicacies and thereby satisfy their curiosity about the regional cultures that made up the Mexican nation. Consuming strange food has always been a necessity for travelers, but Mexico has developed an elaborate culture of antojitos to indulge the desire for new tastes. Of course, many migrants became regular patrons of particular cooks, who offered familiar "comfort" foods. At times, these women even acted as surrogate mothers, but such ties did not preclude the occasional novelty, taken on a whim. The young people who predominated in the ranks of rural migrants may have been particularly eager for new experiences, and taco shops allowed them an economical means to travel the country vicariously. A stodgy contributor to *El Universal* expressed disapproval in 1920, grumbling that rustic foods had soiled the capital's most elegant park: "The *paseo* of the Alameda today is an affair of the people from the provinces. Chocolate from Oaxaca, dishes from Guadalajara, sweets from Morelia."[38] Not all the frock-coat crowd was complaining, for there was a long tradition of slumming in pulque shops and curbside kitchens.

Indeed, many liberal Porfirians welcomed maize as central to the national cuisine, and they rejected the tortilla discourse with its idealization of foreign cuisine. Vicenta Torres de Rubio, a cookbook author from a political family in Morelia, Michoacán, suggested boldly in 1896 that pozole and other "secrets of the indigenous classes" would be appropriate for a formal dinner party, although out of deference to her elite audience, she carefully distinguished these recipes with the label *"indigenista."*[39] Even cookbooks published by French editorial houses gradually introduced Náhuatl terminology as definitive proof of a food's Mexican national origins.[40] Meanwhile, the prominent lawyer and land reform advocate Andrés Molina Enríquez challenged the supposed nutritional inferiority of maize. Refuting Senator Bulnes's claim that corn undermined productivity, Molina Enríquez made the obvious point that the working classes performed heroic labors on a Spartan diet of tortillas and chile. He blamed the nation's problems on an unequal distribution of land, which prevented many

Mexicans from eating a more well-rounded diet, and he declared maize to be "in an absolutely indubitable manner the national cuisine."[41]

Mexican high society soon began to bring tacos back into their homes, although carefully distinguishing them from the food sold on the streets. Perhaps the first published recipe appeared on June 2, 1908, in Filomeno Mata's liberal stalwart, *El Diario del Hogar* (The daily of the home). This elaborate version of *tacos de crema* (cream tacos) employed not corn tortillas but rather French crêpes. The recipe instructed readers to "stuff them with pastry cream or some dry conserves and roll like a taco. In the same fashion make all of the tacos that you like; arrange on a platter in the form of a pyramid, cover with meringue and adorn with strawberries, orange blossoms, and violets."[42] Such an elaborate concoction clearly evoked the latest street food, but it made the dish socially acceptable through the use of European cooking techniques, expensive fruits, and edible flowers. More recognizable versions of tacos, made with corn tortillas, became common in subsequent decades, but the quality of ingredients helped to maintain social distinctions.

Meanwhile, proletarian tacos continued to evolve and spread through the social landscape, traveling across the country and employing whatever ingredients that cooks could obtain. Already in 1907, the Londres cantina in Monterrey, a northern industrial center, advertised tacos de carne as a snack with beer.[43] Local variations soon began to appear, and by the 1930s, Mexican tacos had begun to assume many of their modern-day categories. Ana María Hernández's pioneering home economics manual gave recipes for tacos with barbacoa, carnitas, brains, and maguey worms (now an expensive delicacy, but

---

Box 3.1   Recipe for Taquitos Mexicanos

Fry in very fresh pork fat fourteen thin tortillas; after they are fried put in each a strip of fresh cheese; another of avocado; another of chipotle in vinegar, without the seeds; another of onions; a tablespoon of mashed and well-fried frijoles; and a little green tomato salsa. Roll the tortilla and put it on an oval platter garnished with leaves of fresh yellow lettuce, radish, and cilantro. Serve immediately, very hot.

Source: Alejandro Pardo, *Los 30 menus del mes. Manual de la cocina casera. Exclusivamente para la República mexicana* (Mexico City: Talleres Tipográficos de "El Hogar," 1917), 37–38.

at the time considered beyond the pale). Hernández also explained that tacos should be fried a deep golden color or left very smooth, depending on whether they were hard or soft. She suggested serving both varieties with lettuce, which is still the preferred garnish of *tacos dorados* ("golden"), although soft tacos in Mexico today are more often accompanied by chopped onions and cilantro.[44] The taco was adopted so quickly and widely in the early twentieth century precisely because its simplicity made it open to widely different interpretations. The popular classes could enjoy a quick and inexpensive bite with whatever ingredients were readily at hand. The elite, meanwhile, could essentially have their taco and eat it, too, claiming a measure of populist patriotism unavailable from French cuisine while still maintaining their social distance from actual street foods.

Parisian Mole, or Creole Nostalgia around the World

Concepción Lombardo de Miramón, the wife of a conservative general who was executed alongside Maximilian, spent years in exile during the midcentury civil wars and, on her first stay in Paris, she became terribly depressed. As she explained to her friend, Guadalupe, the daughter of Juan Nepomuceno Almonte: "I am crying for the Alameda of Mexico [City], which perhaps I will never see again, for our Mexican cuisine, for our chiles, and for our tortillas." Nevertheless, she confessed in her memoirs that "when I was in my country, I neither went for promenades in the Alameda, nor frequently ate Mexican dishes." Nostalgia for Creole dishes exerted a powerful emotional tug, particularly on Mexicans living abroad. Although many felt embarrassed by the heat of chiles and the unfashionable reputation of Mexican cooking, expatriates went to great lengths to recreate it for intimate gatherings. When foreigners embraced these dishes, it was as if they had become part of the family, too. Thus, Lombardo recorded the tears wept by Maximilian and Carlota when they first tasted mole de guajolote in Acultzingo, Veracruz.[45] Even Mexicans were often surprised at the diversity of regional specialties, and culinary tourism offered an early expression of the search for a national cuisine. Liberals and conservatives of the nineteenth century could agree on few things, but they did share a common understanding of the Creole culinary heritage.

The first Mexican cookbooks, published in the 1830s, guided readers through the regional diversity of the national cuisine, while carefully emphasizing Creole foods. At times, these volumes mentioned foods that were considered to be indigenous, but the spicy heat of mole and adobo and the cloying sweetness of colonial desserts constituted the vast majority of the Mexican recipes. Curious cooks could reproduce the distinctive Creole moles of Puebla or Oaxaca, although not more indigenous versions such as the Oaxacan *mole verde*, a green broth perfumed with the anis flavor of *hoja santa*. To accompany the main course were the frijoles of Veracruz or Guadalajara, and, for dessert, the *manjar real* (almond rice custard) of San Juan del Río or the *chongos* (syrupy cheese curds) of Zamora. By the end of the century, cookbooks had become a medium for communication between women in different regions. In 1896, Vicenta Torres de Rubio began her volume of *Cocina michoacana*, published in installments. This ambitious project soon extended beyond the regional specialties of Michoacán as subscribers from throughout Mexico submitted their own favorite recipes. Thus, a national community began to form in the kitchen, at least among middle-class correspondents.[46] Travel provided another means for exploring Mexico's culinary diversity, particularly with the construction of railroad lines during the Porfirian era. A tourist returning home to the United States commented on the local produce available at train stations along the Mexican Central from the capital to El Paso—guava preserves in San Juan del Río, *cajeta* (goat's milk caramel) in Celaya, strawberries in Irapuato, and honey in Chihuahua—and those were just the foods a gringo was willing to risk. Adventurous eaters could sample a far wider range of delicacies, as Ángel Rabanal observed in his classic *corrido* (ballad) "El Ferrocarril" (The railroad). The lyrics provided a veritable Michelin guide to the regional specialties of ambulant vendors: the fabled chorizo of Toluca, frijoles from Apizaco, enchiladas in Tlalpujahua, "and if they sell you a dog, watch out, it's Chihuahua."[47]

The satirical reference to the Chihuahua suggests the ambivalent location of the northern borderlands within the geographical imagination of nineteenth-century Mexicans. The region was still considered a dangerous frontier, menaced by Apache Indians, and the reference to eating dogs harkened back to an Aztec past. Nevertheless, the high status accorded to Hispanic wheat and livestock gave the northern diet a distinctively Creole character. For example, the poet Ignacio Ramírez had laughed affectionately at the Sonorans' predilection for eating wheat in "tortillas, bread, and atole" and their consumption of beef instead of turkey in the wedding mole, the Creole dish par excellence. Although there are almost no distinctively northern recipes in nineteenth-century Mexican cookbooks, Vicenta Torres did publish a recipe received from a reader in Nuevo Laredo entitled "Hens from the Gastronomic Frontier."[48] Thus, northerners who maintained Hispanic standards of civilization—and resisted the growing cultural lure of Americanization across the border—could qualify as members of the Creole community that lay at the heart of the nineteenth-century nation.

Throughout the country, the public eclipse of Creole foods by French cuisine gave these Mexican dishes even greater symbolic importance as family rituals in the home. Maximilian and Carlota sought to demonstrate their love of Mexico by consuming mole de guajolote—for brunch, not dinner—on December 12, 1865, as they celebrated the Virgin of Guadalupe. Don Porfirio and doña Carmen served intensely flavored black mole and stuffed chiles to guests at their private residence, Casa de Cadenas. These Oaxacan specialties, reflected not only the president's birthplace but also a sense of national pride and republican simplicity. The fabled kitchen of the Jockey Club likewise retained a *cordon bleu*, meaning in French a woman skilled in domestic cookery, as opposed to male chefs. In Mexico, this translated into employing a woman from Puebla, the symbolic center of Creole gastronomy, to prepare mole, adobo, and pipián for club members. Clemente Jacques, as he Mexicanized his name, perceived an emerging mass market for Creole cuisine and expanded his business from importing European foods to canning local dishes such as *chiles en escabeche*, mole de guajolote, and chongos from Zamora. In 1893, his preserves won gold medals at the Columbian Exposition in Chicago.[49]

When Mexicans living abroad such as Señora de Miramón felt a nostalgic hunger for familiar food, they tended to indulge it discreetly at home and not in public banquets. Such domestic meals have left few archival traces, but a slip of paper, preserved in the private letters of José María Calderón y Tapia, documents the early global presence of Creole cuisine. Calderón, the Mexican minister to France, received a brief note on March 30, 1845, from his cousin, Fernando Mangino, announcing simply: "Today we are going to eat mole de guajolote and tamales at the O'Brien home."[50] Despite their Irish name, the O'Briens were prominent Mexican *comisionistas*, importers of French goods, based in Bordeaux, and their mercantile connections no doubt assisted in the task of preparing this festive meal in exile.

Although it may have been served with little fanfare, a Mexican dinner required extensive logistics to prepare in Paris in the days before canned mole—and for many families, even afterward. Finding the appropriate chiles presented the first challenge for the family maid. Of course, any well-stocked Parisian *épicerie* of the nineteenth century had small quantities of chile powder, perhaps from Spain or Hungary, but paprika would never satisfy a Mexican aficionado, who insisted on particular combinations of chiles anchos, pasillas, and mulatos. With regular demand from the Mexican colony, which fluctuated between 250 and 500 members in the second half of the nineteenth century, *l'èpicerie espagnole* on 131 rue St. Honoré began to import chiles from Mexico. Before this source became available, families such as the O'Briens might have requested dried peppers from relatives in Mexico, hoping that they would survive the sea voyage without becoming wet and moldy. They may also have planted seeds as a reminder of home, although the flavor was surely affected by the different climate and soil of Paris.[51]

Obtaining maize for tamales may have posed another dilemma for the O'Briens' cook. The agricultural expert Arthur Young, in his travels through France on the eve of the Revolution, noted that maize was cultivated through-out the southwest, from the Pyrenees to Limoges. Mostly it went to feed ani-mals, but Alexandre Dumas recorded in his *Dictionnaire de Cuisine* that corn flour was used in Paris to make sweet cakes.[52] Milled corn would have been of little use for Mexican cooks—quite apart from the need for husks to wrap and steam the tamales—because the grains had to be processed first into nixtamal and then ground by hand on a metate to obtain the proper texture. This latter step posed additional problems because, unlike the large-grained, floury varieties such as *cacahuazintle* preferred in central Mexico, the flint corn grown commonly in Europe had relatively little starch. Bent over the metate, the O'Brien maid may have cursed the "*¡maíz frances!*". To avoid such annoy-ance, many exiles imported white maize from Mexico to make their own fresh nixtamal. Once finished grinding the maize, the maid added pork fat from any neighborhood butcher and enough broth to spread the dough smoothly over soaked and dried husks. Although tamales may be stuffed with a variety of fill-ings, these were likely steamed plain, with just the savory corn as a foil for the spicy mole.

With tamales and chiles in hand, the rest of the ingredients for the O'Brien mole were readily available. Turkeys had been introduced from the Americas in the sixteenth century and were eaten commonly throughout France. By the mid-nineteenth century, vendors at the Parisian fresh produce market, Les Halles, also sold tomatoes and pumpkins; the latter was needed for seeds to thicken the mole. Shoppers could obtain bread and almonds, two other common thick-eners, from bakers and grocers, while Asian spices, including some combina-tion of black pepper, cinnamon, sesame seeds, aniseed, cloves, coriander, and cumin could be purchased from an épicerie. Only one item remained, cacao, and this may have been the easiest of all to find. French chocolate vendors of the nineteenth century even used Mexican metates to grind their product, although the O'Brien maid doubtless had one of her own. The most essential ingredient for the O'Brien mole would therefore have been the kitchen knowledge possessed by the family maid. Although Spanish and Basque servants were readily available in Paris for house cleaning and laundry, elite families brought along skilled Mexican cooks for the delicate labor of patting out tortillas, rolling tamales, and seasoning mole.[53]

Prominent Mexicans living in the United States, who had been made into expatriates by the Treaty of Guadalupe Hidalgo, often preserved Creole culinary traditions as a link to their homeland, even while adapting to changing social conditions. The Amador family of New Mexico illustrates the fluid cultural life along the border. The patriarch, Martín Amador, had settled in the Mesilla Valley in the 1850s as a young man, and he built a prominent mercantile house and a hotel. In 1859, he returned to Mexico to marry Refugio Ruiz of Chihuahua City. Their eight children continued to move back and forth across the border. The oldest daughter, Emilia, married Jesús García, a deputy sheriff from Bernalillo. In 1894, she wrote to her mother from Ojo de Jémez, New Mexico, to say that her daughters were eating better—peas, oranges, and cake—while two years later she was in Ciudad Juárez having breakfast of atole (a corn drink) and dining on verdolagas (purslane). Another daughter, Clotilde, married Antonio Terrazas, a member of the Chihuahua dynasty, and shared in the French cuisine of the Porfirian elite. On January 21, 1903, Terrazas attended a banquet in his hometown consisting of pea soup, *robalo* (snook) *à la Parisienne*, chicken *à la financiera*, aspic, leg of lamb *à la Francesa*, salad, and fresh fruit. Even though she shopped at Bloomingdales in New York, the mother Refugio maintained connections with her Mexican home through a manuscript cookbook preserving colonial dishes, particularly Creole desserts such as *torta de cielo* (heavenly cake), *jericaya* (custard), *turrón de Oaxaca* (nougat), and *jamoncillos de almendra* (fudge squares).[54]

Cultural ties across the border were also preserved through the performances of Mexican theater companies, who made frequent references to food as a way of evoking nostalgia among their compatriots. The Carlos Villalongin dramatic company, for example, published a play in San Antonio, Texas, in November 1911, based on the life of San Felipe de Jesús. Although the Mexican-born saint had left the Franciscan order to become a merchant in the Philippines, the irreverent playwright had the young cleric exiled because of his love of fine food. In the first scene, a prior discovers Felipe and another initiate secretly eating *bacalao en escabeche* (soused cod), *lomo relleno* (stuffed loin), and *salchichones* (sausages) in their monastic cell. Once in Manila, the youths complain of their inability to find decent bread and chocolate. Felipe recovers his faith before his final martyrdom in Japan in 1597, but his appeals for Mexican delicacies are clearly intended to win the hearts of Mexican migrants in the United States.[55]

Living in the United States in the nineteenth century, Encarnación Pinedo was perhaps the fiercest defender of Mexican national cuisine. She was born in 1848, the daughter of an elite California family that suffered grievously at the hands of Anglo invaders; eight of her relatives were lynched, one of them twice. Having lost the family's vast estates to land grabbers, she never married and was eventually forced to depend on the generosity of her Anglo brother-in-law. In 1898, she published a cookbook, written in Spanish and dedicated to her nieces, that contained more than eight hundred recipes. Almost a fifth of the recipes had been adapted from the *Nuevo cocinero mexicano* (New Mexican chef), a popular volume that was reprinted in multiple editions. Pinedo hoped that her own cookbook would encourage her nieces to preserve their Mexican heritage. She presented a striking reversal of the images of civilization at the time in the United States, which described Latins as the true heirs of western civilization and depicted Anglos as uncouth savages. In the introduction she stated flatly, "there is not a single Englishman who can cook, as their foods and style of seasoning are the most insipid and tasteless that one can imagine."[56]

Pinedo's vast knowledge and eloquent writing make this cookbook one of the first great works of Mexican American literature composed by a woman, yet she displayed considerable ambivalence about her identity. Although drawing her recipes from Mexican sources and traditions, she titled the book *El cocinero español* (The Spanish chef). By claiming European descent, Pinedo sought to avoid the racist slurs often used by Americans against Mexicans.[57] This led to some confusion within her recipes. For example, she used "Spanish tortillas" to make enchiladas, although in Spain "tortilla" actually refers to an omelet, not a flatbread of maize. Pinedo also felt comfortable adopting modern technology, including American stoves. It was clearly a work that saw the Mexican national cuisine in the range between Creole and European, juxtaposing mole de guajolote and *chilaquiles tapatios* with pâté de foie gras and Italian ravioles. Indeed, it is perhaps the single best statement of a distinctively borderland

Figure 3.5. Encarnación Pinedo, a defender of Mexican Creole cuisine in California, c. 1870. H. Schone. Pinedo Photograph Collection. Courtesy of University of Santa Clara.

Creole cuisine, with unique recipes such as *carne asada en la olla de los misioneros* (Missionary style pot roast) and *chiles rellenos de carne seca* (chiles stuffed with dried beef). Indigenous references were strikingly absent, in contrast to contemporary works such as Vicenta Torres's compilation. This oversight may derive in part from borderland images of Indians as marauding Apaches, in contrast to the glories of long-dead Aztecs appropriated by nationalists else-where in Mexico.[58]

The Mexican national cuisine of the nineteenth century was more a product of contention than of consensus. People imagined it in diverse ways, and many did not think that it existed at all. Representations tended to center around three basic images: an indigenous culture little changed from the ancient Aztecs, a Creole country steeped in Hispanic colonial traditions, and a modern nation following the latest fashions from Europe. Dishes were placed into one of these three categories based on social expectations, which were fluid and changing. Foreign authors generally portrayed exotic visions of the ancient Aztecs and titillated readers with tales of disgusting animalitos. Mexican dip-lomats countered such primitive images by reassuring foreigners that they ate the same food as all civilized peoples, which is to say, French. Many were eager to see their preferred Creole dishes gain acceptance alongside continen-tal cuisine, as happened on December 16, 1891, in a banquet at New York's Democratic Club in honor of Minister Matías Romero. Between the relevé of venison saddle with Port sauce and the rôti of English pheasant, Londonderry, was an entrée of mole de guajalote with frijoles veracruzanos.[59] But this was the exception, not the rule, and Creole dishes tended to be reserved for domes-tic occasions, remaining largely unknown to outsiders. In the United States, although women such as Encarnación Pinedo retained close ties to the Creole past, subsequent generations would take the distinctive dishes of the border-lands and give them new cultural identities as Mexican American foods.

THE RISE AND FALL OF
THE CHILI QUEENS

CHAPTER 4

The chili queens were legends of late nineteenth-century San Antonio, Texas. Like countless working women throughout Mexico, they supplemented their household income by cooking for profit in public, especially during religious and civic festivals. Their improvised kitchens turned into sites of nightly pageant after 1877, when tourists began to arrive on the railroad and create a steady demand for their food. Within a few years, a journalist had observed: "Strangers who visit San Antonio are frequently seen about these tables of nights [sic] tasting of this and that out of mere curiosity, and are often surprised to find that many nice things are served up."[1] By 1894, city boosters had transformed these ordinary cooks into mythological sirens, "bright, bewitching creatures [who] put themselves to much trouble to please their too often rowdy customers."[2] The San Antonio *Daily Express* reported: "The fame of the Alamo City 'chile stands' has spread all over the Union."[3] The chili queens' attraction came from the thrill of danger, both culinary and sexual; they were seen as simultaneously alluring and contaminating. Along with a brigade of pushcart tamale vendors in Los Angeles, these San Antonio cooks helped establish the reputation of Mexican food within the United States, creating an image of plebeian authenticity that later traveled around the world. Like the wheat flour tortilla, their chili stews were products of Mexican home cooking along the northern borderlands, but the industrial imitations that they inspired have clouded the view of Mexican food.

Although the vendors were real people, their image was largely invented by Anglos to populate a regional mythology and boost the tourism industry. The chili queen embodied a "fantasy heritage," in the words of the journalist Carey McWilliams, intended to situate the Spanish Southwest in the national history alongside Puritan New England and the plantation Old South. Like the loyal Southern "mammy," the chili queen served to naturalize racial hierarchies and justify white domination. Newcomers to the Southwest accepted the old elite as Spanish dons—including a nostalgic pantheon of "original" chili queens—while relegating the working classes and recent Mexican migrants, contemporary vendors among them, to unskilled labor. Excluded from education, working-class Mexicans had little opportunity to improve their situation. Meanwhile, businessmen from outside the Mexican community made fortunes by selling mass-produced chili con carne, chili powder, and canned tamales, even as health authorities harassed the vendors in San Antonio. Canned chili thus gained a humble place in the national cuisine, like another industrial product that was advertised with a fantasy, "Aunt Jemima" pancake mix.[4]

In the United States, Mexican food came to be associated with chili queens instead of haute cuisine, but it was not for lack of trying by Mexican restaurateurs eager to offer fine dining in San Antonio and Los Angeles. Unfortunately for them, Anglo tourists considered Mexican cookery to be a vestige of the ancient Aztecs, suitable only for the street, and the elegant restaurants soon closed for lack of patronage. While Mexico has a long tradition of street foods, it derives as much from Mediterranean plazas as from Moctezuma's palaces. Progressive reformers in the Southwest sought to limit commerce to private storefronts and banish loiterers to ensure order, efficiency, and their own business interests. Nevertheless, Mexican vendors fought back against efforts to criminalize their cooking, and these conflicts were not simply a struggle between Hispanic tradition and Anglo modernity. Urban reformers in Mexico likewise sought to constrain the bustle of street life, while progressives were torn between visions of modernity and the fantasy heritage.[5] The chili queens finally disappeared from the streets of San Antonio during the New Deal, when middle-class Mexican Americans aspired to establish a more respectable image of their cookery. By then, the street vendors had left enduring images of Mexican food—redolent of danger and drunkenness, but also of romance and desire.

Imagining the Chili Queens

The "discovery" of Mexican food took place in racial and ethnic borderlands between Mexico and the United States, most notably in San Antonio and Los Angeles, where Mexicans maintained a significant presence until an influx of Anglo migrants tipped the balance. Once the Southern Pacific connected these formerly remote cities to national railroad networks in the late 1870s, newcomers no longer felt the need to integrate themselves into the local society and instead began to assert their cultural dominance. At just this moment, nostalgic images of Mexican food began to take shape, based on the belief that local vendors would soon disappear, or remain at most a colorful spectacle within Anglo cities. Chili queens and tamale pushcarts came to represent a form of "safe danger," allowing tourists to indulge the momentary thrill of hot food, rough booze, cheap sex, and petty crime, but within a folkloric setting that seemed to pose little permanent risk to Anglo society.[6] From the perspective of street vendors earning a precarious living, however, these cross-cultural encounters posed very real dangers of harassment from city officials.

The first railroad travelers to arrive in the Southwest had the opportunity to sample Mexican food in elegant surroundings, as the local elite pursued new economic opportunities from the expanding tourist trade. In San Antonio, for example, Salazar Díaz's El Globo Potosino beckoned diners with allusions to the fabulous wealth of the mines of Potosí. Located directly on the Main Plaza, the city's most desirable real estate, it was listed prominently in San Antonio's first directory, published in 1877. Other Mexican restaurants were operated by Jesús Chávez just off Military Plaza and by a widow named Margarita Calsado near Paschal (later Market) Square.[7] In Los Angeles, no less a figure than the former governor Pio Pico mortgaged his property to construct an elegant hotel on the main plaza. Just across the street, Hilario Preciado's Mexican Restaurant served tamales, enchiladas, carne con chile, and *albóndigas* (meatballs), along with Spanish, French, and American dishes, according to classified ads in the *Los Angeles Times*. The Spanish-language newspaper *La Crónica* also contained notices for El Cinco de Mayo, which billed itself as a "Fonda Mexicana."[8]

Mexicans who aspired to participate in the local tourism industry were soon disillusioned, for Anglos considered their food to be unfit for formal occasions and sought to exclude them from their burgeoning cities. Pio Pico lost his property to foreclosure in 1880, and French restaurants quickly replaced Mexican establishments in city directories and newspaper advertisements. As the transition from frontier towns to commercial cities brought growing numbers of female migrants, Anglo-Mexican intermarriage became unfashionable and residential segregation grew. In San Antonio, Mexicans were confined to a barrio west of the San Pedro Creek; at the same time they were also displaced from the central plaza of Los Angeles.[9]

When Mexican food became the subject of culinary tourism, Anglos sought out exotic street food, not elegant restaurants. In 1883, the *Galveston Daily News* reported visitors to San Antonio "taking in the city by gaslight. The features of interest are the plazas, where the Mexicans vend the tortillas, cafe, chili con carne, and tamales."[10] The folklorist John G. Bourke compared these portable feasts, available on both sides of the border, to the "trattoría" of Venice. "The farther to the south one went, the more elaborate was the spread to be noted on these street tables, until at or near San Luis Potosí it might be called a banquet for the poor."[11] Meanwhile, Los Angeles became the capital of tamale pushcarts, a scene described by a local journalist: "Each cart swings into position at the edge of a sidewalk and stools are placed in front." Having posted the bill of fare at dusk, the vendors fed a succession of newsboys, office workers, and, finally, "as midnight grows near all shades of humanity come on to the scene."[12]

Anglo writers collapsed a variety of Mexican dishes into the iconic images of chili con carne and tamales, whose unaccustomed heat obliterated all other tastes. In 1874, the journalist Edward King described a visit to San Antonio, where a "fat, swarthy Mexican mater-familias will place before you various savory compounds, swimming in fiery pepper, which biteth like a serpent; and the tortilla, a smoking hot cake, thin as a shaving, and about as eatable, is the substitute for bread. This meal," he concluded sarcastically, "will be an event in your gastronomic experience."[13] The novelist Stephen Crane concurred: "Mexican vendors with open air stands, sell food that tastes exactly like pounded fire-brick from Hades."[14] Writers competed to invent outlandish metaphors, comparing chili to the lava of Mt. Vesuvius and enchiladas to a "petrified pancake with vulcanizing rubber poured over it for cheese."[15]

Although the tourism industry benefited from chili stands and tamale carts, many officials sought to purge these picturesque vendors. Urban reformers advocated the creation of green spaces to uplift the masses and replace the squalor of street life. In the 1870s, the Los Angeles city council transformed the main plaza into a park and launched a campaign against tamale wagons and other lunch carts, imposing ever more burdensome restrictions on operating times and locations.[16] In San Antonio, the long-serving Irish-Mexican mayor

Figure 4.1. "The features of interest are the plazas, where the Mexicans vend the tortillas, cafe, chili con carne, and tamales." "Chili stands on Military Plaza, c. 1885." UTSA's Institute of Texas Cultures, No. 083–0080. Captain T. K. Treadwell.

Bryan Callaghan likewise began an urban hygiene campaign in the 1880s, inaugurating public works such as an opera house on Alamo Plaza and a new city hall on Military Plaza, thereby transforming the Spanish colonial plazas into an extended parkway.[17] This meant closing off traditional uses of urban space.

The city council had already restricted street vendors to the night hours so that their tables would not interfere with business traffic. Then, in December 1889, the aldermen ordered the vendors out of Alamo Plaza entirely to make way for construction. The women did not go quietly, however. Four months later, the city council had to repeat its proclamation while promising that the change would be temporary and meanwhile allowing chili sales in Milam Plaza, in the barrio west of the San Pedro Creek. Once construction was finished, the women discovered that the supposedly temporary ban was in fact permanent. Moreover, the city did not restrict all commerce around the monument to Texan independence; a few years later, it rented out an old police department shelter on the plaza as a souvenir stand. Thus, San Antonio's two principal tourist attractions were torn asunder, because visitors could no longer eat chili in the shadow of the Alamo.[18]

City boosters lamented the loss of a valuable attraction. In 1895, John Bourke wrote: "Few tourists can have forgotten the 'chile stands' of San Antonio, Texas, once a most interesting feature of the life of that charming city, but abolished within the past two or three years in deference to the 'progressive' spirit of certain councilmen."[19] While declining to assign blame, a local newspaper agreed: "The places to-day, however, are not what they were in the pleasant past, before the new City Hall was erected and before the Plaza of the Alamo became a garden spot.... [N]ow the first question asked by the visitor is, 'Where are those chile stands I have heard so much about?'"[20]

In writing the chili queens' obituary, journalists conjured up a nostalgic and sexualized image of the fantasy heritage. Gone was the "fat, swarthy Mexican mater-familias" observed by Edward King, to be replaced by "Sadie, the acknowledged 'queen' of all 'queens,' on account of her beauty, her vivacity and aptitude at repartee" and "Martha, black-eyed, tall and slender." The chili queens thus helped create a stereotype of dusky, sharp-witted women, waiting to be tamed by Anglo men. One story included a drawing of an attractive woman wearing a Mexican shawl, or *rebozo*, and smoking a cigarette, signaling her lack of propriety. An accompanying illustration portrayed her disreputable friends.[21] In contrast to the stereotyped sexual deviance of the chili queens, carefully chaperoned "Harvey Girls" served familiar New England foods at Harvey House restaurants around the West, providing western railroad travelers with a refuge of Victorian domesticity.[22]

In describing Mexican food, Anglo authors often conflated moral and physical contamination, just as the early modern globalization of Mesoamerican

Figure 4.2. A chili queen depicted with a Mexican shawl (*rebozo*) and cigarette—signaling her lack of propriety—along with her disreputable friends. "A Chili Queen" and "Some of the Chili Queen's Friends." *San Antonio Daily Express*, June 17, 1894.

ingredients had been associated with poverty, sensuality, and disease. "Ignorance in the details of their manufacture is necessary to the complete enjoyment of tamales," wrote one San Antonio journalist, who went on to explain that those who have seen Mexican food being prepared "have been known to swear off on the seductive viands with surprising emphasis. The abstinence seldom lasts long, however, for tamales have too rare a deliciousness to be renounced on account of a trifle of dirt." His conclusion might have referred equally to the hygienic character of the tamales or the supposed racial quality of the women who made them: "Since they can't be washed or disinfected it is well to take them as they are and thank heaven that they were ever made at all."[23] The imagined health risks of tamales were underscored by sensationalized journalistic accounts, for example, of the 1899 poisoning of Maud Hufford—"one of the handsomest shop girls in Los Angeles"—supposedly by a rotten tamale.[24]

Unlike San Antonio, where the image of chili queens overshadowed the presence of male vendors, in Los Angeles the stereotypical tamale pushcart operator was a man. Yet this made little difference in popular culture depictions, because newspapers questioned their sexuality as well. One José Ramírez allegedly attracted a devoted clientele through the "habitual use of silk in daily variety," consisting of some twenty colorful shirts. To allay fears that this tamale cart

Figure 4.3. Tamale pushcart peacock. *Los Angeles Times*, April 17, 1924, A1. Los Angeles Times Staff. Copyright (c) 1924. Los Angeles Times. Reprinted with Permission.

peacock was seducing white women, the author assured readers that the display was intended for an entirely different audience. "Mexican laborers craving chili would walk extra blocks only to see one of the Ramirez shirts."[25] Reporters also depicted the cartmen as hapless victims of youthful hooligans. Following a traffic accident involving a pushcart, "toothsome morsels, steaming hot, were scattered along the street for nearly half a block and formed rich prey for the gaminos, who scented the catastrophe from afar, and hastened to the spot to get a share of the spilled tamales while they were still good and hot."[26]

The deviant sexuality of Mexican street vendors led inevitably to crime, at least according to popular culture and newspaper accounts. Clara Driscoll's 1906 short story, "Philippa the Chili Queen," told of a young man from back east, Jack Talcott, who falls prey to a dark beauty and lingers each night at her chili stand, "cruelly and wantonly careless of his digestive organs."[27] But the romance is interrupted by her former lover, Benito, conveniently released from prison after murdering Philippa's previous admirer. Jack gallantly offers to carry her away, but she cannot escape the brute's will, thus inadvertently saving the Anglo from racial and gastrointestinal doom. In contrast to this dark tale, journalists often depicted criminality in a more humorous fashion to avoid scaring away tourists. In 1895, Los Angeles police detectives reportedly arrested John Thompson for running a "fence" under cover of a tamale wagon, hiding stolen jewelry in corn husks. Alcoholism was also associated with the pushcarts, which tended to cluster around bars. The *Times* noted simply: "Juan Ocaña, the old tamale man, got on one of his periodical drunks."[28]

Mexican food was also seen as a threat to white workers, both through unfair competition and labor radicalism. Nativist opponents of immigrant workers claimed that the Mexican diet of tortillas and chili, like the Chinese staple rice, undermined the nation's standard of living. "No white man can work for Mexican wages," reported one journalist from an El Paso chili stand in 1884. "A bowl of this stuff costs 10 cents," he quoted a down-and-out worker, who made a revealing comparison with another immigrant group. "Days when I make a little more money I take some Irish stew instead of the chili con carne. It costs 15 cents."[29] Mexican food was also associated with anarchism and union organizing. Tamale vendors were blamed for the Christmas Day Riot of 1913, when police raided a labor rally in Los Angeles Plaza. Milam Plaza in San Antonio, where the chili queens worked in the 1920s, was a prominent recruiting ground for migrant workers. Customers could eat their chili while listening to impassioned speeches by anarcho-syndicalists of the International Workers of the World and the Partido Liberal Mexicano.[30]

Fears of pollution and criminality notwithstanding, Mexican food also held a festive aura that appealed to tourists and city boosters alike. Charles Fletcher Lummis, a leading proponent of the fantasy heritage in California, published *The Landmarks Club Cook Book* in 1903 to raise funds for the preservation of crumbling Spanish missions. The volume began with Mexican recipes intended to convey the flavor of old California to newcomers. Cinco de Mayo and Mexican Independence Day entered the Anglo calendar as a time for bohemian recreation. Conventioneers insisted on including tamale picnics in their tours. Political rallies often attracted the voters with barbecued beef, frijoles, and chili con carne.[31]

In the face of Anglo attacks, the Mexican community closed ranks in self-defense, particularly against claims of criminality. *El Fronterizo*, Tucson's Spanish-language newspaper, rejected depictions of immigrants as deserters, criminals, or "tamale vendors" dedicated to "knavery," by observing that local Mexicans were honest workers and that the two "tamaleros" in town had never been in trouble with the police.[32] When a Los Angeles vendor, María Alonzo, was arrested for vagrancy, her neighbors came forward to testify to her character and demand her release, although the media dismissed this act of solidarity with jokes about "tamale connoisseurs" hungry for their favorite treat.[33]

Figure 4.4. When the city council denied requests to allow them to return to Alamo Plaza, Mexican vendors took direct action, staking out their places of business without municipal authorization. "Chili stands on Alamo Plaza, San Antonio, Texas, c. 1905." UTSA's Institute of Texas Cultures, No. 082–0643. Courtesy of Pioneer Flour Mills.

Mexican vendors often took the initiative, defying city authorities with the support and patronage of tourists and boosters. Pushcart operators in Los Angeles responded to burdensome city restrictions by forming a mutual society and hiring lawyers to defend their rights.[34] When the San Antonio city council rejected requests to allow the chili stands to return to Alamo Plaza, the Mexican women took direct action, staking out their places of business without municipal authorization. Although city archives offer few details about their work, a photo taken around 1905 clearly documents their presence near the Alamo. Like prostitutes, their work was considered illicit but nonetheless tolerated, and in 1909, the city council defeated a resolution intended to enforce the ban. A decade later, with the U.S. entry into World War I, San Antonio became an important military training center, and civilian authorities finally acted to restrict street vendors and prostitutes. As a result, the chili stands were banished once again across the San Pedro Creek.[35] Even as Anglo authorities sought to contain Mexican chili in San Antonio, the dish traveled around the country, assuming ever more varied forms.

The Chili Migrations

Competition between the foods of Mexican migrants and Americanized industrial counterparts had begun already in the early twentieth century, as chili con carne traveled out of its Southwestern homeland and across the United States with the expanding industrial economy. Chili spread north and east by way of Gilded Age railroad construction and became fixed in the national consciousness during the Great Depression. Although tales of boom and bust are often told as an American national saga, industrial development integrated the entire North American continent. Food-processing corporations took a leading role in Porfirian modernization, as in Canada and the United States. Mexicans not only imported technologies for brewing and canning, but they were also innovators who mechanized the labor of tortilla making. Despite the availability of Mexican national products, chili con carne dominated the nascent market for Mexican food in the United States. Chicago meatpacking giants held an advantage in both production and advertising; adding another line of canned goods required little extra investment and allowed them to disguise inferior cuts of meat. Even small businessmen benefited; unrestrained by notions of Mexican authenticity, they adapted their products to mainstream preferences. Chili therefore changed dramatically in its migrations, becoming localized as a distinctive regional dish within the United States.

One of the first Mexican foods to be industrialized was the tortilla, although the cultural insistence on freshness placed long-standing limits on the extent of the transformation. As a result, this transnational process of innovation, which began in the late nineteenth century with the mechanization of corn milling, was not completed until nearly a hundred years later with the creation of integrated factories using dehydrated flour. Wheat had been processed for millennia on mechanical mills, but these stones lacked the precision to grind wet nixtamal, and only the nineteenth-century development of steel mills produced acceptable dough for tortillas. Urban dwellers quickly adopted this milling technology, but it took decades to spread to the countryside, mainly because rural women could not afford to pay the modest charges. Nixtamal mills also set up shop in Mexican communities north of the border—Encarnación Pinedo endorsed the Enterprise mill, while the Moctezuma brand

115

was favored in Texas—but there as well many working women continued to grind corn on the metate to save money. By the 1920s, tortilla factories were equipped with a mill, a rotating mold to shape the nixtamal, and a sequence of heated conveyor belts to flip the tortillas while cooking. The Sanitary Tortilla Company, for example, remains to this day a San Antonio institution with legions of customers still loyal to cantankerous machines from the 1920s. The company's success illustrates both the devotion that many Mexicans have for the refined taste of particular tortillas and their insistence on freshly made products, which helped tortilla factories to survive for decades as a cottage industry.[36]

Yet an alternate future of tortilla mass production had been envisioned already in 1909, when José Bartolomé Martínez, a San Antonio corn miller, patented a formula for dehydrated nixtamal flour called Tamalina. Although the local market was not yet ready for a dried product, Martínez's Aztec Mills did a brisk business in the daily delivery of fresh tortillas. Martínez also transformed the leftover masa into the first commercial corn chips, *tostadas*, which he sold in eight-ounce wax bags beginning in 1912. His sudden death in 1924 derailed plans for a tortilla empire extending throughout South Texas and northern Mexico, leaving others to profit from his vision.[37]

Mexican Americans in the borderlands also dominated in the transnational industry of growing and canning chile peppers and other fruits and vegetables. In the first decade of the century, Emilio Ortega transplanted seeds from New Mexico to the fields of Ventura, California. Although Ortega sold largely to Anglo consumers, other packing companies, such as the Los Angeles–based La Victoria, catered to a Mexican clientele. Networks of Mexican businessmen in San Antonio oversaw the import and wholesale distribution of fresh and prepared goods to Mexican markets as far away as the Midwestern United States. Meanwhile in New Mexico, Fabian García sought to transform chile production from a cottage industry focused on dried strings (*ristras*) into a major export crop. A native of Mexico, García graduated in 1894 from the New Mexico College of Agriculture and Mechanic Arts. He began the first scientific breeding program devoted to chiles, and in 1921, his research yielded "New Mexico No. 9," a mild, high-yielding variety that became the standard chile for commercial farmers in southern New Mexico, although traditional landrace chiles continued to predominate in the northern half of the state.[38]

Despite the growing commercialization, migrant workers outside the Southwest usually had to improvise familiar food in the early years. Track

Box 4.1 Recipe for Prepared Red Chile by Mrs. A. Molina, Box 544, El Paso, Texas

Take seeds and veins from red chiles until a five-pound pail is full of the pods; put them into cold water for one-half hour; then turn off cold water and pour on very hot water; let them stand ten minutes and turn off water. Repeat five or six times. The last water leave on and mash the chile with a potato masher through a colander until the pulp is all removed from the skins. Have a skillet with enough lard in which to brown two tablespoonfuls of flour, into this pour the juice of the chile, and add a small whole onion, a small lump of butter and salt to taste. Place on back of stove to boil slowly for an hour. This can be used for seasoning meats, in beans, for making enchiladas, or on any dish that one likes chile.

Source: *Los Angeles Times Cookbook No. 2: One Thousand Toothsome Cooking and Other Recipes Including Seventy-Nine Old Time California, Spanish and Mexican Dishes* (Los Angeles: Times-Mirror Company, c. 1905), 11.

workers were among the first to move around the United States in the 1880s, and by the turn of the century *traquero* communities were well established in the Midwestern railroad junctions of Chicago, St. Louis, Kansas City, and the Quad Cities on the border between Iowa and Illinois. Recruiters supplied the laborers' meals at first through dining cars and commissariats, charging hefty prices for unpalatable rations. Workers preferred to feed themselves, planting chiles and vegetables in rooftop gardens on their boxcar homes, and raising livestock inside. Families worked cooperatively to prepare vats of *chorizo* (sausage) and *menudo* (tripe stew), and when laborers grew restless, companies began to retain Mexican cooks. As communities became more settled, they imported a more extensive range of goods.[39]

By the 1920s and 1930s, commercial networks and local adaptations had developed to ensure supplies of Mexican food to immigrant communities in Chicago and other Midwestern cities. Chicago's first tortilla factory was founded in 1928 by an experienced factory owner from Monterrey, who had fled the revolution and worked the railroads in Texas, Missouri, and Kansas, before learning of the business opportunity from a brother in the Windy City. By contrast, Panadería el Progreso was owned by a former cantina manager from Durango who employed skilled Mexican bakers. A typical grocery, Botica Galinda, stocked dried ancho and pasilla chiles, Tamalina masa flour, *piloncillo* (rustic cones of brown sugar), metates (grinding stones), and *molcajetes* (mortars and pestles), all obtained from San Antonio wholesalers. While many Mexican immigrants lived in the city, merchants delivered bread and groceries by truck to those who settled in Aurora and other suburbs. A downtown restaurant, México Bello, reproduced fonda cooking for homesick migrants living near Hull House. New hybrids were also appearing—an embryonic Midwest-Mex cuisine—including the distinctive East Chicago *tacos suaves*, made with seasoned pork in a flour tortilla. Jackson Bauer, a graduate student at the University of Chicago's School of Sociology, ironically frequented the south side El Rancho Grande in search of authentic Mexican cooking while doing fieldwork intended to assimilate immigrants. Many of those immigrants indeed feared the loss of traditional foods; a letter to *El Heraldo* denounced an unnamed popular restaurant for steaming tamales in waxed paper with a pickle. "What would our ancestors say if they saw the abused [sic] that had been committed upon the tamale?"[40]

Yet, when compared with the Midwest-Mex cooks, Anglo businessmen were taking far greater liberties with Mexican cooking. Cans of "Montezuma Sauce" appeared on grocery shelves as early as the 1870s, and the Franco-American Food Company marketed "W. G. Tobin's Chili Con Carne" a decade later. These formulas have been lost to history, but Texas businessmen created three of the most enduring brands around the turn of the century: Chiltomaline, created by a Fort Worth grocer, D. C. Pendery; Eagle Chili Powder, established by the New Braunfels café owner William Gebhardt; and Mexene, a product formulated by an Austin chemist named T. Bailey Walker. Chicago meatpackers also began to produce their own versions of chili con carne and tamales in the late nineteenth century, and tamale vendors in striped suits and sombreros were even plying the streets of New York City, although the fad did not last long.[41] Mexican producers also sought to participate in national distribution networks. Already in 1904, tacos appeared on a San Antonio banquet menu intended to promote Mexican food to grocers throughout the state.[42] Perhaps one reason for the failure of Mexican versions to gain a foothold within the broader market was the perceived lack of hygiene, already prominent in the earliest stereotypes of the chili queens. Certainly one common advertising theme of Mexican food produced both by corporate manufacturers and by non-Mexican street vendors alike was the emphasis on the cleanliness of their product, often explicitly distancing the food from its origins. Tamale men donned white jackets and used motor cars for delivery in place of antiquated horse-drawn wagons or pushcarts. Publicity photos of immaculate white-gowned workers in Gebhardt's factory reassured customers that the company maintained high standards of sanitation.[43]

Mexican restaurants owned by Anglos sought to claim a similar air of respectability and sanitation, beginning in San Antonio about 1900 with Otis M. Farnsworth's Original Mexican Restaurant. Reportedly a visitor from Chicago who happened to dine in a small but popular café on San Antonio's segregated West Side, Farnsworth opened his restaurant in the center of town to appeal to those who avoided the barrio. He enforced a strict dress code, requiring men to wear jackets, and his dining room was more upscale than most Mexican restaurants, with pristine tablecloths, napkins, and silverware. The formula proved so successful that "Original" Mexican restaurants began appearing in towns across Texas. Although Farnsworth's menu offered a "special supper" consisting of chile con queso, chile con carne, tamales, rice, beans, enchiladas, chile rellenos, dessert, and coffee, they were not served as a combination plate. Instead, waiters in white coats presented each item individually on fine china. One woman who dined there in the 1920s remembered, "Ordinarily Father didn't want to eat anything unless Mother had cooked it, because he didn't think anyone else could cook anything that was 'sanitary.' I think they had him fooled into thinking their food was sanitary by the immaculate manner in which an order was taken and served."[44]

Tourists to Mexico often displayed a similar obsession with hygiene, ensuring the success of Walter and Frank Sanborn's restaurant and soda fountain. Founded in 1910 in the House of Tiles, the former residence of the Jockey Club, Sanborn's provided an early sign of the shift from French to U.S. cultural influence. *Terry's Guide* recommended it as "the premier restaurante in the Mexican Republic," emphasizing that "one can drink the certified pure water with safety," while "the milk is from certified Jersey cows kept on the Sanborn Farm under scrupulously clean conditions."[45] Bess Adams Garner, a visitor from California in the 1930s, wrote, "I believe that a few precautions about food and drinking-water are reasonable and necessary in any strange country. I don't believe that it is necessary to rouse heaven and earth telling about the fact that you are taking them." She recalled two women who "asked for an order of canned salmon and to see the can the salmon came out of." Sanborn's Swedish cook, Mrs. Thimgren, "came out of the kitchen with a can of Del Monte salmon in one hand and one of Iris [brand] in the other. I wish you could have seen her face—and the faces of *los turistas*."[46]

Garner's attempt to distance herself from the canned tuna fetishists expressed a form of tourist cosmopolitanism that sought out social distinction through knowledge of authentic foods and foreign travel. Bohemians often longed for authentic experiences in order to escape the encroaching homogeneity of industrialization represented by canned Mexican food. "The tamale of today is too often a miserable parody of the Simon pure article," bemoaned a critic in 1894.[47] This nostalgic snob appeal reflected in part regional rivalries. One California booster appealed to potential visitors by noting: "Real tamales, frijoles and chili con carne are to be had—not the canned products of a Chicago packing-house."[48] Connoisseurs also identified a recurrent problem with Mexican restaurants in the United States: the labor-intensive nature of the cuisine fed into the temptation to disguise shortcut recipes with excessive chili powder. For leftist intellectuals of the 1920s, who found kindred spirits in revolutionary Mexico, indigenous foods even acquired a radical chic. Anita Brenner, editor of the journal *Mexican Folklore*, wrote enthusiastically: "*Gusanos de maguey*, literally maguey worms, don't shudder, look like nothing you ever saw before. A highland delicacy."[49]

Insects were beyond the pale for most Anglos, who approached even chili con carne and canned tamales with a mixture of fear and masculine bravado. The classic Midwestern and Great Plains chili parlor of the Depression era seems to have its origins in small-town Texas and Oklahoma of the 1890s as an Anglo adaptation of a Mexican café. The marketing efforts of chili powder manufacturers soon spread the dish beyond the Mexican community. Everette Lee DeGolyer, a geologist and chili aficionado, encountered the fabled "bowl of red" chili con carne as a young man in Missouri in the 1890s before making his fortune in the Tampico oil fields around 1910. Between roughnecks and newspaper reporters, the chili parlor was "absolutely masculine," in the words of Westbrook Pegler, who consumed vast quantities of the devil's brew as a United Press correspondent in St. Louis.[50] A political appointee from Texas opened Washington, D.C.'s first parlor in 1901, importing supplies in bulk from back home, and chili remained a hash-house staple for decades, often heated directly in the can. As it spread across the country, chili acquired new forms and flavors. By 1910, African American cooks had made Memphis famous for "chili mac," served with spaghetti, while farther north in Ohio and Michigan hot dogs slathered with chili became known as "coneys." The most distinctive local version, Cincinnati chili, was created in the 1920s by a Macedonian immigrant named Tom Kiradjieff, who added cinnamon and other spices to his recipe, then poured it on top of spaghetti. With optional cheese, onion, and beans, it made a "five-way" meal.[51]

These new forms of chili prompted a backlash among purists, who touted the authenticity of their own versions. Already in the 1920s, newspaper cooking columnists received heated letters from readers critiquing their chili recipes, particularly those that included beans, a version that became more common during the Great Depression. Regional rivalries also arose, as when a Los Angeles journalist derisively observed: "Boston is a long way from the home of chili con carne, and I do not think that the dish has gained any favor in traveling."[52] Yet Springfield, Illinois, also declared itself to be the chili capital of the world, even if few outsiders recognized that claim. Texans angrily insisted on the purity of their dish, while denying its Mexican origins entirely. But the patron saint of chili con carne, Oklahoma's favorite son, Will Rogers, was more ecumenical, proclaiming the dish to be "about the best thing I know for suffering humanity."[53]

The early industrial development of Mexican food occurred along parallel lines: one version was produced and consumed within the Mexican community while the other was accommodated to Anglo palates and divorced from its origins. When these supply chains crossed, bad things could happen. In 1910, for example, the Mexican consul in San Francisco received a desperate appeal from a group of twenty-four migrant workers at the Alaska Packing Company of Naknek River. Their spokesman, José Miranda, complained that they had been recruited with false promises of payment, worked long hours at the salmon cannery, suffered physical abuse from overseers, and paid exorbitant prices for bad food at the company store. Worse still, for these frostbitten exiles, their rations consisted of canned chili con carne and tamales.[54]

Domesticating the Chili Queens

Even as newfangled versions of chili spread across the country, the vendors in San Antonio were squeezed between Anglo demands for assimilation and rivalries within the ethnic community, a struggle that further confirmed the conflicted image of Mexican food in the United States. Local politics, in turn, reflected changing ideas about health and new approaches to social reform based on the goal of assimilating ethnic minorities. New understandings of urban hygiene, which focused on specific diseases rather than a more vague sense of moral order, also encouraged health officials and home economists to intervene more actively in minorities' family lives. When the Great Depression led to calls for immigrant expulsion, a Mexican American middle class began to assert a political voice in many Southwestern communities. Their influence was challenged by a group of exiled Porfirian elites, who had fled revolutionary fighting and were promoting nostalgic ties to their Mexican homeland. Finally, many Anglo politicians, with their own memories of Mexican food, sought to maintain the Mexican community in a paternalistic relationship of political patronage. The myth of the chili queens could not last under the pressure of these conflicting agendas, and efforts to domesticate the vendors instead led to their disappearance.

Although urban reformers of the early twentieth century generally equated U.S. national culture with universal civilization and sought to transform Mexican dietary habits, a few open-minded home economists came to respect the ability of Mexican women to care for their families. Jet Winters, a native of Farmington, Texas, taught in the Fort Worth public schools before earning an M.A. at Columbia University and, in 1926, a Ph.D. at Yale. There she learned the "new nutrition" of vitamins and amino acids. Returning to her alma mater, the University of Texas, she applied this training to Mexicans and other low-income groups in the region. While retaining a belief in the superiority of Anglo diets and encouraging Mexican families to eat less highly seasoned food, she nevertheless appreciated the nutritional value of corn tortillas and beans. She attributed poor health to low incomes rather than bad choices. Indeed, she admitted: "Since the Mexican spends a smaller percentage of money for meat, uses larger amounts of beans, which apparently give the best nutritive return of all the foods...it would seem that his food selection is better than that of the American."[55] For decades, her students applied the latest methods of nutritional measurement and dietary surveys, and, like the school doctor in John Steinbeck's novel *Tortilla Flat*, they kept finding Mexican nutrition to be surprisingly good. "Gentlemen, they are living on what constitutes a slow poison," said the fictional doctor, referring to corn, beans, and chile. Nevertheless, he concluded: "I tell you I have never seen healthier children in my life!"[56]

Over the short term, the assimilation campaigns had only modest success. Dietary surveys collected by Winters's students include a wide range of foods, from hamburgers to chop suey and Post Toasty breakfast cereal, particularly among the relatively well-to-do. Yet some cultural change among migrants may have been less about emulating Anglo teachers than about using their improved income to purchase higher-status Mexican foods, so that they could

eat *pan dulce* instead of corn tortillas. Another source for measuring acculturation comes from an ethnographic study conducted by the Mexican anthropologist Manuel Gamio in the mid-1920s. Most of his informants felt that they
could reproduce a Mexican diet with foods readily available in the Southwest.
Many adopted an Anglo diet or sampled different cuisines— Italian, Chinese,
or Mexican—as the mood took them. Peer pressure and generational differences rather than the example of teachers may have been the most powerful
inducement to abandoning traditional diets. One assimilated youth, Carlos B.
Aguilar, complained that he got sick whenever he visited his parents and they
cooked Mexican food for him. Yet most seem to have retained their basic dietary preferences and cited among other factors the high cost of buying food in
the United States compared with Mexico.[57]

The tremendous increase of migration in the 1910s and 1920s reinforced
existing networks of Mexican culture. The Mexican population of San Antonio,
for example, grew from about 12,000 to 100,000 between 1900 and 1940,
increasing their relative numbers from 25 to 40 percent of the total population. Most newcomers were migrant workers, who used the city as a base for
seasonal agricultural labor as far away as the upper Midwest. Nevertheless, the
presence of wealthy Porfirian exiles together with a native-born middle class
meant that Mexican restaurateurs no longer depended on Anglo tourists and
could prepare their menus according to Mexican tastes. Gamio observed that
these institutions "varied from humble *fondas* with a daily *comida* (prix fixe)
that regularly costs twenty-five cents or less to those that in addition to all
classes of Mexican dishes also serve typically American [foods]."[58] Restaurant
decorations included nationalist images such as the Mexico City landmarks of
the white-peaked mountains Popocatépetl and Iztaccíhuatl, and also pin-ups
of Mexican women dressed in traditional garb, as *charras* or Tehuana Indians,
but with the heart-shaped lips of flappers. Even in Mexican enclaves, Gamio's
research assistant, Luis Felipe Recinos, noted that numerous Anglos and immigrants ("members of foreign colonies," as he called them) had the "desire to
taste Mexican-style dishes and they go to those places because the food is generally cheaper and more abundant than in other restaurants."[59]

Despite the ready availability of Mexican food, fears of assimilation were
pronounced among the exiled Porfirian elite. Their leading spokesman, Ignacio
Lozano, publisher of the regionally distributed newspaper *La Prensa*, adopted a
paternalistic attitude toward working-class Mexicans, and he sought to instill
within them the conservative values of church, education, and nation as a

means of uplifting them spiritually.[60] One vital link to the home country lay in the memories of childhood foods, and La Prensa sought to preserve these national loyalties with articles describing fiestas, jamaicas, and other social events, along with recipes for traditional foods such as barbacoa, tamales, and buñuelos.[61] Longing to return to Mexico, the exiles bemoaned the assimilation of their working-class compatriots and worse still, of their own children, into mainstream society. Gourmets such as José Juan Tablado and Nemesio García Naranjo took particular offense at the Mexican foods they found north of the border. Another exile, the linguist Francisco J. Santamaria, memorably defined chili con carne as a "detestable food with false Mexican title that is sold in the United States of the North."[62] Similar complaints appeared regularly in the pages of La Prensa. A 1919 editorial entitled "News of the Exile" inquired: "Was it some incompetent imitator or one envious of our fatherland and culinary glories who said that chili con carne descends in a straight line from mole...?"[63]

Yet these exile attacks on the San Antonio favorites must have inflamed many Mexican Americans, who considered chili con carne to be a comfort food during their childhoods. Although there are few contemporary accounts of the chili stands written by Mexicans, photographs from the San Antonio Light illuminate this nocturnal world. The camera can hardly contain the excitement of these young women about being the center of attention. Unmarried Mexican women lived under tight patriarchal restrictions and had few opportunities for employment outside the home; most took in piecework as seamstresses and pecan shellers.[64] Chaperones were surely there, perhaps including younger brothers who strutted for the camera or peeked out from the background. But the materfamilias had allowed herself to be shooed out of the picture, no doubt recognizing the advertising value of the youthful chili queen image. The young women appreciated recognition not only for their beauty—although surely that was part of it—but also for their cooking skills. Moreover, the crowds who clamored for chili validated the entire Mexican community, acknowledging their foods as a worthy part of the national culture.

The photographer clearly staged these scenes to heighten the gendered division between chili queens and male customers. While Anglos exaggerated the vendors' sexuality, there was certainly reciprocal flirting across the tables. Traditional patterns of Mexican courtship, with men serenading the women who fed them in return, coexisted alongside modern cultural practices, such as bobbed haircuts, cardigan sweaters, and motorcycle goggles. Racial diversity was also pervasive, ranging from the blond-haired young man sitting at

Figure 4.5. The camera can hardly contain the excitement of these young women about being the center of attention. "Chili stand, Haymarket Plaza, 1936." UTSA's Institute of Texan Cultures, No. L-1433-F. Courtesy of the Hearst Corporation.

the table to the African American youth standing two rows behind him. The chili vendors had even become, in some ways, representatives of modernity, as automobiles drove up between the two rows of tables that lined Haymarket Plaza in the 1920s. Stylish folks sat in their cars, listening to the strolling musicians and eating Mexican food.[65]

The Mexican American middle class of San Antonio did not uniformly support the chili stands. Quite apart from generational conflicts that arose within families, street vendors represented the poor general state of health within the community. Still living in rustic shacks with dirt floors, the vast majority of West Side residents had no running water or indoor plumbing. Mexican Americans suffered five times the death rates from tuberculosis of Anglos and more than twice that of blacks. Malnutrition, diarrhea, and enteritis contributed to an infant death rate of 144 per 1,000 live births among the Mexican community. These health issues were attributed to poor environments, and authorities debated the deportation of Mexicans.[66]

Figure 4.6. Traditional patterns of Mexican courtship of men serenading the women, who fed them in return, coexisted with modern cultural practices, such as bobbed haircuts, cardigan sweaters, and motorcycle goggles. Race mixture was also pervasive, ranging from the blond-haired young man sitting at the table to the African American youth standing two rows behind him. "Chili stand, Haymarket Plaza, 1936." UTSA's Institute of Texan Cultures, No. L-1433-E. Courtesy of the Hearst Corporation.

The issue came to a head in March 1936, on the eve of the centennial celebrations of Texas independence, when a group of citizens protested that the chili stands threatened the health of the neighborhood and demanded their removal. The West Side Improvement and Taxpayers Association spokesman, Dr. S. L. Boccelato, also took the opportunity to request that the old city market, outside of which the chili vendors worked, be torn down and replaced with a New Deal Works Progress Administration building. Mayor C. K. Quin, the heir to Bryan Callaghan's political machine, met with representatives of the Taxpayers Association and the League of United Latin American Citizens (LULAC) to work out a compromise plan, which allowed the vendors to stay but in screened enclosures to ensure proper sanitation. The San Antonio Centennial Association complained that the screening would make the chili stands less picturesque for tourists. These elite Anglo boosters wanted to

Figure 4.7. Mayor C. K. Quin, the San Antonio West Side Taxpayers Association, and LULAC agreed to allow the vendors to stay but in screened enclosures to ensure proper sanitation. "Exterior of chili stands, in screened tents, Haymarket Plaza, March 4, 1936." UTSA's Institute of Texan Cultures, No. L-1433-E. Courtesy of the Hearst Corporation.

take full advantage of the national publicity focused on the celebration and resented the Mexican community's unwillingness to play the feminized role of chili queens in the tableau of Texas history. Drawing his own line in the sand, Dr. Boccelato replied: "The life of one citizen is worth more than the whole Centennial celebration."[67]

The chili vendors remained a political pawn, even as the Mexican American community asserted its power. In September 1937, Mayor Quin adopted an intensive new sanitary regime that drove the women out of Haymarket Plaza entirely. Two years later, Maury Maverick, a New Deal liberal, challenged the old machine, campaigning actively in the Mexican community, and once in office, he combined his populist agenda with city boosterism by becoming a self-styled *patrón* of the chili queens. To bring them into compliance with health codes, he pledged city council funds to build a central commissary kitchen. He also sought to create an improved tourist attraction by ordering all vendors and musicians to wear Spanish-style clothing. When city officials closed the stands two days after the announcement for failing to clean up litter, Maverick paternalistically responded by offering to finance a "Mayor's model chili stand" in order to teach the women proper behavior. The chili stands reopened to a crowd of about three hundred people, and Maverick consumed the ceremonial first bowl. He personally supplied fiestaware cups and saucers, and, to recreate his memories of the golden age of chili, he donated four antique lanterns that he had purchased in Mexico to illuminate the stands.[68]

Nevertheless, social contradictions embodied within the fantasy heritage ended both the mayor's tenure and the chili stands. Maverick gained no Anglo support from his dalliance with the chili vendors and his broader attempt to assert a Mexican essence for San Antonio. Dr. W. B. Russ expressed a widespread Anglo opinion in a 1939 letter: "Our politics, which has made us stench unto high heaven for forty years, smells of chili and beans."[69] Mexican Americans also felt ambivalent about the mayor's attempts to win support, which seemed more concerned with building tourism than addressing the needs of the community. Maverick was defeated in the 1941 election.[70] The vendors persisted a few years longer, but harassment from health officials, and perhaps military officers as well, finally put an end to their work in 1943, as San Antonio turned its attention to wartime preparedness. Once the war was over, another wave of Anglo nostalgia followed, romantically invoking the past and comparing it with the present: "A few wandering chili vendors now have tacos and tamales for sale in glass-enclosed carts. A few small, indoor chili shops remain around the market plaza. But the earthy air and pungent odor of the plaza are gone. The singers still gather around your car and serenade you. But without the chili queens to exchange anatomical insults with them in sonorous Spanish, they seem a bit lackadaisical and depressed."[71]

Concepción Chávez, one of the last of the vendors, gave a more practical interpretation for closing the stands. She told a reporter that sanitation regulations had changed the whole atmosphere of the work, so that it became "too troublesome to make the tiny profit from their arduous work seem worthwhile."[72] As San Antonio emerged from the Depression, new jobs in the expanding garment industry were more appealing than street vending. Although the stands helped to establish the presence of Mexican women in public, the chili vendors may well have been eager to leave for better-paying work in the wartime economy.[73] When the end of the Depression gave Mexican American women alternative options to earn a living than street vending, the chili stands receded into memory. But the stereotypes that emerged around chili, and Mexican food more generally, proved remarkably persistent.

This indelible legacy resulted in part from deep social divisions, both dividing Mexicans from other groups and based on class within the Mexican community. Bryan Callaghan, for example, relied on Mexican votes for reelection while restricting the chili vendors. With an elite Mexican mother, he surely grew up eating tamales and other spicy foods, but class position gave him a very different perspective. Like the Porfirian exiles, he probably associated Mexican cuisine with Creole mole de guajolote prepared at home rather than chili con carne served in public by working-class vendors.[74]

It is unclear what impact these early migratory networks had on the industrial foods of Mexico, although Clemente Jacques and other manufacturers certainly benefited from the demand of nostalgic Mexicans for the familiar taste of mole de guajolote. Meanwhile, Americanized versions of chili were already being shipped around the globe in the early twentieth century. In 1916, the author George Fitch observed: "Man has explored Australia and the deserts of China with the help of tin cans. He has left empty bean cans in Madagascar, preserved pear cans in Thibet [sic], and *Chili con carne* cans under the eaves of the North Pole."[75] Fifty years of chili powder, chili parlors, canned chili, chili dogs, and chili mac—five ways—diluted the exoticism of chili con carne, making it a thoroughly Anglo dish. As chili lost its former identity, Mexican Americans began to develop a new version of their cuisine, centered on a newly arrived dish, the taco. Yet even as they adopted this culinary migrant from Mexico, it would not help them regain the affection of nationalists across the border.

INVENTING THE MEXICAN
AMERICAN TACO

n his authorized biography, *Taco Titan*, Glen Bell staked his claim as the father of the fast-food taco, the man who took Mexican food from the ethnic community to mainstream consumers. From his humble beginnings as a hot-dog vendor in postwar San Bernardino, California, he had watched in admiration as Richard and Maurice McDonald transformed their nearby carhop into a prototype of the fast-food restaurant. Hoping to emulate this model, Bell found another market niche in Mexican food. He claimed to have devised a frame to fry taco shells, modified his chili-dog sauce to use as salsa, and in 1951, sold his first tacos for nineteen cents each. After operating a succession of restaurants in the Inland Empire region east of Los Angeles, he opened the first Taco Bell in Downey, California, in 1962. Franchising provided the tool for building a taco empire, which now numbers more than 5,600 locations and dominates the sale of Mexican fast food in the United States.[1] Given its commanding position, even some Mexican American entrepreneurs have credited Taco Bell with creating the mass market for Mexican food.[2] From the perspective of the 1950s and 1960s, however, Bell appeared not as a towering titan but rather as a small-time businessman, dependent on the Mexican community both for menu ideas and for the tortillas he fried into shells. Mexican Americans actually invented the fast-food taco in the process of adapting their foods to a changing society.

The Mexican American taco was a common element of distinct regional cuisines that took shape in cookbooks and restaurants of the postwar Southwest. Growing out of roots in the colonial borderlands, and eventually hyphenated with names such as Tex-Mex, Cal-Mex, and New Mex, these novel cooking styles combined North American ingredients with Mexican sensibilities. They were created by migrant and ethnic cooks and they reflected an emerging Mexican American identity. Having already begun to demand civil rights in the first decades of the twentieth century, Mexican Americans were empowered by military service and employment opportunities during and after World War II. They also used their growing disposable income to diversify their diets and to engage in culinary tourism. In cities such as Los Angeles and San Antonio, formal restaurants replaced street vendors as the place to go for Mexican food. As a result, the promoters of Mexican cuisine were no longer impoverished chili queens but rather community leaders who offered both a gathering place for insiders and an upstanding public face to outsiders. Although restaurateurs originally called their foods "Mexican" rather than Tex-Mex or Cal-Mex, many Mexicans refused to acknowledge their authenticity. In a similar fashion, an earlier generation of Porfirian exiles had rejected chili con carne based largely on canned versions arising from the food-processing industry.[3]

Ultimately, it was neither Mexican cooks alone nor outsiders like Glen Bell but rather the competition between the two that shaped these Mexican American regional cuisines. The postwar expansion of consumerism, restaurants, and food processing was crucial to this process of cultural formation. Although the total number of restaurants in the United States increased only slightly, from about 127,000 in 1954 to 135,000 in 1967, the seeming stability of these figures conceals rapid turnover within the industry. Sales of restaurant food, a more revealing statistic, doubled during this same period, from seven to fourteen billion dollars, creating an enormous incentive for experimentation, along with countless failures.[4] The food-processing industry likewise offered great potential profits, and TV dinners were one of the most lucrative sectors in this growing market. Under these circumstances, ethnic foods evolved rapidly. Mexican cooks adapted their recipes to build mainstream clienteles, while restaurateurs and food processors outside the Mexican community sought to entice customers with novelties such as tacos. Experimentation and cross-cultural exchange brought together the formerly separate supply chains for ethnic enclaves and mainstream stores toward an emerging Mexican American standard.

At the same time in Mexico, similar social processes were helping to standardize regional cuisines. The revolutionary activism of the early twentieth century gave way to industrial development, even as a self-consciously mestizo middle class began to explore their national cuisine again, not only Creole versions but also dishes that had earlier been rejected as indigenous. Although earlier cookbooks had acknowledged the regional diversity of Mexican food, twentieth-century writers and restaurateurs codified these differences by enshrining particular dishes as being representative of entire states. The revolutionary ideology of indigenismo also helped gain acceptance for foods that had formerly been disdained for their native associations. Thus, Oaxaca became the "land of seven moles" when urban chefs consolidated diverse village festival foods into a weekly round of restaurant specials. Residents of Hermosillo created the modern rituals of Sonora's carne asada out of nostalgia for the rancho at a time when processed foods were entering the diet on an everyday basis.[5] The consolidation and commercialization of regional cuisines through industry and domestic culinary tourism not only created new rituals, but it also led to the extinction of many local traditions. Burritos, which had been eaten in different parts of Mexico in the nineteenth century, largely disappeared, while in the United States, they became exclusively associated with wheat flour tortillas. The formation of national cuisines thus created new boundaries and ideals of authenticity. The foods of Oaxaca and Sonora came to be seen as authentically Mexican, while those of Mexican cultural provinces in South Texas and California were not. By excluding dishes from the U.S. side of the border, Mexican culinary nationalists marginalized recent migrants as well as established Mexican Americans from their vision of authentic Mexican.

Cooking in the "Mexican American Generation"

The Mexican American generation, which came of age during midcentury as the children of immigrants, invented new cuisines to express their distinctive identities. Their recipes diverged not only from the "white-bread" U.S. mainstream, but also from the cooking of their immigrant mothers. As late as the Great Depression, most Mexicans living in the United States ate tortillas, beans, chiles, and a little meat, a diet that had changed little from the frontier days of northern New Spain—or from their contemporaries in rural Mexico. Products and technologies of the food-processing industry such as fresh and canned vegetables, dairy, and ground beef, which had only begun to enter working-class diets in the 1920s and 1930s, became more readily available in the postwar era. Although discrimination remained pervasive, new opportunities for education gave access to better paying jobs. At the same time, Mexican Americans were torn between maintaining family and historical ties to Mexico and forging new identities in the United States. Restaurateurs and home economists served as entrepreneurial cultural brokers between the Mexican community and the mainstream society, helping their neighbors incorporate the products of market society while presenting their foods to outsiders. In doing so, they insisted that Mexican food was healthy, tasty, and "American," thereby claiming a form of cultural citizenship.[6]

Consuelo Castillo de Bonzo, founder of the Los Angeles restaurant Casa La Golondrina (House of the Swallow), exemplified the cultural brokers who built bridges between Mexico and the United States. Born in Aguascalientes in 1897, she had come to California with her widowed mother at the age of two and was completely bicultural. Although many restaurateurs had modest beginnings as ambulant vendors or small shopkeepers, Castillo de Bonzo got her start as a real estate agent in 1920s Los Angeles and soon ran a chain of small restaurants, called La Misión, in downtown L.A., Hollywood, and San Gabriel. When the *Los Angeles Times* publisher Harry Chandler and a society matron named Christine Sterling sought to revitalize the old downtown, they offered her a lease on the landmark Pelanconi House. La Golondrina opened in 1930 as the centerpiece of Olvera Street, an "ethnic theme park" intended to repackage the Spanish fantasy heritage for a new generation of tourists under the slogan: "a Mexican street of yesterday in a city of today."[7] Castillo de Bonzo did not disappoint her sponsors. A consummate promoter, she marketed the restaurant as an exotic destination for Anglos seeking an experience of Old Mexico with promotions such as a night in the floating gardens of Xochimilco. She also gave her Anglo partners credibility within the community and helped convince Mexicans to join in the tourist performance of Olvera Street. Switching easily between multiple roles, she presided over the restaurant in elegant gowns, wore stylized native costumes in the manner of Frida Kahlo, and conducted business as an official of the Los Angeles Restaurant Association while wearing fashionable hats and flared jackets.[8]

Despite collaborations with Anglo politicians, Castillo de Bonzo remained close to her Mexican origins. She insisted on calling La Golondrina a "Mexican restaurant," unlike El Cholo and other competitors, which advertised "Spanish food." The Spanish-language daily, *La Opinión*, which never overlooked signs

Figure 5.1. Consuelo de Bonzo, center, represents the Mexican community in a Cinco de Mayo celebration, 1951, in Café La Golondrina on Olvera Street. Herald Examiner Collection. No. 57105. Courtesy of the Los Angeles Public Library.

of Americanization, pronounced the 1930 inaugural banquet "netamente mexicana" (cleanly and distinctly Mexican).[9] Whereas the chili queens had reluctantly submitted to the patronage of Maury Maverick, the opening of La Golondrina featured as godparents the two most glamorous celebrities in Hollywood's Mexican colony, Ramón Novarro and Dolores del Río. By the 1940s, the restaurant had begun serving combination plates—the Number 4 consisted of a beef taco with Spanish rice and Mexican beans—but the cooking did not stray over the years from her mother's original recipes. Throughout her life, Castillo de Bonzo worked tirelessly for Catholic charities and *mutualista* societies in support of the Mexican community, even as La Golondrina helped to preserve the connections between Mexican American foods and the regional cuisines of Mexico.[10]

By contrast, Felix Tijerina sought economic profit and political influence by adapting Mexican food to mainstream audiences in the United States.

Although the restaurateur later claimed a Texas birthplace, he was baptized in a small town near Monterrey, Mexico. By 1922, he had arrived in Houston, where he found work in the Original Mexican Restaurant, owned by George Caldwell. Starting as a busboy, Tijerina rose to become a manager, and in 1929 he opened his own establishment, the Mexican Inn, just a block from the Original. The restaurant catered largely to an Anglo audience, with mild dishes, and Tijerina soon became active in politics, joining the local council of the Mexican American civil rights organization, LULAC. After a business failure during the Depression and military service in World War II, he built a chain of Felix Mexican Restaurants in Houston and nearby towns. Tijerina kept prices modest, even for the "Felix De Luxe Dinner"—$1.25 in the 1950s for a platter brimming with beef tacos, cheese enchiladas, rice, beans, and his trademark "spaghetti con chile"—and won a loyal clientele, primarily among Anglos. He plowed profits from the restaurant back into politics and from 1956 to 1960 held the presidency of LULAC, opening new councils throughout the Midwest like franchises in his restaurant chain. With his specialty spaghetti and chili gravy, Tijerina represented the Americanized end of a Mexican American spectrum.[11]

Although Mexican restaurants were still uncommon outside the Southwest at midcentury, isolated outposts could be found as far away as New York City. The man who brought Mexican food to Manhattan was one of the unsung prophets of culinary globalization, Juvencio Maldonado. Born in Celaya, León, in 1898, he came to the Yucatán, perhaps as a soldier in the Revolution, and in 1924, sailed from Progreso to New York City. His future wife, Paz, a native of Mérida, joined him four years later. The couple started a Mexican grocery on the Upper West Side, selling fresh masa, tortillas, salsa, and chocolate, but without an established Mexican population, they found little demand. To educate New Yorkers about proper Mexican food, in 1938 they opened a small restaurant in the theater district on West 46th Street called Xóchitl, the Náhuatl word for flower.[12]

Maldonado, a stout man with an elegant manner, introduced guests to the culture and cuisines of Mexico. Admittedly, the dining room combined tourist stereotypes with images of a Manhattan nightclub—a sombrero displayed over an upright piano and wooden American Indian heads along the walls. Despite the questionable décor, Maldonado delighted in teaching his customers about the fine points of Mexican history, starting with the story of the Aztec eagle and serpent, depicted in a large painting in the center of the room. Although he stocked cans of Gebhard's Chili con Carne in deference to tourist requests, he steered diners to other selections on the à la carte menu such as mole, chilaquiles, cactus salad, and tropical fruit preserves. The pride of the restaurant was fresh tortillas, prepared daily from nixtamal under Maldonado's personal supervision. His cooks went through a hundred pounds of tortillas every day in making soft and hard tacos, enchiladas, and tostadas, and as accompaniments to mole.[13]

A technological visionary as well as restaurant impresario, Maldonado patented the first mechanical taco fryer. On his arrival in New York, he had listed his trade as electrician, and he demonstrated technical ingenuity in his patent application, filed in 1947 and registered three years later. His "form for frying tortillas to make fried tacos" consisted of vertically stacked holders in a metal frame that could be immersed in oil then unfolded to release the tortillas. Throughout the 1950s and 1960s, Maldonado sold fried shells as take-out items in addition to tacos for his restaurant. He explained proudly that the invention had restored "peace after open mutiny among his own cooks, who dreaded handling the fried taco orders."[14] This was the technology that Glen Bell later claimed to have created.

Cookbooks provide another indication of the innovations taking place in Mexican home cooking at midcentury. Following in the footsteps of Encarnación Pinedo, home economists such as Fabiola Cabeza de Baca Gilbert began asserting their voice and defining a Mexican American cuisine. Born into a prominent Santa Fe family, C. de Baca was a small, thin woman with a regal bearing, which she maintained only with great effort after a crippling auto accident in 1929, at the age of thirty-five. Shortly before the accident, she had earned a B.S. in Domestic Science from New Mexico Agricultural and Mechanical University, and, once fitted with a prosthetic leg, she went to work as an agricultural extension agent, both as an outlet for her vast energy and to supplement her family's declining fortune in ranching. In the 1930s, she translated recipes and manuals on canning, table manners, and other forms of culinary modernization into Spanish. But her goal was not simply to acculturate rural women but rather to gain acceptance for Hispanic traditions. "In recent years, New Mexican foods have become increasingly popular," she wrote with pride in one manual. "The principal reason, of course, is that the food is good. Another is that recent research has proved that many of our basic foods—chile, beans, purslane, lamb's quarters, goat's cheese, and whole grain cereals, for example—are highly nutritious."[15]

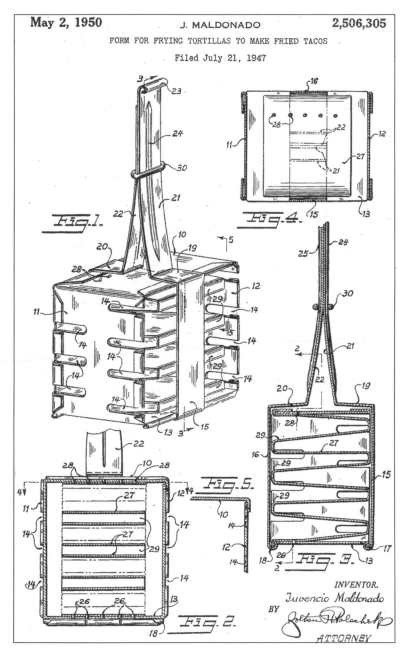

May 2, 1950   J. MALDONADO   2,506,305

FORM FOR FRYING TORTILLAS TO MAKE FRIED TACOS

Filed July 21, 1947

Figure 5.2. The original fast-food taco form, a patent issued to the New York restaurateur Juvencio Maldonado in 1950, when Glen Bell was still flipping hamburgers in San Bernardino, California. Courtesy of the United States Patent and Trademark Office.

For many elite Hispanic women of New Mexico, the work of compiling cookbooks and other folklore served to reclaim their cultural heritage from Anglo interpreters. Cleofas M. Jaramillo published *The Genuine New Mexico Tasty Recipes* (1939) after reading an article in *Holland's* magazine that was "nicely written and illustrated, but very deficient as to knowledge of our Spanish cooking."[16] A few years earlier, Margarita C. de Baca (a distant relation) had published a similar volume with both old favorites like chili verde, posole de chicos, and capirotada, as well as a new recipe for tacos made with chopped meat and potatoes and garnished with lettuce, chili sauce, and grated cheese.[17] Fabiola C. de Baca, in her classic volume *The Good Life* (1949), likewise experimented with the foods of new immigrants. "*Tacos* are definitely a Mexican importation," she observed, "but the recipe given below is a New Mexico adaptation." Her basic formula differed little from the meat and potatoes published earlier, but the domestic science instructor suggested a novel twist, which became almost universal north of the border, by prefrying the tortillas into the characteristic U shape of a taco shell before adding in the filling.[18]

Another prominent midcentury author, Elena Zelayeta, followed an even more remarkable path to becoming a public authority on Mexican cooking. She was born in Mexico City in 1898 and moved with her family to San Francisco during the Revolution. To support her two children, she operated a restaurant until she lost her sight in 1934. After a bout of depression, she taught herself to cook by touch, judging the heat of cooking oil by smell and measuring baking time by listening to programs on the radio. Although she could not maintain the demanding rhythms of restaurant cooking, she eventually, with the assistance of Anglo home economists, began to offer cooking classes and wrote a series of successful cookbooks. She amazed students who could see her boldly flipping tortillas over an open flame and inspired the blind with her independence. Like many contemporaries, Zelayeta was open to new influences. A 1958 recipe for *tacos de carne molida* (ground beef) began with a proper *picadillo*, including almonds, served in taco shells that were fried before filling. She said: "This method may be more American than Mexican, but so what?"[19]

These culinary professionals all had different recipes, but they shared a common insistence on the wholesomeness and acceptability of Mexican food. Restaurateurs of the period may have focused more on taste and affordability, while home economists added an emphasis on healthfulness. Even politicians occasionally felt called upon to defend the cuisine when questioned by outsiders, as in 1951, when the California Department of Public Health announced an inquiry into the nutritional value of the Mexican diet.[20] Edward Roybal, the first Los Angeles city councilman of Mexican descent to be elected for almost seventy years, called a press conference to rebut the accusations. The major newspapers did not see fit to report the story, but the *Los Angeles Examiner* at least sent a photographer. Accompanied by a healthy looking woman in a chef's hat, the charismatic politician juxtaposed for the camera an open-faced taco topped with lettuce and cheese against a bowl of potato chips and bottled soft drinks. Even without the text of his remarks, one could scarcely miss the message that Mexican dishes were better than junk food.

The Mexican American campaign to gain cultural acceptance had mixed results at best. Critics have assailed middle-class leaders for selling out. Felix Tijerina learned to make Mexican food from an Anglo restaurateur, and his

Figure 5.3. "'Is the Mexican diet adequate?' asks the California Health Department. 'Yes,' says Councilman E. R. Roybal. To prove it, he is sending them a tasty open face taco. Tostadas have more health-giving qualities than the American counterpart of cokes, hamburgers and potato chips, according to Roybal." Herald Examiner Collection. No. 37026. Courtesy of the Los Angeles Public Library.

leadership of LULAC was unsympathetic toward the broader civil rights movement. Scholars have likewise questioned the colonizing practices of home
economists like Fabiola C. de Baca. Some might claim that midcentury Mexican
American restaurants and cookbooks had sacrificed Mexico's culinary heritage
to Anglo expectations. Certainly their recipes evolved in different directions
from the tacos that were taking shape in Mexico. Nevertheless, the question
remains of whether public representations actually drove assimilation or simply reflected changes that were already underway in the Mexican American
community. After all, C. de Baca performed invaluable work in preserving local
traditions through her cookbooks, while Tijerina was a tireless advocate of
educating young Mexican Americans.[21] Moreover, the food-processing industry was developing rival versions of Mexican food for mass consumers, and
interactions between these two trends, ethnic home cooking and corporate
food processing, ultimately shaped the final product.

Selling the Fast-Food Taco

The taco shell offered outsiders an entrée that made the mysteries of Mexican
food more accessible. For most Anglos, preparing fresh tortillas was unthinkable and even eating them was an exotic undertaking, as a Los Angeles guide-
book from the 1930s explained: "The Mexican's dexterity with the tortilla is as
amusing to watch as the Italian's business-like disposal of spaghetti and the
chop sticks of the Oriental."[22] Aspiring industrialists faced the dual challenge
of replacing skilled kitchen labor while making consumption appealing and
nonthreatening. Mechanically frying tortillas into shells was the least of these
problems, as Juvencio Maldonado had already demonstrated. Entrepreneurs
seeking to mechanize Mexican cooking benefited from broader social changes
that were moving food preparation out of domestic kitchens to restaurants
and industry, despite the gendered ideal of middle-class women as suburban
homemakers. Moreover, within this changing social landscape, Anglos were
finding new ways of segregating themselves from people of color, which gave a
competitive advantage to businessmen outside the Mexican community.

Glen Bell began his career in Southern California, the epicenter of postwar
suburbanization and fast food. After serving as a Marine cook in World War II,
he watched as Maurice and Richard McDonald created their model of industrial
efficiency, selling standardized, low-cost meals in great volume. Nevertheless,
technology was not the only, or even the primary, cause for the success of fast-

food chains. Ray Kroc, a former restaurant supply salesman who franchised the McDonald's system into a global empire, maintained strict control over franchise holders. The company purchased land and built all restaurants, leasing them back to operators in order to ensure proper upkeep. Kroc recognized that geography was crucial for success, and coming from an upwardly mobile immigrant family, he favored suburban locations. The company selected new restaurant sites carefully, and it worked for middle-class respectability by excluding undesirable elements, including minorities and the working classes. McDonald's later moved downscale as it pursued urban expansion, but it was "in the real estate business"—and a central tenet of that business was to maintain property values by attracting the right sort of people.[23]

Glen Bell followed more in the footsteps of Ray Kroc, the aggressive franchiser, than of the technically innovative McDonald brothers. Bell was not the first to sell tacos outside the Mexican community; the Taco House of Los Angeles, operating already in 1946, spawned a host of imitators, including Alice's Taco Terrace, Bert's Taco Junction, and Frank's Taco Inn. Although Bell described his experiments with taco fryers in the early 1950s—unaware that Maldonado had beaten him to the patent office—his authorized biography revealed the soul of a California real estate man. Passing quickly over technology, he waxed lyrical over bricks, mortar, and traffic flow. Bell had grown up reading Helen Hunt Jackson's romantic novel of Old California, *Ramona*, and he sought to package this pastoral experience for Anglo audiences. Each new restaurant celebrated its grand opening with an anachronistic mix of Mexican mariachi bands, straw sombreros, and dancing women with Spanish castanets. This image was carefully sanitized for mainstream sensibilities. When a consultant suggested the name "La Tapatia" (the lady from Jalisco) for one of his early restaurants in the 1950s, he chose instead a nonsense Spanish phrase "Taco Tia" (Taco Aunt) to make it more accessible to English-speaking customers. In the 1960s, Taco Bell continued the miniature theme-park image with faux adobe walls, a mission-style bell tower, and an elaborate courtyard fountain, which was later discarded as the chain expanded into regions where outdoor dining was impossible year-round.[24]

Bell clearly marketed his restaurants to Anglo customers, but the question remains of who actually ate at any given restaurant. One way to track the clientele for early fast-food tacos is by mapping the physical location of restaurants in Los Angeles County from the 1940s to the 1960s. Although residential patterns might seem unimportant in the car culture of Southern California, even

restaurants on busy thoroughfares depended largely on neighborhood customers—apparently people would not drive far to eat fast food.[25] The dots on the
map indicate restaurants listed under Spanish surnames in the 1941 city directory. Large numbers of Mexicans were concentrated downtown and to the east
in Boyle Heights, but Los Angeles was a surprisingly integrated city on the eve
of World War II, and Mexicans also lived, and owned restaurants, everywhere
from West Hollywood to the largely Jewish West Side and African American
neighborhoods of Southeast Los Angeles.[26] Wartime racial tensions such as the
1943 Zoot Suit Riots, in which servicemen clashed with Mexican youth, accel-
erated a process of resegregation in the postwar era. Taking advantage of the
housing boom of the 1950s, Anglos abandoned the integrated neighborhoods
of downtown and East Los Angeles for distant suburbs around the periphery
of the city, ranging from the San Fernando Valley and Whittier in the north
to Lakewood and Orange County to the south. The city's minority populations grew even more rapidly during this period, and African American and
Mexican enclaves likewise appeared in suburbs from Pasadena to Long Beach.
Yet despite a 1948 Supreme Court ruling against restrictive covenants, zoning
laws and homeowners' associations helped ensure that these neighborhoods
remained separate.

The rise of the taco shop in the postwar era made it possible for non-Mexicans
to satisfy their desire for exotic food without venturing across lines of segregation. The triangles on the map indicate restaurants listed in the Los Angeles
Yellow Pages with the word "taco" in their names. They followed a very different spatial distribution than had the Mexican-owned restaurants of 1940. One
striking conclusion is that Mexicans did not generally use the word "taco" in
naming restaurants—just two of these fifty were located in Mexican East Los
Angeles. Although some small places may not appear for lack of telephone service, restaurants seeking to attract customers from within the Mexican community clearly evoked regional specialties by using Spanish-language names
such as Café Orizaba, Guadalajara Pues, or even Arizona. By contrast, self-
proclaimed taco shops expanded into the white suburbs of Glendale, Pasadena,
and the San Fernando Valley, as well as south into the African American community of Watts, which also had a substantial Mexican minority. Correlating
these taco shops with tract-level racial profiles from the 1960 census reveals a
striking degree of segregation. Of the fifty restaurants, twenty-seven were in
majority white neighborhoods, twelve in majority black neighborhoods, and
only eight in majority Mexican neighborhoods. No more than a third of the

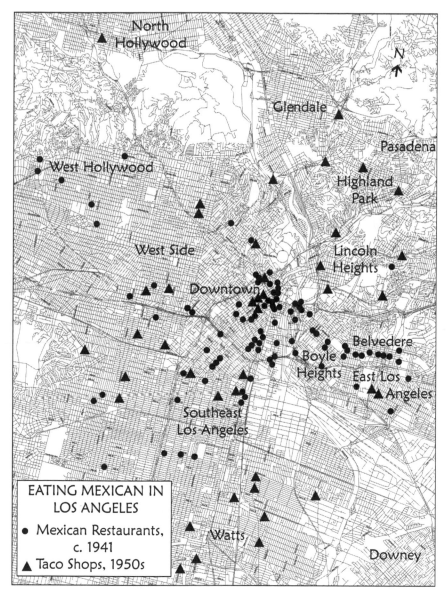

Figure 5.4. Taco shops, as indicated by 1950s and early 1960s telephone directories, moved out of Mexican neighborhoods in central and eastern Los Angeles into predominantly Anglo and African American suburbs to the north and south. Drawn by the author.

143

restaurants operated in neighborhoods with even a modicum of racial or ethnic balance indicated by two or more groups each constituting a minimum of 20 percent of the population. These tended to be in the near north or south, areas such as Lincoln Heights or Watts, or in the business district downtown.[27]

This is not to say that tacos spread across Los Angeles in a completely segregated fashion. They were, after all, about the cheapest food around, and many people bought them for a quick and convenient lunch. Many taco shops doubtless relied on Mexicans in the kitchen, preparing the same foods they served at home. Other culinary border crossings resulted from local particularities of markets and marriages. Lalo's Tacos of El Sereno, for example, specialized in pastrami tacos and burritos, a kosher alternative to the usual pork carnitas and chorizo. Lalo's personal story—whether a Jewish-Mexican mixed marriage or a restaurateur seeking to expand his clientele in this multiethnic neighborhood—may be lost to history. Yet a similar Los Angeles institution called the Kosher Burrito, founded in 1946 by a Jewish man who married a Sonoran woman, still exists on the corner of First and Main.[28]

Mexican food had a mixed reception among other groups, as the African American example demonstrates. Blacks migrated to California in large numbers in the 1940s, and many of them came with a taste for tamales and chili con carne acquired in Texas, the Mississippi Delta, and elsewhere. While these newcomers often found Los Angeles Mexican food to be quite alien, they quickly made it their own. The Tamale Factory of Inglewood, operated by a mixed couple, Earl and Jovita Senior, catered to Mexican and African American tastes with both green chile and chili con carne tamales. Hank Silva, the owner of Bill's Taco House, made tacos with seasoned hamburger patties, grilled and cut into three pieces, with cheese slices and chili gravy on top. Loyal customers included the basketball star Kareem Abdul-Jabbar and the soul music legend Barry White. Not all cross-cultural experiments were as successful; a short-lived restaurant of the 1950s dubbed black-eyed peas in a taco shell as "African Tacos." If nothing else, shops in South Central and Watts often had more creative names, such as Taco Th' Town, than the usual variation on "taco house." But not all commentators were pleased. A *Los Angeles Sentinel* columnist, Stanley G. Robinson, denounced tacos as a bane on the African American community. His editorials of the 1960s and 1970s regularly denounced "losers" and "pushers" hanging out on the streets eating tacos. By the mid-1970s, *Sentinel* readers had begun to complain about the lack of racial solidarity among Chicanos and blacks as expressed in the antitaco tirades.[29]

Notwithstanding the proliferation of restaurants, people still ate most of their meals at home in the 1950s, and supermarket sales contributed to the growing interest in Mexican food. It is difficult to define this market with precision, but arguably the most popular single item was Fritos corn chips. The company founder, Elmer Doolin, claimed to have purchased the recipe in the 1930s from an unknown Mexican in San Antonio. Some have questioned this story, saying the rights actually belonged to Bartolomé Martínez's Tamalina Company. Regardless, Frito-Lay marketed the snack primarily to children by using an Anglo cowboy mascot, the Frito Kid. By contrast, one of the most popular Mexican American foods at midcentury, Velveeta, took little note of its Mexican market. Popularized in the 1920s by Kraft Foods, this processed cheese food product had the perfect melting consistency, and it was used throughout the Southwest for enchiladas, stuffed chiles, and chile con queso.[30]

Customers looking for Mexican convenience foods labeled as such on supermarket shelves had two basic options: canned and frozen. Particular brands were still regional at this point, centered on California and Texas. Pacific Coast companies, including Ortega and Rosarita, the latter founded in 1946 by Pedro Guerrero of Mesa, Arizona, tended to focus on local markets, selling canned chiles, frijoles, and enchilada sauce to mainstream consumers with knowledge of Mexican food. Texas-based firms led the national expansion of Mexican foods. The current market leader, Old El Paso, grew out of the Mountain Pass Canning Company, founded during World War I. By the 1950s, their canned enchiladas and frijoles were available in specialty shops as far away as New York City. But in the early days, a cross-town rival, Ashley Foods, offered a more innovative product line. Starting with a successful El Paso restaurant, George Ashley expanded into canning for regional markets in 1931. By the 1950s, Ashley had a wide range of products, including canned tortillas, enchilada sauce, rice, and beans. The company may also have packaged the first taco dinner kit, in 1955, complete with canned tortillas, frijoles, and taco sauce, and a hand-held taco fryer, all for $1.89.[31]

Frozen Mexican dinners likewise developed through regional markets with similar products. In 1955, within a year of Swanson pioneering the TV dinner, Los Angeles consumers could purchase a quick-frozen combination plate with enchilada, tamale, refried beans, and Spanish rice. By the early 1960s, XLNT, Gordo's, Moreno's, and Rosarita brands were competing for the California market, all offering the same tamale with chili gravy, beef and cheese enchilada, and beef taco dinners. In San Antonio, Texas, the electrical engineer H. E.

Stumberg and his sons Louis and Edward founded Patio Foods in 1947. They started canning chili and tamales but soon developed a line of frozen foods, including the usual tamales, enchiladas, and combination dinners, as well as a Patio original, cocktail beef tacos. After spreading across Texas, the company expanded into Midwestern markets in the 1960s, assuring customers that their entrees contained no bland imitation but rather a "sizzling sauce with the authority of real Mexican hot food."[32]

Despite the convenience of canned and frozen products, kitchen knowledge remained the most fundamental limitation on the marketing of Mexican food outside the community. New industrial products such as taco shells and enchilada kits allowed consumers to savor the exoticism of Mexican cuisine without having to go to Mexico or even to a Mexican American barrio. Yet in many parts of the country, there were few such opportunities, even for those who might want them, and commercial products served as the only connection with Mexico. Jeremy Dillon lovingly described the dinners prepared by his California-born father in 1960s Omaha, Nebraska. "He used store bought corn tortillas for the tacos and would fry and bend them in an old iron pan. His enchiladas were made with store-bought flour tortillas and Old El Paso enchilada sauce. Browned hamburger, shredded cheddar cheese, chopped iceberg lettuce, and diced tomatoes accompanied both dishes."[33] Although perhaps not authentic, such foods offered Midwesterners a welcome break from tuna casseroles.

A Proliferation of Mex's

Texas and California set national patterns for Mexican food within the United States in the postwar era. The regional cuisines that eventually became known as Tex-Mex and Cal-Mex were inherited in part from the frontier culture of New Spain. Recent migration patterns also introduced more modern Mexican foods such as tacos. In both places, aspiring food processors helped to disseminate local specialties around the country. One telling difference between the two states was the importance of cookbooks and other literary texts in formalizing distinctive cuisines. Californians produced abundant written texts, and perhaps as a result, local chefs were highly self-confident about the originality of their foods. In Texas, by contrast, cooking styles developed largely in family restaurants, whose owners often maintained closer connections with regional cuisines of Mexico. Yet even in the absence of culinary literature, restaurant menus and décor became standardized in Texas, as in California, through widespread borrowing of novel approaches, thereby helping to formalize the local cooking style as a regional cuisine. Meanwhile, the foods of New Mexico and Arizona maintained their distinctiveness simply by being overlooked during this period, both because of their smaller urban populations and limited access to tourist markets.

In Texas, public representations of Mexican food were most prominent in restaurants. Apart from a few Mexican recipes in community cookbooks of the San Antonio Symphony Society and the Dallas Junior League, there was little attempt to produce a regional culinary literature.[34] Unlike the masculine space of the chili parlor, the 1950s-era Mexican restaurant was essentially a family institution. When customers sat down, they received not chips and salsa but rather packets of saltine crackers or perhaps wheat flour tortillas and butter. The menus often included regular and special plates, with various combinations of taco, tamales, enchiladas, tostadas, and chalupas, accompanied by chile con queso, rice, beans, tortillas, coffee, and sherbet. Although inspired by San Antonio's Original Mexican Restaurant, Otis Farnsworth's elegant practice of serving the items as separate courses was replaced by overcrowded plates— occasionally more than one—heated to the same volcanic temperatures as the chili gravy that was poured on top.[35]

Restaurant menus may have been standardized, but they were far from stagnant, and each new innovation was rapidly copied by competitors.[36] One distinctively Texan food from the 1940s and 1950s was the puffy taco, made by patting out fresh nixtamal masa into the shape of a tortilla and then deep-frying it rather than cooking it on a comal. Filled with typical Mexican American taco condiments, ground beef, lettuce, and cheese, they were served with plenty of napkins. Claims for having invented this high-cholesterol treat ran from Rosita's in Laredo to the venerable Dallas chain, El Fenix. The chicken and sour cream enchilada, a Texan version of enchiladas suizas that appeared in the 1950s, has similarly disputed origins. Both John Cuellar, of the Dallas-based El Chico chain, and his nephew and cross-town rival, Edward Gámez, of Pulido's in Fort Worth, have attributed the recipe to their respective chefs, Joe Valdez Caballero and Juan García. At least the nacho has a recognized lineage, deriving from Ignacio "Nacho" Anaya, who popularized the chip, cheese, and jalapeño combo at a Piedras Negras border club in the early 1940s. The dish that ultimately symbolized Tex-Mex cooking, *fajitas*, appeared only at the end of this period, in the late 1960s. The folklorist Mario Montaño has traced its origins to borderland barbacoas, especially around Laredo, where the diaphragm muscle of the cow, called *faja* or *arrachera* in Spanish, was cheap enough for working-class people. Although tough when cooked as steak, Mexican techniques for barbacoa and carne asada transformed the flavorful meat into a gourmet delight. In 1973, "Mama" Ninfa Laurenzo, a Houston restaurateur, brought this border specialty to mainstream audiences, helping to popularize a self-consciously Tex-Mex cooking style.[37]

Yet many restaurateurs disclaimed this assimilated style of cooking and its heavy hand with cheese and chili gravy. Dave Cortez of Mi Tierra, a popular San Antonio restaurant founded in 1941 by his Guadalajara-born father, distinguished the local restaurant food from Mexican regional cooking: "Tex-Mex is crisp tacos, cheddar cheese, and puffy tacos. If you eat tamales with cheddar cheese on top, it is more Tex-Mex." The owners of Joe T. Garcia's, a Fort Worth institution founded in 1935 by a migrant from Michoacán, likewise sought to preserve Mexican flavors. "A lot of restaurants would put chili over everything, but we did not do that," explained Joe T.'s daughter, Hope Garcia Lancarte. "Our chiles rellenos and flautas are like we make them in Mexico."[38] Chili gravy, the kitchen secret of casual-dining Mexican restaurants, was simply basic Southern brown gravy with chili powder added, which was smothered indiscriminately over enchiladas, tamales, and other menu items. Claims for authentic Mexican in Texas during this period derived from the connections to Mexico or from home cooking. Albert Villareal, a longtime chef at Casa Rio, a San Antonio restaurant that catered to tourists, explained: "Mexican-Americans don't eat chili gravy at home."[39]

Such claims raise the question of whether Tex-Mex food was segregated in the same ways as California fast food during this period. Although Mexican Americans may have avoided Casa Rio, Anglos and Mexicans certainly rubbed shoulders in many restaurants. If Villareal preferred the grilled meats of Monterrey to his own restaurant cooking, when cookbooks finally began to appear in Mexican South Texas, they revealed a less categorical distinction between Anglo restaurants and Mexican American home cooking. In 1977, Elvira Ramírez published a small book with "many of the recipes used in the homes of Americans of Mexican extraction in Texas." The very first recipe in the book, Vera's Enchiladas, sprinkled grated cheddar cheese ("don't be stingy") over gravy made with chili powder, garlic powder, and mole powder. While giving recipes for *carne guisada*, beef tongue, and menudo, she did not hesitate to save time using canned hominy.[40] Likewise, Lucy Garza, a Falfurrias High School home economics teacher, could cook her way through a steer or kid from

Box 5.1   Recipe for Enchiladas Verdes

4 cups chicken breasts, cooked and cut finely

Oil for frying

12 tortillas

½ pint sour cream

4 cups green enchilada sauce

1. Lift tortillas, one at a time, with kitchen tongs and dip into ½" heated oil in skillet (heat tortillas just for a few seconds; only long enough to soften).
2. Lift tortilla from oil; dip immediately into heated enchilada sauce.
3. Spoon about 1 tablespoon of shredded chicken into the center. Top with 2 teaspoons sour cream. Roll. 4. (Rolled enchiladas should be placed seamside down to keep filling in place.)
4. When all the tortillas have been stuffed, pour the remaining sauce over them and top with sour cream.
5. Bake for 15–20 minutes.
6. Serve at once. Serves 4–6.

Salsa Verde (Green Enchilada Sauce)

6 fresh green *tomatillos*, cooked and chopped

2 green chili peppers, minced

¼ cup onion, chopped

¼ cup fresh coriander (cilantro)

1 teaspoon salt

¼ cup chicken broth

1. (*Tomatillos* are green tomatoes which have a dry husklike covering.) Remove husk covering, rinse, and boil tomatoes in 2 cups water until tender. Drain and chop tomatoes.
2. Blend tomatoes, onion, chili peppers, coriander, broth, and salt in a blender. Cover; blend until pureed.
3. Transfer to saucepan; heat thoroughly. Serves 3–4.

Source: Lucy M. Garza, *South Texas Mexican Cook Book* (Austin, Texas: Eakin Press, 1982), 26, 52.

cabeza (head) to *machitos* (intestines), but her *South Texas Mexican Cookbook* (1982) included recipes for *chile con queso* with Velveeta, *carne picada con elote* ("hamburger corn supreme"), and her mother's adaptation of Southern fried chicken, *conejo frito*, made with cottontail rabbits hunted by her father.[41]

In contrast to Texas, where cooks sought to maintain their connections to Mexico, California was developing a self-consciously distinctive regional cuisine in which authenticity was based on connections to Old California, either through family ties or through the fantasy heritage. California cookery was already an established genre in tourist works including Charles Lummis's *Landmarks Club Cook Book* (1903) and Pauline Wiley-Kleeman's *Ramona's Spanish-Mexican Cookery* (1929). Yet there were also elite California women who claimed social status based on Spanish roots, for example, Ana Bégué de Packman, author of *Early California Hospitality* (1938). Restaurants, such as Joe and Emma Todd's Cal-Mex Café, also promoted California Mexican cooking as a distinct cuisine as early as 1964. Journalists often acted as cultural brokers to publicize such establishments. In 1944, the *Los Angeles Times* columnist Fred Beck discovered the tamales and enchiladas at a particular stand in the city farmers' market. The owner, Consuelo Castillo, was reportedly a sophisticated sixth-generation Californian who had studied law but found her true calling in the kitchen. "Consuelo prefers to think of her cuisine as Californian," Beck explained. "The particular flair and twist she achieves have no direct counterpart in the cookery of either Spain or Mexico."[42] Joe Reina, the longtime chef at Los Angeles's El Cholo, was quite dismissive of food across the border: "I have been to Mexico many times and I haven't learned anything I can apply here."[43]

Burritos were the most distinctive icon of California's Mexican cooking, although they were only beginning to assume their modern form wrapped in large, wheat flour tortillas. As late as 1938, Ana Bégué de Packman had assured readers that corn tortillas would work just fine.[44] Both varieties of tortilla were common in the nineteenth century until the industrial flour milling industry began to displace corn with wheat. By 1930, a social worker named Helen Douglas observed that working-class Mexicans ate a steady diet "of flour tortillas (the corn ones are too expensive)," a reverse of the usual calculation in Mexico.[45] California's corn-tortilla drought abated after the Great Depression, as new migrants from central Mexico began opening modern tortilla factories in the 1940s and 1950s. Without access to these industrial products, Glen Bell might never have progressed beyond hamburgers and hot dogs. But by this point, the burrito had become indelibly associated in the public mind with wheat flour tortillas.[46]

Focused on burritos and tacos, the menus of Mexican restaurants in Anglo neighborhoods were still quite rudimentary at midcentury, and they carefully explained items to customers. For example, a 1950s menu for La Fonda, in Glendale, helpfully included a glossary: "Mexican food consists of: Tacos—beef, sauce, lettuce, corn tortilla; Burritos—milk [and wheat flour] tortilla, meat, beans, sauce; Enchiladas—corn tortilla, olives, onions, cheese, sauce." To reassure cautious newcomers, the restaurant provided a familiar American option in Mexican guise: "Bar-b-q tacos—corn tortilla, bar-b-q meat, sauce." The final option, perhaps most reflective of future Cal-Mex cuisine, was the tostada: "Crisp corn tortilla, avocado, beans, lettuce, fresh tomato, grated cheese, sauce."[47] Nor was this unusually abbreviated; longer menus of the period simply consisted of multiple combinations of a few standard items. Even Taco Bell offered just five selections, including a hamburger, until the 1980s.[48]

Exotic restaurant décor may have been as much of an attraction as the food. While a few restaurants evoked the muralist movement championed by Diego Rivera with stylish art deco interiors, most sought to reproduce a stereotyped hacienda theme with images of cacti, sleeping peons, and china poblanas in low-cut peasant dresses. Taco Bell exemplified the Spanish mission image, while the Pancho Villa restaurant chain adopted a gun-slinging bandito mascot. Yet another variation on this theme, the Baja cantina, was taken up in 1954 by El Torito, a chain founded by a Korean War veteran named Larry Cano. The original location, in Encino, had formerly housed a Polynesian-themed restaurant, and Cano made cosmetic changes to transform the coconut hut into a Spanish hacienda, adding tacos and enchiladas to the menu and replacing Mai Tais with tequila drinks. While swapping Baja for Tahiti, he preserved the exotic sense of place that Californians expected in a bar and restaurant, thereby providing a West Coast model for Mexican casual dining.[49]

New Mexico cooking styles may have changed less than those of Texas and California, although the commercial economy was starting to make inroads even for rural folk. Culinary literature in Santa Fe was dominated by elite Hispanas like Fabiola C. de Baca and Cleofas Jaramillo, who were determined to preserve local traditions. Nevertheless, home economists did help promote new practices such as canning, which became common among farm women in the 1930s. With an investment in mason jars, they could extend the range of foods available in winter, canning green chiles, fruits, and vegetables to supplement the dried versions preserved with traditional methods.[50] Culinary tourism was confined to a few transit stations for transcontinental railroads. La Posta, a Mesilla Valley restaurant founded in 1939, served T-bone steak and carne adobada along with tacos, tamales, and enchiladas to travelers stopping over on the Southern Pacific Railroad. Meanwhile, the growing towns of Albuquerque and Santa Fe had cafés serving local favorites such as chile verde and sopaipillas. Yet restaurants outside the regular tourist destinations struggled to attract diners. The town of Chimayó, southwest of Santa Fe, was renowned locally as a pilgrimage destination for its reputed healing powers, as well as for the quality of its chile peppers. Nevertheless, Arturo Jaramillo struggled for years after transforming his grandparents' home into the Rancho Hacienda Chimayó hotel and restaurant. Even a glowing review in 1965 from the *New York Times* critic Craig Claiborne brought only a trickle of visitors. Financial success was not assured until population growth and local tourism began to pick up in the 1970s.[51]

Arizona was if anything even more isolated than New Mexico, preserving the dried beef and wheat flour tortillas of the late colonial era. In the 1920s, Luis Recinos explained that Tucson's Mexican restaurants lacked menus; "the waiters told the clients what they had, which was almost always beans, rice, enchiladas, chile con carne, eggs to taste, gorditas, and from time to time mole."[52] Nor did a local tradition of culinary literature emerge from the Mexican community. This did not imply a lack of innovation; for example, the application of deep-frying technology to the flour tortilla burrito produced the chimichanga, an Arizona original. But the nondescript storefronts of Mexican restaurants in Tucson as late as 1980 indicate the slow development of culinary tourism in the state.[53]

The early consolidation of regional cuisines in Texas and California ensured that they, rather than New Mexico or Arizona, shaped the image of Mexican food in the United States and ultimately around the world. Meanwhile in Mexico, the middle classes were not lagging behind in commercializing their own food. Indeed, it was the process of industrialization and the looming competition with U.S. industrial foods that prompted Mexicans to invent "authentic" regional cuisines at midcentury.

National Tacos in Mexico

Even as Mexican Americans sought to gain acceptance for their tacos within a proudly industrialized food market, the taco in Mexico came to symbolize a rival and nostalgic national cuisine. A revealing example of this culinary patriotism appeared in the gossip column of a Mexico City newspaper in 1946: "It would appear that the 'sandwich' and the 'hot dog,' debility of *pochos* [a derogatory term for Mexican Americans], have been unable to definitively defeat the very Mexican taco. One notices a new and growing affection for tacos, which is a symptom of the preservation of Mexican identity [*lo mexicano*]."[54] The column was entirely frivolous, advertising a fashionable restaurant of the moment, Al Guajolote (To the turkey), where the celebrities Dolores del Río and Emilio Fernández went for a late-night snack. Yet the seeming contradiction of a "new and growing affection for tacos" ensuring the "preservation" of a nostalgic past was consistent with the workings of nationalist ideology, which invented traditions to endow the nation with an aura of timelessness. The society reporter emphasized the patriotism of the actress del Río, who had returned to the national cinema from Hollywood, by contrasting her predilection for tacos with hot dogs, which were supposedly preferred by Mexican Americans. That growing numbers of Mexicans were consuming industrial processed food, much of it imported from the United States, provided a strong impetus to imagine an authentic national cuisine.

As allies in World War II, Mexico and the United States had fostered close economic integration, and in the postwar era, these ties continued through civilian industries. The historian Sandra Aguilar-Rodríguez has demonstrated the importance of new kitchen technologies in giving Mexican women a sense of modernity in both urban and rural areas. Blenders eased the work of grinding mole sauce, while pressure cookers facilitated the preparation of beans. Even imported goods were invariably Mexicanized or adapted to local tastes; for example, women learned to boil cans of condensed milk to make the popular caramel dessert *cajeta*, although they did so at the risk of exploding cans.[55] The modernization of Mexican food businesses depended in part on small entrepreneurs such as Pedro Marcos Noriega, founder of the snack giant Sabritas, who began to fry potato chips in his kitchen in 1943 and then hired bicycle vendors to sell them locally. As demand grew, he automated production, established retail distribution networks, and in 1966 made a deal to become a distributor for Pepsico, which assured his own supremacy in the Mexican snack-food market. Producers of Mexican food in the United States likewise depended on cross-border expertise. Luis Romero Soto, a Mexican mechanical engineer and tortilla innovator, collaborated in research and development with both George Ashley and H. E. Stumberg. Tortilla factories were a common business venture for Mexican migrants to the United States, thereby ensuring the regular transfer of the latest technologies from Mexico.[56]

The integration of Mexico into a North American capitalist agricultural system through the so-called Green Revolution brought even more sweeping social changes. Mexican agronomists had begun breeding experiments during the 1930s, and they expanded their research program during World War II with the assistance of a scientific mission funded by the Rockefeller Foundation. Plant breeders developed high-yielding seeds, which, along with tractors, irrigation, chemical fertilizers, and pesticides, increased agricultural productivity dramatically. The resulting surpluses from commercial farms, particularly wheat growers in the northwestern states of Sonora and Sinaloa, allowed the Mexican government to create an elaborate welfare bureaucracy and provide subsidized food to urban consumers. As food prices fell, peasant farmers with small, rain-fed cornfields saw their incomes plummet. Unable to make a living on the land, millions migrated in search of industrial jobs.[57] Many of them ended up doing agricultural work in the United States, which had responded to wartime labor shortages by establishing a guest-worker *bracero* program that continued until 1964. Growers in the United States employed cheap labor and new forms of mechanization to replace union workers. In the lettuce fields of Salinas, California, for example, the adoption of vacuum chilling technology in the late 1940s led to the closing of union packinghouses, as noncitizen braceros harvested and packed lettuce in the fields. The subsequent union organization of itinerant fieldworkers under the United Farm Workers of America, led by Cesar Chávez, was a crucial movement in the rise of Mexican American political power.[58]

In Mexico, a rising middle class, internal tourism, restaurants, and a resurgence of nationalist culinary literature helped to codify regional cuisines in the same ways that Cal-Mex and Tex-Mex took shape in the United States. Josefina Velázquez de León, the leading cooking teacher in Mexico, traveled tirelessly through the country while producing more than 150 cookbooks that incorporated local recipes into a national cuisine. Restaurateurs likewise cultivated regional specialties, particularly in tourist destinations. For example, *ceviche*, raw seafood "cooked" in the acid from lime juice in which it soaked, emerged in Acapulco as a popular variation of the colonial *escabeche*. Mexico City's nascent tourist center, the Zona Rosa, attracted restaurants promoting a variety of regional cuisines, including the Yucatán, Guadalajara, and Puebla. José Inés Loredo, a flamboyant former mayor of Tampico, built an upscale restaurant empire around *carne asada a la tampiqueña*, a combination plate of local dishes including a paper-thin steak, a green enchilada, beans, and grilled cheese. Judith Martínez Ortega de van Beuren meanwhile explored the delicacies of Creole cookery, especially colonial desserts, in her Fonda el Refugio.

Although Creole images continued to dominate midcentury constructions of the national cuisine, the revolutionary ideology of indigenismo began to give new status to foods that were seen as being indigenous. The effective end of revolutionary reform by the late 1930s relieved fears of radicalism and encouraged the middle classes to embrace the formerly disdained peasantry, at least from a distance. Frida Kahlo went shopping at indigenous markets for traditional festival foods, while the caterer Mayita Parada introduced peasant dishes to the mansions of Lomas de Chapultepec. But to gain acceptance, formerly disdained Indian foods as *cuitlacoche* (corn smut) had to be ritually purified. Jaime Saldívar, a gourmet chef, reputedly first devised an acceptable way of presenting corn fungus in *crêpes* with béchamel sauce. The poet and diplomat Alfonso Reyes, meanwhile, won applause for his embassy in Buenos Aires by presenting a simple dish of refried black beans under the name of "Mexican caviar."[59]

The spread of tacos out from Mexico City also helped to propagate this emerging national cuisine by providing an inexpensive vehicle for exploring new dishes. Regional versions of tacos began to appear, such as a San Luis Potosí specialty of tacos with potato, carrot, and pickled trotters in chile colorado sauce, or a Sonoran taco made of a wheat flour tortilla filled with roasted green chiles and salsa.[60] Migrants also contributed to the growth of taco culture; for example, in the 1920s, migrants from the Middle East introduced *shwarma*, lamb cooked on a vertical rotisserie. When served on wheat flour tortillas, like thin pita bread, they became known as *tacos árabes* (Arab tacos). This technique was Mexicanized in the 1950s and 1960s, by second-generation Lebanese Mexicans, who cooked pork in the same fashion, put it on corn tortillas with a slice of pineapple, and called it tacos al pastor. These tacos were first served in restaurants such as Tizoncito and Kaliman, located in the affluent Mexico City neighborhood of Condesa.[61] Neighboring restaurants were meanwhile serving gentrified *tacos al carbon* (grilled tacos) using expensive cuts of meat such as *bifstek* (beefsteak) and *chuletas* (pork chops). Despite these upscale versions, tacos remained a food of the common people, as the popular songwriter Salvador "Chava" Flores emphasized in his ballad "Platillos

Figure 5.5. Taco vending becomes an increasingly masculine occupation with the mechanization of tortilla production. Men selling tacos at a stand, Mexico City, c. 1950. Nacho López. Col. SINAFO-INAH. Inventory number 382183. Courtesy of the Instituto Nacional de Antropología e Historia, Mexico.

Mexicanos" (Mexican dishes), which declared his patriotic love for tacos made with carnitas, tongue, and heart.[62]

Mexicans in the provinces were equally interested in promoting their own cuisine and discovering the foods of other regions. In Hermosillo during the 1950s, carne asada was served on improvised dinner tables in the streets, reimagining the barbacoas of the ranchos. Local politicians held court at these tables, bolstering their populist credentials, and a few improvised stands grew into prosperous tourist restaurants. Xochimilco, one of the leading destinations for carne asada in the city, began as a stand at a traffic stop on the road to Guaymas. Even while developing their own foods, Sonorans took an increasing interest in the cuisines of others. Ernesto Camou Healy recalled that when his father drove from Hermosillo to Phoenix on business, he liked to eat at a restaurant called Ochoa's in Casas Grandes, Arizona, because it served dishes from central Mexico that were unknown in Sonora. The border-straddling *maquiladora* industry soon began to overcome this regional isolation, drawing migrants from farther south to work in assembly plants. In the 1960s, when the first Yucatecan restaurant opened in Hermosillo, its name Chichen Itza sounded Chinese to many Sonorans. The restaurant's special, "Escabeche Oriental," admittedly confuses even some Yucatecans, who are no longer familiar with this archaic reference to the city of Valladolid as "oriental," meaning east of Mérida.[63]

Likewise in the northern industrial capital of Monterrey, urbanization spurred the growth of cabrito restaurants as a nostalgic recreation of a rural past, even as migrant workers began introducing tacos from other parts of the country. Informal food markets in the city date back at least to *fritangas* (fried-food shops) of the 1930s, a decade of revolutionary unrest, when union strife threatened the social supremacy of Porfirian industrial groups. Restaurants of the period such as Los Norteños and El Principal had little more than a grill for roasting cabrito, a cauldron to fry the organ meats, and a comal for heating tortillas, but customers waited in line to get the cheap, local comfort food. Jesús Alberto Martínez worked as a youth in fritanga kitchens of the 1950s, standing on soft-drink cases to reach the comal, before he went on to establish one of the city's leading tourist restaurants, El Rey del Cabrito (King of Kid). At the same time, migrant workers in more peripheral barrios introduced their own culinary traditions, including *tacos rojos* (red tacos) from Matehuala, tacos dorados (golden fried tacos) from Querétaro, barbacoa from San Luis Potosí, tacos al pastor from Puebla, and *tacos al vapor* (steamed tacos) from Zacatecas. Thus, even as the middle classes developed a taste for rustic cabrito as a local symbol, the working classes adopted a more cosmopolitan dining culture reflecting the rich variety of Mexican cuisine.[64]

Ethnic and National Cuisines

Similar forces of industrialization and nationalism helped to consolidate Mexican and Mexican American regional cuisines in the mid-twentieth century.

The power of nationalism to standardize cultures within borders while exaggerating cross-border differences can finally explain the curious evolution of the burrito. Formerly a regional antojito in nineteenth-century Guanajuato, the burrito was likely obliterated by the spread of the upstart taco in the first half of the twentieth century, reaching out from the nation's capital to achieve a form of gastronomic and linguistic hegemony. The burrito survived in Sonora and California by taking on a new and distinct identity, cloaked in a wheat flour tortilla, which was itself a relative culinary novelty. Even in California, the taco made inroads, particularly during the formative period of the 1930s and 1940s. While soft tacos came to be associated with relatively small flour tortillas, corn tortillas were transformed into hard tacos, the model for the taco shell. The subsequent spread of Mexican American fast food out of Los Angeles helped to establish what had been a peculiar local nomenclature—burritos and hard and soft tacos—throughout the United States. Migration and food processing thus created an industrial image of Mexican food that was almost completely unrecognizable in Mexico.

Despite these national differences, transnational ties persisted even among the Mexican American generation. Already in 1977, for example, the Monterrey restaurant Regio was serving a recognizable plate of fajitas. Founded as a small fritanga in 1962 by José Inés Cantú Venegas, the restaurant had expanded into a large, elegant dining room, complete with waiters in black and purple uniforms, serving exquisite Hereford meat from local pastures. A Mexican food critic observed: "As a curious detail, meats are not charcoal broiled but broiled with Mexican mesquite shrub kindling, served on a wooden board and on a hot stainless steel plate."[65]

Although Mexican American foods developed in a distinctive fashion, they were not completely alienated from home cooking, at least at the time. After all, Mexican American cooks invented the fast-food taco and it was only much later that corporate formulators reworked it. One testament to the power of food to symbolize both Mexican cultural identity and United States citizenship came from Marine Sergeant Roberto Luis Ferrera, who was born in San Luis Potosí and won both the Silver Star and the Purple Heart at Saipan during World War II. Returning home to Los Angeles, he told an interviewer from *La Prensa* that his greatest wish was "not to be taken from the United States and put in a place where I cannot eat 'burritos' and 'taquitos.'"[66]

This is not to deny the consequences of segregation in Mexican restaurants, particularly at a psychological level for Mexican workers forced to tolerate rude treatment from clients and the ubiquitous imagery of sombrero-clad peasants. Nevertheless, such stereotypes had become increasingly outdated by the end of this period. In 1967, when Frito-Lay attempted to market their corn chips to Mexicans for the first time, they made a classic advertising blunder by creating the character of the Frito Bandito. The Mexican American community was outraged by the revival of "bandito" stereotypes and forced the company to withdraw the campaign. A decade later, President Gerald Ford suffered from another culinary gaffe while campaigning in San Antonio. Eager to win the support of minority voters, he bit into a tamal without stopping to remove the husk. The image was broadcast on television newscasts, and although it may not have cost him the election, it certainly reminded politicians of the growing influence of the Mexican American community.[67]

By the 1970s, Mexican American foods had begun to gain a nationwide following, far beyond the Mexican community. A wave of mergers within the food-processing industry and the growing search for new product lines further consolidated the importance of this ethnic food market. The standardization of Mexican American food would wane already in the 1980s as a new generation of migrants began arriving with their own regional cuisines. But before this could happen, Anglos had already begun to carry Mexican American tacos around the world, thereby establishing global reputations and intensifying the competition with culinary nationalists in Mexico.

PART III

Global Tacos

THE FIRST WAVE OF GLOBAL MEXICAN

I n the summer of 1964, a young American high school gym teacher named Thomas Estes was sitting in an Amsterdam coffee shop, inhaling a cloud of sweet-smelling smoke and thinking that he had finally found the place where he belonged. There was just one problem: the famously tolerant Dutch society was not open to foreigners perceived as freeloaders, including hippies from the United States. To obtain a permanent residency visa, he had to be self-employed, so when summer vacation ended, he returned to his teaching job in East Los Angeles. But the dream of living in Amsterdam never left him, and a few years later, on a road trip to Panama, inspiration struck—he would open Europe's first Mexican restaurant. Making a U-turn on the Inter-American Highway, he headed back toward California, stopping along the way to pick up decorations and menu ideas for the restaurant. He struck it rich in Mazatlán when the family of a former student put him in touch with an executive at the Pacífico Brewery, who filled his Volkswagen bus with ashtrays, signs, t-shirts, and other old promotional materials. Estes never made it to Panama, but in 1976, he opened the Café Pacífico in Amsterdam's Red Light District, the only real estate he could afford. With pioneers like Estes, Mexican food entered the global stage with a Southwestern accent and a reputation for beaches and beer.[1]

Most of these early entrepreneurs were not Mexican themselves, but they felt such a strong attachment to the food that they went to great efforts to recreate it abroad. By establishing restaurants and specialty grocery stores, they built communities of people who shared this desire for foods that were not so much Mexican American as American Mexican. Such businesses sprang up wherever expatriates congregated, around military bases, oil fields, tourist destinations, even remote surfing beaches. Like the first Mexican migrants traveling beyond the Southwestern United States half a century earlier, these pioneers needed considerable ingenuity to reproduce an ethnic cuisine outside of its traditional source of supply. The simplest foods were often the most difficult to reproduce, particularly fresh corn tortillas. Fortunately for these postwar migrants, Mexican engineers had developed affordable, portable technology for mechanizing tortilla production in rural areas. But this was not always enough, and, contrary to the hippie ethic of returning to the land and renouncing corporate production, Mexican food pioneers often depended on canned goods from Old El Paso. Yet even this was not so different from the olive oil and cheese imported by Italian migrants as a flavor from home or the soy sauce and dried mushrooms that the Chinese diaspora used to recreate their cuisine. The global spread of the taco was, in short, a classic immigrant story, but, this time, the ethnics carrying Mexican food abroad were Americans.[2]

The images and dishes first established by taco aficionados were eventually followed by corporate vendors, who used their greater financial resources to create more reliable supply chains and to build markets through large-scale advertising. These food processors also came mainly from the United States, and their international sales grew directly out of the infrastructure first developed to supply North American markets. But as Mexican food acquired global recognition, local firms in Europe and Australia also began to develop homegrown versions, and because they were closer to the customers they were serving, if not to the original Mexican models, they were often able to compete effectively against giants like Old El Paso. Just as the early modern globalization of ingredients such as maize and chiles inspired countless local cooking experiments, Mexican food was adapted to fit the culinary sensibilities of cultures around the world. Mexican firms were relatively late arrivals on this field and, rather than seek to assert claims of authenticity, they were often willing to follow patterns that were already well engrained, recognizing that their local knowledge of Mexican consumers would be of little use in global markets.

Figure 6.1. "Takos" in the former Yugoslavia. Mexican restaurant in Maribor, Slovenia. Photo by Donna R. Gabaccia.

The periodization of Mexico's global cuisine followed the history of the Cold War. During World War II, servicemen and women began to carry chili con carne around the world, and in the postwar era, the taco spread internationally in parallel with its U.S. diffusion. Perhaps the granddaddy of overseas restaurants, founded in 1967 by the Californian Bill Chicote on Australia's Gold Coast, is called Taco Bill. Relatively few Mexicans participated in the global migration of their food during this period, although they established some of the most interesting restaurants. Thus, the weight of numbers ensured that Mexican American models predominated. With the fall of the Iron Curtain, Tex-Mex came into its own, further distancing these restaurants from ties to Mexico. In 1995, for example, the *Financial Times* declared: "Moscow in Throes of Tex-Mex Craze."[3] As the first wave of global Mexican food crested around the millennium, a diverse international marketplace had been created, with well-established stereotypes but also considerable space for new adaptations.

The Pioneers

"In response to many requests we have pleasure in offering a complete range of Mexican foods now available for the first time in this country." Thus began a classified advertisement posted in the London *Observer* in 1960 by a grocer called Gray's in the Midlands town of Worcester. The standard package included an eight-ounce tin of tortillas along with enchilada sauce, chili con carne, and assorted condiments, shipped for £2.50. The advertisement did not specify a brand name but it did conclude with a warning, or perhaps a promise: "These specialties are very hot."[4] Gray's may not have been the first commercial distributor of Mexican food in the United Kingdom, but it represented an early example of patterns that came to dominate global food supplies. The combined promise and warning about the heat of Mexican food conveyed a sense of exoticism. Meanwhile, tins of tortillas, sauce, and the like were the most convenient, if not the most satisfying, way of provisioning Mexican food on a global scale, given the lack of widespread knowledge about cooking and eating it. Finally, the spread of Mexican food benefited from the tremendous growth of the restaurant industry in the final decades of the twentieth century, not only in North America, but also in Western Europe, Australia, and Japan.[5]

As an emerging superpower in the postwar era, the United States projected its military influence around the world, leading to the large-scale deployment of soldiers and support personnel, whose taste for Mexican food added an entirely new dimension to the concept of cultural imperialism. The many requests that Gray's received for Mexican food were no doubt from American visitors, although it remains a mystery why the store was located in the Midlands of England, rather than in the east, where military bases were concentrated, or around a tourist center such as London. The original inquiry at Gray's may have come from a single individual, perhaps a serviceman from Texas who had married a local woman and wanted to spice up the family table. Mexican food certainly made it into individual care packages, although they left little mention in the historical record.

Military personnel who were born or stationed in the U.S. Southwest seem to have developed particular cravings for Mexican food while on duty abroad. Troops had acquired this taste already on the frontier in the late nineteenth century. During World War I, Lieutenant Morrison Wood, a Midwesterner undergoing training in San Antonio, claimed that a bowl of chili con carne made by a regimental cook named Jesús Mendoza saved his life when the icy winds of a Texas storm caught him unaware. During World War II, the army shipped vast quantities of canned chili to the front, prompting the humorist Art Buchwald to imagine the Eastern European principality of Lovlost, where the "gastronomic regional specialties" included "Heinz pork and beans, Hormel's Spam, and Mother O'Hara's chili con carne. Most of it was left over from the war when the American army had a food supply depot just outside the capital."[6] Don Dedera, a member of the Arizona National Guard, added a personal testimony: "Wherever the Arizona [National] Guard goes, it takes a pack of Mañanaland spices. In the Pacific in World War II, the Bushmasters ate C-rations tacos. During the Berlin crisis, they invented wiener-schnitzel tamales."[7]

Although the quartermaster's bureaucracy could imagine little beyond chili con carne, units with Mexican cooks tasted more interesting fare. Jesse Arrambide, founder of the Mexican cafeteria chain Pancho's, got his start in food service in the galley of a navy ship during World War II. He varied the standard-issue rations with his mother's recipes for tamales, enchiladas, and tacos.[8] Nor were U.S. soldiers the only ones to project chile power in the global struggle for democracy. Mexico's 201st Fighter Squadron, serving in the Philippines in 1945, supplemented their rations with familiar tropical produce foraged from the countryside, including mangos, coconuts, and papayas. On one occasion, the vagaries of military supply lines delivered a large cache of pinto beans to a neighboring unit of U.S. pilots, who gladly traded with the Mexicans, allowing the 201st a feast of frijoles.[9]

Over time, military supply chains began to branch out in recognition of the multicultural origins of military personnel. Texas food processors such as Patio Foods acquired lucrative military contracts. Joe B. Martínez of the Alamo Masa Company explained: "It also helps business in San Antonio that military people try Mexican food, like it, and come back for more."[10] International companies also saw potential profits from the demand for spicy foods by U.S. troops stationed abroad. For example, "in 1965 a West German store chain, Karstadt, opened a special department handling 'genuine Texas foods,' in the vicinity of American military bases."[11] Even small-scale producers such as Don Perfecto Mancha, a sausage maker from Eagle Pass, Texas, took advantage of military logistics systems to ship his renowned chorizo to army bases in Vietnam.[12]

The crew-cut crowd shared the taco predilection with long-haired hippies, and although soldiers had an institutional structure to satisfy their Mexican food cravings, members of the counterculture had the time and energy for entrepreneurship. Surfers, in particular, needed to support their habit or at least feed themselves between sets, and tacos were a cheap and readily available food in the areas that they frequented. The Polynesian art of surfing had been introduced to California and Australia in the early twentieth century, but participants remained a small community until Hollywood discovered the sport around 1960. Malibu was an early hub of surfing in Southern California, but aficionados traveled frequently up and down the coast, searching for perfect waves on deserted beaches. On one road trip to Baja, Estes carried bags of avocados, which were cheap at harvest time in the fields north of San Diego, and he bartered them on the beaches for tacos. The informal nature of the sport ensured that even prominent surfers lived and ate simply. In the late 1950s, the big-wave surfer Pat Curren flew "to Hawaii one season with no luggage save a ten-pound sack of flour for making tortillas."[13] Pop culture recognized the Malibu-Mexican food connection in the 1970s television series *Rockford Files*, starring James Garner as a down-and-out private detective with a taste for tacos.

Members of the counterculture who wanted to support themselves making tacos needed considerable expertise in the early days of the global supermarket. In 1967, "Taco Bill" Chicote traveled from Southern California to open a Mexican restaurant on the Gold Coast of Queensland, a surfing haven near the Great Barrier Reef, with just a corn grinder and tortilla machine, confident that he could improvise the rest. Estes carried even less to Amsterdam, just a hand-cranked tortilla roller with an oval blade, a common device in rural Mexico. Rather than use fresh corn, he imported dried masa from the Valley

Grain Company of Madeira, California, clearing customs through a Rotterdam grain agent. He purchased a pair of used domestic stoves at a flea market and fitted them with sheet metal plates as griddles. Like thousands of Mexican women in the countryside, Estes started work early in the morning to make the tortillas and spread them out around the kitchen to cool so they would not turn moldy. He had to recreate these provisioning networks when opening new outlets in London in 1982 and Paris in 1984. At first, he supplied the restaurant chain through informal means, smuggling tortillas on the channel ferry from Holland to England in a hippie "Magic Bus." By contrast, in 1976, the Swedish founder of El Sombrero, Stockholm's first Mexican restaurant, could afford to recreate a small tortilla factory, although he had to send off to Mexico for replacement parts when the machine broke down.[14]

The problem of acquiring ingredients was also shared by expatriates from the Southwest. Earlene Ridge, an Arizona native, recalled the difficulty of assembling a Mexican meal while living in Paris in the early 1980s. She could reproduce by hand the Sonoran wheat flour tortillas of her youth using French wheat. To buy fresh green chile peppers similar to jalapeños, she made a pilgrimage to Algerian markets in the *banlieu*, picking up pinto beans and cumin along the way. A combination of grated Cantal and Edam provided an acceptable substitute for longhorn cheese, and hamburger meat, tomato, and limes were also readily available in local supermarkets. The avocados used to garnish the meal were shipped across the Atlantic, which, together with tequila, were the only ingredients that actually came from Mexico. In each new location, émigrés had to source the ingredients necessary for their Mexican food addiction. When Dennis Cogan arrived in Israel in the 1990s, he wrote to the *Jerusalem Post* to find a local version of Monterey Jack cheese suitable for enchiladas. The food columnist recommended Tirani, Gilboa, or Emek.[15]

Not all the pioneers of global Mexican food came from the United States. Oshima Bari, the chef and owner of La Bamba restaurant in Osaka, Japan, told a similar story of supplying ingredients across the Pacific Rim. Like Estes, a member of the international counterculture, Bari studied Spanish at a Japanese university and spent two years backpacking in Peru and Mexico before returning home. By the time he opened his restaurant in 1986, it was possible to find packaged tortillas in Japan, but they arrived quite stale after the transoceanic voyage, and so he decided to make his own from imported masa. Bari obtained dried chiles and other ingredients through a personalized importing network that consisted of taking regular vacations to Mexico and Los Angeles, where he stuffed a hundred kilograms of kitchen supplies into his luggage. Even with the airline's excess weight charges, he saved money on the import fees. Provisioning the restaurant grew easier as Japanese consumers gained interest in exotic commodities. For example, avocados were difficult to find in the mid-1980s but had become cheaply available in local supermarkets a decade later.[16]

In addition to establishing supply chains that extended both to Mexico and the United States, these early pioneers helped to create a countercultural image of Mexican food beyond the Americas. Despite Estes's aspirations, Café Pacifico was not the first Mexican restaurant in Europe. La Cucaracha had opened in London in 1969, a year after the Mexico City Olympics, although it did not last long, both because the somber décor in a whitewashed former monastery did not meet English expectations of a Mexican atmosphere and because the food was bad.[17] When Estes settled in Amsterdam in the early 1970s, he found a small taco shop, also with a countercultural image, operated by a "beach bunny from Malibu named Debbie and her Dutch boyfriend Herman."[18] Estes owed the menu to his partner and cook, Dennis Real, who prepared chili colorado and tacos California using family recipes. Bicycling around Amsterdam wearing Pacifico T-shirts, the pair advertised the restaurant as a hippie hangout.

In France, meanwhile, Mexican food became firmly associated with a "Wild West" Tex-Mex image in the 1980s. Robb Walsh has attributed the sudden popularity of Tex-Mex to Jean-Jacques Beineix's hugely popular film, *Betty Blue* (1986), about a mentally unbalanced woman and her tequila-swigging, chili-con-carne-cooking lover, Zorg. When the film premiered, a struggling Tex-Mex restaurant in the Marais neighborhood of Paris called Le Studio, founded a few years earlier by a French-Jewish-Texan named Frank Shera, became an overnight success and spawned a dozen imitators with bizarre names such as the Indiana Tex-Mex Café.[19]

Unlike the hippie and Wild West image elsewhere in Europe, the continent's leading consumers of Mexican food, Norwegians, think of tacos as a taste of home. In 1971, inspired by the Mexico City Olympics, the import firm of Oluf Lorentzen began selling Old El Paso products in its six Oslo shops. The novelties did not move quickly off the shelves, and five years later, when Sverre Lorentzen invited his closest friends for a taco party, most had never tasted Mexican food. Sales began to pick up in 1986, when Mexico hosted the World Cup, and by 1990, one magazine estimated an annual national consumption of ten million tacos, or about two per capita. Two decades later, nearly half of all Norwegians reported eating tacos at least once a month. The typical Nordic

Figure 6.2. Café Pácifico founders Thomas Estes (top) and Dennis Real, Amsterdam, 1976. Courtesy of Philippe Salaün.

taco contains the usual Cal-Mex combination of ground beef, lettuce, tomato, and mild salsa, but with white cheese, sour cream, and more vegetables, including cucumber and canned corn. A few full-service and fast-food restaurants have opened in Norway, but the vast majority of sales remain in groceries. In fact, *Fredagstacoen* (Friday tacos) had become a domestic ritual, almost to the

Box 6.1   Cod Tacos, a Norwegian Recipe with a South-of-the-Border Twist

Place the ingredients for the marinate [sic] in a large bowl and mix before adding fish fillets. 1 can (14.5 oz) diced tomatoes; 1 can black beans, strained; 2 tablespoons wine vinegar; onions of choice, chopped; juice of 1 lemon; 2 cloves garlic, minced; ½ or less jalapeno pepper, chopped; 1 teaspoon salt. Add filets and marinate 1 hour or more and strain. Pour 1 tablespoon olive oil into large pan and add strained ingredients. Saute until fish is flaky.

Build fish tacos: Place the following ingredients in taco shells, corn or flour tortillas. Sauteed fish fillets, beans, and vegetables; Roma tomatoes firm, chopped; green onions, chopped; sharp cheddar cheese, shredded; black olives, sliced; lettuce, finely sliced; sour cream; jalapeno peppers for those who lit it hot; salsa, hot, medium or mild.

Source: "Cod Tacos," available at http://www.norway-hei.com/cod-tacos.html (accessed July 10, 2011).

point of boredom, and hosts risked derision if they served tacos to guests. One woman sniffed: "It's like serving frozen pizza."[20]

Because relatively few Mexicans were coming to Europe, entrepreneurs from other countries filled the growing demand for tacos. Migrants from throughout Latin America opened restaurants and groceries under a Mexican guise, even if they had only the most tangential connection. For example, Berlin's Casa Fiesta, a "Spanische-Mexicanische restaurant" founded by an Argentine named Cacho Gallardo, offered not a single Mexican dish on its menu. After the fall of the Iron Curtain, the Hungarian American entrepreneur George Hemmingway opened the Acapulco Restaurant in Budapest. The relationships that brought Mexican food to particular locations were often quite circuitous. Eckart Wieske was born in Leipzig, and as a young man, he fled with his family from communist East Germany. He eventually made his way to Houston, where he found work in the oil industry. With the reunification of Germany, he sought to return to the country of his birth and invest there. Because West German firms dominated industry, the comparative advantage that he had at the time was his knowledge of Mexican food, so he opened a restaurant.[21]

This is not to say that Mexicans accepted these Tex-Mex stereotypes; indeed, many individuals felt a patriotic mission to present the national cuisine in a more favorable light. In the mid-1990s, Cristina Prun opened Anahuacalli, a temple of Mexican gastronomy on the Left Bank of Paris not far from the Cathedral of Notre Dame. Stepping into the small restaurant is like entering an elegant Mexico City fonda, complete with the blue-rimmed glasses on the tables and avant-garde Latin American art tastefully decorating the walls. Menu items, including *quesadillas de cuitlacoche* (fritters stuffed with corn fungus), pork and chicken tamales, and mole de guajolote, could likewise hold their own against those of a Mexico City restaurant. Prun, the wife of a French mathematician, felt an educational mission to inform Parisians about the foods of her native land. While still depending largely on a North American tourist clientele, she gradually gained a following among French men and women who overcame initial fears of hot mole sauces. Students were among her first customers, and they introduced their parents to the restaurant as well. Over time, the educational campaign made progress. At first, she had to serve wheat bread on the table, but eventually she replaced it with corn tortillas. Thus, restaurants founded by Mexicans tended to emphasize their distinctiveness from Tex-Mex as a marketing strategy of authenticity.[22]

Many other Mexicans have also carried on this culinary evangelism, even without Prun's financial resources. In the 1980s, Jaime and Victor Casasus, engineers who grew up running a family canning firm in Mexicali, established the first tortilla factory in the United Kingdom with incentives from the Liverpool Department of Trade and Industry. In order to create demand for their product, they opened a restaurant called El Macho's Mexican Village, serving traditional favorites such as mole de guajolote. Victor explained, "We want to show Britain that there's more to Mexican food than enchiladas and taco shells."[23] Chef Carlos Hernández Cedillo, a native of Guadalajara, moved to Buenos Aires with his wife, an Argentine pastry chef, in 1997. He worked in a succession of Mexican restaurants, trying to raise the standards of their cooking, and eventually opened his own place, Quinta Escencia (The fifth sense), on the fashionable Avenida de la Libertadora. Although he made his own tortillas from nixtamal in-house, his efforts to introduce regional dishes such as *birria*, pozole, and *tortas ahogadas* met with a lukewarm reception. The most popular menu item among Argentine customers was a massive sampler platter of fajitas, tacos, and burritos—all with beef.[24]

As Mexican food expanded into new markets, from Britain and Australia in the 1960s to Eastern Europe and Israel in the 1990s, restaurateurs followed similar patterns to develop supply lines. Behind the scenes, this expansion depended on serious logistical efforts involving shipping consolidators and customs brokers, who sourced chile peppers and supplied fresh tortillas. In unfamiliar territory, rival Mexican restaurants sometimes collaborated to obtain ingredients more cheaply. Knowledgeable customers were likewise essential for the spread of tacos, not just tourists in the Latin Quarter of Paris, but also the roughnecks and oil executives who helped develop the North Sea oil fields in the 1980s and who demanded burritos and enchiladas rather than mince and tatties in the pubs of Aberdeen, Scotland.[25] Once individuals had done the work of creating a global Mexican cuisine, food-processing corporations rushed in to profit from the growing trend.

The Corporate Takeover

Tex-Mex rode to popularity on a millennial wave of globalization in the mid-1990s, more than three decades after U.S. soldiers and surfers established the first taco beachheads in Europe and Australia. This international fad grew in part from the vagaries of popular culture, such as the French craze for *Betty Blue*, but it was also the result of persistent marketing. Whereas pioneering restaurants and specialty shops catered to a small, knowledgeable clientele of tourists and expatriates, building mass markets required expensive advertising campaigns and efficient commodity chains. Corporate globalization grew directly out of the U.S. food-processing industry, which had developed packaged goods for non-Mexican consumers around midcentury and then scaled up production for the North American market in the 1970s and 1980s. Meanwhile, tequila and beer manufacturers, the first Mexican firms to compete internationally, had little incentive to challenge Tex-Mex stereotypes. Those with a more refined vision for Mexican cuisine such as Cristina Prun or even Oshima Bari were invisible on the corporate landscape. As one U.S. industry observer noted: "About the only thing missing from the boom is Mexicans, who have less and less to do with defining this country's—and now the rest of the world's—taste for their native food."[26]

Chips and salsa, the classic gringo snack, also served as an appetizer for consumers around the world beginning in the late 1980s. The combination offered a cheap and nonthreatening introduction to Mexican food—chips required even less manual dexterity than a taco shell, and the "mild" label on salsa jars alleviated fears of painful mouth burns. In the United States, journalists were already reporting on "sauce wars" between Pace Picante and its rivals by the mid-1980s, and salsa famously surpassed catsup in sales in 1991. By this point, chips and salsa had become common in British supermarkets and pubs, from which they spread to Europe and Asia. The tomato and jalapeño blend was particularly appealing for food processors because of the low cost of materials, which allowed profits as high as 30 percent, more than those for soft drinks and most other junk foods. Variants on the lucrative salty chip and hot sauce model soon began to proliferate. Gooey-yellow-cheese-smothered nachos became a standard concession item in North American movie theaters and were then exported around the world along with Hollywood blockbusters. Guacamole meanwhile transcended its Mexican origins with the help of a media blitz by the California avocado growers to associate the snack with the Super Bowl.[27]

For managers at Old El Paso, the challenge was to translate the growing popularity of hot sauce to a wider range of Mexican-themed food products. Pet Milk, which purchased the brand in 1969, focused on domestic expansion in the 1970s, and did not form an international group to manage exports until 1982. Moving first into the UK and Switzerland, the company sought to cultivate a posh image by introducing the brand at the upscale retailer, Harrods. In the pre-Internet days, distributors helpfully supplied promotional cookbooks with adaptations of familiar Anglo recipes such as "Chili Potato Puffs" and "Taco Scrambler" to complement the more exotic "South of the Border Enchiladas." Although international markets remained small in the 1980s, the company gradually expanded into continental Europe, Australia, and Japan. Old El Paso became a truly global brand in 1995 when purchased by the London-based Grand Metropolitan. The British market for Mexican food was still only 68 cents per capita at the time, but GrandMet predicted global sales would soon exceed $1 billion annually. To help achieve that goal, its corporate headquarters sent in experts from another subsidiary, Pillsbury, whose engineers applied technologies such as corrugated light-bulb packaging to resolve the "dread taco-shell breakage problem."[28]

As Mexican food gained a global following, rival corporations felt that they could not neglect this growing market segment. Campbell's Soup became a major competitor with the acquisition of Pace in 1994, and the canned-soup giant's advertising weight leveraged picante sales from Winnipeg to Düsseldorf. Yet corporate consolidation did not deter local firms from entering the market and even challenging established giants. For example, Discovery Foods of Daventry, England, started in 1989 as a supplier of food service tortillas but later expanded into supermarket sales and bottled sauces, including

Figure 6.3. A Tokyo department store display of Old El Paso canned foods. Photo by the author.

Mexican mole and Indian curry, to accompany its flat breads. Mexican food was therefore considered to be less a national cuisine than a spicy product line adaptable to any new trend. Perhaps the most successful contender for this market was the Swedish brand Santa Maria Tex Mex. Launched in 1991 as an Old El Paso knockoff by a company called Nordfalks, it benefited from a growing Scandinavian taste for home-cooked Mexican meals. A decade after its introduction, Tex-Mex had become Nordfalks's best-selling line, and the parent company changed its name to Santa Maria AB. By 2010, the company had overtaken Old El Paso in European market share and had also developed export markets as far away as Bangalore. Thus, Santa Maria had learned yet another global marketing lesson of using business expatriates familiar with the brand as an international sales force.[29]

International advertisements often straddled a hazy mental borderland between Mexico and Texas. Grocers selling to housewives learned from the marketing disaster of the Frito Bandito and avoided the cantina imagery favored by many restaurants. Pace executives expressed a desire to change the name "picante," if it had not already defined the salsa market. Meanwhile, Old El Paso's yellow labels evoked an exotic but anonymous desert landscape of cacti and mesas. As the market leader, Old El Paso had a significant investment in the Mexican food category, and managers developed it with great care. In 2005, the brand's new owners, General Mills, commissioned a U.K. cable channel to produce an unusual advertising campaign in the form of a cooking series starring the celebrity chef Gino D'Acampo entitled "An Italian in Mexico." The six episodes of the first season highlighted basic ingredients of Mexican cooking: tortillas, beans, chiles, meat, seafood, and chocolate. Like similar shows, the series featured cooking demonstrations by guest chefs and visits to markets, including Mexico City's gargantuan Central de Abastos. The handsome spokesman had little credibility with industry insiders, who considered him more of an entertainer than a serious chef, and he seemed to convey authority on Mexican cuisine to British viewers through the force of a thick Italian accent. Company officials explained that the goal of the campaign was simply to improve viewers' opinions of Mexican cuisine and to deliver one basic message: it's not too hot. They bargained, no doubt correctly, that watching Mexican women pat out fresh corn tortillas or grind chiles on a metate would convince many consumers to purchase taco shells and bottled salsas.[30]

The millennial fad for Mexican food also benefited the drink industry. Tequila exports had begun on a small scale already in the nineteenth century, but it was only in the 1940s that the rustic Mexican moonshine developed into a high-tech distilling industry. Eladio Sauza, a prominent distiller and hacienda owner in Tequila, Jalisco, had anticipated revolutionary land reform by diversifying his assets with the purchase of urban real estate in nearby Guadalajara and the city's first commercial radio station. Sauza's media connections and stable of mariachi musicians helped launch an advertising campaign to change tequila's working-class image. Popular *ranchero* movies featured obligatory cantina scenes with paeans to tequila by Pedro Infante and other singing cowboys. The worm at the bottom of the tequila bottle was another invented tradition. According to legend, the pickled gusano provided a rustic indication of alcohol content (if too low, the worm would rot), but in fact, it was added in the 1940s as a marketing gimmick by modernizing distillers seeking to enshrine tequila within a homespun national identity.[31]

Sauza and his leading rival, José Cuervo, also laid the foundations for global marketing, although it took another half century to achieve their desired image. In 1950, the *New York Times* informed readers how to drink tequila "in the approved manner, preceded by a lick of salt, followed by a taste of lime."[32] Daring souls could even buy gusanos, canned, at Bloomingdales. Bartenders meanwhile invented a range of cocktails, and by the early 1960s, Los Angeles restaurants were advertising "the famous Margarita."[33] Yet despite efforts to make tequila upscale, the drink retained an edgy bordertown image, best suited to the masculine excess of fraternity parties. It gained wider acceptance only in the 1990s, and probably not as a result of advertising; indeed, the sudden boom surprised producers, who faced a severe agave shortage. Instead of marketing, experts attributed tequila sales to tourism, increased consumption by women, and renewed acceptance by the Mexican middle classes, for whom the drink had fallen out of fashion after the decline of ranchero movies.[34]

Whatever the cause, industry leaders sought to manage the windfall by cultivating more upscale consumers, particularly women. Production focused on smooth, high-end *añejo* (aged for at least one year in oak casks) tequilas made from 100 percent blue agave, rather than the rough 51 percent *mixto* blended with other alcohols. Marketing campaigns employed distinctive rustic bottle designs and the rarified language of the sommelier. "Tequila is just as complicated as a fine wine when it comes to aromatic components," explained Ana Maria Romero, master taster for Sauza. "The blue agave grown in the highlands of Jalisco contains more water while agave from the flatlands has more herbal notes and more fiber."[35] Advertisers even devised a new etiquette for customers unwilling to spend hundreds of dollars a bottle only to mask the flavors with salt and lime. "Rather than swirling tequila, place your palm over the mouth of the glass and shake the liquid to release its aromas. One hundred percent blue agave tequila will smell of white pepper, pine needles and fresh herbs. Mixto tequila may exude an off aroma of burnt rubber."[36]

Mexico's leading brewer, Grupo Modelo, also shared in the export bonanza, and its best-selling brand, Corona, helped to push Mexican food onto a global stage. Founded in Mexico City in 1925, the company expanded out of its regional market in the 1950s and 1960s by purchasing other local beers, including Victoria, Pacífico, and León. When it began exporting Corona to the United States in 1979, Modelo adapted to local preferences by using ordinary brown bottles in place of the distinctive clear-glass longnecks with a painted crown logo sold in Mexico. After a few years of disappointing sales, the company reintroduced the brand in Texas and Southern California, this time with clear bottles, and it soon took off. Corona was popular first among surfers and other visitors to Mexico, who recognized the familiar bottles from Baja beaches and bordertown bars. In 1986, it broke out of niche markets. Shortages were reported throughout the Southwest, and the formerly regional distribution rapidly expanded nationwide. Sales rose from 1.6 million cases in 1984 to more than 12 million two years later. Consumers were found to be overwhelmingly young professional and college-aged men.[37]

Bartenders and brewers alike were baffled by Corona's sudden popularity. The former reported bizarre ritual behavior among young men who asked for bottles, rather than mugs, along with a slice of lime. They pushed the lime into the bottle and drank the beer, leaving the lime at the bottom. Modelo spokespeople focused instead on the high quality of the beer and said nothing about its plebeian reputation in Mexico. Competitors insisted that the fad would soon pass, given the fickle nature of Corona's young, male market. To hurry the decline of this foreign upstart, rival distributors began spreading rumors that the beer was contaminated with urine. These claims were all the more inflammatory given the widespread restrictionist outcry over Mexican migration in the mid-1980s. Barton Brands, the licensed importer, sued and obtained a settlement that including written statements from competitors attesting to the purity of Corona.[38]

Modelo took the rumors very seriously, and sales continued to rise. Mexican reporters, who were equally surprised by Corona's dramatic surge, gained access to inside information unavailable to journalists in the United States. According to the national press, Modelo had conducted focus groups with their primary demographic, North American male college students. When asked to explain their preference, large numbers responded, no doubt smirking, "It looks like another liquid."[39]

Far from worrying about impurities, hip young consumers laughed at the scatological joke. Modelo directors embraced the Spring Break image their beer conveyed and built an enduring ad campaign around the beach vacation. Abandoning their initial slogan, "Go for the border," they recruited as a pitchman the singer Jimmy Buffett of "Margaritaville" fame, who was already a well-known customer. In 1992, the company rolled out a new slogan, "Change your whole latitude." Similar inane but catchy promotions enthralled youth around the world. In Europe, Corona sponsored events such as the Swedish "Rock Train" music tour and a German coed naked volleyball championship. The keepers of Teutonic brewing traditions were soon bewailing the uncouth behavior of "yuppies" pushing slices of lime down longneck bottles of *Aztekenbier* in Munich discotheques. In many Asian markets, by contrast, tourists were the principal consumers, particularly in beach resorts, and the 2004 tsunami caused a temporary sales crisis throughout the Indian Ocean basin.[40]

Despite its plebeian origins, Corona commanded premium prices in international markets, and formerly dismissive rivals sought to imitate it. Anheuser-Busch introduced a lime-flavored product called Tequiza, which flopped, and it more profitably purchased a minority stake in Modelo to benefit from the Mexican success. In two decades, Corona catapulted to number four in international sales. No longer just a Mexican beer, it became a global brand that happened to be made in Mexico.

The arrival of corporate chains and affluent investors in the 1990s also transformed the nature of Mexican restaurants. When Russell Ramsland, Sr., a Midland, Texas, oil magnate, decided that London needed a good place to get nachos and a margarita, there was no question that he would be making tortillas in the morning. After a long search, Ramsland found a suitable location for his grandiosely named Texas Embassy Cantina near London's Trafalgar Square in the building that had once housed the ticket office of the Titanic. Unfortunately, when he arrived to close the deal wearing a snakeskin blazer and cowboy boots, the real estate agent judged him an inappropriate tenant for the site, in plain view of Admiral Nelson's statue. It took a full year to secure the lease, and even longer to renovate the site. Ramsland spared no expense, hiring a prominent design firm to recreate an Old Texas bordertown with everything but dust and "live horses at the bar."[41] North American chains such as Chi-Chi's and El Torito also established an international presence, although they had to compete with local versions such as the bizarrely named Parisian restaurant chain, Indiana Tex-Mex.

Taco Bell, curiously, has struggled to build global markets for fast-food Mexican, despite its association with KFC and Pizza Hut in Yum!, the world's largest restaurant group. In the late 1970s, the company launched its first international ventures in Canada and Guam, the latter benefiting from both a substantial U.S. military presence and a local population long familiar with tortillas. Although Taco Bell subsequently opened stores in countries such as Argentina, Australia, China, Costa Rica, Poland, Singapore, and even Mexico, these efforts in the 1990s and 2000s generally ended in failure. Defense Department contracts enabled Taco Bell to operate on military bases around the world, but these outlets were restricted to service personnel and dependents. A disgruntled group of young American expatriates in South Korea organized an Internet campaign to make the chain more readily available to civilians. A branch duly opened in 2010 as part of yet another expansion effort that also included stores in India and Greece. It remained to be seen whether Korean youth would transfer their

Figure 6.4. A Taco Bell international success story, near the San José campus of the Universidad de Costa Rica. Photo by the author.

loyalty from kimchi to fire sauce. Although KFC, McDonald's, and other global chains have adapted their menus to local tastes, Mexican fast food has proven more difficult to market in this fashion, and Taco Bell continues to search for a viable international formula.[42]

The need for skilled kitchen labor led to many unusual connections as Mexican food spread around the world. In the early days, restaurant supply companies like Discovery literally had to build the industry from the ground up, educating chefs on how to make a taco or quesadilla, explaining costs and price points. Aspiring international chains sent local workers to Mexico or, perhaps more often, to the United States for training. For example, when the Tex-Mex chain Mama Ninfa's opened in Leipzig, the German chef Sven Hofmann traveled to Houston to learn the menu. Although he quickly mastered the signature fajitas, Hofmann admitted: "My tortillas are German tortillas. They are square. But I will learn how to make them round before the restaurant opens."[43] Existing networks of middle- and working-class migration often took advantage of each new restaurant fad. In Paris, Lebanese reportedly ran many

Mexican restaurants, employing workers from former French colonies in North and West Africa. One restaurant had so many kitchen workers from India that Parisians called it "the home of the Tamil tamale."[44] Yet skillful cooks could often produce credible versions of Mexican food, regardless of national origins. After eating a "terrific" enchilada at the unpromising Restaurant O'Mexico in Paris, John Henderson, a Denver journalist, discovered that the owner, Sam Melhotra, had come from Delhi to study restaurant management, and the cook was from Nepal. A Mexican restaurant in Ulan Bator, Mongolia, apparently relied on a Cuban cook who had been studying in Tashkent when the Soviet Union dissolved.[45]

This complicated mixing should come as no surprise; Italians historically opened French restaurants in the United States, while Greeks took over Italian pizza kitchens, and Chinese now dominate the Thai sector. The international spread of Mexican food has been dominated largely by U.S. corporations, to the point that industry figures referred to the market as "gringo food."[46] Although the modern globalization of Mexican food began with North American packages and stereotypes, they no longer capture the full range of local adaptations.

Of Cactus and Cannibals

The twin icons of Tex-Mex and Aztecs have competed to define the image of Mexican food on a global stage, but they share common stereotypes of exoticism and youthful excess. The more common of the two has been the Tex-Mex bordertown, replete with cacti and sombreros. Indians, another standard motif in restaurants such as this, were more likely to be drawn from Hollywood depictions of Great Plains warriors, or perhaps a drugstore wooden Indian, than from Aztecs or Maya. Also common were images of Pancho Villa and Emiliano Zapata, although these revolutionary heroes may often be conflated in tourists' minds with nondescript banditos, also a stock figure in Hollywood Westerns. The anthropologist Rachel Black, who worked as a waitress at Lyon's El Sombrero while studying French, described the appeal of such restaurants as a *non-lieu*, or "no-place," a grown-up Disneyland where customers could act out Hollywood fantasies. A tall, striking woman, Black played the part with cowboy boots, hat, holster, and a whistle, which she blew when customers drank tequila shots. Her elementary French at the time was a genuine asset in conveying Texas exoticism to visitors who cared little that she spoke with a Canadian accent.[47]

Such Texan associations have a long history in the United States, and early international restaurants such as Stockholm's El Sombrero picked up on them. When restaurants arrived in the former Communist bloc in the 1990s, they advertised Tex-Mex dishes from the beginning and made no pretense of serving Mexican food. For a time, Santa Fe was one of the most fashionable restaurants in Moscow, while the Tequila House took Kiev by storm. One of the first expatriate restaurants to open in Beijing with economic liberalization was called Mexican Wave, although about the only gestures to Mexico were Corona, tequila, cacti, sombreros, and bandito murals. The Chinese cooks in the kitchen actually specialized in pizza.[48]

The beachfront cantina offers a variant on the Tex-Mex image, often drawing more inspiration from California than from Texas. Although the cactus and sombrero remain ubiquitous in these establishments, the desert imagery competes with ocean scenes such as Acapulco cliff diving and, at Café Pacifico, a marlin mascot mounted on the wall. Surfing associations have been particularly prominent in Australia, not just with the original Taco Bill restaurants,

Figure 6.5. Surfers and Aztecs on the Gold Coast of Australia. Photo by the author.

but also among rival chains such as Montezuma's, a Brisbane chain that claimed outlets "from the Sun Coast to the Gold Coast."

The Aztec calendar logo of Montezuma's illustrates a second major source of imagery for Mexican restaurants, the ruins of pre-Hispanic civilizations. A literary work that helped to establish this association in the modern European imagination was Italo Calvino's short story, "Sotto il sole giaguaro" (Under the jaguar sun, 1985), about a tourist couple fighting against the backdrop of savage Oaxaca. The passion of their struggle arouses their hunger for the equally barbaric splendors of Mexican food, chiles, mezcal, gorditas, and tropical fruits. The unfolding story line turns on a supposed cannibalistic instinct in the Mexican past and in the contemporary lovers. Such imagery, and even quotes from Calvino, appeared in Las Rosas, a Mexican restaurant founded in Turin, Italy, in 1993 by Alexander Franco Gaviria, who rejected the Tex-Mex image and insisted that he offered the "real" Mexico of Moctezuma, mole, and the Virgin of Guadalupe.[49] Calvino's tourists were, like many young people, influenced by New Age spiritualism who sought to discover new experiences and ancient spirituality among the ruins of Maya pyramids. The construction of the Cancún beach resort in the 1970s made these archaeological sites even more accessible. Thus, Aztec imagery became a marker of authenticity, although no less commercialized, in a restaurant world crowded with Tex-Mex stereotypes.[50]

Those who wished to reproduce these experiences at home could turn to one of the first Mexican cookbooks published in Europe, Ilona Steckhan's *Die Küche der Azteken: Rezepte einer versunkenen Kultur* (The kitchen/cuisine of the Aztecs: Recipes of a lost culture, 1987). Along with recipes for mole de guajolote, pit-roasted suckling pig, and hamburger taco filling, Steckhan recounted the indigenous legends of pulque, vanilla, and cacao.[51] Germans who lacked the energy to cook Mexican could visit restaurants such as Farolito (Little lighthouse) in the Südstern neighborhood of Berlin. The presentation of the dishes at this restaurant may have reflected the hippie nature of German tourists to Mexico. Although the restaurant was not strictly vegetarian, nonmeat options filled the menu. Those expecting a carnivorous meal would be disappointed, for even the beef tostadas were balanced precariously atop a pyramid of greens.

These international perceptions of primitivism were often mediated through the Mexican middle class and its exotic nationalist fantasies, as can be clearly seen in another Berlin restaurant named Frida Kahlo. Painted the exact shade of the artist's Blue House in Coyoacán, the restaurant featured Aztec calendar glyphs and a sign announcing "Pulquería Mexicana." The clientele consisted primarily of university students who had taken over crumbling apartment blocks in Prenzlauer Berg in the former East Berlin. Even as these unauthorized urban squatters ate their late afternoon breakfast, they left their feather bedding to air on the balconies in tidy bourgeois German fashion. The restaurant catered to this crowd by serving breakfast until 5 P.M., and only the names on the menu bore any connection to Mexico. Thus, the "Poblano" referred to neither mole nor chiles but rather a Nutella sandwich, while the "D.F." consisted of *schinken und käse* (ham and cheese), and the "Yucatan" featured smoked salmon, horseradish, and chopped boiled egg. The most Mexican dish—or perhaps the closest overlap in the two cuisines—was *helotes*, boiled corn on the cob slathered with mayonnaise, grated cheese, and chile powder.

Aztec exoticism reached the pinnacle of sophistication in the 1990s with the marketing of artisanal chocolate. Seeking to differentiate their chocolate from cloying, mass-produced Belgian products, French chocolatiers reduced the sugar content to reveal the complex, bitter flavors of cacao. Advertising campaigns associated this more refined chocolate with exotic images of the Aztecs, the mythical Quetzalcoatl, and Moctezuma quaffing chocolate as an aphrodisiac before visiting his concubines. Another publicity boost came from Joanne Harris's popular novel *Chocolat* (1999), which featured a modern-day sorceress with vaguely Mayan origins who enlivens a French provincial town with magical chocolate. Fueled by these images of ancient Mexico, gourmet French chocolate soon became an export industry of its own, with elite outposts such as Quetzalcoatl Chocolatier near the Piazza di Spagna in Rome and Jacques Torres and La Maison du Chocolat in New York City. Searching for authenticity, these chocolatiers blended ancho and chipotle peppers and bits of cornmeal into products with names such as Aztec Elixir. Journalists also contributed to this savage imagery, describing an unsweetened 70 percent cacao brand called Maya as "a true shock to the system, a reminder that chocolate was once drunk by high priests, before a sacrifice."[52]

A decade into the new millennium, it became possible to find better-informed versions of Mexican food claiming authenticity through references to trendy street food. The British celebrity chef Thomasina Meirs opened one such restaurant in London called Wahaca, which used sustainably raised, locally sourced, and seasonally available ingredients to prepare credible taquitos, tostadas, and quesadillas. In a similar fashion, when a Turin chef, Alexander Gaviria, opened a second branch of Las Rosas, he made it a taquería. But not all of these

Mexican street foods were yuppie translations. Turkish entrepreneurs in many German cities added burritos and nachos to the döner-kebab and pizza served at *Imbiße* (snack shops) for working customers.[53]

The dueling exotics of Mexican cuisine, Tex-Mex and Aztecs, were not mutually exclusive but overlapped with one another, while also incorporating other images of Mexico that conveyed local meanings. The Hispanic world was replete with stereotypes of Mexico, and the crudest versions were often adopted for youth-oriented venues; for example, Córdoba's first Mexican restaurant was El Hijo de la Chingada (son of a bitch).[54] Meanwhile, the Spanish pop singer Joaquín Sabina opened a Madrid restaurant called La Mordida, which literally means "bite" but is also Mexican slang for a bribe. The logo featured a woman's mouth, with brightly painted lips, biting a chile jalapeño, yet another sexual innuendo. In other parts of the world, Mexico had virtually no local references, and the food blended into a homogeneous contemporary modernity. One journalist, stumbling upon an incongruous luxury hotel in Allahabad, India, noted: "Every effort had been made to make it conform to international specifications. The menu at the coffee shop offered Mexican and Italian food."[55] As in most theme parks, the exotic scenery was often more of an attraction than the food. Shinichirou Hosokawa, an eccentric fashion designer, opened Japan's most expensive Mexican restaurant, Fonda de la Madrugada, in order to recreate a hacienda courtyard in the vast space of a Tokyo basement. Along with ceramic tiles and rustic furniture, he imported a chef from Oaxaca and mariachi musicians.[56]

Music and drinking have become expected features of Mexican restaurants. While some establishments have sought the cantina atmosphere of roving mariachis, others have opted for a more Pan-American theme with salsa dancing. A review for Down Mexico Way, a now-defunct London restaurant, explained: "It's billed as a restaurant for a quiet, romantic dinner, but I have to say that for most people, live, energetic Latin music punctuated by deafening taped music to accompany the floor show of Salsa dancing is not the ideal accompaniment to seduction over the Fajitas!"[57] The centrality of booze has become almost a joke: two Mexican chefs went to India on tour and stayed for more than a month in Delhi to train the staff of a Mexican restaurant. They soon discovered that, despite the countries' similar culinary traditions, the local clientele was less interested in food than alcohol, especially shots of tequila served up by bartenders dressed as cowboys.[58] Pacífico's Tom Estes made a second career as a tequila importer, promoting the latest top-shelf varieties and producing his own single-source house brand. The London restaurant's most expensive tequila, José Cuervo Colección, sold for £100 a shot. "One hundred pounds almost seems like an investment," Estes said. "By the end of the first week on sale we'd 'brokered' five shots."[59]

After all this alcohol, some might not even notice the changing taste of Mexican food as it traveled the world, yet cooks have invariably adapted recipes to their culturally conditioned flavor principles. Travelers to Paris complained that chicken fajitas tasted like *coq au vin*, while visitors to British Tex-Mex restaurants may wonder if Indian cooks have gone so heavy on the cumin that the salsa resembles Balti curry, an Anglicized tomato-based dish. In some cases the change in taste may be the result of the local sourcing of ingredients, at times fortuitously. Robb Walsh declared the Paris Pacífico's cheese enchilada, made with aged Gruyère, to be the best version he ever ate. Some tastes intrinsic to Mexican cuisine have turned out to be simply inedible for many people. The extensive use of chile peppers is the most obvious example of adverse reactions, and toned-down Mexican versions are the most common adaption. Curiously, Mexican food seems not to have caught on particularly well in countries with strong traditions of spicy food, such as India and Korea, which suggests that many find the heat itself more interesting than the particular flavors experienced by those with a tolerance for capsaic acid.[60]

Perhaps more difficult to overcome in the long run has been an inexplicable but widespread cultural distaste for maize. Arturo Warman, an anthropologist and government official, explained that "a Mexican agricultural delegation visiting China recently was astonished to be asked if they knew of any method of removing the smell from maize pancakes (the aroma of tortillas which Mexicans find so appetizing), as it made the average Chinese feel sick."[61] A traveler in Chengdu Province described a restaurant called Carol's by the River, run by a Chinese woman who once lived in Texas, which served tortillas made of rice flour. Europeans often substituted wheat for corn; a French Tex-Mex cookbook gave a recipe for wheat flour nachos, while Socorro and Fernando del Paso's Franco-Mexican transnational family history and cookbook suggested serving mole in miniature vols-au-vent.[62]

As the vols-au-vent illustrate, Mexican food has been transformed from the work of cooks fitting new flavors into recognized categories. Of course, that same process of localization took place during the early modern globalization of ingredients such as maize, chiles, and chocolate. The difference today is that cooks around the world now consider Mexican cuisine to be desirable, something to serve with pride at the table, even if they seek to interchange particular flavors.

A similar phenomenon of adaptation is apparent in the commercial sales of Mexican food. When Tel Aviv experienced a sudden fashion for taco shops in 2006, the foods were often adaptations of Middle Eastern pita fare, while many Russians perceived tortillas as Armenian lavash. Dutch restaurateurs placed Mexican food in the category of Spanish tapas, serving jalapeño poppers and *humitas* (Ecuadorean tamales) along with calamares and olives, perhaps an association derived from beach vacations on the Costa del Sol. Snack foods became another way of incorporating Mexican exoticism into everyday foods. Moving beyond the prosaic chips and salsa, the European Langnese Ice Cream Company created a half-moon-shaped ice cream sandwich, which they marketed in Germany as "Winner Taco: Der Powersnack." The Japanese were even more inventive with Mexican-themed snacks such as "Don Tacos," corn tortilla chips sold in three flavors: Mexican chili, seafood, and Super Hot chili. Although not previously known for habañero consumption, many Japanese youth have suddenly become chile addicts; one popular brand is revealingly called "Bokun [tyrant] Habañero."[63]

People seem to find themselves reflected in the global culture that they consume—including their Mexican food. New Age spiritualists following the Maya trail, urban cowboys hungering for the Wild West, and salsa dancers in need of sustenance can all receive a satisfying experience in a Mexican restaurant. While every cook introduces her own personal flavor to Mexican food, her tastes as well as the food change through the encounter, a point revealed by Japanese youth in their newfound devotion to the chile tyrant. Now firmly established as a global cuisine, Mexican food will continue to evolve, together with the tastes of its countless aficionados. Who will profit from the sale of Mexican food remains to be seen.

CHAPTER 7

exican food began to achieve a global presence in the 1980s primarily because it had become so fashionable in the United States. Taco shells and burritos expanded beyond their Southwestern origins to become truly national as fast-food taco chains and full-service restaurants entered regions where they had once been rare, including parts of the Midwest, the South, and even the Northeast. Corona beer also took the country by storm in the mid-1980s, making Cinco de Mayo into a south-of-the-border St. Patrick's Day. Meanwhile, *Good Housekeeping* magazine brought this fad home with recipes and advertisements for a "tasty taco supper" and Spam enchiladas.[1] Tex-Mex fajitas became wildly popular, and in 1991, salsa surpassed catsup as the best-selling condiment in the country. Upscale versions of this pop culture phenomenon also appeared in the "New Southwestern" cuisine, a gourmet movement created by classically trained chefs in Santa Fe, Los Angeles, and Dallas, who presented the street foods of the chili queens as trendy fine dining: lobster tacos, caviar on blue corn tortillas, and sea-bass mousse tamales. In 1987, the food writer M. F. K. Fisher groaned: "If I hear any more about chic Tex-Mex or blue cornmeal, I'll throw up."[2] Despite her protests, a blue corn bonanza was waiting for businessmen if they could sell burritos, taco shells, and fajitas around the world under the name of Mexican food.

Mexicans quickly perceived the economic consequences of this struggle between globalization and national sovereignty, as the demand for industrial Tex-Mex food threatened to crowd Mexico's regional cooking out of surging international markets. For decades, the labeling of canned chili con carne as Mexican food had offended patriotic pride, but the national cuisine acquired new significance with the boom in culinary tourism and high-value agricultural exports. Culinary professionals seeking to reclaim their national heritage from industrial competitors abroad cultivated a new image of authentic Mexican as the food of the ancient Aztecs and Maya. In creating this nouvelle cuisine, called the *nueva cocina mexicana*, they reversed the nineteenth-century hierarchy that put Indians at the bottom of the social pyramid. Their primordial vision of the national cuisine not only fit with the prevailing ideology of *indigenismo*, but it also appealed to European and North American countercultural tourists, aging hippies who were hungry for Third World authenticity as an antidote to processed food at home. Yet the Mexican national cuisine was no more homogeneous at the end of the twentieth century than it had been a hundred years earlier. Although nationalist authors declared Mexican food to be a mestizo blend of Creole, Indian, and French influences, these nineteenth-century categories continued to divide the national cuisine, even as they became configured in new ways.

The struggle between Mexico and the United States for the international market in Mexican food took place on three distinct levels: trend-setting haute cuisine, mass-market restaurants and prepared foods, and basic agricultural exports. At each level, U.S. producers held significant political and economic advantages. The North American Free Trade Agreement (NAFTA), implemented in 1994, allowed subsidized Midwestern corn and beans to move freely across the border, devastating small farms in Mexico, while the United States used nontariff barriers to restrict Mexican agricultural exports. The growth of Mexican migration, an unintended consequence of NAFTA, actually helped to promote the spread of Mexican regional cooking through the opening of family restaurants across the continent. Nevertheless, these small businesses had to survive not only the competition from corporate chains but also raids by immigration officials. The United States even controlled the high end of the market through an infrastructure of cookbook publishers, food critics, and corporate sponsors with considerable power to shape the global image of Mexican food. As a result, the new vision of indigenous cuisine as authentically Mexican gained wide acceptance, but it was often considered

not as a form of culinary artistry, reflecting the talent and originality of individual cooks, but rather as "primitive art," a collective expression of village
and street traditions that were best experienced, and appropriated, through
ethnography.[3]

Haute Mexican: Artistry and Ethnography

For a brief moment around 1980, the most fashionable restaurant in Mexico
City was not a French place in the tourist Zona Rosa, but rather a fonda called
Don Chon in the barrio of La Merced. Black limousines crowded the narrow
streets on the wrong side of the Zócalo, carrying politicians and businessmen
to sample the novelty of a "pre-Hispanic" menu. Powerful men, who ordinarily would have squished xumiles with their Gucci loafers, were eating the bugs
with guacamole. The indigenous chic of Don Chon matched the gritty zeitgeist
of populism and corruption in Mexican politics. The ruling party had lost its
legitimacy a decade earlier with a 1968 massacre of peaceful student protesters, and its economic policies bogged down in the 1970s stagflation. A peso
collapse in 1982 and a fraudulent presidential election in 1988 compounded
the social unrest. Thus, the nueva cocina was born at a time when the national
bourgeoisie was painfully unable to shoulder the burden of conspicuous consumption. As a result, foreigners continued to influence notions of authentic
Mexican, even as culinary professionals sought to counter Tex-Mex versions
of the national cuisine.

The Mexican haute cuisine of the 1980s was a transnational product of the
1960s student movement, sought after by aging and affluent hippies from
both Mexico and the United States. For the North American counterculture,
the goals of this movement were to challenge corporate bureaucracy, conform-
ist suburban lifestyles, and environmental pollution. The historian Warren
Belasco has noted two basic rules of the alternative food culture: "Don't eat
anything you can't pronounce (i.e., no propylene glycol alginate, a stabilizer
used in bottled salad dressing) and if worms, yeast, and bacteria grew on it,
then it must be natural, for no self-respecting bug would eat plastic. Inverting
established notions of spoilage, the countercuisine equated preservatives with
contamination and microbes with health."[4] Thus, gusanos, grasshoppers, and
other peasant foods were seen as a more natural alternative to corporate processed foods. Meanwhile, Mexican youth of the 1960s focused their protests
on the authoritarian one-party state, which voiced revolutionary slogans but

stifled democracy. Many young people registered their discontent by listening to rock music instead of mariachis and calling themselves *xipitecas* (pronounced "hippie-tecas," like Aztecas). In this way, they claimed a nationalist attachment to an indigenous past while maintaining cosmopolitan connections with student rebels around the world.[5]

In creating the nueva cocina, Mexican chefs reworked the nineteenth-century tropes of indigenous, Creole, and foreign cuisines, thereby blending formerly distinct social positions to fit modern sensibilities. Some of the earliest proponents of the nueva cocina were, like most restaurant workers, humble migrants from the countryside. Fortino Rojas Contreras, the innovative chef at Fonda Don Chon, arrived in Mexico City in 1941, at the age of six, an orphan from the small town of Reyes de Juárez, Puebla. He started out selling tacos around the wholesale produce market of La Merced and eventually went to work at Fonda Don Chon, which was owned by a migrant from Tlaxcala named Encarnación Reyes García. Reyes had operated a popular taco stand for decades in a plaza next to the House of Tiles before saving enough money to open a small restaurant on the other side of town. Rojas began washing dishes at Fonda Don Chon in the early 1960s and had become a line cook by the time Reyes passed away in the mid-1970s. When the owner's heirs asked him to take over as chef, Rojas began to expand the Creole fonda menu with foods that he remembered—and at times imagined—his mother cooking for him: *albóndigas de armadillo* (armadillo meatballs), *quelites de ceniza* (lamb's quarters), and the festive *mole de chito* from the annual goat slaughter of Tehuacán, Puebla.

In developing his pre-Hispanic cuisine, Rojas blended Mexico's nineteenth-century indigenous and Creole cuisines, presenting rural festival foods in an urban fonda setting. The restaurant's location, in a rough neighborhood a few blocks from the National Palace on the Zócalo, offered politicians a convenient opportunity to appear at once populist and macho. Intellectuals likewise flocked to Don Chon for the frisson of danger and sophistication. But after a few years, the economic collapse made slumming less appealing and more dangerous, driving wealthy diners back to the secure neighborhoods of Condesa and Polanca. Even after the fashionable crowd had moved on, Rojas continued to develop his cuisine by using ingredients that were still available in obscure corners of the Merced market: grasshoppers, salamanders, iguana, wild boar, possum, and other so-called animalitos. Unlike later exponents of pre-Hispanic cuisine, who attributed their exotic creations to research in old codices, the chef had no need to establish his indigenous credentials and

Figure 7.1. Chef Fortino Reyes Contreras, the founder of the pre-Hispanic menu and the nueva cocina mexicana, in Restaurante Chon, Mexico City. Photo by Fernando Calderón.

freely admitted to inventing his recipes. His art was to recreate for a contemporary restaurant menu rural dishes whose preparation depended on ample female labor and that had been consumed in ritual situations. His market— apart from the neighbors, because his prices were reasonable—consisted of tourists and intellectuals searching for ethnic exoticism.[6]

While Rojas pioneered an indigenous-Creole version of the nueva cocina in a simple fonda, Arnulfo Luengas Rosales developed a foreign-Creole cuisine as the executive chef of the Banco Nacional de México, the country's most aristocratic bank. The two men shared similar rural backgrounds, but the fortunes of patronage set Luengas on a far different career path. Born in 1934 in the pueblo of Huajuapan de León, in the Sierra Mixteca of Oaxaca, he likewise arrived in Mexico City as a young migrant in 1951. Making his way down the Paseo de la Reforma one day, he happened upon an open door to the kitchen of the Ambassadeurs restaurant. There he worked his way from dishwasher to sous chef under the guidance of Chef Emmanuel Descamps, cooking for the Mexican elite and even Charles de Gaulle, the visiting French president. Luengas moved on to serve as chef for the Jalisco Club de Industriales and for the Hotel del Prado, before taking over the executive dining room at Banamex in 1970. The bank encouraged his professional development by providing French-language study and the opportunity to take working leaves in Parisian restaurants, just as the nouvelle cuisine swept France. Returning to Mexico in the early 1980s, Luengas incorporated these new ideas into a culinary repertoire that combined national ingredients with French techniques.

Luengas's artistry glorified Mexico's Creole heritage for a select company of bank executives and guests. Founded in 1884, Banamex displayed its aristocratic lineage with a corporate headquarters in the colonial Palacio de los Condes de San Mateo Valparaíso. The continental service of the bank's executive dining room set a refined atmosphere that allowed for populist flourishes, for example, an appetizer of taquitos de barbacoa before a main course of venison or duck. Following Jaime Saldivar, the midcentury inventor of *crepas de cuitlacoche*, Luengas added chile poblano to Beef Wellington and served *cabuches* (cactus flower buds) in vol-au-vent. Although tourists could gaze at reproductions of these dishes in a coffee-table cookbook, *The Cuisine of Banamex* (2000), the originals were reserved for international bankers, whose trips to Mexico were thereby assured of culinary sophistication, if not monetary stability.[7]

While Luengas served his international-Creole dishes in a wood-paneled executive dining room, Patricia Quintana gave the nueva cocina its public face at the intersection of indigenous and foreign cuisines. Of French, English, and Swiss ancestry, she started giving private cooking classes within her elite circle by the age of eighteen, and in her early twenties she became enamored of Michel Guérard's diet-conscious nouvelle cuisine. In 1979, while consulting for Van de Kamp's on a line of frozen Mexican food, she gave cooking classes in Los Angeles presenting her own version of this approach, for example, garnishing dishes with yogurt instead of thick cream and serving chiles rellenos without the deep-fried egg batter. Quintana also ran a successful catering company, wrote food columns for *Mexican Vogue* and *Novedades*, and became the first Mexican to publish a major cookbook in the United States, *Tastes of Mexico* (1986), which was followed by more than a dozen other volumes. With her political contacts, she was named the executive chef for the Mexican Ministry of Tourism, a diplomatic platform she used to denounce U.S. stereotypes of "goopy burritos and tacos smothered in processed cheese." Quintana explained: "My style of cooking brings sophistication to traditional recipes and [gives] Mexican food the recognition and honor it deserves."[8]

Upscale restaurateurs like Quintana combined Rojas's goal of reinterpreting pre-Hispanic civilization as the modern national cuisine with Luengas's reliance on the techniques of international haute cuisine. As former members of the xipiteca counterculture, they had a natural affinity for indigenous cultures, although Quintana inherited a special interest in the ancient past from her mother, a university-trained archaeologist who conducted excavations on the family's Veracruz rancho. Chef Quintana explained: "The origins of much of what I do lie with the Mayans, whose grand civilizations rose and fell long before the Spanish conquistadors stepped foot in the New World."[9] The feminist movement was another cornerstone of the nueva cocina, as a number of wealthy and talented women decided to use their domestic skills for more than advancing their husbands' careers. The *nuevas cocineras* channeled their ambitions into restaurants, beginning in the mid-1980s with Carmen Ortuño's Isadora, Mónica Patiño's La Galvia, and Alicia Gironella De'Angeli's El Tajín. When Quintana opened her own restaurant, Izote, shortly after the turn of the millennium, it became one of the most sought-after destinations in Mexico. Her signature dish harkened back to the original historical tacos described by Manuel Payno—a simple tortilla with avocado—but she transformed it by presenting the guacamole on rounds of *jícama*, an indigenous, vaguely apple-flavored root, sliced paper-thin like a tortilla.[10]

Quintana, as a self-conscious culinary ambassador, staged her nationalist artistry for international audiences and remained keenly aware of the latest trends. Although smartly dressed Mexicans could always be seen at Izote and its neighbors, tourists were a vital market for the nueva cocina both in restaurants and cookbooks, particularly when the peso declined. Nevertheless, many prominent restaurateurs who had built their reputations on Creole classics such as mole de guajolote condemned the nueva cocina as a misrepresentation of Mexico's culinary traditions.

The "goopy" stereotypes of Mexican American cooking that Quintana found so offensive also provided a common point of departure for international chefs. Venturing out as ethnographers in search of authentic Mexican cuisine, they were less comfortable blending the nineteenth-century tropes of indigenous, Creole, and foreign than were their Mexican counterparts. The leading interpreter of indigenous cooking, Diana Southwood Kennedy, had experienced the privations of World War II as a young woman in England, and she hungrily devoured the writings of Elizabeth David on the still-exotic foods of southern France. Arriving in Mexico in 1957 to marry the *New York Times* reporter Paul Kennedy, she set out in the spirit of her gastronomic heroine to explore a similar rural landscape in search of simple, honest food. After her husband's death in 1967, Kennedy began to teach Mexican cooking classes in New York and wrote *The Cuisines of Mexico* (1972). This was not the first authoritative English-language cookbook on Mexico, but, like Julia Child's volume on preparing French classics a decade earlier, it became enormously popular by providing detailed instructions for such Creole classics as mole de guajolote, red snapper Veracruz, and Yucatecan pit-roasted pig. Kennedy vigorously distinguished her own recipes from the assimilated foods that were widely available in the United States and thereby appealed to countercultural audiences eager for authenticity.

Over the decades, as North Americans gained more knowledge about Mexican regional cuisine, Kennedy continued her ethnographic pursuit of indigenous foods, thereby setting standards for Mexico's culinary tourism industry. Whereas her first book had offered a few mole sauces common throughout Mexico, *The Art of Mexican Cooking* (1989) explored the variety of Oaxaca's iconic seven moles, and her culinary memoir, *My Mexico* (1998), gave recipes for the singular moles of particular towns as prepared by individual chefs. In the latter volume, she frequently assured readers of the authenticity of recipes with statements such as "For local residents of Puerto Vallarta there is no *pozole* to compare with that of Señora Rafaela Villaseñor."[11] By recognizing her informants, Kennedy acknowledged her intellectual debts and gave international recognition to local women, thereby bolstering their status within their communities. Yet such claims have also become essential marketing tools on an increasingly crowded cookbook shelf. For aficionados who wanted a more direct experience of indigenous foods, Kennedy collaborated with the chef and impresario Marilyn Tausend to offer tours of Mexico's regional cuisines, complete with market visits and cooking classes. Thus, her works set a benchmark for ethnographic culinary tourism.[12]

While Kennedy explored the indigenous countryside, John Rivera Sedlar and other French-trained chefs created the New Southwestern as a border-crossing version of Mexico's nueva cocina. In the early 1980s, at his Los Angeles–area restaurant Saint Estèphe, Sedlar first began to incorporate childhood flavors from New Mexico with continental cuisine to create such dishes as cactus-and-chile bouillabaisse and ravioli with carne adobado. He drew eclectically from a range of indigenous groups, such as New Mexico Pueblos, the ancient Maya, and contemporary Mexican peasants. The *zaca-huil*, a pit-roasted tamal from Veracruz large enough to feed an entire village, became a favorite for Hollywood parties when stuffed with lobster. Like their Mexican counterparts, New Southwestern chefs were driven by the search for a national cuisine, as one restaurant reviewer put it, "something—anything—that can convincingly be labeled American."[13] Mark Miller of Coyote Café in Santa Fe complained after one banquet that "three people came up and asked me if there was raspberry vinegar on the quail. Raspberry vinegar! That's the mentality you have to fight. Because it's good and beautiful, it has to be French. The whole point of the dinner was that it doesn't have to be."[14] Yet in a cookbook entitled *Tamales* (2002), which asserted its authenticity through a dedication to Patricia Quintana and the Zapotec cooks of Teotitlán del Valle, Oaxaca, the coauthors Sedlar, Miller, and Stephan Pyles, a Dallas chef, suggested blue corn with rabbit, foie gras and pineapple mole, and elote with black truffles. Clearly, they maintained an ambivalent relationship with their French teachers.[15]

The New Southwestern chefs practiced a modern art of *épatée le bourgeois*, serving street foods on silver platters. Sedlar recalled: "When I first began serving tortillas, tamales, and chiles in a fine dining environment, people gasped."[16] Having grown up around the artist colony of Georgia O'Keefe in Abiquiu, New Mexico, Sedlar emphasized visual presentation; for one dish "he made a lattice by weaving strips of salmon and seabass into a square, sauced with chimayo green chile."[17] Despite efforts to differentiate themselves from French trends, the movement soon became associated with the excesses of 1980s nouvelle cuisine, prompting critics to dub their salsa paintings "squeeze-bottle cuisine."[18] Meanwhile, Latino intellectuals denounced the neocolonialist exploitation of the New Southwestern cuisine, comparing anthropologist-chefs to modern-day Baron von Humboldts, who harvested "tempting flavors and exotic ingredients" for the Armani-suit crowd.[19]

Between Kennedy's documentation of indigenous cuisine and Sedlar's innovative international cuisine, Rick Bayless sought to reinterpret Mexico's regional Creole cuisines for North American audiences. Bayless grew up in postwar Oklahoma City eating Mexican American foods alongside the barbecue served in his family's restaurant. As a graduate student in linguistics and anthropology, he conducted fieldwork on the food and culture of Mexico, but, rather than write up his notes as a dissertation, he published them as a cookbook, *Authentic Mexican* (1987), while opening a Chicago restaurant, Frontera Grill.

Bayless explained his artistry in linguistic terms: "You can read really good translations of poetry that can make your heart soar. Then you can read another translation of the same poem that falls flat. There's a real strong sense that the translator that made your heart soar not only understood the insides of the poem but also had the artistic ability to express it in the other language." Bayless and his chefs sought to translate the flavors of Mexico for U.S. audiences, creating a distinctive style of roasting ingredients over wood fires and achieving a particular balance of flavors. "I'm trying to express that same feeling that I found in a dish in Mexico," he said. "When the diners have it, when they enjoy it, hopefully, they too will have that same kind of reaction to it that I had in its original place." Perhaps the most difficult part of the translation was obtaining ingredients that matched the flavors of Mexican regional produce. While importing dried chiles from Oaxaca for his signature black mole, he sourced local goods from the Midwest whenever possible, emphasizing taste and technique over ethnic origins. Thus, he sought out an Amish cheesemaker from Indiana to reproduce the Mennonite cheese of Chihuahua, and he turned to an old-school Italian baker for the bread in the torta sandwiches at his quick-service outlet Xoco.

Of course, Bayless was no less commercial than other celebrity chefs, with a line of supermarket chips and salsa as well as promotions for Burger King. Nevertheless, by remaining faithful to local traditions, rather than imposing chiles on European models, he affirmed the intrinsic value of Mexican cuisine. While basing his work on ethnography, Bayless self-consciously avoided the impulse to indigenous exoticism: "People often ask me, 'What's the weirdest thing you've ever eaten in Mexico? I heard that they eat armadillos.' It's saying, 'They're weird down there.' "[20]

Although chefs in Mexico and the United States have clearly followed different paths, any typology will oversimplify, just as nineteenth-century Mexicans created artificial distinctions between indigenous, Creole, and French cuisines. Thus, Fortino Rojas served a mousse of *huauhzontle* (an indigenous herb) at Restaurante Chon, while Arnulfo Luengas offered *chapulín* (grasshopper) tamales at Banamex, and Patricia Quintana prepared classic Creole moles at Izote. North American interpreters have been similarly eclectic, and even international boundaries have become increasingly porous. Diana Kennedy has promoted indigenous foods to middle-class Mexicans, receiving the country's highest honor awarded to foreigners, the Order of the Aztec Eagle. Mexican chefs have meanwhile established a foothold in the United States. Zarela Martínez, a native of Sonora, won fame in the 1990s as an interpreter of the nueva cocina at her eponymous New York City restaurant, before rediscovering Mexico's indigenous roots with cookbooks about Oaxaca and Veracruz. Likewise, Richard Sandoval, the scion of an Acapulco restaurant dynasty and a graduate of the Culinary Institute of America, has built a chain of Modern Mexican restaurants in leading North American cities.

The shape of this transnational cuisine, like all forms of border crossing, was determined by unequal power relationships, particularly control of the gourmet infrastructure that connected Mexican chefs to global audiences through media, manufacturers, advertisers, cooking schools, and the like. Consider the story of María Dolores Torres Yzábal, a prominent Sonoran woman who took a job as executive chef for a Monterrey industrial group when she divorced her husband. After decades of innovative cooking, she finally had the opportunity to publish her recipes in a book entitled *The Mexican Gourmet* (1995), part of a series edited by an Australian firm, Weldon Russell Ltd. Unfortunately, the test kitchens down under had no idea of what Mexican food should look like, and they produced glossy photos of decrepit *chiles rellenos*, which had not been skinned before stuffing, and, even worse, moles that were chopped in a food processor instead of in a blender and had a disgustingly chunky, brown consistency.[21]

Nevertheless, Mexicans have begun to challenge the structural inequalities by developing their own gourmet infrastructure. Cooking schools, such as the gastronomy program at the Universidad Claustro de Sor Juana, the first hospitality curriculum in a Mexican university, offered professional training for aspiring culinary professionals. Mexican chefs increasingly have turned away from Paris and sought inspiration in East Asia or in the avant-garde cuisine

---

Box 7.1 Chef Rick Bayless Describes the Ezquites at Chef Enrique Olvera's Mexico City Restaurant, Pujol

When you order ezquites at his very beautiful, very contemporary restaurant, out comes a small glass and it's filled with three different kinds of corn, boiled fresh field corn, *nixtamal* or fully cooked pozole, and some sweet corn, and then it's layered with powdered red chile, *queso fresco* or *añejo*, one or the other, I can't remember which it is, and then he adds crab meat into this mix. The server pours a beautiful braising liquid over the whole thing. A lot of those vendors will have mayonnaise that they just dollop on the top. And you can stir it in to the broth to make it creamy. Enrique has taken mayonnaise and put gelatin in, and you pour broth over this mayonnaise that's on top, it melts down into the whole thing, turning the street vendor dish into one of the most exquisite things that you've ever eaten. That's the perfect example of what I would call real *nueva cocina mexicana*. It's a brilliant dish.

Source: Telephone interview with Rick Bayless, November 21, 2006.

---

of Catalonia. Enrique Olvera, for example, created a deconstructed version of ezquites, the simple dish of roasted corn kernels that borderlands chronicler Alonso de León had compared, during a colonial famine, to "the most delicate and suave dish of the finest *hosteria* of Italy." In Olvera's Mexico City restaurant, Pujol, it did not take a famine to make ezquites into such a "delicate and suave dish."

Cooking columns that chronicled this gourmet movement, such as the "Buena Mesa" (Good Table) section of the Mexico City newspaper *Reforma*, began to challenge the trendsetting powers of North American critics. Certainly in Mexico, the English-language press has limited influence. Iliana de la Vega Arnaud, for example, won plaudits from the *New York Times* and other critics for her innovative nueva cocina approach to Oaxacan cooking. Although her restaurant, El Naranjo (The orange), quickly became a favorite with tourists, it failed to win over Oaxacan traditionalists, and when social unrest disrupted the tourism industry in 2006, it was forced to close. Ultimately, de la Vega was able to parlay her international connections into a faculty position at the San Antonio campus of the Culinary Institute of

America, which opened in 2010 with funding from Kit Goldsbury, heir to the Pace Picante fortune, in order to help Latinos advance in the restaurant industry.[22]

One point of commonality between Mexican and U.S. versions of the nueva cocina has been the marginality of Mexican Americans and indigenous Mexicans. Mexican American home cooks cannot be held responsible for the industrial versions of their cooking that have received such abuse from gourmets on both sides of the border. Nevertheless, they have been tarred with the same "goopy" brush of Americanization as Taco Bell and Old El Paso. Meanwhile, even as ancient Aztecs and Maya were exalted as the source of Mexican authenticity, present-day Indians in Mexico have been viewed through a lens of ethnographic exoticism. Their foods were treated as primitive art, a product of traditional societies that were best appreciated by ethnography. Rather than acknowledge the artistry of native chefs, members of the cultural industry have instead used them to enhance their own prestige. Thus, they demonstrate their discerning palates by "discovering" the foods of village festivals and street markets while braving the threat of "Montezuma's Revenge." A few indigenous chefs, such as Abigail Mendoza, a Zapotec woman from Teotitlán del Valle, have been acknowledged for their personal taste. Both *Gourmet* and *Saveur* magazines ran feature articles on her, and the *New York Times* declared her village restaurant, Tlamanalli, to be one of the top ten culinary experiences in the entire world. The "authenticity" of being an ethnic minority has provided Mendoza with a business opportunity and helped her to overcome patriarchal social restrictions, but the culinary tourism that has made her personal success possible depends on the continued marginality of her people.[23]

The creation of a Mexican haute cuisine has been a transnational project of chefs and cookbook authors collaborating and competing on both sides of the Rio Grande. Although they have greatly advanced the recognition of Mexican food, they still have a long way to go when measured by restaurant checks. Very few Mexican restaurants can command prices comparable to those of French restaurants, even when using the same fresh ingredients and, in many cases, the same Mexican workers. Customers have simply refused to consider the two cuisines as equals. A noted sociologist has suggested that large-scale immigration is inversely related to the acceptance of fine dining in the United States, and clearly the presence of migrant workers has not raised the status of Mexican food.[24] However, this conclusion must be qualified because these social inequalities are as common in Mexico City as in New York City. When Mexican food has gone upscale in either country, it has generally been experienced as a form of slumming. Although this reputation may reflect, in part, artistic choices made by particular chefs, enduring stereotypes of Aztecs and chili queens have also shaped perceptions. These negative associations persisted not only in exclusive restaurants but also in everyday dining as Mexican food spread across North America.

Everyday Mexican: Malls and Migrants

In seeking to explain the rapid spread of Mexican restaurants across the United States at the end of the twentieth century, it is tempting to attribute it to the surge of working-class migration, but the relationship between the migrants and tacos is not as straightforward as one might imagine. While many of these new restaurants have catered to growing ethnic populations, with migrants serving regional foods to their compatriots, other newly arrived cooks quickly reproduced the Mexican American style of the 1950s. At the same time, corporate versions of Mexican food have expanded rapidly into new geographic regions as well as market segments such as "wraps" and "Fresh-Mex." The competition between malls and migrants for the ethnic food market gained particular significance at the turn of the century, as politicians heatedly debated the desirability of Mexican migration. Chains such as Taco Bell, rather than encouraging acceptance of migrant foods, have distanced their products from the ethnic community, and thereby they have reproduced earlier patterns of segregation dating back to the chili queens and the postwar taco shops.

Although scholars have devoted considerable attention to the social nuances of fine dining, far less is known about larger trends in the restaurants where most people eat. One notable exception, the geographer Wilbur Zelinsky's pioneering 1980 survey drawn from telephone books, found not surprisingly that the three most popular cuisines, Chinese, Italian, and Mexican, made up fully 70 percent of ethnic restaurants in the United States. Comparing restaurants with population figures, he concluded that entrepreneurial cooks were more important than ethnic dining communities, most notably in the case of Chinese restaurants, which achieved a near universal presence in North America despite quite modest populations in most regions. Nevertheless, the relative weight of Italian, Chinese, and Mexican restaurants closely followed earlier patterns of labor migration: Italians dominated the eastern seaboard and much of the Midwest; the Mexican presence radiated out from the Southwest; and Chinese filled in residual areas without strongly controlling any one region. Moreover, as a leading immigration historian has observed, these three nations sent the largest numbers of predominantly male migrants, for whom inexpensive restaurants provided a substitute for domestic cooking.[25]

Focusing on the Mexican case, Zelinsky recognized the striking growth taking place around 1980. Although the Southwest still had the greatest concentration, Mexican restaurants were already widespread in the West and parts of the Midwest. This cuisine had also become familiar to cosmopolitan consumers in major cities throughout the country. By contrast, Mexican restaurants remained largely unknown in smaller cities of the South, Northeast, and parts of the Midwest, as well as in Canada except for the "southwestern" cities of Vancouver and Calgary. Nevertheless, Zelinsky observed: "If the Mexican-American population is growing rapidly in numbers and territorial range, its foodways are hurtling northward and eastward at an even faster pace." He predicted that the map "may have captured a major example of cultural diffusion in mid-flight."[26]

Figure 7.2. "If the Mexican American population is growing rapidly in numbers and territorial range, its foodways are hurtling northward and eastward at an even faster pace." Map of Mexican Restaurant cuisines, reprinted from *Geoforum*, vol. 16, no. 1, Wilbur Zelinsky, "The Roving Palate: North America's Ethnic Restaurant Cuisines." Copyright 1985, with permission from Elsevier.

The disparity between population growth and the spread of ethnic restaurants points to significant lags in the movement of food from ethnic enclaves to mainstream society. A long-term study of Omaha, Nebraska, found that the first Mexican restaurant opened there in the 1920s, within a decade after railroad jobs began attracting migrants, but the food remained confined within the Mexican community until the 1950s. The number of Mexican restaurants grew modestly for the next few decades and then took off in the 1970s, although Mexican migrants did not begin arriving in large numbers until the 1990s. This uneven chronology resulted from generational transitions, particularly among other ethnics. Central European immigrants who had tasted Mexican American tacos and enchiladas as children ate them regularly as adults. Thus, as they entered the cultural mainstream, they brought with them a taste for once-exotic foods.[27]

Newcomers from Mexico may have had even less of an influence on shaping images of Mexican food in the eastern United States, where restaurant chains from California and Texas were already well established by the time migrants began arriving. Taco Bell began franchising outside of California in the 1960s, and it had reached the Northeast by the early 1980s. Although the only national taco chain, it nevertheless faced a variety of competitors in different regions of the country, including Taco Time (founded in Eugene, Oregon, in 1959) and Taco Tico (Wichita, Kansas, 1962). Meanwhile, the Dallas-based chain El Chico led the way in opening full-service restaurants in the South, with nearly two dozen outlets from Baton Rouge to Atlanta by the late 1970s. Imitators such as Chi-Chi's (established in Minneapolis in 1976) grew even more rapidly, opening 150 outlets within a decade. As with the international spread of Mexican food, personal connections often had a snowball effect. Family ties led Jimmy and Nonie McClure, the founders of an Amarillo restaurant, El Palacio, to open their second location in Huntsville, Alabama, in the mid-1960s. It proved to be a fortuitous choice when NASA opened a facility and Tex-Mex aficionados began visiting from Mission Control in Houston. Wernher von Braun, a German rocket scientist, became a regular customer. A decade later, when the space program scaled back, unemployed engineers purchased the franchising rights and built El Palacios throughout the Southeast.[28]

Corporate representations of Mexican food, while becoming more diverse, still presented an image of safe danger—exoticism without contamination—that had earlier been used to sell canned tamales and chili con carne. At times, this amounted to simple appropriation of tribal names, as when food-processing companies claimed trademarks for "Hopi Blue Popcorn" or "Zuni Gold Popcorn" brands. Taco Bell took this process of inauthenticity even further as it expanded its franchising base in the 1980s. In doing so, it added new menu items—fajitas, nachos, taco salads, and, in the 1990s, gorditas, a Mexican-themed pita. The company continued to position itself at the low end of the fast-food market, pioneering the "value menu" approach and engaging in perennial price cutting. Kitsch advertisements like the talking Chihuahua, which spoofed Latino culture, projected a sanitized image in opposition to actual migrants. One executive explained the company's dismissive attitude toward the Mexican community: "We're trying to bring together tastes and concepts that people who are not as familiar—or trustful—of Mexican can recognize as beef, cheese, and corn."[29]

Fresh-Mex restaurants, a market segment combining the "quick service" format with higher-quality ingredients, catered to a more upscale clientele while also often showing more respect for Mexicans. Taco Cabana, a San Antonio firm founded in 1978 by brothers Felix and Mike Stehling, gave this image a Tex-Mex face with salsa bars and neon pastels. Rubio's Baja Grill, created by a surfer named Ralph Rubio in 1983, introduced diners to the fish tacos of Baja California. So-called Mission burritos from San Francisco became another popular market segment. The most successful of the Fresh-Mex chains was Steve Ells's Chipotle, which opened in Denver in 1993 and went national with financing from McDonald's. A graduate of the Culinary Institute of America, Ells combined a postindustrial Maya image with locally sourced, organic ingredients, thereby appealing to a new generation of environmentally conscious consumers.[30]

Full-service Mexican dining has also expanded rapidly, driven more by bar tabs than by food, in a trend that might be called "Wet-Mex." Many new chains were direct offshoots of established market leaders; both Abuelo's and On the Border, for example, were founded by former El Chico executives. These new brands did little to alter the cantina atmosphere and menu format. The most significant growth was in the size of the drinks. This trend can be dated to 1971, when the Dallas restaurateur Mariano Martínez, Jr., developed a Slurpee-style machine to serve frozen margaritas, the original of which is now displayed at the Smithsonian Institution in Washington, D.C. At the time, the El Fenix chain of Dallas, for example, served "regular" margaritas in martini glasses of about five ounces, the small size dictated by the desire to keep the drink cold. Even El Fenix's "king-size" version came in a rounded cup

Figure 7.3. Full-service Mexican dining has also expanded rapidly, driven more by bar tabs than by food, in a trend that might be called "Wet-Mex." An illuminated sombrero draws young revelers to the Gonzalez y Gonzalez restaurant on Lower Broadway, New York City. Photo by the author.

of the same diameter. With improved technology—refrigeration, blenders, and Slurpee machines—patrons have come to expect margaritas that are sixteen ounces or larger—alcoholic bird baths. Product development in these restaurants has consisted largely of the search for new drinks such as top-shelf tequilas and the so-called *chelada*, combining beer, lime, salt, and ice, a Yucatecan combination. An entire genre of restaurant-bars grew up around the supposed multicultural marriage of drinking traditions, with names such as Carlos Murphy's or José Muldoon's and satirical narratives about the bandit son of an Irish soldier-of-fortune and a wayward Mexican debutante. But the appetite for this Wet-Mex was not completely insatiable, and declining sales around the turn of the century led many chains to move beyond the suburbs into smaller, more rural communities.[31]

Yet corporate chains and crossover diners alone cannot explain the spread of Mexican food. Migrants were an important force both as cooks and consumers. An updated map confirms Zelinsky's general predictions about the continental spread of Mexican restaurants, but regional patterns are still clearly evident. The data from 2010 reveal a clear correlation between Mexican restaurants and the ethnic population.[32] The Southwest continued to have the highest percentage of Mexican restaurants, all in double digits, with peaks as high as 20 percent along the Rio Grande from Albuquerque, New Mexico, to McAllen, Texas. The biggest change over those three decades came in the Southeast, where economic opportunities drew large numbers of migrant workers. In towns that had neither Mexicans nor tacos before Ronald Reagan's presidency, Mexican restaurants constituted upward of 5 percent of all establishments by the end of George W. Bush's term. This figure was twice the average percentage of restaurants in the Northeastern rustbelt, where declining industries attracted few migrants. Canada likewise had few Mexicans or restaurants, once again excepting Vancouver and Calgary, which formed border-crossing cultural regions. The surfing-skateboarding-snowboarding counterculture extended from Southern California to British Columbia, and cattle-and-oil economies linked Texas and Alberta.

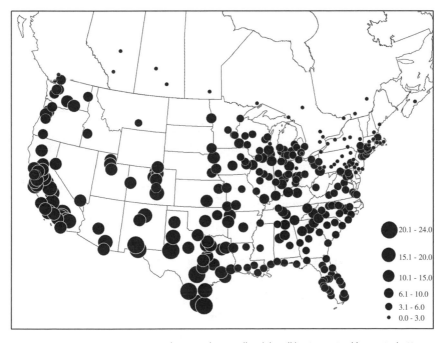

Figure 7.4. Mexican restaurants continued to expand nationally, while still leaving noticeable gaps in the Upper Midwest and Northeastern "rustbelt." Map of Mexican establishments as a percentage of total restaurants from YellowPages.com, 2010. Drawn by David Van Riper.

Between the peso crisis and neoliberal union busting, large numbers of migrants entered the United States beginning in the 1980s to work in meat-packing, construction, and other hazardous, labor-intensive industries in the Great Plains and the Deep South. From Idaho to North Carolina, and from Atlanta to Queens, migrants converted strip malls to ethnic grocery stores and operated taco trucks outside worksites and Sunday afternoon soccer fields. Although some of these new restaurants presented unmistakable varieties of Mexican regional cooking, it was also possible to see the increasing effects of nationalization in Mexican menus. For example, tacos al pastor, pozole, and shrimp cocktail were once regional dishes that have become increasingly common throughout Mexico. The nationalization of Mexican cuisine has also taken place in the United States, as migrants from different regions intermingle in restaurants and worksites. Yet, even with a growing Mexican national homogenization, chefs remain proud of their hometowns and will gladly explain their local culinary twists. Indigenous populations offer the most distinctive cuisines, and the Oaxacan community of Los Angeles has become a mecca for aficionados. Fernando López, a Zapotec from Matatlán, established himself as a community leader both by opening the Guelguetza restaurant chain and publishing El Oaxaqueño. The restaurants, like the newspaper, helped to preserve a sense of community through news and tastes of the homeland such as *clayudas* (enormous corn tortillas), *cecina* (marinated dried pork), and *asiento* (browned pork fat with cracklings).[33]

Constructing supply chains to reproduce such foods in the United States involved both local agriculture and long-distance trade. Fernando Martínez, a migrant disappointed with the quality of Mexican foods available in eastern North Carolina, where he worked on a two-hundred-acre tree farm, convinced his employer to allow him to plant specialty crops on a small patch of land. He soon built a following among migrant workers for his fresh chiles and *quintoniles* (greens), which he sold at farmers' markets. Likewise, Agustín Juárez spent his days working in the kitchen of an Italian restaurant in New York but supplemented his income by planting seeds from his native Oaxaca on an acre-and-a-half plot on Staten Island. Meanwhile, shipping firms supplied migrants with specialties that could not be grown in the United States. La Internacional, a family-run export business in San Agustín Yatareni, delivers chapulines and other local delicacies to Oaxacan communities throughout the United States. At times, such enterprises combine traditional recipes with the latest food-processing technology. Real Sazón, an Hidalgo-based firm, ships half-kilo containers of vacuum-packed barbacoa, complete with consommé and salsa, to migrants eager for a taste of home.[34]

Mexicans have become quite skilled at presenting their foods to diverse North American audiences, whether they were workers looking for a cheap meal or affluent foodies in search of an exotic experience. The South Texas breakfast taco, for example, had begun to appear on menus already by the 1970s but became increasingly popular in the 1980s as an alternative to the bacon-and-egg tacos of fast-food giants like Burger King. Regional variations soon emerged, with more barbacoa and beans near the border while Anglo bacon, eggs, and country sausage predominated in Austin and parts north. In the Rio Grande Valley, there have even been taco wars as rival chains battle for customers.[35] Other immigrant entrepreneurs have been able to move upscale and present their foods to more affluent audiences. The Montreal restaurant Rey del Taco (King of the Taco) started out as a lunch counter attached to a tortilla factory in the Mile End neighborhood. After several years of saving, the owners moved into a more prominent location at the bustling Jean Talon Market in Little Italy, where they staged an experience of Mexico City street life for Quebecois customers, with outdoor dining and serving aguas frescas as smoothies. Migrant restaurants thus have acquired a following at all levels of North American society.

The spread of Mexican food across North America offers examples of globalization from above and below, driven by both corporate marketing and migrant entrepreneurship. Although Taco Bell retains a commanding lead on the sale of fast food, new arrivals have increasingly challenged these stereotypes. Certainly in Los Angeles, Mexican tacos with fresh corn tortillas have all but replaced Mexican American taco shells. Nationwide, migrants were arguably more influential than chains in driving the spread of restaurants since the 1980s, as evidenced by the growing disparity between Mexican food in the South and New England. Yet migrant businesses depend on employment opportunities in the wider economy, and the crash of 2008 has wreaked havoc on the construction and hospitality industries. Without a constant influx of new migrants, the melting pot will reassert itself in the future, as it did with the Mexican American generation, although it is hard to predict what forms it will take. The future of Mexican food is all the more uncertain, given the increasing integration of North American markets.

Figure 7.5. El Rey del Taco in the Jean Talon Market, Montreal, Canada. Photo by Lorenzo Cancian.

Terroir in the Time of NAFTA

The blue corn bonanza, the international competition between alternate visions of Mexican food, has occurred within a context of social and economic convergence between the United States and Mexico. This has not been a marriage of equals; the U.S. government has dominated the relationship politically, while Mexican family farms have struggled to survive through the collective labor both of migrants and of those who stayed behind on the land. Moreover, the inequalities arising from this convergence have resulted as much from urban disdain for rural dwellers both in Mexico and in the United States as from conflicts between the two countries. When negotiating the agricultural provisions of NAFTA, Mexican President Carlos Salinas de Gortari gave away the farm.[36] Unable to compete with subsidized commodity maize from Iowa, some Mexican farmers have tried to grow higher-value crops, either through off-season fruits and vegetables or by following the European *terroir* model, which cultivates a "taste of place" in the hopes that knowledgeable consumers will pay more for distinctive goods. Other *campesinos* (rural workers) have migrated to Iowa to labor on the commercial farms that undercut their livelihoods at home. Because NAFTA lowered barriers to the trade in goods but not to the migration of people, these two forms of movement—one deemed legal, the other illegal—have been inextricably connected. Many observers, fearing the onslaught of migrants, trade goods, or both, have seen this as a battle between the Americanization of Mexico and the Mexicanization of the United States. Both trends are evident, and their outcome promises to shape the future of Mexican food.

At first glance, the United States and Mexico seem to represent two completely different models of food production: the former exemplifying global, industrial agriculture and fast food, and the latter retaining local, alternative agriculture and slow food. Indeed, the United States is home to giant seed companies and food processors, while large numbers of Mexican farmers are undercapitalized smallholders. Nevertheless, this dichotomy fails to capture the complexity of capitalist agriculture. The Mexican farm sector is quite differentiated, with transnational agrifood corporations, large commercial farms, and moderate-sized holdings alongside a mass of tiny plots held by impoverished campesinos.[37] Access to "traditional peasant food" is also highly skewed. Consumers in the industrialized nations of Western Europe and North America eat the greatest quantities of organic produce, grown without pesticides or artificial fertilizers. Some 98 percent of Mexican organic food is exported, mostly to its northern neighbors, and much of the rest is sold locally by upscale supermarkets.[38] This is not a new phenomenon; peasants have long been integrated into global capitalism, selling their best produce to urban consumers while gleaning subsistence from markets.

Although both countries combine industrial and alternative agricultural systems, one difference between them is that U.S. producers have valued maize not so much as a food in its own right but rather as a component in larger industrial processes. Midwestern farmers of the early nineteenth century marketed their crop by distilling it into corn mash whiskey or by feeding it to pigs to be driven across the Appalachian Trail or slaughtered in Cincinnati packinghouses. At the turn of the twentieth century, John Harvey Kellogg began marketing flaked corn kernels, the first instant breakfast cereal.

Industrial applications multiplied with the introduction of high fructose corn syrup in the 1960s, followed by the large-scale distilling of ethanol motor fuel and designer industrial starches for use in everything from diapers to plastic wrap. With its high starch and low fiber, maize also became the preferred feed for the livestock industry. To meet the growing demand for burgers and Cokes, in the 1970s the U.S. Department of Agriculture (USDA) reversed New Deal programs and encouraged the planting of fields "from fencepost to fencepost." Midwestern farmers followed this advice, transforming diversified agriculture into a monotonous landscape of maize and soybean fields. The resulting decline in commodity prices drove many farmers into bankruptcy by the 1980s. Yet chemical and seed companies pushed ahead with the development of genetically modified organisms (GMOs), claiming that proprietary seeds would lower costs by allowing farmers to use fewer chemicals. Some of the first commercial brands were Aventis's StarLink Bt maize, implanted with bacterial genes lethal to pests, and Monsanto's Roundup Ready, with genetic immunity to the company's herbicide. Government regulators first approved Bt maize in 1996 but only for animal feed; within five years, a fourth of all maize grown in the United States was genetically modified.[39]

Promoters of agribusiness have often depicted peasant cultivators as a problem to be overcome through development, but industrial agriculture actually depends on campesinos as a reservoir of cheap labor. Mechanized farms of the early twentieth century employed migrants until the Great Depression, when displaced "Arkies" and "Okies" became a source of transient labor in peak seasons. With the mobilization for World War II, Mexicans returned to the fields as braceros and continued to migrate informally long after the guestworker program expired in 1964. Commentators fiercely debate the social consequences of migration, but there can be no questioning their contribution to the U.S. economy. At the turn of the millennium, an estimated seven million Mexican-born workers accounted for about 5 percent of the civilian labor force in the United States, and more than half of them worked in construction and service occupations, particularly food preparation and domestic work. Migrants were particularly important for the organic food industry, which replaced industrial inputs of chemical pesticides and herbicides with labor-intensive practices made affordable by low-paid workers. The Mexican economy depended even more heavily on migrants, with some 14 percent of its labor force located in the United States. In 2005, the Bank of Mexico estimated that remittances back to Mexico totaled $16 billion annually, which was more than tourism or foreign investment, although the amounts declined during the subsequent recession.[40]

Modern industrial monoculture depended equally heavily on the biodiversity created by peasant cultivators. Teosinte, for example, conferred resistance to seven important plant diseases after it was "rediscovered" in Mexico in 1977. An economist calculated the value of perennial corn bred from teosinte at $8.6 billion per year, but Mexico received no compensation. International property law ensured that seed companies such as Monsanto and Aventis profit from the germplasm of commercial varieties while treating peasant landraces as a natural resource with no economic value. Nevertheless, as one scholar explained: "It is important to recognize, as Marx did, that the germplasm of domesticated species is not a free gift of nature, but is the product of millions and millions of hours of human labor. Whatever the contribution of plant scientists, they are not the sole producers of utility in the seed."[41]

The Mexican government was less interested in protecting the rights of small farmers than in supporting private firms such as Maseca, short for Molinos Aztecas, or Aztec Mills, an industrial producer of dehydrated tortilla flour. For most of the twentieth century, the Mexican government emphasized the production of basic grains to ensure political stability and to help subsidize national industry. As late as 1980, officials announced a major program to achieve food sovereignty and reduce dependence on imports, in part because of concern about the U.S. grain embargo against the Soviet Union following its invasion of Afghanistan in 1979. With the peso collapse of 1982, the Mexican government shifted to a neoliberal approach, privatizing business and slashing welfare programs that provided cheap food for urban residents.[42] Maseca, founded in 1949, had benefited from decades of government support for research in tortilla flour, although consumers overwhelmingly preferred tortillas made of freshly ground dough. The crisis of the 1980s forced hungry Mexicans to put aside long-standing prejudices, especially as fresh products became increasingly difficult to find. Tortilla makers denounced Maseca as "Masa Seca" (dried-out tortilla dough), but their outrage counted for little in the face of neoliberal reforms. Unable to find alternative sources of maize, many were reduced to outlets for the multinational company. The market share for masa flour soared from 5 percent in 1975 to more than 50 percent by the end of the century. Critics also denounced the manipulation of differential regional corn subsidies; one journalist estimated that government support for the company amounted to $300 million. The renowned journalist Alma Guillermoprieto wrote: "When the privatization program of Mexico's notorious former President Carlos Salinas delivered the future of the tortilla into their hands... [magnates] served up to the Mexican people the rounds of grilled cardboard that at present constitute the nation's basic foodstuff."[43]

With limited potential for further domestic growth, Maseca began to focus on international expansion. The company had entered the California market in 1978 with the purchase of Mission Foods and focused at first on the local Mexican community, buying out small factories, advertising heavily in Spanish-language media, and building efficient distribution networks. Within East Los Angeles neighborhoods, the company made store deliveries daily or even two or three times a day to satisfy Mexican demand for the freshest possible tortillas. In the United States, as in Mexico, small competitors referred to the company as an "evil empire." By the 1990s, the company had built a network of tortilla factories stretching across the country, and it had also launched international ventures in South America, Europe, Australia, and China. Reaching beyond the Mexican community in the relentless search for profits, Maseca shifted from fresh corn tortillas to other product lines, including wheat flour tortillas, chips, and taco shells; investment in China was spurred by the demand for KFC chicken wraps. The anthropologist Carolina Bank Muñoz described Maseca as "a Mexican company trying to impersonate a U.S. company that is impersonating Mexican culture."[44]

Globalization has also transformed food retailing in Mexico, lowering prices for middle-class consumers while crowding out public markets that catered to the working classes. Wal-Mart first entered Mexico in 1991 and has become the country's largest private employer with more than two thousand retail outlets, including local subsidiaries. Its annual sales of $15 billion in 2005 accounted for three out of every ten pesos that Mexicans spent on food. The company revolutionized retail supply chains by creating parallel procurement systems, bypassing public wholesale markets, where ambulant vendors rubbed shoulders with the purchasing agents of local supermarket chains. Moreover, the *New York Times* claimed that executives resorted to a sweeping campaign of bribery to ensure rapid growth and to beat out competitors.[45] Fearing for their survival, rival firms emulated Wal-Mart's famously efficient distribution centers, computer systems, and grower contracts, although small vendors lacked the resources to adapt to the new business environment. One group of researchers concluded: "Given its market power and impact on its domestic competitors, consumers and suppliers, it is perhaps more appropriate to speak of the walmartization, rather than globalization, of food retailing in Mexico."[46] Direct procurement has drawn farm cooperatives into larger supply chains, but under contracts that require investment in expensive refrigeration and handling equipment. Although in theory capitalization should allow growers to compete on a global basis, in practice, restructuring has led to a growing privatization of Mexican wholesale markets on which the working classes depend for food without significantly benefiting small-scale farmers.[47]

Wal-Mart's Mexican operations reflect the deeply unequal structures of trade under NAFTA. Corporations and commodities moved freely southward, while people and goods from Mexico faced a maze of border restrictions and nontariff barriers. Mexican government officials made a strategic decision to specialize in farm products that would be viable in international markets, shifting from basic grains to nontraditional agricultural exports to North American consumers.[48] They did not count on a range of nontariff barriers imposed by the United States, ostensibly for the purposes of sanitary inspection or border security, but often with the clear goal of protecting domestic farmers. Frequently changing USDA standards require companies to purchase expensive technology that may need replacement a short time later. Even packing companies that have invested in such equipment have been wiped out by declarations of health quarantines or delays at border crossings. Not even Maseca has been able to circumvent border restrictions, although the company would dearly love to concentrate production in Baja California and export tortillas to Southern California.[49]

Mexican migrant workers face an equally precarious situation in the United States. Congress simply does not allocate employment-based visas to satisfy the demand for manual labor in the U.S. economy. Moreover, the nation's immigration enforcement system has long focused on workers rather than on the employers or consumers who benefit from their labor. As a result, migrants are forced into an underworld of illegality, where they earn significantly less than the minimum wage and have little recourse to the protections of occupational safety or child labor laws. News stories about immigration raids provide regular reminders not only of the number of migrant workers but also of the deplorable conditions in which they labor. As it turned out, the "giant sucking sound" of NAFTA was not the relocation of factory jobs southward that the presidential candidate Ross Perot predicted in 1992 but rather the movement of impoverished Mexican campesinos northward in search of work.[50]

The environmental costs of modern industrial agriculture have also been passed along to Mexico and other countries of the Global South. One area of concern has been the loss of biodiversity from industrial standardization. Maseca gears its machinery to particular varieties of commercial maize and has little use for the idiosyncrasies of peasant landraces, which have different characteristics from region to region. Yet, as the hearth of domestication, Mexico still has the world's greatest variety of maize plants under cultivation, despite pressure from industrial buyers. GM-maize has become an even more sensitive political issue in Mexico, and not only for its potential to contaminate native strains. There are also threats to an important tourist attraction, the Monarch breeding grounds of Michoacán, from the adverse effects of Bt corn on butterfly larvae. Despite a ban on planting GM-maize in Mexico, Maseca legally imports large quantities of such grain to process for tortilla flour through a strategic partnership with Archer Daniels Midland. The industry's argument that GMOs could be controlled in the field had been discredited already in 2000 with the discovery of StarLink, approved in the United States only for animal feed, in Taco Bell taco shells. If North American farmers could not keep their corn straight, there was little hope for Mexico, where peasants cannot afford to be picky. A national scandal erupted just one year later when researchers documented GM-maize growing in fields throughout Oaxaca. Nevertheless, attempts to enforce greater restrictions on biotechnology were blocked by AgroBIO, an industry lobby representing foreign seed companies.[51]

Social and health concerns about the modern food system have spread with the increasing incorporation of Mexico's urban middle class and even rural communities into a transnational consumer society. Affluent customers mobbed the first McDonald's when it opened in Mexico City in 1985, and local chains soon emulated U.S. models. Oxy emerged as the Mexican 7–11, while the venerable Sanborn's battled the Wal-Mart subsidiary Vips for the mantle of Denny's. Each new trend was given a local twist; for example, nachos became a favorite theater snack in the 1990s, with the same goopy yellow cheese but better jalapeños. Remittances from migrant workers have also introduced remote villages to global consumer culture. As young men migrate to the United States in search of higher wages, women have had to take over agricultural labor, leaving less time to cook at home. Across the social spectrum, consumption of processed food has increased, contributing to an alarming incidence of obesity, heart disease, and diabetes, even among poorly nourished rural populations. Mexico now reportedly has the world's second largest percentage of obese citizens, surpassed only by the United States.[52] Festival foods have also been increasingly commercialized and privatized, to the detriment of transnational families that are held together in part by culinary traditions. For weddings and saints' days, when hundreds of guests would formerly have been served mole de guajolote and tamales, smaller numbers often dine on pork chops and applesauce in catered functions. Although festival meals require countless hours of female labor, they serve as investments in communal solidarity and pay valuable dividends in migrant remittances. Young migrants will be less inclined to make the arduous trip home for the holidays if they can find the same pork chops at their local Wal-Mart.[53]

The culinary globalization represented by Wal-Mart, Maseca, and Monsanto has generated widespread calls for local control over the food system. In the United States, this backlash has been channeled into diverse alternative food initiatives such as farmers' markets, organic labeling, urban farming, and political opposition to commodity supports. Mexican resistance to capitalist agriculture took an even more dramatic form with the Zapatista uprising in Chiapas on New Year's Day of 1994, just as NAFTA went into effect. Although the baklava-clad rebels demanded indigenous rights in particular, they were also deeply concerned with the plight of Mexican small farmers under an authoritarian regime that pursued globalization at any cost. Urban protests have also focused on the neoliberal sacrifice of Mexico's food sovereignty, especially in early 2007, when a rush to convert Midwestern maize into biofuel was followed by a dramatic rise in the cost of Mexican tortillas. Food rioters have shown a flair for political theater and an awareness of environmental issues. Protesters pelted the U.S. embassy with corn cobs, symbolically rejecting the import of GM-maize, and marched to demand assistance with the rising cost of living.[54]

The protest against GMOs led to the creation of a cross-class coalition of producers and consumers called "In Defense of Maize" in order to assert Mexican food sovereignty. Intellectuals within the movement demanded the protection of the countryside and rural livelihoods as essential to the nation's health. Campesinos sought to assert their voices in the debate and gain recognition for their deep knowledge of farming, thereby countering industry leaders who dismissed opposition to biotechnology as the stubbornness of backward peasants.[55] The middle classes often framed the question in consumer terms. In September 2001, following the revelation of GM contamination, Greenpeace activists in Mexico City targeted billboards advertising crispy, flute-shaped tacos; the ecological guerrillas changed the slogan from "Flautas with Maseca are tastier," to "Flautas with Maseca are genetically modified."[56]

Local food networks have emerged to link rural producers and urban consumers, thereby challenging the market power of Monsanto and Maseca. For example, Nuestro Maíz (Our maize), a cooperative program of the National Association of Campesino Marketing Associations, established a network of small tortilla factories to utilize the cooperative's production. After a study of industrial applications such as ethanol production, they concluded that the most cost-effective outlet for their crop was to market tortillas of freshly processed maize at a small premium. A second initiative, the Itanoní Tortillería, was founded in Oaxaca City in 2001 to build middle-class and tourist markets for landrace maize. Their tacos and quesadillas acquired such a following that the tortillería opened a restaurant in the historic downtown. Such cooperatives are financially precarious, but for that very reason, the "evil empire" can impose few barriers to entry. When cheap maize became available at the turn of the century through a combination of record U.S. harvests and the dumping of Mexican government stockpiles, fully 10 percent of the factories that had used tortilla flour promptly switched back to fresh corn dough.[57]

The ecologist Victor Toledo envisioned such local initiatives as a potential second Zapatista revolution that could make sustainable agriculture an alternative to traditional development strategies. The Programa de Campesino a Campesino (farmer-to-farmer movement) has exemplified this approach through extension classes conducted not by university agronomists but rather by fellow farmers, often from indigenous communities, who demonstrate the practical value of ecological farming techniques such as animal traction, biodynamic gardening, organic inputs, precision fertilizer, and seed selection. Some of these were novel ideas introduced from other countries; others were skills that had been forgotten through the rush to modernize. Distrustful of their government, working-class Mexicans have a long-tradition of self-help community building through such campesino exchanges and cooperatives. Yet while the benefits of sustainable farming have been well established, economic insecurity puts limits on popular attempts to claim food sovereignty, especially as a younger generation that has become accustomed to the income from migrant labor turns away from an insecure life in the fields.[58]

Perhaps middle-class demand will help sustain local initiatives in the face of corporate competition. Clearly, the campesinos cannot bet their future on the market for bespoke tortillas, if only because urban consumers eat far fewer of them per meal than do rural dwellers. A more promising approach has been to appeal to conscientious consumers in the Global North through the fair-trade movement, which has achieved some success with coffee, chocolate, and other commodities. The goal has been to increase incomes for campesino organizations while encouraging environmentally sound practices and products such as shade-grown coffee. Yet fair-trade initiatives depend on consumers' willingness to spend extra, an uncertain proposition in difficult economic times. In any event, the profits remain largely with middlemen from the Global North. For many small farmers, the labor of cleaning coffee beans or chocolate seeds for gourmet markets is not worth the small financial gains for what is still essentially commodity production.[59] By contrast, the European strategy of developing and marketing high-quality terroir-based luxury goods such as Champagne wine and prosciutto ham has the potential to create permanent income gains. Mexico exports high-quality pork and vegetables, but it receives relatively little income from them because of the lack of global cachet. Efforts to promote agricultural exports have been supported by the Foreign Trade Bank (Bancomext), founded in 1990, yet far more resources are needed to match the European government extension services, which are consciously geared toward identifying distinctive growing conditions and processing methods that can maximize taste and consumer appeal, unlike the interchangeable commodity approach followed in the United States.[60]

Political hurdles must also be surmounted to make terroir an effective strategy, as can be seen in the case of tequila. In 1994 Mexico joined the Lisbon Accord, gaining "denomination of origin" (DOC) status for its iconic drink. A national regulatory council was created to determine standards for what could be sold as "tequila" in signatory nations. Other regional distillers of maguey, from Oaxacan *mezcal* to Sonoran *bacanora*, also began to invest in modern facilities in the hopes of marketing their own distinctive drinks. Unfortunately, the United States, the world's leading consumer of tequila, does not recognize the accord, and more than 80 percent of its tequila is shipped in bulk and bottled by U.S. distillers. This two-tiered structure, with a relatively small market for estate-bottled añejos and mass sales of inferior mixtos, works well for Sauza and Cuervo, who have formed strategic alliances with Allied Domecq and Heublein, transnational conglomerates that coordinate production between Mexican and North American firms. Without political support from leading producers, the Mexican government has made little effort to pressure the United States to restrict tequila bottling and improve quality.[61]

Environmental and social as well as political challenges threaten efforts by Mexican producers to raise the value of their exports. When popular foods have been "discovered" by mass markets, it often leads to scarcity. The fad for fajitas in the United States, for example, caused a dramatic jump in the price of formerly cheap skirt steak, making it unaffordable to the Mexican Americans who invented the dish in the first place. Likewise, ingredients that Chef Fortino Rojas Contreras once used for his pre-Hispanic cuisine have become endangered species. Meanwhile, dualistic labor markets and the lack of educational opportunities have limited the possibilities for minorities. Even in upscale Mexican restaurants in the United States, well-paid chef and sous chef positions often go to Anglos, while immigrants from Latin America fill the ranks of poorly paid dishwashers and busboys.[62]

Although marginalized groups have suffered most from the struggle over Mexican food, the globalization of migrant remittances, campesino exchanges, and marketing of good food offers more hope for an impoverished countryside than does the politics of national sovereignty. Concern for social justice, environmental and personal health, and tasty food has prompted growing numbers of European and North American consumers to pay premiums for healthful, organic foods. Promising examples of Mexican terroir include traditional craft chocolate and tequila. There are also opportunities for experimental projects such as feeding avocados to pigs, which seems to convey healthful antioxidants to pork.[63] Marketing such goods will be difficult in the face of Mexican government neglect and U.S. trade restrictions. Nevertheless, the Chiapas rebels successfully deployed Internet technology to call global attention to their unequal struggle against the Mexican Army, and they could turn this media savvy to selling premium chocolate and ham.[64] Just as First Lady Michelle Obama created a vegetable garden at the White House in 2009, perhaps one day Zapatistas will plant a *milpa* (cornfield) on the Zócalo to symbolize the return of local control over food.

THE BATTLE OF THE TACO TRUCKS

CONCLUSION

I n 2008, the city of Los Angeles declared war on Mexican mobile food
carts. There had already been periodic sweeps of vendors in city parks,
and officers had occasionally ordered taco trucks to move along. But with
a new ordinance, passed on the eve of Cinco de Mayo, the city raised the pen-
alty for loitering, defined as parking in one spot for more than thirty minutes,
from a mere infraction to a misdemeanor punishable by fines and possible
prison time. A diverse coalition of Angelinos rallied in support of the vendors,
forming a website (saveourtacotrucks.org) and declaring that "carne asada
is not a crime." County officials responded that the trucks had become "a big
quality of life issue." This battle of the taco trucks, like campaigns against the
chili queens and tamale pushcarts a century earlier, revealed diverse racial
and communal fault lines in contemporary Los Angeles. Many Latinos already
felt harassed by anti-immigrant campaigns such as the passage in 1994 of the
draconian Proposition 187, which denied basic services to immigrants before
it was repealed by court order. They considered this ordinance to be yet another
form of discrimination against their livelihoods and culture. Nevertheless,
some neighbors thought the trucks were a nuisance because of their late-night
crowds and litter, while Mexican restaurateurs complained about unfair competition. Anglos were likewise split on the issue, with nativists applauding the
crackdown and "chowhounds" defending their favorite vendors. Although a

judge declared the ordinance unconstitutional, cities around the country have engaged in similar battles over public space and the rights of citizenship. New Orleans banned taco trucks in the aftermath of the 2005 Katrina hurricane at a time when Latinos were prominent in recovery efforts.[1]

While taco trucks' public presence has made them a focus for anti-immigrant outrage—even when they are operated by Mexican American citizens—the struggles over street vending have also revealed how the pursuit of culinary authenticity is embedded within complicated relations of race and class. The trucks originally served a predominantly Latino, working-class clientele by setting up shop near factories, plazas, and soccer fields. More recently, however, taco trucks have become sites of culinary tourism for Anglos searching for ethnic exoticism. Gentrified taco trucks, not all of them Mexican, now frequent upscale neighborhoods and corporate centers. Roy Choi's Kogi Korean BBQ taco trucks use Twitter to inform followers of their locations, attracting impossibly long lines of people hungry for short-rib tacos and kimchi quesadillas. New media have been used most effectively by middle-class truck owners, but even plebeian vendors may benefit from online recognition. Blogs and social networking sites offer countless rankings of the most authentic tacos and photos documenting visits to spots ranging from the well known to the unknown. Taco trucks have provided some with an opportunity for entrepreneurship, allowing owners to accumulate enough capital to open a more permanent restaurant. Far more operators work long hours for low wages in leased trucks. Moreover, the pursuit of authentic tacos, whether real or virtual, contains its own cultural politics, not so much a democratic acknowledgment of blue-collar food but rather a new form of distinction. Like art critics who gain status through their knowledge of primitive art, or for that matter, the tourists who went slumming among the chili queens of San Antonio, contemporary taco truck followers acquire a measure of cultural distinction through their command of exotic cuisines and their ability to discern what is truly authentic.[2]

Planet Taco has argued that notions of authentic Mexican food have been invented by promoters of culinary tourism. While often attributed to ancient Aztecs and Maya, such an authentic Mexican cuisine did not exist in pre-Hispanic or even colonial times. In fact, Mexican food, like the nation itself, was the product of globalization, beginning with the Spanish conquest. Foodstuffs from Mesoamerica were also carried around the early modern world, although the kitchen knowledge that would make them Mexican was

Figure C.1. Anaheim Street, Tacos El Gallito. Flikr. Photograph by Joey Zanotti.

largely left behind. Present-day global images of Mexican food have been shaped by the regional cooking of northern New Spain in distinctive dishes such as wheat flour tortillas and chili con carne. After the United States conquered this territory in 1848, the chili queens and other Mexican Americans struggled to gain acceptance in an Anglo-dominated society. Their cooking became the subject of enduring stereotypes of Mexican food as dangerous but alluring, although at the time only a mass-market version of canned and powdered chili crossed over to the mainstream. Meanwhile in nineteenth-century Mexico, intellectuals struggled to reconcile their own national cuisine and identity from among three separate ideals: modern French, nostalgic Creole, and unfashionable Indian foods. Mexican regional cuisines, largely Creole in nature, were consolidated by cookbooks and restaurants of the mid-twentieth century in response to the upheavals of industrialization—on both sides of the border—but Mexican nationalists refused to accept the nascent Tex-Mex and Cal-Mex tacos as legitimate. When industrialized versions of Mexican American home cooking were carried around the world during the Cold War, culinary professionals claimed pre-Hispanic authenticity for Mexican food, even though these modern versions often had little to do with the indigenous Mexicans who supposedly provided their authenticity.

In seeking to historicize authenticity, this book has shown how images of Mexican food have evolved over time and how ideas about what is or is not proper Mexican cooking have been used for political purposes, sometimes to make profits for cultural outsiders but other times to exclude ethnic minorities from citizenship. Perhaps the most compelling sense of authenticity for cultural insiders derives from the familiarity of childhood foods, although this is also the most variable form, because every family has its own particular tastes and traditions. Notions of authenticity can also convey a sense of pride in the shared cultural heritage of ethnic and national communities. Nearly twenty years ago, when I described my doctoral dissertation on the history of Mexican food to a Mexican American working at Joe T. García's restaurant in Fort Worth, Texas, he enthusiastically declared the project "¡auténtico!" But even this communal sense of authentic is inevitably tied to relationships of power and authority, as particular individuals use authenticity to speak for larger groups. Porfirian intellectuals such as Manuel Payno sought to define an authentic national cuisine as a sensual rhetoric for advancing their Creole image of the national community. Maury Maverick tried to revive the chili queens both to promote local tourism and to build political support, although the Mexican community rejected his nostalgic patronage. Those without childhood memories of Mexican food—myself included—have often pursued authenticity as a source of social distinction through arcane knowledge of exotic cultures. Corporate advertising campaigns have even developed forms of satirical, mocking inauthenticity such as the Frito Bandito or the Taco Bell dog.[3]

Narratives of authenticity thus arise through the process of codifying domestic kitchen practices into the formal and public realm of cuisine; after all, home cooks rarely feel the need to claim authenticity for their own family recipes. The regional cuisines of Oaxaca and Sonora, as well as their Tex-Mex and Cal-Mex counterparts, are modern artifacts of culinary tourism, in many ways quite distant from the domestic practices from which they emerged. The culinary literature and restaurant menus that serve to codify recipes are similar to and often allied with the ideological work of forging national identities. Both sets of narratives ground collective memories of an abstract community in concrete representations, creating emotional ties by way of things that can be seen, heard, and tasted, like a flag, anthem, or dish. The historical memories of nations seek to make modern, often accidental, political units appear ancient and natural, while purposely forgetting inconvenient episodes and rivalries. Culinary authenticity likewise derives from genealogies that connect present-day consumers with mythical origins, thereby distorting the social history of times past. Thus, the banquets of ancient Aztec and Maya Indians have been enshrined by Mexican revolutionary indigenismo, while the culinary inventions of Pueblo Indians have been erased from Hispanic memories of New Mexico. The alternate treatment of Indians in these narratives did not reflect more or less egalitarian societies but simply different ideological motivations: celebrations of independence in Mexico as opposed to assertions of whiteness in the United States.[4]

The historically evolving images of Mexican food illustrate some of the ways people form stereotypes of cultures with which they have minimal or no direct contact, particularly during periods of intensifying global contact. In comparing Mexican food to Chinese and Italian, there is a clear difference between who has actually done the globalizing. Whereas Chinese and Italian migrants circled the world in the late nineteenth century, Mexican food has been carried largely by travelers from the United States, although pizza offers a similar example of globalized commodity culture. The process of cultural change has followed from two basic and conflicting human impulses: the desire to take comfort in the familiar and the predilection to experiment with the novel and exotic. Both have been at work since the early modern era at least, when Europeans adapted New World ingredients such as maize, chiles, and chocolate into existing culinary systems, while still projecting onto them fantasies of grand empires as well as fears of disease and immorality. Similar flights of imagination continue to the present day as indigenous exoticism becomes a pathway to instant spirituality. New Age authenticity was central to Sonja Atkinson's cookbook, *The Aztec Way to Healthy Eating* (1992), which advocated a truncated pyramid of Aztec food groups with menus based on the calendar stone.[5]

Mexican food has also provided a vehicle for thinking about citizenship and immigrant incorporation within the United States. Racial panics have often been conflated with culinary difference, from the late nineteenth-century perception of tacos as an indigenous invasion of Mexico City to present-day nativists in the United States who associate the supposed refusal of newcomers to assimilate with the "indigestibility" of their food. Even cross-cultural eating provides no guarantee of social harmony. For example, one Texan began marketing "Minuteman" salsa to benefit a vigilante group of the same name that targets migrant workers. Under such circumstances, a commentator asked: "What does it mean to eat the tacos but expel the trucks?"[6] Nevertheless, such episodes of racial conflict must be balanced by simultaneous histories of accommodation. In a poignant scene, Gloria Anzaldúa recalled the validation her mother, a fieldworker in South Texas, took from having a recipe for *enchiladas coloradas* included in a cooking manual prepared by an Anglo home economist. Moreover, recent immigrants have actually seen Mexican food as a model to be emulated; Asian vendors market their foods as tacos in order to "Americanize" them.[7]

The outcome of the conflicting impulses toward familiarity and novelty has often been determined by structural constraints, particularly racial segregation. Anglo businessmen have profited from the desire for ethnic exoticism, at least since Otis Farnsworth opened the Original Mexican Restaurant in San Antonio. Even when run by Mexican Americans such as Felix Tijerina, restaurants catering to an Anglo clientele offer limited opportunities for cross-racial contact. While Anglos may visit predominantly Mexican restaurants, they often feel out of place. Indeed, the thrill of danger may be part of the attraction, as it probably was for the tourists who sought out chili queens in turn-of-the-century San Antonio. Glen Bell built a taco empire on the combination of exoticism and distrust in the segregated streets of postwar Southern California. Such feelings persist today in small towns in the Midwest, where new migrants have revitalized dwindling communities, even as they provoked the suspicions of many old-timers. Despite their desire for Mexican restaurants that are exotic but not threatening, the boundaries between novelty and familiarity are constantly shifting. After all, those old-timers generally descended from earlier immigrants, who were exotic newcomers at one point.[8]

Corporate constructions of inauthenticity, and the asymmetrical power relations they embody, pose a far greater barrier to immigrant acceptance than small-town ways. The sociologist Sarita Gaytán has demonstrated the pervasiveness of inauthenticity in market-based promotions of Mexican restaurants, whether by insiders or outsiders. Satirical advertising provides a way for companies such as Chi-Chi's or Taco Bell to cleanse their products of ethnicity. "Fire Roasted Zuni Zalza," for example, ironically evoked a mythical Mexican countryside: "The old patrón walked down the mountainside overlooking the jalapeño field. He paused, turned to young Josélito [*sic*] and said, 'Make me a salsa, make me a salsa I can't refuse.'" Advertisements for alcohol, like mobster references, have also perpetuated chili queen stereotypes, frustrating restaurateurs who seek to change popular images. One asked: "Why do people associate Mexican restaurants with total oblivion when it comes to drinking?"[9]

Even Mexican corporations have indulged in creating such inauthenticity when they perceive a market opportunity. Grupo Modelo has not worried about Mexican dignity in promoting Corona beer. Maseca, the industrial tortilla flour giant, seemingly has a competitive advantage in its local knowledge of Mexican food. The company has even sponsored a Mexican corn-mill attraction at Disney's California Adventure theme park, although its educational effort seems directed mostly toward convincing Anglo customers that its products are sanitary. Having locked up the domestic market, Maseca increasingly depends for profits on such international sales. The process of globalization, taking foods out of their ethnic context and adapting them to foreigners, has been standard practice for more than a century in the U.S. food-processing industry. Local knowledge may actually hinder such an enterprise, although Maseca never let authenticity stand in the way of a deal—the company has supplied shells to Taco Bell for twenty years.[10]

The difficulty of pinning down authenticity in global commodity culture is particularly great. Mexican efforts to market authentic regional cuisines are pointless if consumers are actually looking for Tex-Mex tastes. Anne Skoogh, a food blogger and taco fanatic from Stockholm, recognized this crucial point: "People here don't think of tacos as Mexican as much as they think they are American."[11] Indeed, Taco Bell has produced its own forms of authenticity, albeit unanticipated, which became clear when the chain attempted to establish itself in Mexico. The grand opening, in an upscale Mexico City suburb in 1992, prompted skeptics to wonder about "coals to Newcastle." The company spokesmen blithely justified the move with the claim that "the one thing Mexico lacks is somewhere to get a clean, cheap, fast taco." In fact, as the journalist Alma Guillermoprieto observed, countless taquerías offered precisely that, although admittedly "no Mexican taco stand looks like a NASA food-preparation station." Even Taco Bell acknowledged its doubts by obtaining a supply of fresh corn tortillas and offering the standard taquería fare of the 1990s, pork carnitas and shredded beef. But Mexican customers were disappointed, because they could get those tacos anywhere. One woman complained: "This doesn't taste like the real thing, does it? What I wanted was those big taco shells stuffed with salad and Kraft cheese and all *kinds* of stuff, like what you get in Texas."[12] Taco Bell had actually become a form of tourist authenticity for a select group of middle-class Mexicans who could afford to vacation in San Antonio. Yet the novelty of taco shells soon wore off, and repeated efforts by the company to "make a run for the border" have failed.[13]

In Mexico, the pursuit of culinary authenticity has perpetuated what anthropologists call "peasant essentialism," a set of stereotypes that reduces rural workers to timeless and unchanging relics of the ancient past, thereby contributing to their continued marginality. Creole patriots at the end of the eighteenth century imagined the Mexican nation to be a legitimate successor to the Aztec monarchy, but they were reluctant to grant political rights to living Indians, who had supposedly regressed under Spanish colonial oppression. The tortilla discourse of the late nineteenth century shifted the blame for indigenous marginality from political misrule to poor diets. With the fashion for native foods at the end of the twentieth century, Mazatec women wearing indigenous costumes became a regular presence on roadways around Mexico City as they sold authentic tortillas to commuters returning home to affluent suburbs. Their use of colored maize, once looked down on as famine food, added economic value by distinguishing hand-crafted Mazatec tortillas from the uniformly white, industrial Maseca consumed by the urban working classes. While the income helps impoverished communities to survive, the folkloric performances of culinary tourism reinforce their social exclusion.[14] When middle-class residents first noticed the presence of indigenous vendors in the capital during the 1970s, there was a sense of crisis about the failure of modernization. Decades later, marginalized Indians have become familiar, accepted, even valorized. Surely only the challenge of Tex-Mex could have convinced the Mexican political elite to abandon its self-image of modernity and to construct a national cuisine around indigenous primitivism.

The limits of this culinary authenticity became apparent with the recognition of Mexican cuisine by UNESCO as an "intangible patrimony of humanity" in 2010. Celebrated in Mexico as a tremendous coup, the campaign for recognition has a complicated history. Mexico petitioned the United Nations cultural authority for the first time in 2005, arguing that the country's unique culinary artistry needed protection both from fast-food imitators and from genetically modified invaders. Thus, it grew out of the national debate inspired by the coalition In Defense of Maize and reflected the concerns of a wide range of Mexican society. The UN agency, which usually stamps its approval on dance, music, and oral traditions, had never before received a petition about cuisine. Mexican scholars and chefs prepared supporting documentation to address a number of concerns such as how to define the cuisine and to show why the biodiversity of maize needed protection. While such concerns were valid, there was also a tendency within the movement to reify a canon of authentic Mexican dishes, which recalled the exclusivist nineteenth-century constructions of the national cuisine. Ultimately, the researchers compiled nearly ninety pounds of text, plus a video. To support the petition further with cooking demonstrations at the Hotel Bristol in Paris, the Mexican government assembled "a brigade of six Mexican chefs," listed by name on the presidential website, "and five indigenous cooks," listed by region. Once again, the elite perpetuated a distinction between the artistry of classically trained chefs and the ethnography of village cooks.[15]

Yet, ultimately, Mexico's culinary elite found themselves caught in the same trap of primitive art to which they had consigned the "five indigenous cooks." UNESCO rejected the initial petition, and the chefs returned home dejected. By 2010, when the UN body reviewed a new application, the Mexicans were joined by other candidates, including the "gastronomic meal" of the French, gingerbread craft of Northern Croatia, and the Mediterranean diet (a combined petition from Greece, Italy, and Morocco). Domestic politics had also changed, following the 2006 election of President Felipe Calderón. The new petition focused not on the national symbol of maize, but rather on one particular regional cuisine, the "Michoacán paradigm," which happened to feature Calderón's home state. The implicit rivalry between states promised to undermine even further any sense of national solidarity from the project. In the end, UNESCO accepted all of the applicants, thereby preserving international hierarchies of status: France remained the center of gastronomic art, while Mexico became the poster child for regional peasant cooking.[16] Ultimately, this recognition served not to defend rural livelihoods but rather as a fillip for the culinary tourism industry. Even before the announcement was official, I found a "Patrimony of Humanity" combination plate on the menu of a restaurant serving Oaxacan food in Querétaro.

This is not to deny the value of culinary tourism. Producing food is surely the most common form of work in human history, and the people who do it deserve to be rewarded for their labor. Nevertheless, the desire for authentic, noncommercialized food too often reinforces patriarchal restrictions that deny fair compensation for such labor, most notably, to domestic cooks. At times, notions of authenticity may help open market niches for marginalized cooks such as Indian women. Abigail Mendoza, the renowned Zapotec chef, has built a successful restaurant catering to tourists searching for ethnic authenticity. The problem lies in the discriminatory nature of these exchanges: the male chef is paid in cash, while the female is expected to cook for love; the commercial plant breeder earns royalties for his work, while the peasant's seeds are treated as a natural resource that deserve no compensation. Colonial relationships encourage the French chef to experiment with and artistically refine the foods of other cultures, as with the New Southwestern cuisine. By contrast, customer expectations limit the Zapotec chef to the foods of her ethnic community, even if her restaurant is located in Los Angeles.

Admittedly, Mendoza and others may prefer the foods of their childhood; marginalized communities often fall back on their culture in the face of hostile outsiders. One rural woman denounced the inferior foods available to Mexico City residents by declaring: "They say we live like animals here in the countryside, but in the city, they *eat* like animals!"[17] Mexican Americans meanwhile have responded to the Anglo appropriation of chili con carne and fajitas by taking comfort in menudo, a dish that is unlikely to be claimed by the mainstream. Another defensive sentiment in the face of Anglo discrimination was expressed by Victor Villaseñor, in his family memoir, *Rain of Gold*, recalling his immigrant grandmother's words from the 1920s, "don't worry about the police. One day we'll feed them tacos with so much old chile that they'll get diarrhea and their assholes will burn for weeks!"[18] Even elite Mexicans have felt alienated by images of their food encountered when living abroad, and understandably so. While some such as Cristina Prun have had the resources to challenge those stereotypes in public, most expatriates have reserved their cooking for intimate family gatherings, like the O'Briens' dinner of mole and tamales in nineteenth-century Paris. Patricia López Marroquín, a Mexican recently transplanted to Australia, has taken comfort from reviving a family tradition of tortilla making: "As an expat, I have now learned to prepare my own tortillas from scratch.... It is almost the same feeling I had as a child when my grandmother was preparing our meals and handed over a recently cooked tortilla. Those memories never disappear."[19]

The process of localization is inevitable as people adapt novelties to fit with local cultures, and cuisines cannot acquire a global reputation without inspiring people to take liberties with recipes. Mexican travelers have become understandably irritated at misrepresentation of their cuisine: frijoles tasting like British baked beans or party stereotypes of Tex-Mex swagger and Aztec exoticism. Nevertheless, they might take some comfort from the thought that, a century ago, they had been the imitators of a globalized French cuisine. Just as José Juan Tablada insisted on the creativity of French food in Porfirian Mexico—adapted and exaggerated to make it unique—Mexicans may also find something of interest in contemporary experiments with their cuisine. Veronique Wade first encountered Mexican food in Wimberley, Texas, when she took a job in a tamale factory to support her three children while in the midst of a divorce. With her previous experience in commercial kitchens, she was soon running Wimberley's Gourmet Tamale Kitchen and experimenting with new varieties filled with smoked salmon or blue cheese or raspberry chipotle sauce.[20] Equally unlikely culinary combinations have emerged from Mexicans' own complex histories of migration. In McAllen, Texas, for example, an Acapulco-born chef has established an acclaimed Mexican-Japanese fusion restaurant, Yoko Sushi, with a signature dish of spicy tuna sashimi roll made with chili powder and avocado. Or consider the Mennonite restaurant in Canada whose menu juxtaposed *pierogi* and apple cake with enchiladas and tacos. The owner, having grown up in the Mennonite colony of Chihuahua before his family returned to Canada, considered Mexican foods to be just as much a cultural tradition as dishes learned centuries earlier in Holland and Eastern Europe.[21]

It is entirely possible that future historians will dismiss the current polemics over authentic Mexican as inconsequential. The target of authenticity is constantly moving, even as people seek to fix it in a pristine and timeless past. Taco shells caught on in the 1950s as a more authentic alternative to canned chili, but as consumers have become more knowledgeable, they have exchanged taco shells for fresh corn tortillas. Even in Norway, where a modified Cal-Mex taco has become a national icon, demand for soft tortillas is now growing much faster than that for taco shells.[22] Such an outcome was made possible only by the global spread of industrial versions from the United States. Maseca's international factories were founded largely to supply a Tex-Mex market, most notably, for movie theater nachos. The enormous reach of popular media may make Gino D'Acampo's Old El Paso advertisement, "An Italian in Mexico," as important as the UNESCO intangible patrimony in expanding international awareness of Mexican regional cuisines. Of course, some will never get past the grocery store taco kit, but for others, Taco Bell is the gateway drug. A late-night burrito supreme can lead to lunch at Chipotle's, and before long the person is standing at a taco truck ordering a half dozen *al pastor*.

More important than purity of tradition is the legal right to prepare and sell food without harassment. The recent validation of Mexican American food as an American regional cuisine marks a gratifying shift. When Rick Bayless published his first cookbook, *Authentic Mexican* (1987), his editors refused to include recipes for chili-con-carne and other dishes he had grown up eating, preferring to focus on the foods of central and southern Mexico.[23] Two decades later, multiple books have chronicled Tex-Mex cooking, including *Matt Martinez's Culinary Frontier* (1997), Robb Walsh's *The Tex-Mex Cookbook* (2004), and Melissa Guerra's *Dishes from the Wild Horse Desert* (2006).[24] With growing economic and political weight, Mexican Americans have successfully refuted many negative stereotypes of their culture and cuisine, especially as a younger generation of cooks achieves gourmet distinction. Lanny Lancarte II, a great-grandson of Joe T. García, recently opened a fine dining restaurant as an adjunct to the venerable Fort Worth institution. Indigenous Mexicans have also begun to challenge elite attempts to speak for them, as food becomes part of ethnic revivals and indigenous political movements. Perhaps one day Abigail Mendoza will achieve her dream of publishing a Zapotec cookbook.

For better or worse, there has been a growing cultural convergence across the Rio Grande, with Mexican food becoming increasingly American, and vice versa. Long histories of international conflicts of interest and racial discrimination must still be overcome, not least in the persistent stereotypes of Mexicans as chili queens and Aztec cannibals. Nevertheless, Mexican food has been an integral part of the culture, first of the Southwest and increasingly throughout the United States, and for the past fifty years, expatriates have gone to great lengths to recreate it as best they can. Moreover, each generation of Americans has produced a more credible approximation of Mexican regional cuisine, in part because of the continued arrival of new migrants. However unlikely it may seem at a moment of rabid anti-immigrant sentiment, it is possible that food can foster a sense of common culture, providing the thin edge of a taco that may one day help bring down the militarized border currently dividing Mexico and the United States. With desire and enough tortillas, the whole world could be Planet Taco.

NOTES

PREFACE

1. Salvador Novo, *Cocina mexicana, o historia gastronomica de la Ciudad de México* (1967; reprint: Mexico City: Editorial Porrúa, 1993).

2. Sonia Corcuera de Mancera, *Entre gula y templanza: Un aspecto de la historia mexicana*, 3rd ed. (Mexico City: Fondo de Cultura Económica, 1991); Jeffrey M. Pilcher, *¡Que vivan los tamales! Food and the Making of Mexican Identity* (Albuquerque: University of New Mexico Press, 1998); Janet Long-Solís and Luis Alberto Vargas, *Food Culture in Mexico* (Westport, Conn.: Greenwood, 2005); José Luis Juárez López, *Nacionalismo culinario: La cocina mexicana en el siglo XX* (Mexico City: CONACULTA, 2008).

3. Steffan Igor Ayora-Diaz, "Regionalism and the Institution of the Yucatecan Gastronomic Field," *Food, Culture and Society* 13, no. 3 (September 2010): 397–420.

INTRODUCTION

1. "Day Job: Taco Bell Employee," *The New Yorker*, April 24, 2000, 185.

2. George Ritzer, *The McDonaldization of Society* (Thousand Oaks, Calif.: Pine Forge Press, 1993).

3. Quoted in "History," available at http://www.tacobell.com (accessed March 17, 2004).

4. Pascal Ory, "Gastronomy," in *Traditions*, vol. 2 of *Realms of Memory: The Construction of the French Past*, ed. Pierre Nora, trans. Arthur Goldhammer (New York: Columbia University Press, 1997), 445.

5. Some authors have proposed indigenous derivations of the word, including *tlaco*, meaning "half," as in a folded-over tortilla. Salvador Novo attributed the word's origin to the Nahuatl *tacol*, which is usually translated as "shoulder" but refers more expansively to any cylinder surrounding a soft interior, such as the mound of dirt gathered around a newly transplanted tree or a penis filled with semen. Having been viciously taunted for his homosexuality, Novo doubtless enjoyed the thought of taco-munching machos symbolically imitating the act of oral sex.

The linguist Hector Manuel Romero suggested that the word came from *itacate*, a sort of doggie bag handed out at fiestas. At least in some parts of Mexico, such as San Luis Potosí, taco is now used with this colloquial meaning. Any or all of these sources are possible, but historical evidence points to a more likely European origin. Novo, *Las locas, el sexo, los burdeles* (Mexico City: Editorial Novaro, 1972), 61; see also Maribel Álvarez, "Food, Poetry, and Borderlands Materiality: Walter Benjamin at the *Taquería*," *Arizona Journal of Hispanic Cultural Studies* 10 (2006): 205–30; Romero, *Vocabulario gastronómico mexicano* (Mexico City: Coordinación General de Abasto y Distribución del Distrito Federal, 1991), 58.

6. Novo, *Cocina mexicana*, 29.

7. Joan Corominas, *Diccionario crítico etimológico castellano e hispánico*, 6 vols. (Madrid: Editorial Gredos, 1991), 5:368.

8. *Diccionario de la lengua castellana*, 6 vols. (Madrid: Francisco del Hierro, 1726), 6:209–10; Esteban de Terreros y Pando, *Diccionario castellano con las voces de ciencias y artes y sus correspondientes en las tres lenguas Francesa, Latina ó Italiana*, 3 vols. (Madrid: Imprenta Vda. de Ibarra, Hijos y Compañía, 1786–88), 3:569–70.

9. Melchor Ocampo, "Idiotismos Hispano-Mexicanos," in *Obras completas*, ed. Angel Pola and Aurelio J. Venegas, 3 vols. (Mexico City: F. Vázquez, 1900–1901), 3:89–231. For more on taco etymology, see Jeffrey M. Pilcher, "¡Tacos, joven! Cosmopolitismo proletario y la cocina nacional mexicana," *Dimensión Antropológica* 13, no. 37 (mayo–agosto 2006): 87–125.

10. *El cocinero mexicano*, 3 vols. (Mexico City: Imprenta de Galvan a cargo de Mariano Arevalo, 1831), 1:183.

11. David Frye, Lizardi's English translator, provided this citation along with other insightful suggestions. José Joaquín Fernández de Lizardi, *The Mangy Parrot: The Life and Times of Periquillo Sarniento, Written by Himself for His Children*, trans. David Frye (Indianapolis: Hackett, 2004), 408–9.

12. Manuel Payno, *Los bandidos de Río Frío*, 24th ed. (Mexico City: Editorial Porrúa, 2004), 31–32.

13. Feliz Ramos I. Duarte, *Diccionario de mejicanismos: Colección de locuciones i frases viciosas* (Mexico City: Imprenta de Eduardo Dublan, 1895), 469.

14. Doris M. Ladd, *The Making of a Strike: Mexican Silver Workers' Struggles in Real Del Monte, 1766–1775* (Lincoln: University of Nebraska Press, 1988), 10.

15. Archivo Histórico del Distrito Federal (hereafter AHDF), vol. "Licencias diversas," exp. 458, 523; "Mercados," exp. 359, 782; "Vías públicas," 1981, 999. I thank Linda Arnold and Marianne Samayoa for assistance. See also Jesús Flores y Escalante, *Brevísima historia de la comida mexicana* (Mexico City: Asociación Mexicana de Estudios Fonográficos, 1994), 232.

16. Steve Penfold, "Fast Food," in *The Oxford Handbook of Food History*, ed. Jeffrey M. Pilcher (New York: Oxford University Press, 2012), 280.

17. Industry data indicate that by 2010, taco shells accounted for only 2 percent of overall sales, compared to 42 percent for corn tortillas and 43 percent for wheat flour. This represents a dramatic change from a decade ago, when flour tortillas outsold corn by 3 to 1. Jim Kabbani, "Market Overview: 2010 Tortilla Industry Association Technical Conference," available at http://www.tortilla-info.com/downloads/tech_seminar_presentations/Presentation%20-%20Market%20Overview%209-2010.pdf (accessed April 12, 2001). I thank Jim Kabbani for pointing me to this data.

18. There are many approaches to commodity-chain analysis, food regimes, networks, and the like. See André Magnan, "Food Regimes," in Pilcher, *The Oxford Handbook of Food History*.

19. Matthew Caire, "'Sin maíz, no hay país': Corn in Mexico under Neoliberalism" (M.A. thesis, Bowling Green State University, 2010).

20. Lucy M. Long, "Culinary Tourism: A Folkloristic Perspective on Eating and Otherness," in *Culinary Tourism*, ed. Lucy M. Long (Lexington: University Press of Kentucky, 2004), 20–50.

21. Sidney W. Mintz, *Sweetness and Power: The Place of Sugar in Modern History* (New York: Viking, 1985), 151–58.

22. Victor M. Valle and Rodolfo D. Torres, *Latino Metropolis* (Minneapolis: University of Minnesota Press, 2000); Uma Narayan, "Eating Cultures: Incorporation, Identity, and Indian Food," *Social Identities* 1, no. 1 (1995): 63–86; Lisa Heldke, *Exotic Appetites: Ruminations of a Food Adventurer* (New York: Routledge, 2003).

23. Anne Goldman, "'I Yam What I Yam': Cooking, Culture, and Colonialism," in *De/Colonizing the Subject*, ed. Sidonie Smith and Julia Watson (Minneapolis: University of Minnesota Press, 1992), 169–95.

24. See William V. Flores and Rina Benmayor, eds., *Latino Cultural Citizenship: Claiming Identity, Space, and Rights* (Boston: Beacon, 1997).

25. For a historical approach to the origins of regional cuisines through the "naturalization of taste," see Steffan Igor Ayora-Diaz, *Foodscapes, Foodfields, and Identities in Yucatán* (New York: Berghahn, 2012), 114–52.

26. Meredith E. Abarca, "Authentic or Not, It's Original," *Food and Foodways* 12 (2004): 1–25.

27. Octavio Paz, *Convergences: Essays on Art and Literature*, trans. Helen Lane (Orlando: Harcourt, Brace, and Jovanovich, 1987), 83.

28. Gloria Anzaldúa, *Borderlands/La Frontera: The New Mestiza* (San Francisco: Aunt Lute Books, 1999).

29. Robb Walsh, *The Tex-Mex Cookbook: A History in Recipes and Photos* (New York: Broadway, 2004), xvi–xix.

CHAPTER 1

1. Bernardino de Sahagún, *Florentine Codex: General History of the Things of New Spain*, trans. Charles E. Dibble and Arthur J. O. Anderson, 13 parts (Santa Fe: School of American Research, 1961), 2:138, 8:38.

2. Guillermo Bonfil Batalla, *México Profundo: Reclaiming a Civilization*, trans. Philip A. Dennis (Austin: University of Texas Press, 1996); Josée Johnston and Shyon Baumann, *Foodies: Democracy and Distinction in the Gourmet Foodscape* (New York: Routledge, 2010), 69–73.

3. Enrique Florescano, *Memory, Myth, and Time in Mexico: From the Aztecs to Independence*, trans. Albert G. Bork and Kathryn R. Bork (Austin: University of Texas Press, 1994), viii, 186.

4. José Vasconcelos, *The Cosmic Race/La raza cósmica*, trans. Didier T. Jaén (Baltimore, Md.: Johns Hopkins University Press, 1997); Guillermo Bonfil Batalla, ed., *Simbiosis de culturas: Los inmigrantes y su cultura en México* (Mexico City: Fondo de Cultura Económica, 1993).

5. Dennis Tedlock, trans., *Popol Vuh: The Definitive Edition of the Maya Book of the Dawn of Life and the Glories of Gods and Kings*, rev ed. (New York: Simon and Schuster, 1996), 145–46, 288.

6. J. Dorweiler et al., "Teosinte Glume Architecture 1: A Genetic Locus Controlling a Key Step in Maize Evolution," *Science* 262 (1993): 233–35; Y. Matsuoka et al., "A Single Domestication for Maize Shown by Multilocus Microsatellite Genotyping," *Proceedings of the National Academy of Sciences* 99, no. 9 (2002): 6080–84; Hugh H. Iltis, "Origin of Polystichy in Maize," in *Histories of Maize: Multidisciplinary Approaches to the Prehistory, Linguistics, Biogeography, Domestication, and Evolution of Maize*, ed. John E. Staller, Robert H. Tykot, and Bruce F. Benz (San Diego: Elsevier Academic, 2006), 21–53.

7. Dolores R. Piperno and Deborah M. Pearsall, *The Origins of Agriculture in the Lowland Neotropics* (San Diego: Academic Press, 1998).

8. Marshall Sahlins, "The Original Affluent Society," *Stone Age Economics* (London: Tavistock, 1974); Martin Jones, *Feast: Why Humans Share Food* (New York: Oxford University Press, 2007).

9. Donald H. Morris, "Changes in Groundstone Following the Introduction of Maize into the American Southwest," *Journal of Anthropological Research* 46, no. 2 (Summer 1990): 177–94; Jenny L. Adams, "Refocusing the Role of Food-Grinding Tools as Correlates for Subsistence Strategies in the U.S. Southwest," *American Antiquity* 54, no. 3 (1999): 475–98; Jenny L. Adams, *Ground Stone Analysis: A Technological Approach* (Salt Lake City: University of Utah Press, 2002), 120–24; Patricia L. Crown, "Women's Role in Changing Cuisine," in *Women and Men in the Prehispanic Southwest*, ed. Patricia L. Crown (Santa Fe: School of American Research Press, 2000), 239–49.

10. John E. Clark and David Cheetham, "Mesoamerica's Tribal Foundations," in *The Archaeology of Tribal Societies*, ed. William A. Parkinson (Ann Arbor, Mich.: International Monographs in Prehistory, 2002), 281–83; J. Skibo and E. Blinman, "Exploring the Origins of Pottery on the Colorado Plateau," in *Pottery and People*, ed. J. Skibo and G. Feinman (Salt Lake City: University of Utah Press, 1999), 171–83.

11. S. H. Katz, M. L. Hediger, and L. A. Valleroy, "Traditional Maize Processing Techniques in the New World," *Science* 184 (1974): 765–73.

12. Sophie D. Coe, *America's First Cuisines* (Austin: University of Texas Press, 1994), 134–36, 145–50.

13. Michael E. Smith, "The Aztlan Migrations of the Nahuatl Chronicles: Myth or History?" *Ethnohistory* 31, no. 3 (Summer 1984): 153–86; Pilcher, *¡Que vivan los tamales!*, 14–22.

14. Thomas P. Myers, "Hominy Technology and the Emergence of Mississippian Societies," in Staller et al., *Histories of Maize*, 511–20; Katz, Hediger, and Valleroy, "Traditional Maize Processing," 765–73.

15. James Lockhart, ed., *We People Here: Nahuatl Accounts of the Conquest of Mexico* (Berkeley: University of California Press, 1993), 80; Coe, *America's First Cuisines*, 93.

16. Rebecca Earle, "'If You Eat Their Food…': Diets and Bodies in Early Colonial Spanish America," *American Historical Review* 115, no. 3 (June 2010): 688–713; Justo L. del Río Moreno, *Los inicios de la agricultura europea en el nuevo mundo (1492–1542)* (Sevilla: ASAJA-Sevilla, 1991); Arnold Bauer, *Goods, Power, History: Latin America's Material Culture* (Cambridge: Cambridge University Press, 2001), 87–90; José de Acosta, *Natural and Moral History of the Indies*, ed. Jane E. Mangan, trans. Frances M. López-Morillas (Durham, N.C.: Duke University Press, 2002), 228.

17. Alexander von Humboldt, *Political Essay on the Kingdom of New Spain*, trans. John Black, 4 vols. (New York: AMS Press, 1966), 4:33–35; José Luis Juárez López, *La lenta emergencia de la comida mexicana: Ambigüedades criollas, 1750–1800* (Mexico: Editorial Porrúa, 2000), 129.

18. Elinor G. K. Melville, *A Plague of Sheep: Environmental Consequences of the Conquest of Mexico* (Cambridge: Cambridge University Press, 1997), 6, 17–20, 153–55.

19. R. Douglas Cope, *The Limits of Racial Domination: Plebeian Society in Colonial Mexico City, 1660–1720* (Madison: University of Wisconsin Press, 1994).

20. Virginia García Acosta, *Las panaderías, sus dueños y trabajadores. Ciudad de México, siglo XVIII* (Mexico City: CIESAS, 1989), 158.

21. Juan Pedro Viquiera Alban, *Propriety and Permissiveness in Bourbon Mexico*, trans. Sonya Lipsett-Rivera and Sergio Rivera Ayala (Wilmington, Del.: Scholarly Resources, 1999), 153.

22. Kenneth F. Kiple and Kriemhild Coneè Orenlas, eds., *The Cambridge World History of Food*, 2 vols. (Cambridge: Cambridge University Press, 2000), 2:1762; Apicius, *Cookery and Dining in*

Imperial Rome, ed. and trans. Joseph Dommers Vehling (New York: Dover, 1977), 130, 133, 229; Martino of Como, *The Art of Cooking: The First Modern Cookery Book*, ed. Luigi Ballerini, trans. Jeremy Parzen (Berkeley: University of California Press, 2005), 56; Vicenta Torres de Rubio, *Cocina michoacana* (Zamora: Imprenta Moderna, 1896), 18; *Formulario de la cocina mexicana: Puebla, siglo XIX* (Mexico City: CONACULTA, 2002), 99–100.

23. Ikram Antaki, "Al encuentro de nuestra herencia islamo-árabe," in Bonfil Batalla, *Simbiosis de culturas*, 97–98; Bauer, *Goods, Power, History*, 101.

24. Judith A. Carney and Richard Rosomoff, *In the Shadow of Slavery: Africa's Botanical Legacy in the Atlantic World* (Berkeley: University of California Press, 2009); Judith A. Carney, *Black Rice: The African Origins of Rice Cultivation in the Americas* (Cambridge: Harvard University Press, 2001), 13–30; S. Max Edelson, *Plantation Enterprise in Colonial South Carolina* (Cambridge: Harvard University Press, 2006), 66–67; *Dos manuscritos mexicanos de cocina: Siglo XVIII* (Mexico City: CONACULTA, 2002), 28; Colin A. Palmer, *Slaves of the Black God: Blacks in Mexico, 1570– 1650* (Cambridge: Harvard University Press, 1976), 20.

25. Norma Angélica Castillo Palma and Susan Kellogg, "Conflict and Cohabitation between Afro-Mexicans and Nahuas in Central Mexico," in *Beyond Black and Red: African-Native Relations in Colonial Latin America*, ed. Matthew Restall (Albuquerque: University of New Mexico Press, 2005), 128.

26. William L. Schurz, *The Manila Galleon* (New York: E. P. Dutton, 1939); Peter Gerhard, *Pirates on the West Coast of New Spain, 1575–1742* (Glendale, Calif.: Arthur H. Clark, 1960), 40; Jonathan I. Israel, *Race, Class, and Politics in Colonial Mexico, 1610–1670* (Oxford: Oxford University Press, 1975), 75–76; Edward R. Slack, Jr., "The *Chinos* in New Spain: A Corrective Lens for a Distorted Image," *Journal of World History* 20, no. 1 (March 2009): 37–43.

27. Paula de Vos, "The Science of Spices: Empiricism and Economic Botany in the Early Spanish Empire," *Journal of World History* 17, no. 4 (December 2006): 417–24; Fabio López-Lázaro, "Sweet Food of Knowledge: Botany, Food, and Empire in the Early Modern Spanish Kingdoms," in *At the Table: Metaphorical and Material Cultures of Food in Medieval and Early Modern Europe*, ed. Timothy J. Tomasik and Juliann M. Vitullo (Tunnhout: Brepols, 2007), 13.

28. Arturo Warman, *Corn and Capitalism: How a Botanical Bastard Grew to Global Dominance*, trans. Nancy L. Westrate (Chapel Hill: University of North Carolina Press, 2003), xiii. See also Alphonse de Candolle, *Origin of Cultivated Plants* (1884; reprint: New York: D. Appleton and Company, 1902), 389; James A. McCann, *Maize and Grace: Africa's Encounter with a New World Crop, 1500–2000* (Cambridge: Harvard University Press, 2005), 34; Stanley Brandes, "Maize as a Culinary Mystery," *Ethnology* 31, no. 4 (1992): 331–36.

29. Alfred W. Crosby, Jr., *The Columbian Exchange: Biological and Cultural Consequences of 1492* (Westport, Conn.: Greenwood, 1972).

30. Sucheta Mazumdar, "The Impact of New World Food Crops on the Diet and Economy of China and India, 1600–1900," in *Food in Global History*, ed. Raymond Grew (Boulder, Colo.: Westview, 1999), 58–78.

31. Earl J. Hamilton, "What the New World Gave the Economy of the Old," in *First Images of America: The Impact of the New World on the Old*, ed. Fredi Chiappelli, 2 vols. (Berkeley: University of California Press, 1976), 2:859; Antonio Garrido Aranda, "La revolución alimentaria del siglo XVI en América y Europa," in *Los sabores de España y América: Cultura y alimentación*, ed. Antonio Garrido Aranda (Huesca: La Val de Onsera, 1999), 207; Alan Davidson, "Europeans' Wary Encounter with Tomatoes, Potatoes, and Other New World Foods," in *Chilies to Chocolate: Food the Americas Gave the World*, ed. Nelson Foster and Linda Cordell (Tucson: University of Arizona Press, 1992), 1–14.

32. Warman, *Corn and Capitalism*, 104–6; Jonathan D. Sauer, "Changing Perception and Exploitation of New World Plants in Europe, 1492–1800," in *First Images of America: The Impact of the New World on the Old*, ed. Fredi Chiappelli, 2 vols. (Berkeley: University of California Press, 1976), 2:823; McCann, *Maize and Grace*, 63–76

33. George Nicholson, "On Food," in *Radical Food: The Culture and Politics of Eating and Drinking, 1790–1820*, ed. Timothy Morton, 3 vols. (London: Routledge, 2000), 1:87; Warman, *Corn and Capitalism*, 109–10.

34. Daphne A. Roe, *A Plague of Corn: The Social History of Pellagra* (Ithaca, N.Y.: Cornell University Press, 1973), 30, 34, quote from 38.

35. Warman, *Corn and Capitalism*, 132–38.

36. John Parkinson, *Theatrum Botanicum, the theater of plantes* (London: Cotes, 1640), 359; Acosta, *Natural and Moral History*, 206.

37. Huguette Chaunu and Pierre Chaunu, *Séville et l'Atlantique (1504–1650)*, volume 6, part 1, of 8 vols. (Paris: SEVPEN, 1956), 1040, 1044; Jean Andrews, *Peppers: The Domesticated Capsicums* (Austin: University of Texas Press, 1984), 25; Vito Teti, *Storia del peperoncino: Un protagonista delle culture mediterranee* (Rome: Donzelli Editore, 2007), 149.

38. Ken Albala, *Eating Right in the Renaissance* (Berkeley: University of California Press, 2002), 236; Jean-Louis Flandrin, "Dietary Choices and Culinary Technique, 1500–1800," in *Food: A Culinary History from Antiquity to the Present*, ed. Jean-Louis Flandrin and Massimo Montanari, trans. Albert Sonnenfeld (New York: Columbia University Press, 1999), 403–17.

39. Sophie Coe and Michael Coe, *The True History of Chocolate* (London: Thames and Hudson, 1996), 110–15, 133–38, 187–99, 224–25; Piero Camporesi, *Exotic Brew: The Art of Living in the Age of Enlightenment*, trans. Christopher Woodall (Cambridge: Polity Press, 1994), 108, 116.

40. Quoted in Camporesi, *Exotic Brew*, 112; Coe and Coe, *The True History of Chocolate*, 136, 150–51; Marcy Norton, *Sacred Gifts, Profane Pleasures: A History of Tobacco and Chocolate in the Atlantic World* (Ithaca, N.Y.: Cornell University Press, 2008), 170, 296–97.

41. Quoted in Norton, *Sacred Gifts, Profane Pleasures*, 175–79.

42. Coe and Coe, *The True History of Chocolate*, 176–78.

43. Quoted in K. T. Achay, *Indian Food: A Historical Companion* (Delhi: Oxford University Press, 1998), 227; Jean Andrews, "Chilli Peppers," in *The Cambridge World History of Food*, ed. Kenneth F. Kiple and Kriemhild Coneè Orenlas, 2 vols. (Cambridge: Cambridge University Press, 2000), 1:282; Mazumdar, "Impact of New World Food Crops," 60–61; James C. McCann, *Stirring the Pot: A History of African Cuisine* (Athens: Ohio University Press, 2009), 58–61.

44. Andrews, *Peppers*, 86–87; Penny Van Esterik, "From Marco Polo to McDonald's: Thai Cuisine in Transition," *Food and Foodways* 5, no. 2 (1992): 177–94.

45. Warman, *Corn and Capitalism*, 108, 138; William H. McNeill, "American Food Crops in the Old World," in *Seeds of Change: A Quincentennial Commemoration*, ed. Herman J. Viola and Carolyn Margolis (Washington, D.C.: Smithsonian Institution Press, 1991), 43–59.

46. McCann, *Maize and Grace*, 23–38, 42–49.

47. Mazumdar, "Impact of New World Food Crops," 68–69, 72–73; Ping-Ti Ho, "The Introduction of American Food Plants into China," *American Anthropologist* 57, no. 2 (April 1955): 194–95; Francesca Bray, *Agriculture*, vol. 6, pt. 2 of *Science and Civilisation in China*, ed. Joseph Needham (Cambridge: Cambridge University Press, 1984), 455–58; N. N. Kuleshov, "Some Peculiarities of Maize in Asia," *Annals of the Missouri Botanical Garden* 41 (1954): 271–99; Robert B. Marks, *Tigers, Rice, Silk, and Silt: Environment and Economy in Late Imperial South China* (Cambridge: Cambridge University Press, 1998), 310; Victor Lieberman, *Strange Parallels: Southeast Asia in Global Context, c. 800–1830* (Cambridge: Cambridge University Press, 2003), 437.

48. John Leddy Phelan, *The Hispanization of the Philippines: Spanish Aims and Filipino Responses, 1565–1700* (Madison: University of Wisconsin Press, 1959).

49. Domingo de Salazar, "The Chinese and the Parián at Manila," in *The Philippine Islands, 1493–1898*, ed. and trans. Emma Helen Blair and James Alexander Robertson, 55 vols. (Cleveland: Arthur H. Clark, 1903–9), 7:225.

50. Raymond Sokolov, *Why We Eat What We Eat* (New York: Summit, 1991), 56; Elisabeth Rozin, *Ethnic Cuisine: The Flavor Principle Cook-Book* (Lexington, Mass.: S. Greene, 1983).

51. Laura Thompson, *Guam and Its People* (Princeton: Princeton University Press, 1947), 5–6, 24.

CHAPTER 2

1. Merrill Shindler, *El Cholo Cookbook: Recipes and Lore from California's Best-Loved Mexican Kitchen* (Santa Monica: Angel City Press, 1998), 85.

2. Ramos I. Duarte, *Diccionario de mejicanismos*, 98.

3. Ana Bégué de Packman, *Early California Hospitality: The Cookery Customs of Spanish California, with Authentic Recipes and Menus of the Period* (Glendale, Calif.: Arthur H. Clark, 1938), 38.

4. Eugenio del Hoyo, *Historia del Nuevo Reino de León (1577–1723)*, 2 vols. (Monterrey: Instituto Tecnológico y de Estudios Superiores de Monterrey, 1972), 2:375.

5. In New Mexico, this Hispanic renaissance encouraged the production of textiles, *santos* (folk saints), and furniture making—modern-day symbols of regional identity. See Ross Frank, *From Settler to Citizen: New Mexican Economic Development and the Creation of Vecino Society, 1750–1820* (Berkeley: University of California Press, 2000), 122–56, 182–95.

6. Héctor Rodríguez Espinosa, "Dijo realmente Vasconcelos que en Sonora termina la civilización y comienza la carne asada?" *Boletín de la Sociedad Sonorense de Historia* 27 (July–August 1986): 4–6.

7. Sahagún, *Florentine Codex*, 11:171–80.

8. Alfredo López Austin and Leonardo López Luján, *Mexico's Indigenous Past*, trans. Bernard R. Ortiz de Montellano (Norman: University of Oklahoma Press, 2001), 15–47.

9. Alan H. Simmons, "Early People, Early Maize, and Late Archaic Change in the American Southwest," in *Environmental Change and Human Adaptation in the Ancient American Southwest*, ed. David E. Doyel and Jeffrey S. Dean (Salt Lake City: University of Utah Press, 2006), 10–25.

10. Jane H. Hill, "Toward a Linguistic Prehistory of the Southwest: 'Azteco-Tanoan' and the Arrival of Maize Cultivation," *Journal of Anthropological Research* 58 (2002): 457–75; William E. Doolittle and Jonathan B. Mabry, "Environmental Mosaics, Agricultural Diversity, and the Evolutionary Adoption of Maize in the American Southwest," in Staller et al., *Histories of Maize*, 109–21; Robert J. Hard, A. C. Macwilliams, John R. Roney, Karen R. Adams, and William L. Merrill, "Early Agriculture in Chihuahua, Mexico," in Staller et al., *Histories of Maize*, 471–85; Gayle J. Fritz, "The Transition to Agriculture in the Desert Borderlands: An Introduction," in *Archaeology without Borders: Contact, Commerce, and Change in the U.S. Southwest and Northwestern Mexico*, ed. Laurie D. Webster, Maxine E. McBrinn, and Eduardo Gamboa Carrera (Boulder: University Press of Colorado/CONACULTA, 2008), 25–33.

11. Paul E. Minnis, "Prehistoric Diet in the Northern Southwest: Macroplant Remains from Four Corners Feces," *American Antiquity* 54, no. 3 (July 1989): 543–63; Donald H. Morris, "Changes in Groundstone Following the Introduction of Maize into the American Southwest," *Journal of Anthropological Research* 46, no. 2 (Summer 1990): 189–90; Jenny L. Adams, "Refocusing the Role of Food-Grinding Tools as Correlates for Subsistence Strategies in the U.S. Southwest," *American Antiquity* 64, no. 3 (July 1999): 475–98.

12. Marie-Areti Hers, "Zacatecas y Durango. Los confines tolteca-chichimecas," in *La gran chichimeca: El lugar de las rocas secas*, ed. Beatriz Braniff C. (Milan: Jaca Book/CNCA, 2001), 113–54; Patricia Carot and Marie-Areti Hers, "Epic of the Toltec Chichimec and the Purépecha in the American Southwest," in Hard et al., *Archaeology without Borders*, 301–33.

13. Patricia L. Crown and W. Jeffrey Hurst, "Evidence of Cacao Use in the Prehispanic American Southwest," *Proceedings of the National Academy of Sciences* 106, no. 7 (February 17, 2009): 2110–13; W. H. Wills and Patricia L. Crown, "Commensal Politics in the Prehispanic Southwest," in *Identity, Feasting, and the Archaeology of the Greater Southwest*, ed. Barbara J. Mills (Boulder: University Press of Colorado, 2004), 153–72; Mark D. Varien, *Sedentism and Mobility in a Social Landscape: Mesa Verde and Beyond* (Tucson: University of Arizona Press, 1999), 144–49; Michael E. Whalen and Paul E. Minnis, *Casas Grandes and Its Hinterland: Prehistoric Regional Organization in Northwest Mexico* (Tucson: University of Arizona Press, 2001), 125–33.

14. W. Bruce Masse, "The Quest for Subsistence Sufficiency and Civilization in the Sonoran Desert," in *Chaco and Hohokam: Prehistoric Regional Systems in the American Southwest*, ed. Patricia L. Crown and W. James Judge (Santa Fe: School of American Research Press, 1991), 218–19.

15. David H. Snow, "Tener Comal y Metate: Protohistoric Rio Grande Maize Use and Diet," in *Perspectives on Southwestern Prehistory*, ed. Paul E. Minnis and Charles L. Redman (Boulder, Colo.: Westview, 1990), 289–300. On maize varieties, see James M. Potter and Scott G. Ortman, "Community and Cuisine in the Prehispanic American Southwest," in Mills, *Identity, Feasting, and Archaeology*, 178–79.

16. Charles C. Di Peso, John B. Rinaldo, and Gloria J. Fenner, *Casas Grandes: A Fallen Trading Center of the Gran Chichimeca*, 8 vols. (Flagstaff, Ariz.: Northland, 1974), 2:604–11, 6:86; Emil Haury, *The Excavation of Los Muertos and Neighboring Ruins in the Salt River Valley, Southern Arizona*, Papers of the Peabody Museum of American Archaeology and Ethnology, 24, no. 1 (Cambridge: Harvard University, 1945), 109–11.

17. *Documents of the Coronado Expedition, 1539–1542*, ed. and trans. Richard Flint and Shirley Cushing Flint (Dallas: Southern Methodist University Press, 2005), 260.

18. Ibid., 419, 475.

19. Ibid., 164.

20. E. Charles Adams, *The Origin and Development of the Pueblo Katsina Cult* (Tucson: University of Arizona Press, 1991); Patricia L. Crown, *Ceramics and Ideology: Salado Polychrome Pottery* (Albuquerque: University of New Mexico Press, 1994).

21. Frank Hamilton Cushing, *Zuni Breadstuff* (New York: Museum of the American Indian, 1920), 338; Barrett P. Brenton, "Piki, Polenta, and Pellagra: Maize, Nutrition and Nurturing the Natural," in *Nurture: Proceedings of the Oxford Symposium on Food and Cookery 2003*, ed. Richard Hosking (Bristol: Footwork, 2004), 38–41; Adams, *Origin and Development*, 80–82.

22. *Documents of the Coronado Expedition*, 419; Richard I. Ford, "Corn Is Our Mother," in *Corn and Culture in the Prehistoric New World*, ed. Sissel Johannessen and Christine A. Hastorf (Boulder, Colo.: Westview, 1994), 513–25; Ramón Gutiérrez, *When Jesus Came, the Corn Mothers Went Away: Marriage, Sexuality, and Power in New Mexico, 1500–1846* (Stanford: Stanford University Press, 1991), 3–24; Carol Patterson-Rudolph, *Petroglyphs and Pueblo Myths of the Rio Grande* (Albuquerque: Avanyu, 1990), 87–90; Kelley Hays-Gilpin, "Gender Ideology and Ritual Activities," in Crown, *Women and Men in the Prehispanic Southwest*, 126–27; Cushing, *Zuni Breadstuff*, 40–54, 332–36.

23. Linda S. Cordell and Bruce D. Smith, "Indigenous Farmers," in *The Cambridge History of the Native Peoples of the Americas*, vol. 1, *North America*, part 1, ed. Bruce G. Trigger and Wilcomb E. Washburn (Cambridge: Cambridge University Press, 1996), 233.

24. Pedro Tamarón y Romeral, *Demostración del vastísimo obispado de la Nueva Vizcaya—1765*, ed. Vito Alessio Robles (Mexico City: Antigua Librería Robredo, de José Porrúa e Hijos, 1937), 339.

25. John L. Kessell, *Kiva, Cross, and Crown: The Pecos Indians and New Mexico, 1540–1840* (Washington, D.C.: National Park Service, 1979), 339–41.

26. François Chevalier, *Land and Society in Colonial Mexico: The Great Hacienda*, trans. Alvin Eustis (Berkeley: University of California Press, 1963); José Cuello, *Saltillo colonial: Orígenes y formación de una sociedad mexicana en la frontera norte* (Saltillo: Archivo Municipal de Saltillo and Universidad Autónoma de Coahuila, 2004), 93, 137.

27. Of the vast mission historiography, compare John F. Bannon, *The Mission Frontier in Sonora, 1620–1687* (New York: United States Catholic Historical Society, 1955); Cynthia Radding, *Wandering Peoples: Colonialism, Ethnic Spaces, and Ecological Frontiers in Northwestern Mexico, 1700–1850* (Durham, N.C.: Duke University Press, 1997).

28. David Frye, "The Native Peoples of Northeastern Mexico," in *Mesoamerica*, vol. 2 of *Cambridge History of Native Peoples of the Americas*, ed. Richard E. W. Adams and Murdo J. MacLeod (Cambridge: Cambridge University Press, 2000), 102–4.

29. Robert C. West, *The Mining Community in Northern New Spain: The Parral Mining District* (Berkeley: University of California Press, 1949), 57–71; Susan M. Deeds, *Defiance and Deference in Mexico's Colonial North: Indians under Spanish Rule in Nueva Vizcaya* (Austin: University of Texas Press, 2003), 27–29, 64.

30. Tamarón, *Demostración del vastísimo obispado*, 328; Juan Agustin de Morfi, *Viaje de indios y diario del Nuevo México* (Mexico City: José Porrúa e Hijos, 1935), 134, 142; Sergio Antonio Corona Páez, *La vitivinicultura en el pueblo de Santa María de las Parras: Producción de vinos, vinagres y aguardientes bajo el paradigma andaluz (siglos XVII y XVIII)* (Torreón, Coahuila: Ayuntamiento de Torreón, 2004).

31. Quoted in Hank Shaw, "Chasing Angels: The Sweet Wine Angelica," *Gastronomica* 8, no. 3 (Summer 2008): 74.

32. Peter Boyd-Bowman, "Two Country Stores in XVIIth Century Mexico," *The Americas* 28, no. 3 (January 1972): 241, 244; West, *The Mining Community*, 62–72.

33. Alonso de la Mota y Escobar, *Descripción geográfica de los reinos de Nueva Galicia, Nueva Vizcaya, y Nuevo León* (Mexico City: Editorial Pedro Robredo, 1940), 146–48.

34. Cheryl English Martin, *Governance and Society in Colonial Mexico: Chihuahua in the Eighteenth Century* (Stanford: Stanford University Press, 1996), 165–68.

35. Heather Trigg, "Food Choice and Social Identity in Early Colonial New Mexico," *Journal of the Southwest* 46, no. 2 (Summer 2004): 234.

36. See, for example, Juan Bautista Chapa, *Historia de Nuevo León*, ed. Israel Cavazos Garza (Monterrey: Universidad de Nuevo León, 1961), 195; Nan A. Rothschild, *Colonial Encounters in a Native American Landscape* (Washington, D.C.: Smithsonian Books, 2003), 145; Clara Elena Suárez Argüello, *La política cerealera en la economía novohispana. El caso de trigo* (Mexico City: CIESAS, 1985), 95.

37. Charles Perry, "What to Order in Ninth-Century Baghdad," in *Medieval Arab Cookery*, ed. Maxime Rodinson, A. J. Arberry, and Charles Perry (Devon: Prospect Books, 2001), 217–23.

38. Alfonso Toro, *Los Judíos en la Nueva España: Documentos del siglo XVI correspondientes al ramo de Inquisición* (Mexico City: Fondo de Cultura Económica, 1982), 246; David M. Gitlitz and Linda Kay Davidson, *A Drizzle of Honey: The Lives and Recipes of Spain's Secret Jews* (New York: St. Martin's, 1999), 293. I thank Vanessa Fonseca for these citations.

39. West, *The Mining Community*, 63; Martin, *Governance and Society*, 58, 100–106, 111; Phillip L. Hadley, *Minería y sociedad en el centro minero de Santa Eulalia, Chihuahua [1709–1750]* (Mexico City: Fondo de Cultura Económica, 1975), 102–3; Jesús F. de la Teja, "Saint James at the Fair: Religious Ceremony, Civic Boosterism, and Commercial Development on the Colonial Mexican Frontier," *The Americas* 57, no. 3 (January 2001): 395–416; Leslie S. Offutt, *Saltillo, 1770–1810: Town and Region in the Mexican North* (Tucson: University of Arizona Press, 2001), 154.

40. Vito Alessio Robles, *Acapulco, Saltillo y Monterrey en la historia y en la leyenda* (Mexico City: Editorial Porrúa, 1978), 310–11.

41. John R. Van Ness, "Hispanic Land Grants: Ecology and Subsistence in the Uplands of Northern New Mexico and Southern Colorado," in *Land, Water, and Culture: New Perspectives on Hispanic Land Grants*, ed. Charles L. Briggs and John R. Van Ness (Albuquerque: University of New Mexico Press, 1987), 189; John O. Baxter, *Las Carneradas: Sheep Trade in New Mexico, 1700–1860* (Albuquerque: University of New Mexico Press, 1987), 13, 42; Rothschild, *Colonial Encounters*, 141–45; France V. Scholes, "The Supply Service of the New Mexican Missions in the Seventeenth Century," *New Mexico Historical Review* 5 (1930): 93–115, 186–210, 386–404; Radding, *Wandering Peoples*, 39–40, 193–207.

42. Cushing, *Zuni Breadstuff*, 372–76; Robert C. West, *Sonora: Its Geographical Personality* (Austin: University of Texas Press, 1993), 37–38.

43. Manuel J. Espinosa, *The Pueblo Indian Revolt of 1696 and the Franciscan Missions in New Mexico: Letters of the Missionaries and Related Documents* (Norman: University of Oklahoma Press, 1988), 124, 127, 134; Alfredo Jiménez Núñez, *El gran norte de México: Una frontera imperial en la Nueva España (1540–1820)* (Madrid: Tébar, 2006), 323.

44. Thomas E. Sheridan, *Empire of Sand: The Seri Indians and the Struggle for Spanish Sonora, 1645–1803* (Tucson: University of Arizona Press, 1999), 97; Deeds, *Defiance and Deference*, 78, 102, 160, 257–59; Cuello, *Saltillo colonial*, 206; Ignacio del Río, *Conquista y aculturación en la California Jesuítica 1697–1768* (Mexico City: UNAM, 1984), 130–33.

45. Juan Agustín de Morfi, *Viaje de indios y diario del Nuevo México* (Mexico City: José Porrúa e Hijos, 1935), 156; Frye, "Native Peoples," 94, 109, 121–22; Elisabeth Butzer, *Historia social de una comunidad tlaxcalteca: San Miguel de Aguayo (Bustamante, N.L.) 1686–1820* (Saltillo: Archivo Municipal de Saltillo, 2001), 9, 45, 92–93; Javier Fortanelli Martínez, Fernando Carlín Castelán, and Jéssica Grétel Loza León, "Sistemas agrícolas de regadío de origin tlaxcalteca en San Luis Potosí," in *Constructores de la nación: La migración tlaxcalteca en el norte de la Nueva España*, ed. Israel Cavazos Garza et al. (San Luis Potosí: El Colegio de San Luis, 1999), 105–33; Corona Páez, *La vitivinicultura*, 37–38.

46. Deeds, *Defiance and Deference*, 116–19, 193–95; Wendell C. Bennett and Robert M. Zingg, *The Tarahumara: An Indian Tribe of Northern Mexico* (Chicago: University of Chicago Press, 1935), 33–35.

47. *Documents of the Coronado Expedition*, 164; Carroll L. Riley, *The Kachina and the Cross: Indians and Spaniards in the Early Southwest* (Salt Lake City: University of Utah Press, 1999), 276; Bradley J. Vierra and Stanley M. Hordes, "Let the Dust Settle: A Review of the Coronado Campsite in the Tiguex Province," in *The Coronado Expedition to Tierra Nueva: The 1540–1542 Route Across the Southwest*, ed. Richard Flint and Shirley Cushing Flint (Boulder: University Press of Colorado, 1997), 259–60.

48. Radding, *Wandering Peoples*, 167, 193–207; Deeds, *Defiance and Deference*, 195–99; Rothschild, *Colonial Encounters*, 141–45.

49. Alonso de León, *Historia de Nuevo León*, ed. Israel Cavazos Garza (Monterrey: Gobierno de Nuevo León, 1961), 76.

50. Hoyo, *Historia del Nuevo Reino*, 2:380–90; Ida Altman, "A Family and Region in the Northern Fringe Lands: The Marqueses de Aguayo of Nuevo León and Coahuila," in *Provinces of Early Mexico: Variants of Spanish American Regional Evolution*, ed. Ida Altman and James Lockhart (Los Angeles: UCLA Latin American Center, 1976), 260; Nils Jacobsen, "Livestock Complexes in Late Colonial Peru and New Spain: An Attempt at Comparison," in *The Economies of Mexico and Peru during the Late Colonial Period, 1760–1810*, ed. Nils Jacobsen and Hans-Jürgen Puhle

(Berlin: Colloquium Verlag, 1986), 123; Anita Purcell, ed., *Frontier Mexico, 1875–1894: Letters of William Purcell* (San Antonio: The Naylor Company, 1963), 87–88.

51. Jesús F. de la Teja, *San Antonio de Béxar: A Community on New Spain's Northern Frontier* (Albuquerque: University of New Mexico Press, 1995), 98–114; Armando C. Alonzo, *Tejano Legacy: Rancheros and Settlers in South Texas, 1734–1900* (Albuquerque: University of New Mexico Press, 1998), 67–89; Terry G. Jordan, *North American Cattle-Ranching Frontiers: Origins, Diffusion, and Differentiation* (Albuquerque: University of New Mexico Press, 1993), 150–56.

52. Juan Nepomuceno Almonte, *Almonte's Texas: Juan N. Almonte's 1834 Inspection, Secret Report, and Role in the 1836 Campaign*, ed. Jack Jackson, trans. John Wheat (Austin: Texas State Historical Association, 2003), 244; Oakah L. Jones, Jr., *Los Paisanos: Spanish Settlers on the Northern Frontier of New Spain* (Norman: University of Oklahoma Press, 1979), 43; De la Teja, *San Antonio de Béxar*, 91–92, 109, 115; Patricia Osante, *Orígenes del Nuevo Santander, 1748–1772* (Mexico City: UNAM, 1997), 186; John H. Bartlett, *Personal Narrative of Explorations and Incidents*, 2 vols. (New York: D. Appleton and Company, 1854), 2:38.

53. Arnoldo De Leon, *The Tejano Community, 1836–1900* (Albuquerque: University of New Mexico Press, 1982), 93; Gilberto M. Hinojosa and Anne A. Fox, "Indians and Their Culture in San Fernando de Béxar," in *Tejano Origins in Eighteenth-Century San Antonio*, ed. Gerald E. Poyo and Gilberto M. Hinojosa (Austin: University of Texas Press/UTSA Institute of Texas Cultures, 1991), 117.

54. W. Eugene Hollon and Ruth Lapham Butler, eds., *William Bollaert's Texas* (1842; reprint: Norman: University of Oklahoma Press, 1956), 218.

55. Eric J. Votava, Jit B. Baral, and Paul W. Bosland, "Genetic Diversity of Chile (*Capsicum Annuum* var. *Annuum* L.) Landraces from Northern New Mexico, Colorado, and Mexico," *Economic Botany* 59, no. 1 (2005): 8–17.

56. James O. Pattie, *The Personal Narrative of James O. Pattie* (1831; reprint: Philadelphia: J. B. Lippincott, 1962), 39.

57. Susan Shelby Magoffin, *Down the Santa Fe Trail and into Mexico: The Diary of Susan Shelby Magoffin, 1846–1847*, ed. Stella M. Drumm (New Haven: Yale University Press, 1962), 65, 94.

58. Ibid., 107, 135, 165.

59. William H. Emory, *Notes of a Military Reconnaissance from Fort Leavenworth, in Missouri, to San Diego, in California* (Washington, D.C.: Wendell and Van Benthuysen, 1848), 7, 40.

60. Don J. Usner, *Sabin's Map: Life in Chimayó's Old Plaza* (Santa Fe: Museum of New Mexico Press, 1995), 10–11, 169.

61. Ignaz Pfefferkorn, *Sonora: A Description of the Province*, trans. Theodore E. Treutlein (Albuquerque: University of New Mexico Press, 1949), 49–50, 100, 195–96, 288–89.

62. Fay Jackson Smith, *Captain of the Phantom Presidio: A History of the Presidio of Fronteras, Sonora, New Spain, 1686–1735* (Spokane, Wash.: Arthur H. Clark, 1993), 117, 185–86.

63. Quoted in Jiménez Núñez, *El gran norte*, 328.

64. Radding, *Wandering Peoples*, 206, 217, 227, 243.

65. James G. Bell, "A Log of the Texas-California Cattle Trail, 1854," *Southwestern Historical Quarterly* 35 (1932): 47–66.

66. Quoted in Martín González de la Vara, *Tiempos de guerra*, vol. 5 of *La cocina mexicana a través de los siglos*, ed. Enrique Krauze (Mexico City: Editorial Clio, 1997), 14.

67. BANC MSS Eulalia Perez, "Una vieja y sus recuerdos," December 10, 1877, C-D 139, 17; Steven W. Hackel, *Children of Coyote, Missionaries of Saint Francis: Indian-Spanish Relations in Colonial California, 1769–1850* (Chapel Hill: University of North Carolina Press, 2005), 275–76.

68. Georg H. von Langsdorff, *Voyages and Travels in Various Parts of the World* (Carlisle: George Philips, 1817), 435–36.

69. Walter Colton, *Three Years in California* (New York: A. S. Barnes, 1852), 40, 204.

70. Sir George Simpson, *Narrative of a Journey Round the World during the Years 1841 and 1842*, 2 vols. (London: Henry Colburn, 1847), 1:311.

71. BANC MSS José Fernández, "Cosas de California," 1874, C-D 10, 176.

72. Frederick Law Olmsted, *A Journey through Texas* (1860; reprint: Austin: University of Texas Press, 1978), 144.

73. Quoted in Carey McWilliams, *North from Mexico: The Spanish-Speaking People of the United States* (1949; reprint: Westport, Conn.: Greenwood, 1968), 86–87. See also Deena J. González, *Refusing the Favor: Spanish-Mexican Women of Santa Fé, 1820–1880* (New York: Oxford University Press, 1999); Virginia Bouvier, *Women and the Conquest of California, 1542–1840* (Tucson: University of Arizona Press, 2001); Miroslava Chávez-García, *Negotiating Conquest: Gender and Power in California, 1770s to 1880s* (Tucson: University of Arizona Press, 2004).

74. Gustave Aimard, "Stronghand: A Romance of the Prairies," *Saturday Evening Post*, March 4, 1871; J. Homer Thiel et al., *Down by the River: Archaeological and Historical Studies of the León Family Farmstead* (Tucson: Center for Desert Archaeology, 2005), 86–124.

75. Carl Lumholtz, *New Trails in Mexico* (New York: Charles Scribner's Sons, 1912), 216.

76. Patricia Preciado Martin, ed., *Songs My Mother Sang to Me: An Oral History of Mexican American Women* (Tucson: University of Arizona Press, 1992), 129.

77. Arthur L. Campa, *Hispanic Culture in the Southwest* (Norman: University of Oklahoma Press, 1979), 280.

78. Leda Frances Blazek, "Food Habits and Living Conditions of Mexican Families on Four Income Levels in the Upper Rio Grande Valley" (M.S. thesis, University of Texas, Austin, 1938), 6–7.

79. Hoyo, *Historia del Nuevo Reino*, 1:141.

80. H. Bailey Carroll and J. Villasaña Haggard, eds., *Three New Mexico Chronicles* (Albuquerque: Quivira Society, 1942), 37–38.

CHAPTER 3

1. Payno, *Los bandidos de Río Frío*, 31–32.

2. Ibid., 31.

3. See Pablo Piccato, "Urbanistas, Ambulantes, and Mendigos: The Dispute for Urban Space in Mexico City, 1890–1930," in *Reconstructing Criminality in Mexico City*, ed. Carlos Aguirre and Robert Buffington (Wilmington, Del.: Scholarly Resources, 2000), 113–48.

4. Francisco Bulnes, *El porvenir de las naciones Hispano-Americanas ante las conquistas recientes de Europa y los Estados Unidos* (Mexico City: Imprenta de Mariano Nava, 1899), 6, 19.

5. Pilcher, *¡Que vivan los tamales!*, 77–97.

6. Fanny Calderón de la Barca, *Life in Mexico: The Letters of Fanny Calderón de la Barca*, ed. Howard T. Fisher and Marion Hall Fisher (Garden City, N.Y.: Doubleday, 1966), 129; Brantz Mayer, *Mexico as It Was and as It Is* (New York: J. Winchester, 1844), 48; *El Siglo XIX*, February 2, 1853. I thank Pedro Santoni for this reference.

7. Antonio García Cubas, *El libro de mis recuerdos* (1904; reprint: Mexico City: Editorial Porrúa, 1986), 313.

8. Víctor M. Macías-González, "Presidential Ritual in Porfirian Mexico: Curtsying in the Shadow of Dictators," in *Heroes and Hero Cults in Latin America*, ed. Samuel Brunk and Ben Fallow (Austin: University of Texas Press, 2006), 91; William H. Beezley, *Mexican National Identity: Memory, Innuendo, and Popular Culture* (Tucson: University of Arizona Press, 2008), 82–83.

9. Auguste Escoffier, *The Complete Guide to the Art of Modern Cooking*, trans. H. L. Cracknell and R. J. Kaufmann (New York: John Wiley and Sons, 1979), 60. On the flexibility of nineteenth-century culinary labels, see Priscilla Parkhurst Ferguson, *Accounting for Taste: The Triumph of French Cuisine* (Chicago: University of Chicago Press, 2004), 72.

10. Alison Smith, "Eating Out in Imperial Russia: Class, Nationality, and Dining before the Great Reforms," 65, no. 4 (Winter 2006): 761.

11. Archivo de la Secretaría de Relaciones Exteriores (hereafter SRE), Mexico City, Acervo Diplomático, Archivo Genaro Estrada, 18–29-2, newspaper clippings, *Washington Evening Star*, February 25, 1879, February 10, 1880; *The Post*, February 10, 1880.

12. José Juan Tablada, *La feria de la vida* (Mexico City: Ediciones Botas, 1937), 199, 260–65; Auguste Génin, *Notes sur le Mexique: Les Français au Mexique* (Mexico City: Imprenta Lacaud, 1908–10), 3; Auguste Génin, *Les Français au Mexique du XVIe siècle a nos jours* (Paris: Nouvelle Éditions Argo, 1933), 347, 435–36, 441; William Harrison Richardson, *Mexico through Russian Eyes, 1806–1940* (Pittsburgh: University of Pittsburgh Press, 1988), 59; Víctor Manuel Macías-González, "The Mexican Aristocracy and Porfirio Díaz, 1876–1911" (Ph.D. diss., Texas Christian University, 1999), 172, 181, 194.

13. Auguste Escoffier, *Memories of My Life*, trans. Laurence Escoffier (New York: Van Nostrand Reinhold, 1997), 178.

14. Novo, *Cocina mexicana*, 136–37.

15. Génin, *Les Français au Mexique*, 436.

16. Sarah Bak-Geller Corona, "Los recetarios 'afrancesados' del siglo XIX en México: La construcción de la nación Mexicana y de un modelo culinario nacional," *Anthropology of Food* S6 (2009): 3, 9, available at http://aof.revues.org/index6464.html (accessed December 7, 2010).

17. *The Mexican Herald*, January 19, 1908, 3; René Rabell Jara, *La bella época*, vol. 6 of *La cocina mexicana a través de los siglos*, ed. Enrique Krauze (Mexico City: Editorial Clio, 1997), 10.

18. Reau Campbell, *Campbell's New Revised Complete Guide and Descriptive Book of Mexico* (Chicago: Rogers and Smith, 1907), 48; José Luis Juárez López, "La cocina de Alejandro Pardo Landa," *Cuadernos de Nutrición* (Mexico City) 4 (July–August 2001): 186–88; Teresa Alfaro-Velcamp, *So Far from Allah, So Close to Mexico: Middle Eastern Immigrants in Modern Mexico* (Austin: University of Texas Press, 2007), 33.

19. José Angel Espinoza, *El ejémplo de Sonora* (Mexico City: N.p., 1932), 36; Robert Chao Romero, *The Chinese in Mexico, 1882–1940* (Tucson: University of Arizona Press, 2010); *La Guacamaya*, August 18, 1904, quoted by Robert Buffington, "The People Contest the Popular: Representations of Chin Chun Chan in the Mexico City Satiric Penny Press" (paper presented at the Rocky Mountain Council on Latin American Studies, Park City, Utah, March 30, 2012).

20. Génin, *Notes sur le Mexique*, 3; Beezley, *Mexican National Identity*, 36; Jeffrey M. Pilcher, *The Sausage Rebellion: Public Health and Private Enterprise, and Meat in Mexico City, 1890–1917* (Albuquerque: University of New Mexico Press, 2006); Robert Weis, "Las panaderías en la Ciudad de México de Porfirio Díaz: Los empresarios vasco-navarros y la movilización obrera," *Revista de Estudios Sociales* 29 (April 2008): 70–85.

21. Archivo de la Casa Juridica, Hermosillo, Sonora, 1883, caja 36, exp. 104, Proceso Sres. Seldner and von Borstel, April 2, 1883.

22. José Tomás de Cuéllar, *The Magic Lantern*, ed. Margo Glantz, trans. Margaret Carson (New York: Oxford University Press, 2000), 84.

23. *Mexican Herald*, January 19, 1908; Pilcher, *¡Que vivan los tamales!*, 65–66; Alejandro Pardo, *Los 30 menus del mes. Manual de la cocina casera. Exclusivamente para la República mexicana* (Mexico City: Talleres Tipográficos de "El Hogar," 1917), 37–38.

24. Tablada, *La feria de la vida*, 145. Emphasis in the original.

25. Francesco Saverio Clavigero, *The History of Mexico*, trans. Charles Cullen, 2 vols. (London: J. Johnson, 1807), 1:431–33.

26. William Robertson, *The History of the Discovery and Settlement of America* (New York: J. and J. Harper, 1828), 324.

27. William Hickling Prescott, *A History of the Conquest of Mexico* (1843; reprint: New York: Heritage Press, 1949), 56, 254.

28. Lewis H. Morgan, "Montezuma's Dinner," *North American Review* 122 (April 1876): 287–88.

29. Lucien Biart, *My Rambles in the New World*, trans. Mary de Hauteville (London: Sampson Low, 1877), 242.

30. Carl Sartorius, *Mexico about 1850* (1858; reprint: Stuttgart: F. A. Brockhaus Komm, 1961), 114–15.

31. Calderón de la Barca, *Life in Mexico*, 150, 220.

32. Juárez López, *Nacionalismo culinario*, 69–70.

33. Guillermo Prieto (Fidel), "Glorias de Juan Pamuceno," in *El folklore literario de México*, ed. Ruben M. Campos (Mexico City: Talleres Gráficos de la Nación, 1929), 131.

34. AHDF, vol. 2405, "Infracciones taquerías," exp. 2, 3, 7, 12, 17, 19.

35. John Lear, *Workers, Neighbors, and Citizens: The Revolution in Mexico City* (Lincoln: University of Nebraska Press, 2001), 49–54.

36. AHDF, vol. 2405, exp. 15, Ruiz to Municipal President, January 10, 1920.

37. Interview with Evelia Reyes Arias, Mexico City, August 5, 2005.

38. Quoted in Claudio Lomnitz, *Death and the Idea of Mexico* (New York: Zone Books, 2005), 327.

39. Torres de Rubio, *Cocina michoacana*, v.

40. Bak-Geller Corona, "Los recetarios 'afrancesados,'" 47.

41. Andrés Molina Enríquez, *Los grandes problemas nacionales* (1909; reprint: Mexico City: Editorial Era, 1978), 279.

42. *El Diario del Hogar*, June 2, 1908, 4.

43. Juan Mora-Torres, *The Making of the Mexican Border* (Austin: University of Texas Press, 2001), 207.

44. Ana María Hernández, *Libro social y familiar para la mujer obrera y campesina mexicana* (Mexico City: Tipografía Moderna, 1938), 66–67.

45. Concepción Lombardo de Miramón, *Memorias* (Mexico City: Editorial Porrúa, 1980), 332, 473.

46. Pilcher, *¡Que vivan los tamales!*, 67.

47. Aline Desentis Otálora, *El que come y canta...Cancionero gastronómico de México*, 2 vols. (Mexico City: CONACULTA, 1999), 1:383–84; P. F. Parisot, *The Reminiscences of a Texas Missionary* (San Antonio: Johnson Brothers, 1899), 190–91.

48. Torres de Rubio, *Cocina michoacana*, 152; Ramírez was cited in the previous chapter.

49. Instituto Nacional de Antropologia e Historia, box 34, 4th series, leg. 109, doc. 16F, "*Almuerzo del 12 de Dic. 1865*"; personal communication from Víctor Macías-González; Tablada, *La feria de la vida*, 265; Beezley, *Mexican National Identity*, 36.

50. AGN, Fondos Particulares, Colección José María Iglesias, José María Calderón y Tapia papers, Caja 5, Exp. 9, Foja 16, Mangino to Calderón, March 30, 1845. I thank Víctor Macías-González for this citation.

51. Víctor Macías-González, "Le capital social et culturel de la communauté aristocratique mexicaine à Paris, 1850–1914," in *Méxique-Francia, una sensibilidad compartida*, ed. Javier

Pérez-Siller and Jean-Marie Lassus (Puebla and Nantes: Université de Nantes and Benemérita Universidad Autónoma de Puebla, forthcoming), 357–85.

52. Arthur Young, *Travels in France during the Years 1787, 1788, 1789*, ed. Betham-Edwards (London: George Gell and Sons, 1906), 25, 26, 41; Alexandre Dumas, *Grand Dictionnaire de Cuisine* (Paris: A. Lemerre, 1873), 703. I thank Kyri Claflin for help in reconstructing this meal.

53. Armand Husson, *Les consommations de Paris* (Paris: Guillaumin et Cie, 1856), 406, 417; Susan J. Terrio, *Crafting the Culture and History of French Chocolate* (Berkeley: University of California Press, 2000), 75.

54. Rio Grande Historical Collections, New Mexico State University Library, Las Cruces, Amador Family Papers, MS 4, box 7, folder 1, Refugio Ruiz de Amador manuscript cookbook; folder 7, letters from Emilia to Refugio, June 7, 1894, and February 7, May 10, 1896; box 25, folder 5, menu signed by Antonio Terrazas, January 21, 1903.

55. Nettie Lee Benson Latin American Collection, Rare Book Room, University of Texas at Austin, Carlos Villalongin Dramatic Company, Series 1, Plays and Promptbooks, shelf no. 6, "San Felipe de Jesús: Protomartyr Mexicano. Drama histórico en cuatro actos," no date.

56. Encarnación Pinedo, *Encarnación's Kitchen: Mexican Recipes from Nineteenth-Century California: Selections from Encarnación Pinedo's "El Cocinero Español,"* ed. and trans. Dan Strehl (Berkeley: University of California Press, 2003), 48.

57. Victor Valle, "A Curse of Tea and Potatoes: The Life and Recipes of Encarnación Pinedo," in ibid., 1–17.

58. Encarnación Pinedo, *El cocinero español: Obra que contiene mil recetas valiosas y utiles para cocinar con facilidad en diferentes estilos* (San Francisco: E. C. Hughes, 1898), 53, 62, 124, 164, 223. See also Robert McKee Irwin, "Ramona and Postnationalist American Studies: On 'Our America' and the Mexican Borderlands," *American Quarterly* 55, no. 4 (December 2003): 539–67.

59. Matías Romero, *Artículos sobre México publicados en los Estados Unidos de América por Matías Romero en 1891–1892* (Mexico City: Tipografia Palacio Nacional, 1892), 181–82.

CHAPTER 4

1. *San Antonio Express*, June 3, 1879, quoted in Donald E. Everett, *San Antonio: The Flavor of Its Past, 1845–1898* (San Antonio: Trinity University Press, 1975), 32.

2. *San Antonio Daily Express*, June 17, 1894, section 2, page 1.

3. Ibid.

4. McWilliams, *North From Mexico*, 43; Arnoldo de León and Kenneth L. Stewart, *Not Room Enough: Mexicans, Anglos, and Socio-Economic Change in Texas* (Albuquerque: University of New Mexico Press, 1993); Albert Camarillo, *Chicanos in a Changing Society: From Mexican Pueblos to American Barrios in Santa Barbara and Southern California, 1848–1930* (Cambridge: Harvard University Press, 1979). On Aunt Jemima, see Doris Witt, *Black Hunger: Food and the Politics of U.S. Identity* (New York: Oxford University Press, 1999).

5. Richard R. Flores, *Remembering the Alamo: Memory, Modernity, and the Master Symbol* (Austin: University of Texas Press, 2002); Daniel Arreola, *Tejano South Texas: A Mexican American Cultural Province* (Austin: University of Texas Press, 2002); William H. Beezley, Cheryl English Martin, and William E. French, eds., *Rituals of Rule, Rituals of Resistance: Public Celebrations and Popular Culture in Mexico* (Wilmington, Del.: Scholarly Resources, 1994).

6. The term "safe danger" comes from Michael Stephens, "Safe Danger and Virtual Slumming: Gangsta Rap, *Grand Theft Auto* and Ghetto Tourism," *Popmatters*, June 17, 2005, available at http://www.popmatters.com/columns/stephens/050617.shtml (accessed October 17, 2009).

7. *Mooney and Morrison Directory of the City of San Antonio, 1877–1878* (Galveston, Tex.: Galveston News, 1877), 83, 169; *Morrison and Fourny's General Directory City of San Antonio, 1879–1880* (Marshall, Tex.: Jennings Bros., 1879), 292; Flores, *Remembering the Alamo*, 42–43.

8. *Los Angeles Times*, January 7, 1882; Victor Valle and Mary Lau Valle, *Recipe of Memory: Five Generations of Mexican Cuisine* (New York: New Press, 1995), 131.

9. David Montejano, *Anglos and Mexicans in the Making of Texas, 1836–1986* (Austin: University of Texas Press, 1987), 28–29, 92; William David Estrada, *The Los Angeles Plaza: Sacred and Contested Space* (Austin: University of Texas Press, 2008), 85–87.

10. "From San Antonio," *Galveston Daily News*, November 22, 1883, 1.

11. John G. Bourke, "The Folk-Foods of the Rio Grande Valley and of Northern Mexico," *Journal of American Folklore* (1895): 60.

12. "Tamale Man Must File His Wits," *Los Angeles Times*, January 27, 1901, C2.

13. Quoted in Donna R. Gabaccia, *We Are What We Eat: Ethnic Food and the Making of Americans* (Cambridge: Harvard University Press, 1998), 108–9.

14. Stephen Crane, "From San Antonio," *Los Angeles Times*, January 8, 1899, B9.

15. Eric St. Clair, "Adventures in a Mexican Jungle," *Los Angeles Times*, August 16, 1931, K7.

16. "Hot Tamales," *Los Angeles Times*, March 30, 1897, 8; "Hot Tamale Men," *Los Angeles Times*, December 20, 1901, 7; "Tamale Politicians to Petition Council," *Los Angeles Times*, February 7, 1903, 14.

17. Sam Woolford, ed., *San Antonio . . . A History for Tomorrow* (San Antonio: Naylor Company, 1963), 152–60.

18. San Antonio City Council (hereafter SACC), "San Antonio Council Journal and Minutes," manuscript book H, December 16, 1889, 564; April 14, 1890, 775; book K, May 4, 1896, 759.

19. Bourke, "Folk-Foods of the Rio Grande," 60.

20. *San Antonio Daily Express*, June 17, 1894, section 2, page 1.

21. Ibid.

22. Lesley Poling-Kempes, *The Harvey Girls: Women Who Opened the West* (New York: Paragon House, 1989).

23. *San Antonio Express*, August 25, 1897, quoted in Everett, *San Antonio*, 33.

24. Valle and Torres, *Latino Metropolis*, 74–75.

25. "Tamale Hounds Fickle," *Los Angeles Times*, April 17, 1924, A1.

26. "Floyd Got Full," *Los Angeles Times*, May 11, 1895, 9.

27. Clara Driscoll, *In the Shadow of the Alamo* (New York: Knickerbocker Press, 1906), 145–60.

28. "The 'Tamale' Man in Trouble," *Los Angeles Times*, June 18, 1889, 6; "Burglars' Booty," *Los Angeles Times*, April 14, 1895, 9.

29. "The Frontier Tramp," *St. Louis Daily Globe Democrat*, December 14, 1884, 1.

30. Zaragosa Vargas, *Proletarians of the North: A History of Mexican Industrial Workers in Detroit and the Midwest, 1917–1933* (Berkeley: University of California Press, 1993), 19; Estrada, *The Los Angeles Plaza*, 148–52.

31. Charles F. Lummis, *The Landmarks Club Cook Book* (Los Angeles: Out West, 1903), 1–10; "Fiery Hot and Water Scarce," *Los Angeles Times*, September 15, 1912, section 2, page 9; "Monster Free Barbecue," *Los Angeles Times*, September 21, 1911, section 12, page 7.

32. Quoted in Thomas E. Sheridan, *Los Tucsoneses: The Mexican Community in Tucson, 1854–1941* (Tucson: University of Arizona Press, 1986), 106.

33. "She Still Makes 'Em," *Los Angeles Times*, February 18, 1916, I3.

34. "Hot Tamales," *Los Angeles Times*, March 30, 1897, 8; "Hot Tamale Men," *Los Angeles Times*, December 20, 1901, 7; "Tamale Politicians to Petition Council," *Los Angeles Times*, February 7, 1903, 14.

35. SACC, "San Antonio Council Journal and Minutes," book K, April 6, 1896, 720; book O, October 7, 1901, 230; October 14, 1901, 234; book T, August 2, 1909, 160; "Fueron clausurados varios expendios de refrescos," *La Epoca*, June 2, 1918, 2; "Nuevas disposiciones contra las mujeres vagas," *La Epoca*, June 30, 1918, 2.

36. David McLemore, "Tortilla Factory Sticks to Tradition," *Dallas Morning News*, July 22, 2007; Pinedo, *Encarnación's Kitchen*, 134; "La harina de trigo escasea," *La Epoca*, April 14, 1918, 6; Arnold J. Bauer, "Millers and Grinders: Technology and Household Economy in Meso-America," *Agricultural History* 64, no. 1 (Winter 1990): 1–17; Pilcher, *¡Que vivan los tamales!*, 102–5.

37. Vanessa Fonseca, "Fractal Capitalism and the Latinization of the U.S. Market" (Ph.D. diss., University of Texas, Austin, 2003), 28, 43.

38. Margarita Cellja Pinedo, "Los empresarios en el comercio de frutas y hortalizas frescas de México a Estados Unidos," in *Empresarios migrantes mexicanos en Estados Unidos*, ed. M. Basilia Valenzuela and Margarita Calleja Pinedo (Guadalajara: Universidad de Guadalajara, 2009), 307–43; Carmella Padilla, *The Chile Chronicles: Tales of a New Mexico Harvest* (Santa Fe: Museum of New Mexico Press, 1997), 6–7.

39. Jeffrey Marcos Garcilazo, "*Traqueros*: Mexican Railroad Workers in the United States, 1870 to 1930" (PhD diss., University of California, Santa Barbara, 1995), 152, 258, 298.

40. Gabriela F. Arredondo, *Mexican Chicago: Race, Identity, and Nation, 1916–39* (Urbana: University of Illinois Press, 2008), 19–20, 54, quote from 170; Susan L. Palmer, "The Community-Building Experiences of Mexicans in Aurora, Illinois, 1915–1935," *Journal of the Illinois State Historical Society* 98, no. 3 (Autumn 2005): 141 (125–43); BANC, Manuel Gamio, 2322:3, Casa de Don Juan Harvey, VI-27-26, Tienda Mexicana, VIII-6-16; Jackson Bauer Papers, Special Collections, Joseph Regenstein Library, University of Chicago, box 1, folder 1, letter to parents, November 24, 1935. I thank Anne Rubenstein for the document and Arturo Rosales for the *tacos suaves*.

41. Walsh, *The Tex-Mex Cookbook*, 68; "Tamales in New York," *Los Angeles Times*, March 7, 1894, 5.

42. "Grocers Are Ready for State Meeting," *San Antonio Light*, June 5, 1904. I thank Robb Walsh for this citation.

43. "Brevities," *Los Angeles Times*, September 30, 1911, section 2, page 6; "Tamales by Overland," *Los Angeles Times*, January 24, 1915, section 7, page 9.

44. Mary E. Livingston, *San Antonio in the 1920s and 1930s* (Charleston, S.C.: Arcadia, 2000), 41–42; Walsh, *The Tex-Mex Cookbook*, 64–65.

45. T. Philip Terry, *Terry's Guide to Mexico* (Boston: Rapid Service, 1944), 243.

46. Bess Adams Garner, *Mexico: Notes in the Margin* (Boston: Houghton Mifflin, 1937), 24–25.

47. "Tamales Calientes," *Los Angeles Times*, September 23, 1894, 19. See also Fredrick B. Pike, *The United States and Latin America: Myths and Stereotypes of Civilization and Nature* (Austin: University of Texas Press, 1992).

48. Charles Francis Saunders, *Under the Sky in California* (New York: McBride, Nast, and Company, 1913), 160.

49. Anita Brenner, *Your Mexican Holiday* (New York: G. P. Putnam's Sons, 1941), 281; Harry Carr, "The Lancer," *Los Angeles Times*, December 14, 1927, A1; Helen Delpar, *The Enormous Vogue*

of Things Mexican: Cultural Relations between the United States and Mexico, 1920–1935 (Tuscaloosa: University of Alabama Press, 1995).

50. Joe E. Cooper, *With or Without Beans* (Dallas: William S. Henson, 1952), 97, quote from 134.

51. Timothy Charles Lloyd, "The Cincinnati Chili Culinary Complex," *Western Folklore* 40, no. 1 (1981): 28–40; "All Palates Pleased," *Washington Post*, July 14, 1901, 14; "Who Will Concoct a New Dish?" *Los Angeles Times*, May 15, 1910, section 2, page 1.

52. A. D. Wyman, "Oldest Recipe Told in Rhyme," *Los Angeles Times*, January 5, 1921, section 2, page 2; Jane Eddington, "Tribune Cook Book," *Chicago Daily Tribune*, September 5, 1927, 13.

53. Will Rogers, "Slipping the Lariat Over," *New York Times*, June 24, 1923, p. 2; Cooper, *With or Without Beans*, 15–22; Chesly Manly, "A Few Words for Texas," *Chicago Daily Tribune*, April 3, 1959, 12.

54. SRE, vol. 46, fo. 543, Mexican Embassy to San Francisco Consul, August 9, 1910; Embajada Mexicana en los Estados Unidos de América, leg. 356, exp. 4, undated petition.

55. Jet C. Winters, "A Report on the Health and Nutrition of Mexicans Living in Texas," *University of Texas Bulletin: 3127* (July 15, 1931), 30. For comparison, see Sarah Deutsch, *No Separate Refuge: Culture, Class, and Gender on an Anglo-Hispanic Frontier in the American Southwest, 1880–1940* (New York: Oxford University Press, 1987), 77, 99, 185; George J. Sánchez, "'Go After the Women': Americanization and the Mexican Immigrant Woman, 1915–1929," in *Unequal Sisters: A Multi-Cultural Reader in U.S. Women's History*, ed. Ellen Carol DuBois and Vicki L. Ruiz (New York: Routledge, 1990), 250–63.

56. John Steinbeck, *Tortilla Flat* (New York: Grosset and Dunlap, 1935), 227. See also Mary Jean Willard, "A Study of the Diet and Nutritional Status of Latin-American Women" (M.S. thesis, University of Texas, Austin, 1942), 8.

57. BANC, Manuel Gamio, 2322, reel 1, 413, "Conrado Martínez," May 24, 1927; reel 1, 364, "Sr. Manuel Lomelí," May 21, 1927; reel 2, 395, "Carlos B. Aguilar," April 8, 1927; reel 2, 449, "Relato de Luis Aguñaga," April 6, 1927.

58. BANC, Manuel Gamio, 2322, reel 3, "Preliminary Report on Mexican Immigration in the United States," 295. See also Hasia Diner, *Hungering for America: Italian, Irish, and Jewish Foodways in the Age of Migration* (Cambridge: Harvard University Press, 2001); Deutsch, *No Separate Refuge*, 85–86; Sánchez, "'Go After the Women,'" 259–61.

59. BANC, Manuel Gamio, 2322, reel 3, 22, Luis Felipe Recinos, "Datos sobre decoración de cafes y restaurants," April 2, 1927.

60. Richard A. García, *Rise of the Mexican American Middle Class: San Antonio, 1929–1941* (College Station: Texas A&M University Press, 1991), 39, 132.

61. *La Prensa*, February 13, 1913, 2; December 19, 1935, 5, 8; August 22, 1937, 5.

62. Francisco J. Santamaria, *Diccionario de mejicanismos*, 5th ed. (Mexico City: Editorial Porrúa, 1992), 385.

63. "Cosas del destierro: Chili con carne," *La Prensa*, March 16, 1919.

64. Julia Kirk Blackwelder, *Women of the Depression: Caste and Culture in San Antonio, 1929–1939* (College Station: Texas A&M University Press, 1984), 62, 81.

65. John Rosales, "Chili Queens," *San Antonio Light*, May 22, 1987, D1.

66. Lyndon Gayle Knippa, "San Antonio, Texas during the Depression, 1933–1936" (M.A. thesis, University of Texas, Austin, 1971); Blackwelder, *Women of the Depression*, 15, 20, 106, 112; García, *Rise of the Mexican American*, 39, 132.

67. *San Antonio Light*, March 4, 1936, section 2, page 6.

68. *San Antonio Express*, July 5, 1939, 8; July 6, 1939, 8; July 7, 1939, 7; July 10, 1939, 3.

69. Center for American History (hereafter CAH), University of Texas at Austin, Maury Maverick Papers, 2L24, W. B. Russ to C. M. Bumstead, October 3, 1939.

70. García, *Rise of the Mexican American*, 215.

71. Green Peyton, *San Antonio: City in the Sun* (New York: McGraw-Hill, 1946), 144–45.

72. "Former Chili Queen Could Lend Expertise, Spice to New Festival," *San Antonio Light*, May 22, 1987, B5.

73. Blackwelder, *Women of the Depression*, 88, 181.

74. See the special issue edited by Ramona Lee Pérez and Meredith E. Abarca, "Cocinas Públicas: Food and Border Consciousness in Greater Mexico," *Food and Foodways* 15, no. 3–4 (July–December 2007); Psyche A. Williams-Forson, *Building Houses Out of Chicken Legs: Black Women, Food, and Power* (Chapel Hill: University of North Carolina Press, 2006); Psyche Williams-Forson and Carole Counihan, eds., *Taking Food Public: Redefining Foodways in a Changing World* (New York: Routledge, 2012).

75. George Fitch, *Vest Pocket Essays* (New York: Barse and Hopkins, 1916), 99.

CHAPTER 5

1. Debra Lee Baldwin, *Taco Titan: The Glen Bell Story* (Arlington, Tex.: Summit Publishing, 1999), 51–55, 62–65, 76–78.

2. *San Antonio Express News*, November 22, 1981, G1.

3. Walsh, *The Tex-Mex Cookbook*, xvi–xix.

4. Richard Pillsbury, *From Boarding House to Bistro: The American Restaurant Then and Now* (Boston: Unwin Hyman, 1990), 103.

5. Ernesto Camou Healy, "La nostalgia del rancho: Notas sobre la cultura urbana y la carne asada," in *Sociedad, economía y cultura alimentaria*, ed. Shoko Doode and Emma Paulina Pérez (Hermosillo: CIAD, 1994), 421–29.

6. On Mexican American cultural formation, see Vicki L. Ruiz, *From Out of the Shadows: Mexican Women in Twentieth-Century America* (New York: Oxford University Press, 1998).

7. Phoebe S. Kropp, "Citizens of the Past? Olvera Street and the Construction of Race and Memory in 1930s Los Angeles," *Radical History Review* 81 (Fall 2001): 35–60. On "ethnic theme parks," see Jerome Krase, "The Present/Future of Little Italies," June 4, 1999, available at http://academic.brooklyn.cuny.edu/soc/semiotics/v1n1/p9.html (accessed July 9, 2011).

8. *Los Angeles Times*, April 19, 1934, 4; June 2, 1934, 2; "Senora de Bonzo Will Conduct Mexican Tour," *Los Angeles Times*, August 23, 1934, A8; "Southland Cafés," *Los Angeles Times*, April 19, 1940, B25.

9. *La Opinión*, April 22, 1930, 4; Valle and Valle, *Recipe of Memory*, 131; "Roundabout," *Los Angeles Times*, March 8, 1964, D26.

10. Kropp, "Citizens of the Past?" 49; "Casa La Golondrina Menu," available at http://collectibles.bidstart.com/Casa-La-Golondrina-Menu-Olvera-Street-Los-Angeles-1930s-/17021523/a.html (accessed June 24, 2011).

11. Thomas H. Kreneck, *Mexican American Odyssey: Felix Tijerina, Entrepreneur and Civic Leader, 1905–1965* (College Station: Texas A&M University Press, 2001), 17, 33, 53, 107, 271. The Felix dinners are listed in a menu from the 1970s posted by a nostalgic customer, available at http://media.houstonfoodie.com/2007/03/felix-menu.pdf (accessed June 24, 2011).

12. New York Passenger Lists, 1820–1957, Coahuila, October 29, 1924, New York Petitions for Naturalization, No. 5314815, April 12, 1943, library edition, available at http://ancestry.com (accessed April 12, 2009).

13. New York Municipal Archive, box 7, folder 444, roll 144, Sarah Chavez, "Feeding the City," October 15, 1940; "News of Food," *New York Times*, January 31, 1952, 30.

14. United States Patent Office, No. 2,506,305, Juvencio Maldonado, "Form for Frying Tortillas to Make Fried Tacos," May 2, 1950. Quote from "News of Food," *New York Times*, May 3, 1952, 24.

15. Fabiola C. de Baca Gilbert, *Historic Cookery* (1939; reprint: State College: New Mexico College of Agriculture and Mechanic Arts, Agriculture Extension Service, Circular No. 250, 1956), 1–2.

16. Cleofas Jaramillo, *The Genuine New Mexico Tasty Recipes* (Santa Fe: Ancient City Press, 1981), 20.

17. Margarita C. de Baca, *Spanish Foods of the Southwest* (Albuquerque: A. B. C. Co., 1937), 9.

18. Fabiola Cabeza de Vaca Gilbert, *The Good Life: New Mexico Traditions and Food* (1949; reprint: Santa Fe: Museum of New Mexico Press, 1982), 71.

19. Elena Zelayeta, *Elena's Secrets of Mexican Cooking* (Garden City, N.Y.: Doubleday and Company, 1958), 128; Elena Zelayeta, *Elena* (Englewood Cliffs, N.J.: Prentice-Hall, 1960), 96, 112.

20. "State to Study Bean Chili Diet of Mexicans," *Los Angeles Times*, August 23, 1951, 23.

21. Goldman, "'I Yam What I Yam,'" 170–76; Merrihelen Ponce, "The Life and Works of Fabiola Cabeza de Baca, New Mexican Hispanic Woman Writer: A Contextual Biography" (PhD diss., University of New Mexico, 1995), 104–10.

22. Elizabeth Webb Herrick, *Curious California Customs* (Los Angeles: Pacific Carbon & Printing, 1935), 109.

23. John F. Love, *McDonald's: Behind the Arches* (New York: Bantam, 1986); Warren Belasco, "Ethnic Fast Foods: The Corporate Melting Pot," *Food and Foodways* 2 (1987): 1–30; John A. Jakle and Keith A. Sculle, *Fast Food: Roadside Restaurants in the Automobile Age* (Baltimore, Md.: Johns Hopkins University Press, 1999), 143–51; Steve Penfold, *The Donut: A Canadian History* (Toronto: University of Toronto Press, 2008), 80–89.

24. Baldwin, *Taco Titan*, 70–74, 120–22; Jeffrey M. Pilcher, "Was the Taco Invented in Southern California?" *Gastronomica* 8, no. 1 (Winter 2008): 36.

25. Penfold, *The Donut*, 81, 89.

26. George J. Sánchez, *Becoming Mexican American: Ethnicity, Culture and Identity in Chicano Los Angeles, 1900–1945* (Berkeley: University of California Press, 1993), 72–76.

27. My thanks to David Van Riper of the Minnesota Population Center for technical assistance with National Historical Geographic Information System (NHGIS). The historians Albert Camarillo and Philip Ethington have influenced this line of research. For more details, see Pilcher, "Was the Taco Invented?," 35.

28. Interview with the manager of Kosher Burrito, Los Angeles, January 31, 2001.

29. Libby Clark, "Soul Food Solé," *Los Angeles Sentinel*, February 19, 1981, C7; "Henry 'Hank' Silva," *Los Angeles Times*, August 26, 2009; Stanley G. Robinson, "L.A. Confidential," *Los Angeles Sentinel*, May 30, 1963, A7; August 3, 1967, A7; March 1, 1973, A6; "Readers Protest Griffen's 'Black/Chicano' Column," *Los Angeles Sentinel*, January 23, 1975, A6; Pilcher, "Was the Taco Invented?," 36.

30. Gabaccia, *We Are What We Eat*, 165; Fonseca, "Fractal Capitalism," 54–57; Walsh, *The Tex-Mex Cookbook*, 199.

31. *Arizona Republic*, December 20, 2002; *New York Times*, February 21, 1955, 24; February 28, 1990; Matthew Lynn, "GrandMet's Mexican food Is Far Too Hot for the City," *Sunday Times* (London), January 15, 1995, 4; "Bruce Foods Company History," available at http://www.fundinguniverse.com/company-histories/Bruce-Foods-Corporation-Company-History.html (accessed July 27, 2006).

32. *Los Angeles Examiner*, February 10, 1955, section 3, page 2; *Los Angeles Times*, January 28, 1960, E5; February 11, 1960, 21; June 22, 1961, 29; *Chicago Daily Tribune*, September 16, 1960, C12; April 28, 1961, B4; October 4, 1963, B3.

33. Jeremy S. Dillon, Paul R. Burger, and Barbara G. Shortridge, "The Growth of Mexican Restaurants in Omaha, Nebraska," *Journal of Cultural Geography* 24, no. 1 (Fall–Winter 2006): 38.

34. *From Texas Tables: Gourmet Recipes Collected by the Junior League of Dallas*, 5th ed. (N.p., 1961); Symphony Society of San Antonio Women's Committee, *The San Antonio Cookbook* (San Antonio: Prompt Printers, 1962).

35. Walsh, *Tex-Mex Cookbook*, 154–60. See also CAH, Barker Menu Collection, La Fonda, undated, La Casita, 1977.

36. The borrowing of menu items also contributed to the standardization of Chinese restaurants in North America. See Lily Cho, *Eating Chinese: Culture on the Menu in Small Town Canada* (Toronto: University of Toronto Press, 2010).

37. Mario Montaño, "Appropriation and Counterhegemony in South Texas: Food Slurs, Offal Meats, and Blood," in *Useable Pasts: Traditions and Group Expressions in North America*, ed. Tad Tuleja (Logan: Utah State University Press, 1997), 50–67; Walsh, *Tex-Mex Cookbook*, 178–81, 193, 208; *Guardian* (London), May 15, 1989, 39; interview with Edward Gámez, Fort Worth, Texas, March 26, 1992.

38. Patricia Sharpe, "Table Talk: Four Restaurateurs Talk about Tex-Mex, Chile Con Queso, Chips, and Heartburn," *Texas Monthly*, August 2003.

39. Walsh, *The Tex-Mex Cookbook*, 69.

40. Elvira Ramírez, *Recetas de Doña Elvira: A Collection of Dishes from Texas and Mexico* (San Antonio: N.p., 1977), 2–3.

41. Lucy M. Garza, *South Texas Mexican Cookbook* (Austin, Tex.: Eakin Press, 1982), 10, 29, 42, 48.

42. Charles Lummis, ed., *Landmarks Club Cook Book: A California Collection of the Choicest Recipes from Everywhere...Including a Chapter of the Most Famous Old Californian and Mexican Dishes* (Los Angeles: Out West, 1903); Pauline Wiley-Kleeman, *Ramona's Spanish-Mexican Cookery: The First Complete and Authentic Spanish-Mexican Cook Book in English* (Los Angeles: West Coast, 1929); "Farmer's Market Today," *Los Angeles Times*, April 26, 1944, 4; April 18, 1948, 2; "Round About with Art Ryon," *Los Angeles Times*, May 24, 1964, C28.

43. Barbara Hansen, "Head Chef Adapts Mexican Fare to California Taste," *Los Angeles Times*, June 30, 1977, 33.

44. Bégué de Packman, *Early California Hospitality*, 38.

45. Quoted in Douglas Monroy, *Rebirth: Mexican Los Angeles from the Great Migration to the Great Depression* (Berkeley: University of California Press, 1999), 30.

46. "Pat-a-Cake Tortillas Bow to Machine Age," *Los Angeles Times*, March 10, 1947, 7.

47. Los Angeles Public Library, Menu Collection, "La Fonda," available at http://dbase1.lapl.org/images/menus/fullsize/a/13620-inside1.jpg (accessed February 15, 2006).

48. Baldwin, *Taco Titan*, 170.

49. John Gregory, "A Specialty of the House: Atmosphere," *Los Angeles Times*, May 5, 1974, 5; Kirsten Searer, "El Tortito's Fiesta," *Los Angeles Daily News*, July 24, 1999, B1.

50. Joan M. Jenson, "Canning Comes to New Mexico: Women and the Agricultural Extension Service, 1914–1919," in *New Mexico Women: Intercultural Perspectives*, ed. Joan M. Jenson and Darlis A. Miller (Albuquerque: University of New Mexico Press, 1986), 203–7; Carole M. Counihan, *A Tortilla Is Like Life: Food and Culture in the San Luis Valley of Colorado* (Austin: University of Texas Press, 2009), 75, 100–104.

51. Sunny Conley, *A Bite of History: Recipes and Tales from the Mesilla Valley* (Las Cruces: Writing the Southwest, 1999), 11.

52. BANC, Manuel Gamio, 2322:3, 19, Luis Recinos, Tucson, Arizona, April 27, 1927.

53. Daniel Arreola, "Mexican Restaurants in Tucson," *Journal of Cultural Geography* 3 (Spring–Summer 1983): 112.

54. *El Universal Grafico*, July 1, 1946, 10.

55. Sandra Aguilar Rodríguez, "Cooking Modernity: Food, Gender, and Class in 1940s and 1950s Mexico City and Guanajuato" (Ph.D. diss., University of Manchester, 2008), 151, 155, 171.

56. Víctor M. Macías-González and Steven B. Bunker, "Consumption and Material Culture in the Twentieth Century," in *Companion to Mexican History and Culture*, ed. William H. Beezley (Chichester: Wiley-Blackwell, 2011), 83–118; AGN, Luis Romero Soto, vol. 5, exp. 3–5, Romero to Ashley, April 30, 1941; vol. 14, exp. 15, Stumberg to Romero, date illegible.

57. Cynthia Hewitt de Alcántara, *Modernizing Mexican Agriculture: Socioeconomic Implications of Technological Change, 1940–1970* (Geneva: United Nations Research Institute for Social Development, 1976); Joseph Cotter, *Troubled Harvest: Agronomy and Revolution in Mexico, 1880–2002* (New York: Praeger, 2003).

58. Gabriella Petrick, "'Like Ribbons of Green and Gold': Industrializing Lettuce and the Quest for Quality in the Salinas Valley, 1920–1965," *Agricultural History* 80, no. 3 (2006): 269–95; Susan Freidberg, *Fresh: A Perishable History* (Cambridge: Harvard University Press, 2009), 182–84; Susan Ferriss and Ricardo Sandoval, *The Fight in the Fields: Cesar Chavez and the Farmworkers Movement* (New York: Harcourt Brace, 1997).

59. Christopher R. Boyer, *Becoming Campesinos: Politics, Identity, and Agrarian Struggle in Postrevolutionary Michoacán, 1920–1935* (Stanford: Stanford University Press, 2003); Alfonso Reyes, *Memorias de cocina y bodega* (Mexico City: Fondo de Cultura Económica, 1989), 142; interview with Juan Mutizaval Velázquez de León, Mexico City, June 30, 1994; Pilcher, *¡Que vivan los tamales!*, 131.

60. Josefina Velázquez de León, *Cocina de San Luis Potosí* (Mexico City: Ediciones Josefina Velázquez de León, 1957), 76–77; Josefina Velázquez de León, *Cocina de Sonora* (Mexico City: Ediciones Josefina Velázquez de León, 1958), 60–61.

61. Federico López, personal communication, October 6, 2010.

62. Desentis Otálora, *El que come y canta*, 1:300–301.

63. Camou Healy, "La nostalgia del rancho," 426; interview with Ernesto Camou Healy, Hermosillo, February 19, 2008; "Restaurante Chichen Itza," *El Imparcial* (Hermosillo), January 3, 1967, 6.

64. Domingo García Garza, "Una etnografía de los 'tacos' en México. El caso de Monterrey," *Estudios Sociales* 19, no. 37 (January–June 2011): 32–63; Antonio Murray, *El rey del cabrito: Biografía de Jesús Alberto Martínez* (Monterrey: Ediciones Castillo, 2000), 54.

65. Jorge De'Angeli, ed., *Comer como dios manda: Good Dining in Mexico* (Mexico City: Ediciones Culturales DGA, 1977), 168.

66. "Tres años de lucha," *La Prensa*, May 24, 1946, 3.

67. Chon Noriega, *Shot in America: Television, the State, and the Rise of Chicano Cinema* (Minneapolis: University of Minnesota Press, 2000), 46; Samuel L. Popkin, *The Reasoning Voter: Communication and Persuasion in Presidential Campaigns* (Chicago: University of Chicago Press, 1991), 1.

CHAPTER 6

1. Interview with Thomas Estes, Paris, June 1, 1999. This chapter is based on a decade of international fieldwork eating Mexican food on five continents.

2. For immigrant parallels, see Gabaccia, *We Are What We Eat*, 64–92.

3. Chrystia Freeland, "Moscow in Throes of Tex-Mex Craze," *Financial Times*, April 10, 1995.

4. *The Observer*, October 9, 1960, 23.

5. Diane Kirkby, "'From Wharfie Haunt to Foodie Haven': Modernity and Law in the Transformation of the Australian Working-Class Pub," *Food, Culture and Society* 11, no. 1 (March 2008): 37–38.

6. Art Buchwald, "The Tourist Is Welcome Here," *Los Angeles Times*, August 4, 1959; Morrison Wood, "For Men Only!" *Chicago Daily Tribune*, October 30, 1948, 14.

7. Phyllis Pooler, *Hon-Dah a la Fiesta Cook Book* (Phoenix: Arizona Messenger Printing Co., 1968), 21.

8. R. Lee Sullivan, "Raise the Flag," *Forbes*, April 25, 1994, 84.

9. Stephen I. Schwab, "The Role of the Mexican Expeditionary Air Force in World War II," *Journal of Military History* 66, no. 4 (October 2002): 1115–40.

10. Vicki Vaughan, "S.A. Anglos Taking to Tacos," *San Antonio Express News*, November 22, 1981, G1.

11. Ella K. Daggett Stumpf, "Cheers for Chili Con Carne!" *San Antonio Magazine*, March 1978, 47.

12. Mario Montaño, "The History of Mexican Folk Foodways of South Texas: Street Vendors, Offal Foods, and *Barbacoa de Cabeza*" (Ph.D. diss., University of Pennsylvania, 1992), 285.

13. Matt Warshaw, *The History of Surfing* (San Francisco: Chronicle, 2010), 146; *Café Pacifico: Twenty-Five Years of Mexican Madness* (London: Ian Selman, 2001), 16.

14. AGN, Romero Soto, vol. 5, exp. 48, [illegible] to Ana Maria Romero, 1976.

15. Earlene Ridge, "Cook Who Makes Mexican Food in Paris Has to Go by Way of the Arab Market," *Arizona Daily Star* (Tucson), December 18, 1996; *Phyllis Glazer*, "Feedback," *Jerusalem Post*, June 25, 1998, 12.

16. Interview with Oshima Bari, Osaka, Japan, September 10, 2000.

17. "Eating Out," *The Times* (London), May 10, 1969, 27.

18. Interview with Estes.

19. Walsh, *The Tex-Mex Cookbook*, 247.

20. Øyvind Holen, "Taco Nation," *Fredag*, May 6, 2011, 18.

21. *Budapest Sun*, October 19, 1995; Greg Hassell, "Guten Tag, Frau Ninfa," *Houston Chronicle*, January 16, 1996, 1.

22. Interviews with Cristin Prun, Paris, June 3, 1999, and June 16, 2004.

23. "The North Bites Back," *Guardian*, June 19, 1987, 20.

24. Interview with Carlos Hernández Cedillo, Buenos Aires, Argentina, March 3, 2009.

25. "Scotland's Oil Rush Town," *The Irish Times*, June 16, 1981, 10.

26. Glenn Collins, "With Mexican Food Tamed, Big Business Looks Abroad," *New York Times*, January 9, 1997, D1.

27. Ibid.; Susan Lindee, "Sauce Wars," *San Antonio Light*, January 13, 1985, 19–23; Deirdre McQuillan, "Chip Off the Old Block; Mexican Food," *Sunday Times*, August 14, 1988; Jeffrey Charles, "Searching for Gold in Guacamole: California Growers Market the Avocado, 1910–1994," in *Food Nations: Selling Taste in Consumer Societies*, ed. Warren Belasco and Philip Scranton (New York: Routledge, 2002), 149.

28. Quotes from Collins, "With Mexican Food Tamed," D1; *Favourite Mexican Recipes* (Sydney: Marketing Machine, n.d.), 5, 11; Lisa Buckingham, "GrandMet Pays £1.7bn to Spice Up U.S. Food Rivalry," *Guardian*, January 10, 1995, 13.

29. "Feeling Hot! Hot! Hot!" *Financial Times*, January 10, 1995; "Tortilla Trends," *Snack Food and Wholesale Bakery*, August 2006; Gregory Rodriguez, "Swedish Mexican Food, Straight from the U.S.," *Los Angeles Times*, September 24, 2006, A11; Holen, "Taco Nation," 11; "Santa Maria

World," available at http://www.ie.santamariaworld.com/jsp/company/c1a.jsp (accessed April 28, 2009).

30. Ian Darby, "General Mills Commissions Old El Paso Series," *PRWeek*, September 30, 2005; Raymond Snoddy, "IDS Salve Steals March on Thinkbox," *Marketing*, September 6, 2006, 16; Gabaccia, *We Are What We Eat*, 220.

31. José Orozco, "Gabriel Espíndola Martínez: Tequila Master," in *The Human Tradition in Mexico*, ed. Jeffrey M. Pilcher (Wilmington, Del.: Scholarly Resources, 2003), 225–33; Tim Mitchell, *Intoxicated Identities: Alcohol's Power in Mexican History and Culture* (New York: Routledge, 2004), 153, 163; Matthew DeBord, "Más Tequila!" *Wine Spectator* 28, no. 2 (May 15, 2003): 90.

32. "News of Food," *New York Times*, April 13, 1950, 33.

33. *Los Angeles Times*, May 28, 1961, 16; "Variety of South American Foods," *New York Times*, April 13, 1950, 33.

34. Ioan Grillo, "On the Tequila Express," *Latin Trade* 11, no. 10 (October 2003): 68–69.

35. In Patricia Alisau, "Discovering Mexico's Liquid Treasure," *Business Mexico* 14, no. 11 (November 2004): 56.

36. DeBord, "Más Tequila!," 90.

37. Bruce Horovitz, "Corona Beer a Big Success: Import's Popularity Baffles the Analysts," *Los Angeles Times*, March 30, 1986, 1; Dianne Klein, "Mexico's Poor-Man's Brew Makes Big Splash in U.S.," *Houston Chronicle*, August 3, 1986, 1.

38. Bob Greene, "Solving the Mystery of a Beer with Lime," *Chicago Tribune*, September 3, 1986, 1; Jonathan Peterson, "Weird Rumor No Joke When It's about Your Firm's Product," *Minneapolis Star and Tribune*, August 24, 1987, 3.

39. "Impresionante, la demanda que tiene la cerveza Corona en EU," *El Universal*, September 11, 1986; "Corona se coloca como la cerveza Mexicana de mayor venta en EU," *Excelsior*, September 8, 1986.

40. Alejandro Claps, "Se logro la aperture del mercado Sueco," *Excelsior*, April 17, 1992; "Cervezas mexicanas conquistan Europa," *El Financiero*, August 25, 1992; Dietmar H. Lamparter, "Getränkemarkt Durst auf Exoten," *Die Zeit*, February 21, 1992, 9; "Miss Mexico Helping Promote Corona Beer," *Bangkok Post*, June 3, 2005.

41. Tara Parker-Pope, "Texans Bite Off All They Can Chew in U.K. Restaurant," *Wall Street Journal* (Europe), December 2, 1994; "Rex Kirby Design," available at http://www.rexkirbydesign .com/texas-embassy-cantina.html (accessed August 12, 2009).

42. Lisa Takeuchi Cullen, "When Eat Meets West," *Time*, January 28, 2008, 44–46; "Wikipedia: Taco Bell," available at http://en.wikipedia.org/wiki/Taco_Bell (accessed June 30, 2011). See also "We Want Taco Bell," available at http://www.youtube.com/watch?v=nwqgZLOGAqk (accessed June 30, 2011). I thank Laura Coco for the Korean taco report.

43. Hassell, "Guten Tag, Frau Ninfa," 1; Amanda *Richards,* "The Foodie Who Found His Feet," *Marketing*, November 10, 1994, 22.

44. Clotilde Luce, "Texas, Paris," *Texas Monthly*, February 1996, 98; interview with Prun.

45. John Henderson, "Enchiladas in Paris? C'est Bon," *Denver Post*, August 3, 2005; "Marie's World Tour 2001: The Hurd's the Word," available at http://mjavins.fatcow.com/mwt.2001/ www/index.html (accessed May 20, 2012).

46. Collins, "With Mexican Food Tamed," D1.

47. Rachel Black, personal communication, June 7, 2008.

48. Freeland, "Moscow in Throes of Tex-Mex Craze"; "Wild, Wild, East," *The Economist*, August 31, 1996; Jim Harkness, personal communication, March 4, 2011.

49. Italo Calvino, *Bajo el sol jaguar*, trans. Aurora Bernárdez (Mexico City: Editorial Patria, 1992); Elena Muzzarelli, "Las Rosas: Mexico algo màs," *Torino Magazine*, May 2005, 154–55.

50. Quetzil E. Castañeda, "The Aura of Ruins," in *Fragments of a Golden Age: The Politics of Culture in Mexico since 1940*, ed. Gilbert Joseph, Anne Rubenstein, and Eric Zolov (Durham, N.C.: Duke University Press, 2001), 453, 458.

51. Ilona Steckhan, *Die Küche der Azteken: Rezepte einer versunkenen Kultur* (Freiburg: Dreisam-Verlag, 1987).

52. Ligaya Mishan, "Winter's Pleasures, Sip by Sip," *New York Times*, December 24, 2008, D6; *New York Times*, December 2, 2007, Travel, 16; Joanne Harris, *Chocolat: A Novel* (New York: Viking, 1999).

53. Gisela Williams, "Street Food with Ambition," *New York Times*, November 12, 2006, TR4.

54. Pablo Piccata, personal communication, February 5, 2009.

55. Pankaj Mishra, *Temptations of the West: How to Be Modern in India, Pakistan, Tibet, and Beyond* (New York: Farrar, Straus and Giroux, 2006), 27.

56. "Tokyo Online Magazine," available at http://www.coolgirlsjapan.biz/fonda_E.html (accessed February 5, 2008).

57. Lisa Teoh, "Dine-online," available at http://www.dine-online.co.uk/downmex.htm (accessed July 3, 2007).

58. "A Slice of Mexico on Your Platter," *Hindustan Times* (New Delhi), February 4, 2005.

59. *Café Pacifico*, 15.

60. Walsh, *Tex-Mex Cookbook*, 245; *The Berkeley Guides: Paris '96* (New York: Fodor's, 1995), 153.

61. Quoted in Francesca Bray, *Agriculture*, part 2 of *Biology and Biological Technology*, vol. 6 of *Science and Civilisation in China*, ed. Joseph Needham (Cambridge: Cambridge University Press, 1984), 458.

62. Jim Benning, "Eating Fajitas in France," available at http://www.worldhum.com/features/travel-stories/eating_fajitas_in_france_20070409 (accessed March 1, 2010); Jean-Michel Maumont, *La Cuisine Tex-Mex* (Ingersheim: Editions S.A.E.P., 1995), 38; Socorro del Paso and Fernando del Paso, *Douceur et passion de la cuisine mexicaine* (Marseille: Éditions de l'aube, 1991), 177.

63. Hannah Weitzer, "The Tel Aviv Tortilla," *Jerusalem Post*, July 19, 2007, 10; Nozomi Kobayashi, "Japan's 'Habanero' Boom Saves Mexican Chili Industry," *Kyodo News International* (Tokyo), November 2, 2004.

CHAPTER 7

1. *Good Housekeeping*, October 1980, 6; April 1985, 80.

2. Quote from Sylvia Lovegren, *Fashionable Food: Seven Decades of Food Fads* (New York: Macmillan, 1995), 378.

3. Shelly Errington, *The Death of Authentic Primitive Art and Other Tales of Progress* (Berkeley: University of California Press, 1998).

4. Warren J. Belasco, *Appetite for Change: How the Counterculture Took on the Food Industry* (Ithaca, N.Y.: Cornell University Press, 1993), 40.

5. Eric Zolov, *Refried Elvis: The Rise of the Mexican Counterculture* (Berkeley: University of California Press, 1999); Claudio Lomnitz-Adler, *Exits from the Labyrinth: Culture and Ideology in the Mexican National Space* (Berkeley: University of California Press, 1992), 255–56.

6. Interview with Fortino Rojas Contreras, Mexico City, June 4, 2006; "Restaurant Bar 'Chon,'" available at http://www.restaurantechon.com (accessed July 15, 2008).

7. *La cocina del banco nacional de México* (Mexico: Fomento Cultural Banamex, 2000), 95–107.

8. "Star Chefs," available at http://www.starchefs.com/chefs/PQuintana/html/bio.shtml (accessed July 14, 2008); Barbara Hansen, "Aficionado of Mexican Cuisine," *Los Angeles Times*, July 26, 1979, G1.

9. "Alta Cocina Patricia Quintana," available at http://jamesbeard.starchefs.com/old/events/1999/10/029.html (accessed May 20, 2012).

10. Patricia Sharpe, "Mix Masters," *Texas Monthly*, June 1991, 42–49; Florence Fabricant, "Mexican Chefs Embrace a Lighter Cuisine of Old," *New York Times*, May 3, 1995, B1.

11. Diana Kennedy, *My Mexico: A Culinary Odyssey* (New York: Clarkson Potter, 1998), 56; Diana Kennedy, *The Cuisines of Mexico* (New York: Harper and Row, 1972).

12. Jeffrey M. Pilcher, "From 'Montezuma's Revenge' to 'Mexican Truffles': Culinary Tourism across the Rio Grande," in *Culinary Tourism*, ed. Lucy M. Long (Lexington: University Press of Kentucky, 2004), 76–96.

13. Luis Dwan, "A Cuisine That's Truly American," *Los Angeles Times*, February 20, 1983, S87.

14. Ruth Reichl, "Chefs Pledge Allegiance to the Southwest," *Los Angeles Times*, September 30, 1984, K87.

15. Mark Miller, Stephan Pyles, and John Sedlar, *Tamales* (New York: Wiley, 2002), 33, 85, 131.

16. Quoted in Barbara Fenzl, *Savor the Southwest* (San Francisco: Bay Books, 1999), 14.

17. Reichl, "Chefs Pledge Allegiance," K88.

18. William Grimes, "Squirt! Splat! Gone!" *New York Times*, July 26, 2000, B13.

19. Vanessa Fonseca, "Nuevo Latino: Rebranding Latin American Cuisine," *Consumption, Markets, and Culture* 8, no. 2 (June 2005): 99; Valle and Torres, *Latino Metropolis*, 88.

20. Rick Bayless, interview in *Chef's Story*, ed. Dorothy Hamilton and Patric Kuh (New York: HarperCollins, 2007), 38–40; telephone interview with Rick Bayless, November 21, 2006; Rick Bayless with Deann Groen Bayless, *Authentic Mexican: Regional Cooking from the Heart of Mexico* (New York: William Morrow, 1987).

21. María Dolores Torres Yzábal and Shelton Wiseman, *The Mexican Gourmet: Authentic Ingredients and Traditional Recipes from the Kitchens of Mexico* (Sydney: Gold Street, 1995).

22. Kent Black, "In Oaxaca, a Cook Creates a Stir," *New York Times*, August 14, 2002, D1; interview with Iliana de la Vega Arnaud, Santa Fe, New Mexico, January 26, 2007.

23. Pilcher, "From 'Montezuma's Revenge,'" 89–91.

24. Krishnendu Ray, "Ethnic Succession and the New American Restaurant Cuisine," in *The Restaurants Book: Ethnographies of Where We Eat*, ed. David Beriss and David Sutton (Oxford: Berg, 2007), 97–114.

25. Wilbur Zelinsky, "The Roving Palate: North America's Ethnic Restaurant Cuisines," *Geoforum* 16, no. 1 (1985): 51–72; Gabaccia, *We Are What We Eat*, 80–81.

26. Zelinsky, "The Roving Palate," 64.

27. Dillon, Burger, and Shortridge, "Mexican Restaurants in Omaha," 37–65.

28. *Campell Taggert Annual Report*, 1977, 17; Paul Goldstein, "Chi-Chi's Profit under Pressure," *Globe and Mail* (Toronto), April 22, 1985, B7; Mike Marshall, "Huntsville's Oldest Mexican Restaurant," available at http://blog.al.com/huntsville-times-business/2010/01/owner_recalls_beginnings_of_hu.html (accessed July 13, 2010); Tom Spencer, personal communication, August 10, 2000.

29. Quoted in Marie Sarita Gaytán, "From Sombreros to Sincronizadas: Authenticity, Ethnicity, and the Mexican Restaurant Industry," *Journal of Contemporary Ethnography* 37, no. 3

(June 2008): 335. See also Richard A. Guest, "Intellectual Property Rights and Native American Tribes," *American Indian Law Review* 20, no. 1 (1995/1996): 130–32.

30. "Fresh Mex Profiles," *Restaurant Finance Monitor* 10, no. 7 (1998): 6–11; Jane Black, "In Trial Run, Chipotle Heads to the Farm," *Washington Post*, March 26, 2008, F1.

31. I thank Rayna Green and Alvis Dunn for their technical expertise. See also Patricia Sharpe, "Slush Fun," *Texas Monthly*, May 2001; Steffan Igor Ayora-Diaz and Gabriela Vargas-Cetina, "Romantic Moods: Food, Beer, Music, and the Yucatecan Soul," in *Drinking Cultures: Alcohol and Identity*, ed. Thomas Wilson (Oxford: Berg, 2005), 166; Tim Weiner, "Pour Beer, Add Volcano and Drink," *New York Times*, August 15, 2001; Teresa Gubbins and Mary Brown Malouf, "The Tex-Mex Trail," *D: Dallas/Fort Worth*, November 1, 2006, 58; Karen Robinson-Jacobs, "Mexican Eateries Try Smaller Markets to Fight Sales Slump," *Dallas Morning News*, July 19, 2005.

32. Unlike Zelinsky's actual count of restaurants from telephone books, this map is based on Mexican establishments as a percentage of total restaurants on yellowpages.com and in its Canadian counterpart, collected in spring 2010.

33. Nicole M. Christian, "Mexican Immigrants Lead a Revival," *New York Times*, May 21, 2000; Barbara Hansen, "The Oaxaca Connection," *Los Angeles Times*, May 1, 2002, H1.

34. Dánica Coto, "Making Room for Tomatillos," *Charlotte Observer*, August 3, 2005, E1; Sarah Kramer, "From New York Soil, the Taste of Home," *New York Times*, September 21, 2008, City 1; Jeffrey H. Cohen et al., "*Chapulines* and Food Choices in Rural Oaxaca," *Gastronomica* 9, no. 1 (Winter 2009): 64; Alejandro Ascencio, "Envían a paisanos menudo y barbacoa," *Reforma*, July 4, 2006, Negocios 2.

35. Karen Haram, "Tac'o the Morning," *San Antonio Express*, November 6, 1991, 1B; telephone interview with Melissa Guerra, April 6, 2008.

36. See Juan M. Rivera, Scott Whiteford, and Manuel Chávez, eds., *NAFTA and the Campesinos: The Impact of NAFTA on Small-Scale Agricultural Producers in Mexico and the Prospects for Change* (Scranton: University of Scranton Press, 2009); Magdalena Barros, *From Maize to Melons: Struggles and Strategies of Small Mexican Farmers* (Amsterdam: CEDLA, 2000).

37. Hubert C. de Grammont, ed., *Empreses, reestructuración productiva y empleo en la agricultura mexicana* (Mexico City: Editorial Plaza y Valdés, 1999); M. Guadalupe Rodríguez Gómez, *El frijol en México: Elementos para una agenda de soberanía alimentaria* (Guadalajara: Universidad de Guadalajara, 2006).

38. Johnston and Baumann, *Foodies*, 4.

39. Ellen Messer, "Maize," in Kiple and Orenlas, *The Cambridge World History of Food*, 1:107–8; Warman, *Corn and Capitalism*, 174–90; Harvey Levenstein, *Revolution at the Table: The Transformation of the American Diet* (New York: Oxford University Press, 1988), 33; Deborah Fitzgerald, "Eating and Remembering," *Agricultural History* 79, no. 4 (Autumn 2005): 393–408.

40. "Mexican-Born Persons in the U.S. Civilian Labor Force," Migration Policy Institute Fact Sheet Number 14, November 2006, available at http://www.migrationpolicy.org/pubs/FS14_MexicanWorkers2006.pdf (accessed July 20, 2010); Julie Guthman, *Agrarian Dreams: The Paradox of Organic Farming in California* (Berkeley: University of California Press, 2004); Susan Rose and Robert Shaw, "The Gamble: Circular Mexican Migration and the Return of Remittances," *Mexican Studies/Estudios Mexicanos* 24, no. 1 (Winter 2008): 79–111.

41. Jack Kloppenburg, *First the Seed: The Political Economy of Plant Biotechnology, 1492–2000*, 2nd ed. (Madison: University of Wisconsin Press, 2004), 186.

42. Enrique Ochoa, *Feeding Mexico: The Political Uses of Food since 1910* (Wilmington, Del.: Scholarly Resources, 2000).

43. Quote from Alma Guillermoprieto, "In Search of the Real Tortilla," *The New Yorker*, November 29, 1999, 46; José Ferrer Pujol, "Racionalización de subsidios y liberación de precios del sector," in *La industria de la masa y la tortilla: Desarrollo y tecnología*, ed. Felipe Torres (Mexico City: UNAM, 1996), 39–48; Carolina Bank Muñoz, *Transnational Tortillas: Race, Gender, and Shop-Floor Politics in Mexico and the United States* (Ithaca, N.Y.: Cornell University Press, 2008), 30. A recent investigation by Mexican authorities has reportedly uncovered no evidence of wrongdoing. See Marla Dickerson and Jerry Hirsch, "Investment Money Pours in from Mexico," *Los Angeles Times*, May 5, 2007.

44. Bank, *Transnational Tortillas*, 32, 35; "Wrapping the Globe in Tortillas," *Business Week*, February 26, 2007; "Food Manufacture," *Processing News* 75, no. 1 (January 2000): 7.

45. David Barstow, "Vast Mexico Bribery Case Hushed Up by Wal-Mart after Top-Level Struggle," *New York Times*, April 21, 2012, 1.

46. James J. Biles et al., "Globalization of Food Retailing and Transformation of Supply Networks: Consequences for Small-Scale Agricultural Producers in Southeastern Mexico," *Journal of Latin American Geography* 6, no. 2 (2007): 59.

47. Ibid., 55–75.

48. Flavia Echánove and Cristina Steffen, "Coping with Trade Liberalization: The Case of Mexican Grain Producers," *Culture and Agriculture* 25, no. 2 (Fall 2003): 1–12; Steven E. Sanderson, *The Transformation of Mexican Agriculture: International Structure and the Politics of Rural Change* (Princeton: Princeton University Press, 1986); Cynthia Hewitt de Alcántara, ed., *Economic Restructuring and Rural Subsistence in Mexico: Corn and the Crisis of the 1980s* (San Diego: Center for U.S.-Mexican Studies, University of California, San Diego, 1994); Deborah Barndt, *Tangled Routes: Women, Work, and Globalization on the Tomato Trail* (Lanham, Md.: Rowman and Littlefield, 2002).

49. Robert R. Alvarez, Jr., *Mangos, Chiles, and Truckers: The Business of Transnationalism* (Minneapolis: University of Minnesota Press, 2005); Lori Ann Thrupp, *Bittersweet Harvests for Global Supermarkets: Challenges in Latin Americas Agricultural Export Boom* (Washington, D.C.: World Resources Institute, 1995); Wayne A. Cornelius and David Myhre, *The Transformation of Rural Mexico: Reforming the Ejido Sector* (La Jolla: Center for U.S.-Mexico Studies, University of California, San Diego, 1998); Echánove and Steffen, "Coping with Trade Liberalization," 7–8; Biles et al., "Globalization of Food Retailing," 68; Bank Muñoz, *Transnational Tortillas*, 31.

50. Douglas S. Massey, Jorge Durand, and Nolan J. Malone, *Beyond Smoke and Mirrors: Mexican Immigration in an Era of Economic Integration* (New York: Russell Sage Foundation, 2003); Alberto Arroyo, "NAFTA in Mexico's Promises, Myths and Realities," *Lessons from NAFTA: The High Cost of Free Trade*, Hemispheric Social Alliance Research Report (June 2003): 5–22.

51. Elizabeth Fitting, *The Struggle for Maize: Campesinos, Workers, and Transgenic Corn in the Mexican Countryside* (Durham, N.C.: Duke University Press, 2011), 59–64; Kathleen McAfee, "Corn Culture and Dangerous DNA: Real and Imagined Consequences of Maize Transgene Flow in Oaxaca," *Journal of Latin American Geography* 2, no. 1 (2003): 18–42; Edit Antal, Lauren Baker, and Gerard Verschoor, *Maize and Biosecurity in Mexico: Debate and Practice*, Cuadernos del CEDLA 22 (Amsterdam: CEDLA, 2007); Rachel A. Schurman and Dennis Doyle Takahashi Kelso, eds., *Engineering Trouble: Biotechnology and Its Discontents* (Berkeley: University of California Press, 2003).

52. John Parker, "The 9 Billion-People Question," *The Economist*, February 26, 2011, 15.

53. Frances Abrahamer Rothstein, *Globalization in Rural Mexico: Three Decades of Change* (Austin: University of Texas Press, 2007), 116, 121; Marie Elisa Christie, *Kitchenspace: Women, Fiestas, and Everyday Life in Central Mexico* (Austin: University of Texas Press, 2008).

54. Caire, "'Sin maíz, no hay país.'"

55. Fitting, *The Struggle for Maize*, 65–71.

56. "Greenpeace etiqueta anuncio espectacular de Maseca," Boletín 173, September 6, 2001, available at http://www.greenpeace.org.mx/php/gp.php?target=%2Fphp%2Fboletines. php%3Fc%3Dtrans%26n%3D173 (available April 22, 2004).

57. Lauren Baker, "Regional Maize Marketing Initiatives," in *Maize and Biosecurity in Mexico*, 55–83; Andrea Mandel-Campbell, "Tortilla Move Puts Corn Flour Groups through the Mill," *Financial Times*, October 11, 2000.

58. Víctor M. Toledo, *La paz en Chiapas: Ecología, luchas indígenas y modernidad alternativa* (Mexico City: Ediciones Quinta Sol, 2000); Eric Holt-Giménez, *Campesino a Campesino: Voices from Latin America's Farmer to Farmer Movement for Sustainable Agriculture* (Oakland: Food First, 2006); Fitting, *The Struggle for Maize*, 159, 200.

59. Maria Elena Martinez-Torres, *Organic Coffee: Sustainable Development by Mayan Farmers* (Athens: Ohio University Press, 2006).

60. Kolleen Guy, *When Champagne Became French: Wine and the Making of a National Identity* (Baltimore: Johns Hopkins University Press, 2003); Amy B. Trubek, *A Taste of Place: A Cultural Journey into Terroir* (Berkeley: University of California Press, 2008).

61. Gabriel Torres, "The Agave War: Toward an Agenda for the Post-NAFTA Ejido," in *The Future Role of the Ejido in Rural Mexico*, ed. Richard Snyder and Gabriel Torres (La Jolla: Center for U.S.-Mexico Studies, University of California, San Diego, 1998), 73–100; "Storm in a Tequila Bottle," *The Economist*, October 4, 2003.

62. Valle and Torres, *Latino Metropolis*, 92–99.

63. David Barkin, *Wealth, Poverty and Sustainable Development* (Mexico City: Editorial Jus, 1998), 68. See also Cornelia Flora, ed., *Interactions between Agroecosystems and Rural Communities* (Boca Raton, Fla.: CRC Press, 2001).

64. Sarah Lyon, "Maya Coffee Farmers and Fair Trade: Assessing the Benefits and Limitations of Alternative Markets," *Culture and Agriculture* 29, no. 2 (Fall 2007): 100–112; Echánove and Steffen, "Coping with Trade Liberalization," 7; Barros, *From Maize to Melons*, 147.

CONCLUSION

1. Vicki Ruiz, "Citizen Restaurant: American Imaginaries, American Communities," *American Quarterly* 60, no. 1 (March 2008): 1–21; Jennifer Steinhauer, "In Taco Truck Battle, Mild Angelenos Turn Hot," *New York Times*, May 3, 2008, 1; "Carne Asada Is Not a Crime," available at http://saveourtacotrucks.org (accessed December 20, 2011).

2. Joaquín Contreras, "The Taco Truck: Morphology and Assemblage of an American Object" (M.A. thesis, University of Minnesota, 2011).

3. Heldke, *Exotic Appetites*, 23–44, 56–59; Johnston and Baumann, *Foodies*, 69–95.

4. Emiko Ohnuki-Tierney, *Rice as Self: Japanese Identities through Time* (Princeton: Princeton University Press, 1993); Ferguson, *Accounting for Taste*, 22–25; Richard Wilk, *Home Cooking in the Global Village: Caribbean Food from Buccaneers to Ecotourists* (Oxford: Berg, 2006); Benedict Anderson, *Imagined Communities: Reflections on the Origin and Spread of Nationalism*, rev ed. (London: Verso, 1991); Meredith Abarca, *Voices in the Kitchen: Views of Food and the World from Working-Class Mexican and Mexican American Women* (College Station: Texas A&M University Press, 2006), 120–22.

5. Sonja G. Atkinson, *The Aztec Way to Healthy Eating* (New York: Paragon House, 1992).

6. Kirsten Silva Gruesz, "Lexical Snacks at the Citizen Restaurant: A Response to Vicki Ruiz," *American Quarterly* 60, no. 1 (March 2008): 38; Ruiz, "Citizen Restaurant," 9; Amy Bentley, "From

Culinary Other to Mainstream America: The Meanings and Uses of Southwestern Cuisine," in Long, *Culinary Tourism*, 209–25.

7. Anzaldúa, *Borderlands/La Frontera*, 31; Jennifer Steinhauer, "For a New Generation, Kimchi Goes with Tacos," *New York Times*, February 25, 2009, D1; John T. Edge, "The Tortilla Takes a Road Trip to Korea," *New York Times*, July 28, 2010, D1.

8. Ann V. Millard and Jorge Chapa, *Apple Pie and Enchiladas: Latino Newcomers in the Rural Midwest* (Austin: University of Texas Press, 2004), 4–5; Heldke, *Exotic Appetites*, 17–22.

9. Alex Witchel, "The Latest Thing? Who Needs It?" *New York Times*, March 31, 2010, D3; Gaytán, "From Sombreros to Sincronizadas," 314–41.

10. Dan Malovany, "Tortilla Trends," *Snack Food and Wholesale Bakery*, August 2006; "Wrapping the Globe in Tortillas," *Business Week*, February 26, 2007.

11. Gregory Rodriguez, "Swedish Mexican Food, Straight from the U.S.," *Los Angeles Times*, September 24, 2006, A11.

12. Alma Guillermoprieto, *The Heart That Bleeds* (New York: Vintage, 1994), 248.

13. Mark Stevenson, "Taco Bell Runs for the Border," *Minneapolis Star Tribune*, October 10, 2007, A13.

14. Ivonne Vizcarra Bordi, "The 'Authentic' Taco and Peasant Women: Nostalgic Consumption in the Era of Globalization," *Culture and Agriculture* 28, no. 2 (Fall 2006): 101–2. On peasant essentialism, see Michael Kearney, *Reconceptualizing the Peasantry: Anthropology in Global Perspective* (Boulder, Colo.: Westview, 1996).

15. Mónica Delgado, "A la conquista de París," *Reforma*, September 30, 2005, from the presidential webpage of Vicente Fox, available at http://fox.presidencia.gob.mx/buenasnoticias/?contenido=20979&pagina=190 (accessed April 23, 2007); Arturo Cruz Barcenas, "Fallo en contra de la comida mexicana," *La Jornada*, November 26, 2005.

16. "Intangible Heritage Lists: 2010," available at http://www.unesco.org/culture/ich/index.php?lg=en&pg=00011 (accessed July 10, 2011).

17. Quoted in Fitting, *The Struggle for Maize*, 173.

18. Victor Villaseñor, *Rain of Gold* (New York: Delta, 1991), 350.

19. Patricia López Marroquín, "Miss Conception," manuscript in possession of the author. On the construction of national cuisines in exile, see Arjun Appadurai, "How to Make a National Cuisine: Cookbooks in Contemporary India," *Comparative Studies in Society and History* 30, no. 1 (January 1988): 3–24; Richard Wilk, "Food and Nationalism: The Origins of 'Belizean' Food," in *Food Nations: Selling Taste in Contemporary Societies*, ed. Warren Belasco and Philip Scranton (New York: Routledge, 2002), 67–89.

20. I-Pei Hsiu Hodge, "Healthy Tamales Made the Old Fashioned Way," *Hill Country Sun* (Austin, Tex.), December 2008, 12–13. I thank Carla Phillips for this citation.

21. "Contempo: The Lifestyle Magazine for the Rio Grande Valley," available at http://issuu.com/tmagana/docs/contempo_magazine_november_2008 (accessed May 18, 2012); Roy Lieuven, personal communication, October 24, 2008.

22. Øyvind Holen, "Taco Nation," *Fredag*, May 6, 2011, 18.

23. Rick Bayless, personal communication, December 15, 2011.

24. Matt Martinez and Steve Pate, *Matt Martinez's Culinary Frontier: A Real Texas Cookbook* (New York: Broadway, 1997); Melissa Guerra, *Dishes from the Wild Horse Desert: Norteño Cooking of South Texas* (New York: Wiley, 2006).

GLOSSARY

Adobo Paste of vinegar, herbs, and chiles, originally used to preserve meat.

Aguardiente "Burning water": a potent alcohol distilled from maguey or sugar cane.

Albóndigas Meatballs.

Almuerzo Brunch, an informal family meal taken at about ten o'clock in the morning.

Animalitos "Little animals," a derogatory term used by Spaniards to refer to meats consumed by the Indians.

Antojitos "Little whimsy," corn-based foods such as *gorditas*, *chalupas*, or *tamales*, typically eaten on the street.

Arid America Geographical term for regions of present-day northern Mexico and the southwestern United States, inhabited in pre-Hispanic times by nomadic and semisedentary peoples.

Asiento Pork fat cooked with cracklings, commonly used in the cooking of Oaxaca.

Ate Conserves of mamey or other fruit, a colonial dessert.

Atole Corn *masa* gruel.

Bacanora Distilled liquor made from local magueys of Sonora.

Barbacoa Pit-roasted meat. *Barbacoa de cabeza de vaca*, the entire head of a cow, was a festival dish of the borderlands. Today, barbacoa is often prepared in stainless steel containers.

Birria Spicy goat stew, a specialty of Jalisco.

Bizcocho   Colonial biscuit, like hardtack; also a cookie.

Buñuelo   Deep-fried yeast dough topped with brown sugar or honey, a popular festival dish.

Burrito   Wheat flour tortilla filled with beans, meat, or other stuffings, common to Sonoran and Cal-Mex cooking; a particularly large version, the Mission burrito, filled with rice and beans, originated in San Francisco.

Cabrito   Kid, a regional specialty of Monterrey.

Cabuches   Cactus flower buds.

Cacahuazintle   Variety of corn used for making *nixtamal*, particularly in central Mexico.

Cajeta   Caramelized syrup, particularly of goat's milk, a regional specialty of the Bajío region of central Mexico.

Camote   Sweet potato; candied sweet potatoes were a colonial dessert.

Capirotada   Bread pudding.

Carne adobada   Meat marinated in chile paste, a specialty of New Mexico.

Carne asada   Grilled meat, a common dish of northern Mexico.

Carnitas   Bits of fried meat, particularly pork.

Cecina   Salted beef or pork, also known as *tasajo* and, in Sonora, *carne seca*.

Cemitas   Whole-grain bread, also a sandwich made from this bread.

Cena   Supper, an informal meal often eaten out as late as ten o'clock at night.

Ceviche   Fresh, raw seafood "cooked" with lime juice.

Chalupa   Open-faced *antojito* from central and southern Mexico.

Champurrado   Maize *atole* mixed with chocolate.

Chapulín   Small grasshopper commonly eaten in southern Mexico

Chicha   Fermented corn beverage of Andean South America.

Chichimecas   "Dog people," a derogatory Nahua term for nomadic peoples of Arid America.

Chilaquiles   Dish of chile pepper sauce and leftover tortillas.

Chile con queso   Appetizer made with melted cheese and green chiles.

Chile relleno   Stuffed chile peppers, often poblanos, filled with cheese or meat and fried with egg batter.

Chile verde   Green chile stew, a specialty of New Mexico.

Chili con carne   Stew of Texas Mexican origin, typically containing meat, dried red chiles, oregano, and garlic, also referred to as *carne con chile*. A chili gravy thickened with roux is commonly used as a sauce for enchiladas and other dishes in Tex-Mex restaurants.

Chiltepines   Wild chile pepper common to northern Mexico; small, round, and very hot.

Chimichanga Deep-fried burrito.

Chito Deep-fried goat, a festival dish in central Mexico.

Chongos Dessert formerly made of bread, cheese, and syrup; also cooked milk curds, a specialty of Zamora, Michoacán.

Chorizo Sausage spiced with chile peppers.

Clayudas Large tortilla served with *asiento*, a specialty of Oaxaca.

Cocado Candied coconut, a colonial dessert.

Comal Earthenware griddle.

Comida Main meal of the day, typically eaten about two o'clock.

Comiscal Oval-shaped "Tandoor-style" oven from the Isthmus of Tehuantepec.

Creole Person of European descent born in the Americas, also an adjective referring to Hispanic American culture.

Cuitlacoche Black fungus (*Ustilago maydis*) that grows on corn and is used in both *antojitos* and the *nueva cocina mexicana*.

Envuelto Nineteenth-century *antojito*, a cross between a taco and an enchilada.

Epazote Distinctively flavored herb (*Chenopodium ambrosioides*) often cooked with beans.

Escabeche Pickle used in colonial times to preserve meat, fish, and vegetables.

Ezquites Toasted grains of maize, a common street food in Mexico.

Fajitas Northern Mexican *carne asada* made from the *faja* or *arrachera*, the diaphragm muscle of a cow.

Flautas "Flutes," a form of hard taco.

Fonda Informal restaurant.

Fritanga Fried-food shop.

Gorda "Fattie," thick *antojito* stuffed with meat or other fillings; also called *gordita*.

Gusano Larval worm that feeds on maguey leaves, often added to *mezcal* or tequila to convey a rustic authenticity.

Huauhzontle An herb (*Chenopodium spp*) often cooked like *chiles rellenos*.

Indigenismo Revolutionary nationalist ideology seeking to incorporate Native Americans into Mexican society.

Jamoncillos de almendra Fudge squares, a colonial dessert.

Jericaya Custard.

Jícama A tuber of a vine (*Pachyrrhizus erosus*); has brown skin and potatolike flesh, often eaten in salads.

Maguey Century plant (*Agave sp.*), fermented to make *pulque* or distilled into *mezcal* or tequila.

Manjar real Almond rice custard.

Mano Stone "rolling pin" used to grind *nixtamal* on a *metate*.

Menudo   Tripe stew made with chile peppers.

Mesoamerica   Geographical region encompassing central Mexico, the Yucatán, and northern Central America.

Mestizo   Person of mixed race, from the colonial system of castes, often referred to with derogatory names such as "coyote."

Metate   Basalt grinding stone used to prepare *nixtamal*.

Mezcal   Spirit distilled from the fermented juice of the maguey plant.

Mole de guajolote   Turkey with chile pepper sauce.

Nixtamal   Alkaline-processed maize, ground into a dough for making tortillas and tamales, or cooked whole in stews such as *pozole*.

Nopal   A cactus (*Opuntia sp.*) with dark green, oval-shaped paddles, often grilled or eaten as a salad.

Norteño   A person from northern Mexico, also an adjective referring to northern culture.

Nueva cocina mexicana   Gourmet movement originating in the 1980s.

Oasis America   A geographical region where pre-Hispanic societies practiced sedentary agriculture in river valleys of the present-day southwestern United States and northwestern Mexico.

Panadería   Bakery.

Pellagra   Nutritional deficiency caused by inadequate niacin intake, common to populations with diets based on corn made without alkaline processing (*nixtamal*).

Picadillo   Chopped meat stuffing made with nuts and candied fruit.

Pico de gallo   "Rooster's beak," salsa of tomato and green chile.

Piki bread   Thin blue-corn bread made among the Hopi, Zuni, and other Pueblos.

Piloncillo   Rustic brown sugar, made in a cone shape.

Pinole   Maize porridge.

Pipián   Pumpkin seed and chile pepper sauce often served with poultry.

Pozole   Stew of whole grains of *nixtamal*; in New Mexico, *pozole de chicos* is made with a particular variety of corn.

Puchero   Spanish stew.

Pulque   A thick, white alcoholic beverage fermented from the sap of the maguey plant.

Quelites de ceniza   Lamb's quarters, an herb of the *Chenopodium* family often eaten in salads or soups.

Quesadilla   *Antojito* shaped like a corn tortilla, folded around a stuffing of cheese or vegetable, and then deep-fried or cooked on a comal.

Queso Chihuahua   Soft, white cow's milk cheese produced by Mennonites in northern Mexico.

Queso de tuna   Candied prickly pear fruit.

Recado negro   Yucatecan spice mixture.

Sopaipillas   Fried pastry of Iberian Muslim origin eaten with honey in New Mexico

Taco   A common *antojito* first documented in late nineteenth-century Mexico
City. In Mexico, soft tacos are made with fresh corn tortillas and meats such as
barbacoa and organ meats, often garnished with diced onion and cilantro. Hard
tacos, called *tacos dorados* (golden tacos), are rolled into a cylinder shape, fried,
and often served with lettuce, salsa, and cream on top. *Tacos al carbon* (grilled
tacos) began to appear in upscale restaurants in the 1960s with fancy meats
such as *bifstek* (steak) and *chuleta* (pork chops). *Tacos al pastor* were introduced by
second-generation Lebanese Mexicans, who adapted lamb gyros (also known as
tacos arabes) to Mexican ingredients, preparing chile-flavored pork on a vertical
rotisserie served with pineapple. In the United States, soft tacos are often made
with wheat flour tortillas, while hard tacos are served in prefried taco shells.
Puffy tacos are a distinctively Tex-Mex variation, made with a deep-fried round of
nixtamal dough in place of a tortilla.

Taco shell   Corn tortilla fried into a U-shaped container.

Tasajo   Salted meat, also known as *cecina* or *carne seca*.

Teosinte   A grass of the *Zea* family, common to Mexico and Central America, and
the source for domesticated maize.

Tlemolito   Chile broth.

Tostada   Open-faced taco.

Verdolagas   Purslane, a succulent (*Portulaca oleracea*) eaten in salads and stews.

Xumiles   An insect (*Atizies taxcoensis*) native to Guerrero.

Yemitas   Candied egg yolks, a colonial dessert.

ARCHIVES AND LIBRARIES

Archivo de la Casa Jurídica, Hermosillo, Sonora

Archivo de la Secretaría de Relaciones Exteriores, Mexico City (SRE)
    Acervo Diplomático, Archivo Genaro Estrada
    Embajada Mexicana en los Estados Unidos de América

Archivo General de la Nación, Mexico City, Fondos Particulares (AGN)
    Colección José María Iglesias, José María Calderón y Tapia Papers
    Colección Luis Romero Soto

Archivo Histórico del Distrito Federal (AHDF)

Bancroft Library, University of California, Berkeley (BANC)
    Manuscripts Eulalia Perez, José Fernández
    Manuel Gamio Collection

Center for American History, University of Texas at Austin (CAH)
    Maury Maverick Papers

Instituto Nacional de Antropología e Historia, Mexico City

Joseph Regenstein Library, University of Chicago, Special Collections
    Jackson Bauer Papers

Los Angeles Public Library, Menu Collection

Nettie Lee Benson Latin American Collection, Rare Book Room, University of Texas at Austin
    Carlos Villalongin Dramatic Company

New York City Municipal Archive

Rio Grande Historical Collections, New Mexico State University Library, Las Cruces
    Amador Family Papers

San Antonio City Council Archive (SACC)

United States Patent Office

BOOKS, ARTICLES, AND THESES

Abarca, Meredith E. "Authentic or Not, It's Original." *Food and Foodways* 12 (2004): 1–25.

———. *Voices in the Kitchen: Views of Food and the World from Working-Class Mexican and Mexican American Women*. College Station: Texas A&M University Press, 2006.

Achay, K. T. *Indian Food: A Historical Companion*. Delhi: Oxford University Press, 1998.

Acosta, José de. *Natural and Moral History of the Indies*. Edited by Jane E. Mangan. Translated by Frances M. López-Morillas. Durham, N.C.: Duke University Press, 2002.

Adams, Jenny L. "Refocusing the Role of Food-Grinding Tools as Correlates for Subsistence Strategies in the US Southwest." *American Antiquity* 54, no. 3 (1999): 475–98.

———. *Ground Stone Analysis: A Technological Approach*. Salt Lake City: University of Utah Press, 2002.

Aguilar-Rodríguez, Sandra. "Cooking Modernity: Food, Gender, and Class in 1940s and 1950s Mexico City and Guanajuato." Ph.D. diss., University of Manchester, 2008.

Albala, Ken. *Eating Right in the Renaissance*. Berkeley: University of California Press, 2002.

Alessio Robles, Vito. *Acapulco, Saltillo y Monterrey en la historia y en la leyenda*. Mexico City: Editorial Porrúa, 1978.

Alfaro-Velcamp, Teresa. *So Far from Allah, So Close to Mexico: Middle Eastern Immigrants in Modern Mexico*. Austin: University of Texas Press, 2007.

Alonzo, Armando C. *Tejano Legacy: Rancheros and Settlers in South Texas, 1734–1900*. Albuquerque: University of New Mexico Press, 1998.

Alvarez, Robert R., Jr. *Mangos, Chiles, and Truckers: The Business of Transnationalism*. Minneapolis: University of Minnesota Press, 2005.

Anderson, Benedict. *Imagined Communities: Reflections on the Origin and Spread of Nationalism*. Rev. ed. London: Verso, 1991.

Andrews, Jean. *Peppers: The Domesticated Capsicums*. Austin: University of Texas Press, 1984.

Antal, Edit, Lauren Baker, and Gerard Verschoor. *Maize and Biosecurity in Mexico: Debate and Practice*. Cuadernos del CEDLA 22. Amsterdam: CEDLA, 2007.

Anzaldúa, Gloria. *Borderlands/La Frontera: The New Mestiza*. San Francisco: Aunt Lute Books, 1999.

Arredondo, Gabriela F. *Mexican Chicago: Race, Identity, and Nation, 1916–39*. Urbana: University of Illinois Press, 2008.

Arreola, Daniel. "Mexican Restaurants in Tucson." *Journal of Cultural Geography* 3 (Spring–Summer 1983): 108–114.

———. *Tejano South Texas: A Mexican American Cultural Province*. Austin: University of Texas Press, 2002.

Arroyo, Alberto. "NAFTA in Mexico's Promises, Myths and Realities." *Lessons from NAFTA: The High Cost of Free Trade*. Hemispheric Social Alliance Research Report (June 2003): 5–22.

Ayora-Diaz, Steffan Igor. *Foodscapes, Foodfields, and Identities in Yucatán*. New York: Berghahn, 2012.

———. "Regionalism and the Institution of the Yucatecan Gastronomic Field." *Food, Culture and Society* 13, no. 3 (September 2010): 397–420.

Bak-Geller Corona, Sarah. "Los recetarios 'afrancesados' del siglo XIX en México: La construcción de la nación Mexicana y de un modelo culinario nacional," *Anthropology of Food* S6 (December 2009). http://aof.revues.org/index6464.html.

Baldwin, Debra Lee. *Taco Titan: The Glen Bell Story*. Arlington, Tex.: Summit Publishing, 1999.

Bank Muñoz, Carolina. *Transnational Tortillas: Race, Gender, and Shop-Floor Politics in Mexico and the United States*. Ithaca, N.Y.: Cornell University Press, 2008.

Barkin, David. *Wealth, Poverty and Sustainable Development*. Mexico City: Editorial Jus, 1998.

Barndt, Deborah. *Tangled Routes: Women, Work, and Globalization on the Tomato Trail*. Lanham, Md.: Rowman and Littlefield, 2002.

Barros, Magdalena. *From Maize to Melons: Struggles and Strategies of Small Mexican Farmers*. Amsterdam: CEDLA, 2000.

Bauer, Arnold. *Goods, Power, History: Latin America's Material Culture*. Cambridge: Cambridge University Press, 2001.

Beezley, William H. *Mexican National Identity: Memory, Innuendo, and Popular Culture*. Tucson: University of Arizona Press, 2008.

Belasco, Warren J. *Appetite for Change: How the Counterculture Took on the Food Industry*. Ithaca, N.Y.: Cornell University Press, 1993.

———. "Ethnic Fast Foods: The Corporate Melting Pot." *Food and Foodways* 2 (1987): 1–30.

Bentley, Amy. "From Culinary Other to Mainstream America: The Meanings and Uses of Southwestern Cuisine." In *Culinary Tourism*, edited by Lucy Long, 209–25. Lexington: University Press of Kentucky, 2003.

Biles, James J., et al. "Globalization of Food Retailing and Transformation of Supply Networks: Consequences for Small-Scale Agricultural Producers in Southeastern Mexico." *Journal of Latin American Geography* 6, no. 2 (2007): 55–75.

Bonfil Batalla, Guillermo. *México Profundo: Reclaiming a Civilization*. Translated by Philip A. Dennis. Austin: University of Texas Press, 1996.

———, ed. *Simbiosis de culturas: Los inmigrantes y su cultura en México*. Mexico City: Fondo de Cultura Económica, 1993.

Bouvier, Virginia. *Women and the Conquest of California, 1542–1840*. Tucson: University of Arizona Press, 2001.

Boyer, Christopher R. *Becoming Campesinos: Politics, Identity, and Agrarian Struggle in Postrevolutionary Michoacán, 1920–1935*. Stanford: Stanford University Press, 2003.

Brandes, Stanley. "Maize as a Culinary Mystery." *Ethnology* 31, no. 4 (1992): 331–36.

Bray, Francesca. *Agriculture*, vol. 6, pt. 2 of *Science and Civilisation in China*, edited by Joseph Needham. Cambridge: Cambridge University Press, 1984.

Brenton, Barrett P. "Piki, Polenta, and Pellagra: Maize, Nutrition and Nurturing the Natural." In *Nurture: Proceedings of the Oxford Symposium on Food and Cookery 2003*, edited by Richard Hosking, 36–50. Bristol: Footwork, 2004.

Butzer, Elisabeth. *Historia social de una comunidad tlaxcalteca: San Miguel de Aguayo (Bustamante, N.L.) 1686–1820*. Saltillo: Archivo Municipal de Saltillo, 2001.

Caire, Matthew. "'Sin maíz, no hay pais': Corn in Mexico under Neoliberalism." M.A. thesis, Bowling Green State University, 2010.

Calderón de la Barca, Fanny. *Life in Mexico: The Letters of Fanny Calderón de la Barca*. Edited by Howard T. Fisher and Marion Hall Fisher. Garden City, N.Y.: Doubleday, 1966.

Calleja Pinedo, Margarita. "Los empresarios en el comercio de frutas y hortalizas frescas de México a Estados Unidos." In *Empresarios migrantes mexicanos en Estados Unidos*, edited by M. Basilia Valenzuela and Margarita Calleja Pinedo, 307–43. Guadalajara: Universidad de Guadalajara, 2009.

Camarillo, Albert. *Chicanos in a Changing Society: From Mexican Pueblos to American Barrios in Santa Barbara and Southern California, 1848–1930*. Cambridge: Harvard University Press, 1979.

Camou Healy, Ernesto. "La nostalgia del rancho: Notas sobre la cultura urbana y la carne asada." In *Sociedad, economía y cultura alimentaria*, edited by Shoko Doode and Emma Paulina Pérez, 431–29. Hermosillo: CIAD, 1994.

Campa, Arthur L. *Hispanic Culture in the Southwest*. Norman: University of Oklahoma Press, 1979.

Carney, Judith A. *Black Rice: The African Origins of Rice Cultivation in the Americas*. Cambridge: Harvard University Press, 2001.

Carney, Judith A., and Richard Rosomoff. *In the Shadow of Slavery: Africa's Botanical Legacy in the Atlantic World*. Berkeley: University of California Press, 2009.

Castañeda, Quetzil E. "The Aura of Ruins." In *Fragments of a Golden Age: The Politics of Culture in Mexico since 1940*, edited by Gilbert Joseph, Anne Rubenstein, and Eric Zolov, 452–67. Durham, N.C.: Duke University Press, 2001.

Castillo Palma, Norma Angélica, and Susan Kellogg. "Conflict and Cohabitation between Afro-Mexicans and Nahuas in Central Mexico." In *Beyond Black and Red: African-Native Relations in Colonial Latin America*, edited by Matthew Restall, 115–36. Albuquerque: University of New Mexico Press, 2005.

Chávez-García, Miroslava. *Negotiating Conquest: Gender and Power in California, 1770s to 1880s*. Tucson: University of Arizona Press, 2004.

Chevalier, François. *Land and Society in Colonial Mexico: The Great Hacienda*. Translated by Alvin Eustis. Berkeley: University of California Press, 1963.

Cho, Lily. *Eating Chinese: Culture on the Menu in Small Town Canada*. Toronto: University of Toronto Press, 2010.

Christie, Marie Elisa. *Kitchenspace: Women, Fiestas, and Everyday Life in Central Mexico*. Austin: University of Texas Press, 2008.

Clark, John E., and David Cheetham. "Mesoamerica's Tribal Foundations." In *The Archaeology of Tribal Societies*, edited by William A. Parkinson, 278–339. Archaeological Series 15. Ann Arbor, Mich.: International Monographs in Prehistory, 2002.

Coe, Sophie D. *America's First Cuisines*. Austin: University of Texas Press, 1994.

Coe, Sophie D., and Michael Coe. *The True History of Chocolate*. London: Thames and Hudson, 1996.

Cohen, Jeffrey H., et al. "*Chapulines* and Food Choices in Rural Oaxaca." *Gastronomica* 9, no. 1 (Winter 2009): 61–65.

Contreras, Joaquín. "The Taco Truck: Morphology and Assemblage of an American Object." M.A. thesis, University of Minnesota, 2011.

Cope, R. Douglas. *The Limits of Racial Domination: Plebeian Society in Colonial Mexico City, 1660–1720*. Madison: University of Wisconsin Press, 1994.

Corcuera de Mancera, Sonia. *Entre gula y templanza: Un aspecto de la historia mexicana*. 3rd ed. Mexico City: Fondo de Cultura Económica, 1991.

Cornelius, Wayne A., and David Myhre, eds. *The Transformation of Rural Mexico: Reforming the Ejido Sector*. La Jolla: Center for US-Mexico Studies, University of California, San Diego, 1998.

Corominas, Joan. *Diccionario crítico etimológico castellano e hispánico*. 6 vols. Madrid: Editorial Gredos, 1991.

Corona Páez, Sergio Antonio. *La vitivinicultura en el pueblo de Santa María de las Parras: Producción de vinos, vinagres y aguardientes bajo el paradigma andaluz (siglos XVII y XVIII)*. Torreón, Coahuila: Ayuntamiento de Torreón, 2004.

Cotter, Joseph. *Troubled Harvest: Agronomy and Revolution in Mexico, 1880–2002*. New York: Praeger, 2003.

Counihan, Carole M. *A Tortilla Is Like Life: Food and Culture in the San Luis Valley of Colorado*. Austin: University of Texas Press, 2009.

Crosby, Alfred W., Jr. *The Columbian Exchange: Biological and Cultural Consequences of 1492*. Westport, Conn.: Greenwood, 1972.

Crown, Patricia L. "Women's Role in Changing Cuisine." In *Women and Men in the Prehispanic Southwest*, edited by Patricia L. Crown, 221–66. Santa Fe: School of American Research Press, 2000.

Crown, Patricia L., and W. Jeffrey Hurst. "Evidence of Cacao Use in the Prehispanic American Southwest." *Proceedings of the National Academy of Sciences* 106, no. 7 (February 17, 2009): 2110–13.

Cuello, José. *Saltillo colonial: Orígenes y formación de una sociedad mexicana en la frontera norte*. Saltillo: Archivo Municipal de Saltillo and Universidad Autónoma de Coahuila, 2004.

Cushing, Frank Hamilton. *Zuni Breadstuff*. New York: Museum of the American Indian, 1920.

Davidson, Alan. "Europeans' Wary Encounter with Tomatoes, Potatoes, and Other New World Foods." In *Chilies to Chocolate: Food the Americas Gave the World*, edited by Nelson Foster and Linda Cordell, 1–14. Tucson: University of Arizona Press, 1992.

de Grammont, Hubert C., ed. *Empreses, reestructuración productiva y empleo en la agricultura mexicana*. Mexico City: Editorial Plaza y Valdés, 1999.

de la Teja, Jesús F. "Saint James at the Fair: Religious Ceremony, Civic Boosterism, and Commercial Development on the Colonial Mexican Frontier." *The Americas* 57, no. 3 (January 2001): 395–416.

———. *San Antonio de Béxar: A Community on New Spain's Northern Frontier*. Albuquerque: University of New Mexico Press, 1995.

De León, Arnoldo. *The Tejano Community, 1836–1900*. Albuquerque: University of New Mexico Press, 1982.

De León, Arnoldo, and Kenneth L. Stewart. *Not Room Enough: Mexicans, Anglos, and Socio-Economic Change in Texas*. Albuquerque: University of New Mexico Press, 1993.

de Vos, Paula. "The Science of Spices: Empiricism and Economic Botany in the Early Spanish Empire." *Journal of World History* 17, no. 4 (December 2006): 399–427.

Deeds, Susan M. *Defiance and Deference in Mexico's Colonial North: Indians under Spanish Rule in Nueva Vizcaya*. Austin: University of Texas Press, 2003.

del Hoyo, Eugenio. *Historia del Nuevo Reino de León (1577–1723)*. 2 vols. Monterrey: Instituto Tecnológico y de Estudios Superiores de Monterrey, 1972.

del Río Moreno, Justo L. *Los inicios de la agricultura europea en el nuevo mundo (1492–1542)*. Sevilla: ASAJA-Sevilla, 1991.

Desentis Otálora, Aline. *El que come y canta … Cancionero gastronómico de México*. 2 vols. Mexico City: CONACULTA, 1999.

Deutsch, Sarah. *No Separate Refuge: Culture, Class, and Gender on an Anglo-Hispanic Frontier in the American Southwest, 1880–1940*. New York: Oxford University Press, 1987.

Di Peso, Charles C., John B. Rinaldo, and Gloria J. Fenner. *Casas Grandes: A Fallen Trading Center of the Gran Chichimeca*. 8 vols. Flagstaff, Ariz.: Northland Press, 1974.

Diccionario de la lengua castellana. 6 vols. Madrid: Francisco del Hierro, 1726.

Dillon, Jeremy S., Paul R. Burger, and Barbara G. Shortridge. "The Growth of Mexican Restaurants in Omaha, Nebraska." *Journal of Cultural Geography* 24, no. 1 (Fall–Winter 2006): 37–65.

Diner, Hasia. *Hungering for America: Italian, Irish, and Jewish Foodways in the Age of Migration*. Cambridge: Harvard University Press, 2001.

Documents of the Coronado Expedition, 1539–1542. Edited and translated by Richard Flint and Shirley Cushing Flint. Dallas: Southern Methodist University Press, 2005.

Dorweiler, J., et al. "Teosinte Glume Architecture 1: A Genetic Locus Controlling a Key Step in Maize Evolution." *Science* 262 (1993): 233–35.

Earle, Rebecca. "'If You Eat Their Food . . .': Diets and Bodies in Early Colonial Spanish America." *American Historical Review* 115, no. 3 (June 2010): 688–713.

Echánove, Flavia, and Cristina Steffen. "Coping with Trade Liberalization: The Case of Mexican Grain Producers." *Culture and Agriculture* 25, no. 2 (Fall 2003): 1–12.

Edelson, S. Max. *Plantation Enterprise in Colonial South Carolina.* Cambridge: Harvard University Press, 2006.

Errington, Shelly. *The Death of Authentic Primitive Art and Other Tales of Progress.* Berkeley: University of California Press, 1998.

Estrada, William David. *The Los Angeles Plaza: Sacred and Contested Space.* Austin: University of Texas Press, 2008.

Ferguson, Priscilla Parkhurst. *Accounting for Taste: The Triumph of French Cuisine.* Chicago: University of Chicago Press, 2004.

Fernández e Lizardi, José Joaquín. *The Mangy Parrot: The Life and Times of Periquillo Sarniento, Written by Himself for His Children.* Translated by David Frye. Indianapolis: Hackett, 2004.

Ferrer Pujol, José. "Racionalización de subsidios y liberación de precios del sector." In *La industria de la masa y la tortilla: Desarrollo y tecnología,* edited by Felipe Torres et al., 39–48. Mexico City: Editorial Cambio XXI, 1994.

Fitting, Elizabeth. *The Struggle for Maize: Campesinos, Workers, and Transgenic Corn in the Mexican Countryside.* Durham, N.C.: Duke University Press, 2011.

Fitzgerald, Deborah. "Eating and Remembering." *Agricultural History* 79, no. 4 (Autumn 2005): 393–408.

Flandrin, Jean-Louis. "Dietary Choices and Culinary Technique, 1500–1800." In *Food: A Culinary History from Antiquity to the Present,* edited by Jean-Louis Flandrin and Massimo Montanari and translated by Albert Sonnenfeld. New York: Columbia University Press, 1999.

Flora, Cornelia, ed. *Interactions between Agroecosystems and Rural Communities.* Boca Raton, Fla.: CRC Press, 2001.

Flores, Richard R. *Remembering the Alamo: Memory, Modernity, and the Master Symbol.* Austin: University of Texas Press, 2002.

Flores, William V., and Rina Benmayor, eds. *Latino Cultural Citizenship: Claiming Identity, Space, and Rights.* Boston: Beacon, 1997.

Flores y Escalante, Jesús. *Brevísima historia de la comida mexicana.* Mexico City: Asociación Mexicana de Estudios Fonográficos, 1994.

Florescano, Enrique. *Memory, Myth, and Time in Mexico: From the Aztecs to Independence.* Translated by Albert G. Bork and Kathryn R. Bork. Austin: University of Texas Press, 1994.

Fonseca, Vanessa. "Fractal Capitalism and the Latinization of the U.S. Market." Ph.D. diss., University of Texas, Austin, 2003.

———. "Nuevo Latino: Rebranding Latin American Cuisine." *Consumption, Markets, and Culture* 8, no. 2 (June 2005): 95–130.

Ford, Richard I. "Corn Is Our Mother." In *Corn and Culture in the Prehistoric New World,* edited by Sissel Johannessen and Christine A. Hastorf, 513–25. Boulder, Colo.: Westview, 1994.

Frank, Ross. *From Settler to Citizen: New Mexican Economic Development and the Creation of Vecino Society, 1750–1820.* Berkeley: University of California Press, 2000.

Fredi Chiapelli, ed. *First Images of America: The Impact of the New World on the Old.* 2 vols. Berkeley: University of California Press, 1976.

Freidberg, Susan. *Fresh: A Perishable History.* Cambridge: Harvard University Press, 2009.

Fritz, Gayle J. "The Transition to Agriculture in the Desert Borderlands: An Introduction." In *Archaeology without Borders: Contact, Commerce, and Change in the US Southwest and*

Northwestern Mexico, edited by Laurie D. Webster, Maxine E. McBrinn, and Eduardo Gamboa Carrera. Boulder: University Press of Colorado/CONACULTA, 2008.

Frye, David. "The Native Peoples of Northeastern Mexico." In *Mesoamerica*, vol. 2 of *Cambridge History of Native Peoples of the Americas*, edited by Richard E. W. Adams and Murdo J. MacLeod, 89–135. Cambridge: Cambridge University Press, 2000.

Gabaccia, Donna R. *We Are What We Eat: Ethnic Food and the Making of Americans*. Cambridge: Harvard University Press, 1998.

García, Richard A. *Rise of the Mexican American Middle Class: San Antonio, 1929–1941*. College Station: Texas A&M University Press, 1991.

García Acosta, Virginia. *Las panaderías, sus dueños y trabajadores. Ciudad de México, siglo XVIII*. Mexico City: CIESAS, 1989.

García Garza, Domingo. "Una etnografía de los 'tacos' en México. El caso de Monterrey." *Estudios Sociales* 19, no. 37 (January–June 2011): 32–63.

Garcilazo, Jeffrey Marcos. "*Traqueros*: Mexican Railroad Workers in the United States, 1870 to 1930." Ph.D. diss., University of California, Santa Barbara, 1995.

Garrido Aranda, Antonio, ed. *Los sabores de España y América: Cultura y alimentación*. Huesca: La Val de Onsera, 1999.

Gaytán, Marie Sarita. "From Sombreros to Sincronizadas: Authenticity, Ethnicity, and the Mexican Restaurant Industry." *Journal of Contemporary Ethnography* 37, no. 3 (June 2008): 314–41.

Goldman, Anne. "'I Yam What I Yam': Cooking, Culture, and Colonialism." In *Decolonizing the Subject: The Politics of Gender in Women's Autobiography*, edited by Sidonie Smith and Julie Watson, 169–95. Minneapolis: University of Minnesota Press, 1992.

González, Deena J. *Refusing the Favor: Spanish-Mexican Women of Santa Fé, 1820–1880*. New York: Oxford University Press, 1999.

González de la Vara, Martín. *Tiempos de guerra*, vol. 5 of *La cocina mexicana a través de los siglos*, edited by Enrique Krauze. Mexico City: Editorial Clío, 1997.

Gruesz, Kirsten Silva. "Lexical Snacks at the Citizen Restaurant: A Response to Vicki Ruiz." *American Quarterly* 60, no. 1 (March 2008): 33–42.

Guest, Robert A. "Intellectual Property Rights and Native American Tribes." *American Indian Law Review* 20, no. 1 (1995/1996): 111–39.

Guillermoprieto, Alma. *The Heart That Bleeds*. New York: Vintage, 1994.

Guthman, Julie. *Agrarian Dreams: The Paradox of Organic Farming in California*. Berkeley: University of California Press, 2004.

Gutiérrez, Ramón. *When Jesus Came, the Corn Mothers Went Away: Marriage, Sexuality, and Power in New Mexico, 1500–1846*. Stanford: Stanford University Press, 1991.

Guy, Kolleen. *When Champagne Became French: Wine and the Making of a National Identity*. Baltimore, Md.: Johns Hopkins University Press, 2003.

Hackel, Steven W. *Children of Coyote, Missionaries of Saint Francis: Indian-Spanish Relations in Colonial California, 1769–1850*. Chapel Hill: University of North Carolina Press, 2005.

Hadley, Phillip L. *Minería y sociedad en el centro minero de Santa Eulalia, Chihuahua [1709–1750]*. Mexico City: Fondo de Cultura Económica, 1975.

Heldke, Lisa. *Exotic Appetites: Ruminations of a Food Adventurer*. New York: Routledge, 2003.

Hers, Marie-Areti. "Zacatecas y Durango. Los confines tolteca-chichimecas." In *La gran chichimeca: El lugar de las rocas secas*, edited by Beatriz Braniff C, 113–54. Milan: Jaca Book/CNCA, 2001.

Hewitt de Alcántara, Cynthia. *Modernizing Mexican Agriculture: Socioeconomic Implications of Technological Change, 1940–1970*. Geneva: United Nations Research Institute for Social Development, 1976.

————, ed. *Economic Restructuring and Rural Subsistence in Mexico: Corn and the Crisis of the 1980s*. San Diego: Center for US-Mexican Studies, University of California, San Diego, 1994.

Ho, Ping-Ti. "The Introduction of American Food Plants into China." *American Anthropologist* 57, no. 2 (April 1955): 191–201.

Holt-Giménez, Eric. *Campesino a Campesino: Voices from Latin America's Farmer to Farmer Movement for Sustainable Agriculture*. Oakland, Calif.: Food First, 2006.

Iltis, Hugh H. "Origin of Polystichy in Maize." In *Histories of Maize: Multidisciplinary Approaches to the Prehistory, Linguistics, Biogeography, Domestication, and Evolution of Maize*, edited by John E. Staller, Robert H. Tykot, and Bruce F. Benz, 21–53. San Diego: Elsevier Academic, 2006.

Israel, Jonathan I. *Race, Class, and Politics in Colonial Mexico, 1610–1670*. Oxford: Oxford University Press, 1975.

Jakle, John A., and Keith A. Sculle. *Fast Food: Roadside Restaurants in the Automobile Age*. Baltimore, Md.: Johns Hopkins University Press, 1999.

Javerluk, Terrence W. "Chile Peppers and Identity Construction in Pueblo, Colorado." *Journal for the Study of Food and Society* 6, no. 1 (Winter 2002): 45–59.

Jenson, Joan M. "Canning Comes to New Mexico: Women and the Agricultural Extension Service, 1914–1919." In *New Mexico Women: Intercultural Perspectives*, edited by Joan M. Jenson and Darlis A. Miller, 201–26. Albuquerque: University of New Mexico Press, 1986.

Jiménez Núñez, Alfredo. *El gran norte de México: Una frontera imperial en la Nueva España (1540–1820)*. Madrid: Tébar, 2006.

Johnston, Josée, and Shyon Baumann. *Foodies: Democracy and Distinction in the Gourmet Foodscape*. New York: Routledge, 2010.

Jones, Martin. *Feast: Why Humans Share Food*. New York: Oxford University Press, 2007.

Juárez López, José Luis. *La lenta emergencia de la comida mexicana: Ambigüedades criollas, 1750–1800*. Mexico: Editorial Porrúa, 2000.

————. *Nacionalismo culinario: La cocina mexicana en el siglo XX*. Mexico City: CONACULTA, 2008.

Katz, S. H., M. L. Hediger, and L. A. Valleroy. "Traditional Maize Processing Techniques in the New World." *Science* 184 (1974): 765–73.

Kearney, Michael. *Reconceptualizing the Peasantry: Anthropology in Global Perspective*. Boulder, Colo.: Westview, 1996.

Kessell, John L. *Kiva, Cross, and Crown: The Pecos Indians and New Mexico, 1540–1840*. Washington, D.C.: National Park Service, 1979.

Kiple, Kenneth F., and Kriemhild Coneè Orenlas, eds. *The Cambridge World History of Food*. 2 vols. Cambridge: Cambridge University Press, 2000.

Kirkby, Diane. "'From Wharfie Haunt to Foodie Haven': Modernity and Law in the Transformation of the Australian Working-Class Pub." *Food, Culture and Society* 11, no. 1 (March 2008): 29–48.

Kloppenburg, Jack. *First the Seed: The Political Economy of Plant Biotechnology, 1492–2000*. 2nd ed. Madison: University of Wisconsin Press, 2004.

Kropp, Phoebe S. "Citizens of the Past? Olvera Street and the Construction of Race and Memory in 1930s Los Angeles." *Radical History Review* 81 (Fall 2001): 35–60.

Ladd, Doris M. *The Making of a Strike: Mexican Silver Workers' Struggles in Real del Monte, 1766–1775*. Lincoln: University of Nebraska Press, 1988.

Lear, John. *Workers, Neighbors, and Citizens: The Revolution in Mexico City*. Lincoln: University of Nebraska Press, 2001.

Levenstein, Harvey. *Revolution at the Table: The Transformation of the American Diet*. New York: Oxford University Press, 1988.

Lieberman, Victor. *Strange Parallels: Southeast Asia in Global Context, c. 800–1830.* Cambridge: Cambridge University Press, 2003.

Limón, José. *Dancing with the Devil: Society and Cultural Poetics in Mexican American South Texas.* Madison: University of Wisconsin Press, 1994.

Lind, David, and Elizabeth Barham. "The Social Life of the Tortilla: Food, Cultural Politics, and Contested Commodification." *Agriculture and Human Values* 21 (2004): 47–60.

Lloyd, Timothy Charles. "The Cincinnati Chili Culinary Complex." *Western Folklore* 40, no. 1 (1981): 28–40.

Lomnitz-Adler, Claudio. *Exits from the Labyrinth: Culture and Ideology in the Mexican National Space.* Berkeley: University of California Press, 1992.

Long, Lucy M. "Culinary Tourism: A Folkloristic Perspective on Eating and Otherness." In *Culinary Tourism*, edited by Lucy M. Long, 20–50. Lexington: University Press of Kentucky, 2004.

———, ed. *Culinary Tourism.* Lexington: University Press of Kentucky, 2004.

Long-Solís, Janet, and Luis Alberto Vargas. *Food Culture in Mexico.* Westport, Conn.: Greenwood, 2005.

López Austin, Alfredo, and Leonardo López Luján. *Mexico's Indigenous Past.* Translated by Bernard R. Ortiz de Montellano. Norman: University of Oklahoma Press, 2001.

López-Lázaro, Fabio. "Sweet Food of Knowledge: Botany, Food, and Empire in the Early Modern Spanish Kingdoms." In *At the Table: Metaphorical and Material Cultures of Food in Medieval and Early Modern Europe*, edited by Timothy J. Tomasik and Juliann M. Vitullo, 3–28. Tunnhout: Brepols, 2007.

Lyon, Sarah. "Maya Coffee Farmers and Fair Trade: Assessing the Benefits and Limitations of Alternative Markets." *Culture and Agriculture* 29, no. 2 (Fall 2007): 100–112.

Macías-González, Víctor M. "Le capital social et culturel de la communauté aristocratique mexicaine à Paris, 1850–1914." In *Méxique-Francia, una sensibilidad compartida*, edited by Javier Pérez-Siller and Jean-Marie Lassus, 357–85. Puebla and Nantes: Université de Nantes and Benemérita Universidad Autónoma de Puebla, forthcoming.

———. "The Mexican Aristocracy and Porfirio Díaz, 1876–1911." Ph.D. diss., Texas Christian University, 1999.

———. "Presidential Ritual in Porfirian Mexico: Curtsying in the Shadow of Dictators." In *Heroes and Hero Cults in Latin America*, edited by Samuel Brunk and Ben Fallow, 83–108. Austin: University of Texas Press, 2006.

Macías-González, Víctor M., and Steven B. Bunker. "Consumption and Material Culture in the Twentieth Century." In *Companion to Mexican History and Culture*, edited by William H. Beezley, 83–118. Chichester: Wiley-Blackwell, 2011.

Magnan, André. "Food Regimes." In *Oxford Handbook of Food History*, edited by Jeffrey M. Pilcher, 370–88. New York: Oxford University Press, 2012.

Marks, Robert B. *Tigers, Rice, Silk, and Silt: Environment and Economy in Late Imperial South China.* Cambridge: Cambridge University Press, 1998.

Martin, Cheryl English. *Governance and Society in Colonial Mexico: Chihuahua in the Eighteenth Century.* Stanford: Stanford University Press, 1996.

Martin, Patricia Preciado, ed. *Songs My Mother Sang to Me: An Oral History of Mexican American Women.* Tucson: University of Arizona Press, 1992.

Martinez-Torres, Maria Elena. *Organic Coffee: Sustainable Development by Mayan Farmers.* Athens: Ohio University Press, 2006.

Massey, Douglas S., Jorge Durand, and Nolan J. Malone. *Beyond Smoke and Mirrors: Mexican Immigration in an Era of Economic Integration.* New York: Russell Sage Foundation, 2003.

Matsuoka, Y., et al. "A Single Domestication for Maize Shown by Multilocus Microsatellite Genotyping." *Proceedings of the National Academy of Sciences* 99, no. 9 (2002): 6080–84.

Mazumdar, Sucheta. "The Impact of New World Food Crops on the Diet and Economy of China and India, 1600–1900." In *Food in Global History*, edited by Raymond Grew, 58–78. Boulder, Colo.: Westview, 1999.

McAfee, Kathleen. "Corn Culture and Dangerous DNA: Real and Imagined Consequences of Maize Transgene Flow in Oaxaca." *Journal of Latin American Geography* 2, no. 1 (2003): 18–42.

McCann, James A. *Maize and Grace: Africa's Encounter with a New World Crop, 1500–2000.* Cambridge: Harvard University Press, 2005.

———. *Stirring the Pot: A History of African Cuisine.* Athens: Ohio University Press, 2009.

McNeill, William H. "American Food Crops in the Old World." In *Seeds of Change: A Quincentennial Commemoration*, edited by Herman J. Viola and Carolyn Margolis. Washington, D.C.: Smithsonian Institution Press, 1991.

McWilliams, Carey. *North from Mexico: The Spanish-Speaking People of the United States.* 1949. Reprint, Westport, Conn.: Greenwood, 1968.

Melville, Elinor G. K. *A Plague of Sheep: Environmental Consequences of the Conquest of Mexico.* Cambridge: Cambridge University Press, 1997.

Millard, Ann V., and Jorge Chapa. *Apple Pie and Enchiladas: Latino Newcomers in the Rural Midwest.* Austin: University of Texas Press, 2004.

Mills, Barbara J., ed. *Identity, Feasting, and the Archaeology of the Greater Southwest.* Boulder: University Press of Colorado, 2004.

Minnis, Paul E. "Prehistoric Diet in the Northern Southwest: Macroplant Remains from Four Corners Feces." *American Antiquity* 54, no. 3 (1989): 543–63.

Mintz, Sidney W. *Sweetness and Power: The Place of Sugar in Modern History.* New York: Viking, 1985.

Mitchell, Tim. *Intoxicated Identities: Alcohol's Power in Mexican History and Culture.* New York: Routledge, 2004.

Monroy, Douglas. *Rebirth: Mexican Los Angeles from the Great Migration to the Great Depression.* Berkeley: University of California Press, 1999.

Montaño, Mario. "Appropriation and Counterhegemony in South Texas: Food Slurs, Offal Meats, and Blood." In *Useable Pasts: Traditions and Group Expressions in North America*, edited by Tad Tuleja, 50–67. Logan: Utah State University Press, 1997.

———. "The History of Mexican Folk Foodways of South Texas: Street Vendors, Offal Foods, and *Barbacoa de Cabeza*." Ph.D. diss., University of Pennsylvania, 1992.

Montejano, David. *Anglos and Mexicans in the Making of Texas, 1836–1986.* Austin: University of Texas Press, 1987.

Mora-Torres, Juan. *The Making of the Mexican Border.* Austin: University of Texas Press, 2001.

Morris, Donald H. "Changes in Groundstone Following the Introduction of Maize into the American Southwest." *Journal of Anthropological Research* 46, no. 2 (Summer 1990): 177–94.

Myers, Thomas P. "Hominy Technology and the Emergence of Mississippian Societies." In *Histories of Maize: Multidisciplinary Approaches to the Prehistory, Linguistics, Biogeography, Domestication, and Evolution of Maize*, edited by John E. Staller, Robert H. Tykot, and Bruce F. Benz, 511–22. San Diego: Elsevier Academic, 2006.

Narayan, Uma. "Eating Cultures: Incorporation, Identity, and Indian Food." *Social Identities* 1, no. 1 (1995): 63–86.

Noriega, Chon. *Shot in America: Television, the State, and the Rise of Chicano Cinema.* Minneapolis: University of Minnesota Press, 2000.

Norton, Marcy. *Sacred Gifts, Profane Pleasures: A History of Tobacco and Chocolate in the Atlantic World*. Ithaca, N.Y.: Cornell University Press, 2008.

Novo, Salvador. *Cocina mexicana, o historia gastronomica de la Ciudad de México*. 1967. Reprint, Mexico City: Editorial Porrúa, 1993.

———. *Las locas, el sexo, los burdeles*. Mexico City: Editorial Novaro, 1972.

Ocampo, Melchor. "Idiotismos Hispano-Mexicanos." In *Obras completas*, edited by Angel Pola and Aurelio J. Venegas. 3 vols. Mexico City: F. Vázquez, 1900–1901.

Ochoa, Enrique. *Feeding Mexico: The Political Uses of Food since 1910*. Wilmington, Del.: Scholarly Resources, 2000.

Offutt, Leslie S. *Saltillo, 1770–1810: Town and Region in the Mexican North*. Tucson: University of Arizona Press, 2001.

Ohnuki-Tierney, Emiko. *Rice as Self: Japanese Identities through Time*. Princeton: Princeton University Press, 1993.

Orozco, José. "Gabriel Espíndola Martínez: Tequila Master." In *The Human Tradition in Mexico*, edited by Jeffrey M. Pilcher, 225–33. Wilmington, Del.: Scholarly Resources, 2003.

Ory, Pascal. "Gastronomy." In *Traditions*, vol. 2 of *Realms of Memory: The Construction of the French Past*, edited by Pierre Nora and translated by Arthur Goldhammer, 442–67. New York: Columbia University Press, 1997.

Palmer, Colin A. *Slaves of the Black God: Blacks in Mexico, 1570–1650*. Cambridge: Harvard University Press, 1976.

Payno, Manuel. *Los bandidos de Río Frío*. 24th ed. Mexico City: Editorial Porrúa, 2004.

Paz, Octavio. *Convergences: Essays on Art and Literature*. Translated by Helen Lane. Orlando: Harcourt, Brace, and Jovanovich, 1987.

Penfold, Steve. *The Donut: A Canadian History*. Toronto: University of Toronto Press, 2008.

———. "Fast Food." In *The Oxford Handbook of Food History*, edited by Jeffrey M. Pilcher, 279–301. New York: Oxford University Press, 2012.

Pérez, Ramona Lee, and Meredith E. Abarca, eds. "Cocinas Públicas: Food and Border Consciousness in Greater Mexico." A special issue of *Food and Foodways* 15, no. 3–4 (July–December 2007).

Petrick, Gabriella. "'Like Ribbons of Green and Gold': Industrializing Lettuce and the Quest for Quality in the Salinas Valley, 1920–1965." *Agricultural History* 80, no. 3 (2006): 269–95.

Phelan, John Leddy. *The Hispanization of the Philippines: Spanish Aims and Filipino Responses, 1565–1700*. Madison: University of Wisconsin Press, 1959.

Piccato, Pablo. "Urbanistas, Ambulantes, and Mendigos: The Dispute for Urban Space in Mexico City, 1890–1930." In *Reconstructing Criminality in Mexico City*, edited by Carlos Aguirre and Robert Buffington, 113–48. Wilmington, Del.: Scholarly Resources, 2000.

Pilcher, Jeffrey M. "From 'Montezuma's Revenge' to 'Mexican Truffles': Culinary Tourism across the Rio Grande." In *Culinary Tourism*, edited by Lucy M. Long, 76–96. Lexington: University Press of Kentucky, 2004.

———. *¡Que vivan los tamales! Food and the Making of Mexican Identity*. Albuquerque: University of New Mexico Press, 1998.

———. *The Sausage Rebellion: Public Health and Private Enterprise, and Meat in Mexico City, 1890–1917*. Albuquerque: University of New Mexico Press, 2006.

———. "Taco Bell, Maseca, and Slow Food: A Postmodern Apocalypse for Mexico's Peasant Cuisine?" In *Fast Food/Slow Food: The Cultural Economy of the Global Food System*, edited by Richard Wilk, 69–81. Walnut Creek, Calif.: Altamira, 2006.

———. "¡Tacos, joven! Cosmopolitismo proletario y la cocina nacional mexicana." *Dimensión Antropológica* 13, no. 37 (mayo–agosto 2006): 87–125.

————. "Was the Taco Invented in Southern California?" *Gastronomica* 8, no. 1 (Winter 2008): 26–38.

Pillsbury, Richard. *From Boarding House to Bistro: The American Restaurant Then and Now*. Boston: Unwin Hyman, 1990.

Pinedo, Encarnación. *Encarnación's Kitchen: Mexican Recipes from Nineteenth-Century California: Selections from Encarnación Pinedo's "El Cocinero Español."* Edited and translated by Dan Strehl. Berkeley: University of California Press, 2003.

Piperno, Dolores R., and Deborah M. Pearsall. *The Origins of Agriculture in the Lowland Neotropics*. San Diego: Academic Press, 1998.

Ponce, Merrihelen. "The Life and Works of Fabiola Cabeza de Baca, New Mexican Hispanic Woman Writer: A Contextual Biography." Ph.D. diss., University of New Mexico, 1995.

Radding, Cynthia. *Wandering Peoples: Colonialism, Ethnic Spaces, and Ecological Frontiers in Northwestern Mexico, 1700–1850*. Durham, N.C.: Duke University Press, 1997.

Ramos I. Duarte, Feliz. *Diccionario de mejicanismos: Colección de locuciones i frases viciosas*. Mexico City: Imprenta de Eduardo Dublan, 1895.

Ray, Krishnendu. "Ethnic Succession and the New American Restaurant Cuisine." In *The Restaurants Book: Ethnographies of Where We Eat*, edited by David Beriss and David Sutton, 97–114. Oxford: Berg, 2007.

Restall, Matthew, ed. *Beyond Black and Red: African-Native Relations in Colonial Latin America*. Albuquerque: University of New Mexico Press, 2005.

Ritzer, George. *The McDonaldization of Society*. Thousand Oaks, Calif.: Pine Forge, 1993.

Rivera, Juan M., Scott Whiteford, and Manuel Chávez, eds. *NAFTA and the Campesinos: The Impact of NAFTA on Small-Scale Agricultural Producers in Mexico and the Prospects for Change*. Scranton: University of Scranton Press, 2009.

Rodríguez Gómez, M. Guadalupe. *El frijol en México: Elementos para una agenda de soberanía alimentaria*. Guadalajara: Universidad de Guadalajara, 2006.

Roe, Daphne A. *A Plague of Corn: The Social History of Pellagra*. Ithaca, N.Y.: Cornell University Press, 1973.

Romero, Héctor. *Vocabulario gastronómico mexicano*. Mexico City: Coordinación General de Abasto y Distribución del Distrito Federal, 1991.

Romero, Robert Chao. *The Chinese in Mexico, 1882–1940*. Tucson: University of Arizona Press, 2010.

Rose, Susan, and Robert Shaw. "The Gamble: Circular Mexican Migration and the Return of Remittances." *Mexican Studies/Estudios Mexicanos* 24, no. 1 (Winter 2008): 79–111.

Rothstein, Frances Abrahamer. *Globalization in Rural Mexico: Three Decades of Change*. Austin: University of Texas Press, 2007.

Rozin, Elisabeth. *Ethnic Cuisine: The Flavor Principle Cook-Book*. Lexington, Mass.: S. Greene, 1983.

Ruiz, Vicki L. "Citizen Restaurant: American Imaginaries, American Communities." *American Quarterly* 60, no. 1 (March 2008): 1–21.

————. *From Out of the Shadows: Mexican Women in Twentieth-Century America*. New York: Oxford University Press, 1998.

Sahagún, Bernardino de. *Florentine Codex: General History of the Things of New Spain*. 13 parts. Translated by Charles E. Dibble and Arthur J. O. Anderson. Santa Fe: School of American Research, 1961.

Sahlins, Marshall. "The Original Affluent Society." In *Stone Age Economics*. London: Tavistock, 1974.

Sánchez, George J. *Becoming Mexican American: Ethnicity, Culture and Identity in Chicano Los Angeles, 1900–1945*. Berkeley: University of California Press, 1993.

———. "'Go After the Women': Americanization and the Mexican Immigrant Woman, 1915–1929." In *Unequal Sisters: A Multi-Cultural Reader in U.S. Women's History*, edited by Ellen Carol DuBois and Vicki L. Ruiz, 250–63. New York: Routledge, 1990.

Sanderson, Steven E. *The Transformation of Mexican Agriculture: International Stucture and the Politics of Rural Change*. Princeton: Princeton University Press, 1986.

Schurman, Rachel A., and Dennis Doyle Takahashi Kelso, eds. *Engineering Trouble: Biotechnology and Its Discontents*. Berkeley: University of California Press, 2003.

Sheridan, Thomas E. *Los Tucsoneses: The Mexican Community in Tucson, 1854–1941*. Tucson: University of Arizona Press, 1986.

Skibo, J., and E. Blinman. "Exploring the Origins of Pottery on the Colorado Plateau." In *Pottery and People*, edited by J. Skibo and G. Feinman, 171–83. Salt Lake City: University of Utah Press, 1999.

Slack, Edward R., Jr. "The *Chinos* in New Spain: A Corrective Lens for a Distorted Image." *Journal of World History* 20, no. 1 (March 2009): 35–67.

Smith, Michael E. "The Aztlan Migrations of the Nahuatl Chronicles: Myth or History?" *Ethnohistory* 31, no. 3 (Summer 1984): 153–86.

Snow, David H. "Tener Comal y Metate: Protohistoric Rio Grande Maize Use and Diet." In *Perspectives on Southwestern Prehistory*, edited by Paul E. Minnis and Charles L. Redman, 289–300. Boulder, Colo.: Westview, 1990.

Sokolov, Raymond. *Why We Eat What We Eat*. New York: Summit, 1991.

Soleri, Daniela, and David Cleveland, et al. "Gifts from the Creator: Intellectual Property Rights and Folk Crop Varieties." In *Intellectual Property Rights for Indigenous Peoples: A Sourcebook*, edited by Tom Greaves, 21–40. Oklahoma City: Society for Applied Anthropology, 1994.

Staller, John E., Robert H. Tykot, and Bruce F. Benz, eds. *Histories of Maize: Multidisciplinary Approaches to the Prehistory, Linguistics, Biogeography, Domestication, and Evolution of Maize*. San Diego: Elsevier Academic, 2006.

Suárez Argüello, Clara Elena. *La política cerealera en la economía novohispana. El caso de trigo*. Mexico City: CIESAS, 1985.

Tablada, José Juan. *La feria de la vida*. Mexico City: Ediciones Botas, 1937.

Tedlock, Dennis, trans. *Popol Vuh: The Definitive Edition of the Maya Book of the Dawn of Life and the Glories of Gods and Kings*. Rev. ed. New York: Simon and Schuster, 1996.

Thiel, J. Homer, et al. *Down by the River: Archaeological and Historical Studies of the León Family Farmstead*. Tucson: Center for Desert Archaeology, 2005.

Thrupp, Lori Ann. *Bittersweet Harvests for Global Supermarkets: Challenges in Latin America's Agricultural Export Boom*. Washington, D.C.: World Resources Institute, 1995.

Toledo, Víctor M. *La paz en Chiapas: Ecología, luchas indígenas y modernidad alternativa*. Mexico City: Ediciones Quinta Sol, 2000.

Torres, Gabriel. "The Agave War: Toward an Agenda for the Post-NAFTA Ejido." In *The Future Role of the Ejido in Rural Mexico*, edited by Richard Snyder and Gabriel Torres, 73–100. La Jolla: Center for US-Mexico Studies, University of California, San Diego, 1998.

Trigg, Heather. "Food Choice and Social Identity in Early Colonial New Mexico." *Journal of the Southwest* 46, no. 2 (Summer 2004): 223–52.

Trubek, Amy B. *A Taste of Place: A Cultural Journey into Terroir*. Berkeley: University of California Press, 2008.

Valle, Victor M., and Rodolfo D. Torres. *Latino Metropolis*. Minneapolis: University of Minnesota Press, 2000.

Valle, Victor M., and Mary Lau Valle. *Recipe of Memory: Five Generations of Mexican Cuisine.* New York: New Press, 1995.

Van Esterik, Penny. "From Marco Polo to McDonald's: Thai Cuisine in Transition." *Food and Foodways* 5, no. 2 (1992): 177–94.

Vargas, Zaragosa. *Proletarians of the North: A History of Mexican Industrial Workers in Detroit and the Midwest, 1917–1933.* Berkeley: University of California Press, 1993.

Varien, Mark D. *Sedentism and Mobility in a Social Landscape: Mesa Verde and Beyond.* Tucson: University of Arizona Press, 1999.

Vasconcelos, José. *The Cosmic Race/La raza cósmica.* Translated by Didier T. Jaén. Baltimore, Md.: Johns Hopkins University Press, 1997.

Viquiera Alban, Juan Pedro. *Propriety and Permissiveness in Bourbon Mexico.* Translated by Sonya Lipsett-Rivera and Sergio Rivera Ayala. Wilmington, Del.: Scholarly Resources, 1999.

Vizcarra Bordi, Ivonne. "The 'Authentic' Taco and Peasant Women: Nostalgic Consumption in the Era of Globalization." *Culture and Agriculture* 28, no. 2 (Fall 2006): 97–107.

Votava, Eric J., Jit B. Baral, and Paul W. Bosland. "Genetic Diversity of Chile (*Capsicum Annuum* var. *Annuum* L.) Landraces from Northern New Mexico, Colorado, and Mexico." *Economic Botany* 59, no. 1 (2005): 8–17.

Walsh, Robb. *The Tex-Mex Cookbook: A History in Recipes and Photos.* New York: Broadway, 2004.

Warman, Arturo. *Corn and Capitalism: How a Botanical Bastard Grew to Global Dominance.* Translated by Nancy L. Westrate. Chapel Hill: University of North Carolina Press, 2003.

West, Robert C. *The Mining Community in Northern New Spain: The Parral Mining District.* Berkeley: University of California Press, 1949.

———. *Sonora: Its Geographical Personality.* Austin: University of Texas Press, 1993.

Whalen, Michael E., and Paul E. Minnis. *Casas Grandes and Its Hinterland: Prehistoric Regional Organization in Northwest Mexico.* Tucson: University of Arizona Press, 2001.

Wilk, Richard. *Home Cooking in the Global Village: Caribbean Food from Buccaneers to Ecotourists.* Oxford: Berg, 2006.

Williams-Forson, Psyche A. *Building Houses Out of Chicken Legs: Black Women, Food, and Power.* Chapel Hill: University of North Carolina Press, 2006.

Williams-Forson, Psyche A., and Carole Counihan, eds. *Taking Food Public: Redefining Foodways in a Changing World.* New York: Routledge, 2012.

Wills, W. H., and Patricia L. Crown. "Commensal Politics in the Prehispanic Southwest." In *Identity, Feasting, and the Archaeology of the Greater Southwest,* edited by Barbara J. Mills, 153–72. Boulder: University Press of Colorado, 2004.

Zelinsky, Wilbur. "The Roving Palate: North America's Ethnic Restaurant Cuisines." *Geoforum* 16, no. 1 (1985): 51–72.

Zolov, Eric. *Refried Elvis: The Rise of the Mexican Counterculture.* Berkeley: University of California Press, 1999.

NEWSPAPERS

Arizona Daily Star (Tucson)
Arizona Republic (Phoenix)
Atlanta Daily World
Bangkok Post
Budapest Sun
Charlotte [N.C.] *Observer*

Chicago Daily Tribune
Chicago Defender
Dallas Morning News
Denver Post
El Diario del Hogar (Mexico City)
The Economist (London)
La Epoca (San Antonio)
Excelsior (Mexico City)
Financial Times (London)
El Financiero (Mexico City)
Galveston [Tex.] *Daily News*
Guardian (Manchester)
Hindustan Times (New Delhi)
Houston [Tex.] *Chronicle*
El Imparcial (Hermosillo)
The Irish Times (Belfast)
Jerusalem Post
Kyodo News International (Tokyo)
Los Angeles Examiner
Los Angeles Sentinel
Los Angeles Times
The Mexican Herald (Mexico City)
Minneapolis Star and Tribune
New York Amsterdam News
New York Times
The Observer (London)
La Opinión (Los Angeles)
Pittsburgh Courier
The Post (Washington, D.C.)
La Prensa (San Antonio)
Reforma (Mexico City)
St. Louis Daily Globe Democrat
San Antonio Daily Express
San Antonio Express News
San Antonio Light
El Siglo XIX (Mexico City)
Sunday Times (London)
The Times (London)
El Universal (Mexico City)
El Universal Gráfico (Mexico City)
Wall Street Journal (Europe)
Washington Evening Star (Washington, D.C.)
Die Zeit (Hamburg)

INDEX